Peopling the Russian Periphery

Though usually forgotten in general surveys of European colonization, the Russians were among the greatest colonizers of the Old World, eventually settling across most of the immense expanse of Northern Europe and Asia, from the Baltic and the Pacific, and from the Arctic Ocean to Central Asia. This book makes a unique contribution to our understanding of the Eurasian past by examining the policies, practices, cultural representations, and daily-life experiences of Slavic settlement in non-Russian regions of Eurasia from the time of Ivan the Terrible to the nuclear era.

The movement of tens of millions of Slavic settlers was a central component of Russian empire-building and of the everyday life of numerous social and ethnic groups. It remains a crucial regional security issue today, yet is relatively understudied. *Peopling the Russian Periphery* redresses this omission through a detailed exploration of the varied meanings and dynamics of Slavic settlement from the sixteenth century to the 1960s. Providing an account of the different approaches to settlement and expansion that were adopted in different periods of history, it includes detailed case studies of particular episodes of migration.

Written by up and coming and established experts in Russian history, and with exceptional geographical and chronological breadth, this book provides a thorough examination of the history of Slavic settlement and migration from the Muscovite to the Soviet era. It will be of great interest to students and scholars of Russian history, comparative history of colonization, migration, interethnic contact, environmental history, and European Imperialism.

Nicholas B. Breyfogle is Associate Professor of History at The Ohio State University. He is the author of *Heretics and Colonizers: Forging Russia's Empire in the South Caucasus*, which received the 2006 Outstanding Publication Award from the Ohio Academy of History.

Abby Schrader is Associate Professor of History at Franklin and Marshall College. She is the author of *Languages of the Lash: Corporal Punishment and Identity in Imperial Russia*.

Willard Sunderland is Associate Professor of History at the University of Cincinnati. He is the author of *Taming the Wild Field: Colonization and Empire on the Russian Steppe*.

BASEES/Routledge series on Russian and East European studies

Series editor:
Richard Sakwa, Department of Politics and International Relations, University of Kent

Editorial Committee:
Julian Cooper, Centre for Russian and East European Studies, University of Birmingham
Terry Cox, Department of Central and East European Studies, University of Glasgow
Rosalind Marsh, Department of European Studies and Modern Languages, University of Bath
David Moon, Department of History, University of Durham
Hilary Pilkington, Department of Sociology, University of Warwick
Stephen White, Department of Politics, University of Glasgow

Founding Editorial Committee Member:
George Blazyca, Centre for Contemporary European Studies, University of Paisley

This series is published on behalf of BASEES (the British Association for Slavonic and East European Studies). The series comprises original, high-quality, research-level work by both new and established scholars on all aspects of Russian, Soviet, post-Soviet and East European Studies in humanities and social science subjects.

1 **Ukraine's Foreign and Security Policy, 1991–2000**
Roman Wolczuk

2 **Political Parties in the Russian Regions**
Derek S. Hutcheson

3 **Local Communities and Post-Communist Transformation**
Edited by Simon Smith

4 **Repression and Resistance in Communist Europe**
J.C. Sharman

5 **Political Elites and the New Russia**
Anton Steen

6 **Dostoevsky and the Idea of Russianness**
Sarah Hudspith

7 **Performing Russia – Folk Revival and Russian Identity**
Laura J. Olson

8 **Russian Transformations**
Edited by Leo McCann

9 **Soviet Music and Society under Lenin and Stalin**
The baton and sickle
Edited by Neil Edmunds

10 **State Building in Ukraine**
The Ukranian parliament, 1990–2003
Sarah Whitmore

11 **Defending Human Rights in Russia**
Sergei Kovalyov, dissident and human rights commissioner, 1969–2003
Emma Gilligan

12 **Small-Town Russia**
Postcommunist livelihoods and identities: a portrait of the intelligentsia in Achit, Bednodemyanovsk and Zubtsov, 1999–2000
Anne White

13 **Russian Society and the Orthodox Church**
Religion in Russia after communism
Zoe Knox

14 **Russian Literary Culture in the Camera Age**
The word as image
Stephen Hutchings

15 **Between Stalin and Hitler**
Class war and race war on the Dvina, 1940–6
Geoffrey Swain

16 **Literature in Post-Communist Russia and Eastern Europe**
The Russian, Czech and Slovak fiction of the changes 1988–98
Rajendra A. Chitnis

17 **Soviet Dissent and Russia's Transition to Democracy**
Dissident legacies
Robert Horvath

18 **Russian and Soviet Film Adaptations of Literature, 1900–2001**
Screening the word
Edited by Stephen Hutchings and Anat Vernitski

19 **Russia as a Great Power**
Dimensions of security under Putin
Edited by Jakob Hedenskog, Vilhelm Konnander, Bertil Nygren, Ingmar Oldberg and Christer Pursiainen

20 **Katyn and the Soviet Massacre of 1940**
Truth, justice and memory
George Sanford

21 **Conscience, Dissent and Reform in Soviet Russia**
Philip Boobbyer

22 **The Limits of Russian Democratisation**
Emergency powers and states of emergency
Alexander N. Domrin

23 **The Dilemmas of Destalinisation**
A social and cultural history of reform in the Khrushchev Era
Edited by Polly Jones

24 **News Media and Power in Russia**
Olessia Koltsova

25 **Post-Soviet Civil Society**
Democratization in Russia and the Baltic states
Anders Uhlin

26 **The Collapse of Communist Power in Poland**
Jacqueline Hayden

27 **Television, Democracy and Elections in Russia**
Sarah Oates

28 **Russian Constitutionalism**
Historical and contemporary development
Andrey N. Medushevsky

29 **Late Stalinist Russia**
Society between reconstruction
and reinvention
Edited by Juliane Fürst

30 **The Transformation of Urban
Space in Post-Soviet Russia**
*Konstantin Axenov, Isolde Brade
and Evgenij Bondarchuk*

31 **Western Intellectuals and the
Soviet Union, 1920–40**
From Red Square to the Left Bank
Ludmila Stern

32 **The Germans of the Soviet
Union**
Irina Mukhina

33 **Re-constructing the Post-Soviet
Industrial Region**
The Donbas in transition
Edited by Adam Swain

34 **Chechnya – Russia's "War on
Terror"**
John Russell

35 **The New Right in the New
Europe**
Czech transformation and right-
wing politics, 1989–2006
Seán Hanley

36 **Democracy and Myth in Russia
and Eastern Europe**
*Edited by Alexander Wöll and
Harald Wydra*

37 **Energy Dependency, Politics and
Corruption in the Former Soviet
Union**
Russia's power, oligarchs' profits
and Ukraine's missing energy
policy, 1995–2006
Margarita M. Balmaceda

38 **Peopling the Russian Periphery**
Borderland colonization in
Eurasian history
*Edited by Nicholas B. Breyfogle,
Abby Schrader and
Willard Sunderland*

39 **Russian Criminal Justice in the
Age of Reform, 1855–1917**
Theories, practice and legacy
Frances Nethercott

40 **Political and Social Thought in
Post-Communist Russia**
Axel Kaehne

41 **The Demise of the Soviet
Communist Party**
Atsushi Ogushi

42 **Russian Policy towards China
and Japan**
The El'tsin and Putin periods
Natasha Kuhrt

43 **Soviet Karelia**
Politics, planning and terror in
Stalin's Russia, 1920–39
Nick Baron

Peopling the Russian Periphery

Borderland colonization in Eurasian history

**Edited by
Nicholas B. Breyfogle,
Abby Schrader, and
Willard Sunderland**

 **Routledge**
Taylor & Francis Group

LONDON AND NEW YORK

First published 2007
by Routledge
2 Park Square, Milton Park, Abingdon, Oxon, OX14 4RN

Simultaneously published in the USA and Canada
by Routledge
270 Madison Avenue, New York, NY 10016

Routledge is an imprint of the Taylor & Francis Group, an informa business

Transferred to Digital Printing 2008

© 2007 Nicholas B. Breyfogle, Abby Schrader and Willard Sunderland

Typeset by Bookcraft Ltd, Stroud, Gloucestershire

British Library Cataloguing in Publication Data
A catalogue record for this book is available from the British Library

Library of Congress Cataloging in Publication Data
Peopling the Russian periphery: borderland colonization in Eurasian
history / edited by Nicholas B. Breyfogle, Abby Schrader and Willard
Sunderland.
    p. cm. – (BASEES/Routledge series on Russian and East European
studies)
    Includes bibliographical references and index.
    1. Russia—Territorial expansion—History. 2. Emigration and
immigration—Russia—History. 3. Emigration and immigration—Soviet
Union—History. I. Breyfogle, Nicholas B., 1968–II. Schrader,
    Abby M. III. Sunderland, Willard, 1965–
DK43.P46 2007
307.2–dc22   2007016526

ISBN10: 0-415-41880-1 (hbk)
ISBN10: 0-203-93376-1 (ebk)

ISBN13: 978-0-415-41880-5 (hbk)
ISBN13: 978-0-203-93376-3 (ebk)

Contents

List of illustrations   x
List of contributors   xi
Preface   xiii
Archives and abbreviations   xv

Russian colonizations: an introduction   1
NICHOLAS B. BREYFOGLE, ABBY SCHRADER, AND
WILLARD SUNDERLAND

PART I
Muscovy, expansion, and the limits of migration   19

1 **Claiming Siberia: colonial possession and property holding
   in the seventeenth and early eighteenth centuries**   21
   VALERIE KIVELSON

2 **Containment vs. colonization: Muscovite approaches
   to settling the steppe**   41
   BRIAN J. BOECK

3 **Grant, settle, negotiate: military servitors in the
   Middle Volga region**   61
   MATTHEW P. ROMANIELLO

PART II
Colonization on the Imperial Russian frontier   79

4 **Agriculture and the environment on the steppes in the
   nineteenth century**   81
   DAVID MOON

5 **The "ethic of empire" on the Siberian borderland: the
   peculiar case of the "rock people," 1791–1878**   106
   ANDREI A. ZNAMENSKI

6 **Resettling people, unsettling the empire: migration and
   the challenge of governance, 1861–1917**   128
   CHARLES STEINWEDEL

7 **Progress or peril: migrants and locals in
   Russian Tashkent, 1906–14**   148
   JEFF SAHADEO

PART III
Population politics and the Soviet experiment   167

8 **Acclimatization, the shifting science of settlement**   169
   CASSANDRA CAVANAUGH

9 **The aesthetic of Stalinist planning and the world of the
   special villages**   189
   LYNNE VIOLA

10 **"Those who hurry to the Far East": readers, dreamers,
    and volunteers**   213
    ELENA SHULMAN

11 **The "planet of one hundred languages":
    ethnic relations and Soviet identity in the Virgin Lands** 238
    MICHAELA POHL

PART IV
Conclusions   263

12 Colonizing Eurasia   265
ALFRED J. RIEBER

Glossary   280
Index   281

Illustrations

Figures

I.1   Settlers traveling to their land allotments in Siberia, late
      nineteenth century   12
1.1   Semen Remezov's copy of the Godunov Map of all Siberia
      (1666/7)   29
3.1   Engraving of Kazan, seventeenth century   63
5.1   Engraving of "rock people," Altai region, early nineteenth
      century   119
6.1   P.A. Stolypin and A.V. Krivoshein touring Siberia (1910)   136
7.1   Tashkent horseracing track (1900)   157
9.1   A utopian drawing of special settlement (1936)   202
10.1 "Meeting the women patriots" (newspaper illustration, 1939)   219
11.1 "Come with us to the Virgin Lands!" (poster, 1954)   243
12.1 Peasant migrants with their makeshift tents, late
      nineteenth century   269

Tables

4.1   The male peasant and Cossack populations of the open
      steppes of southeastern European Russia, eighteenth
      and nineteenth centuries   84
4.2   Changes in land use in the open steppe region of southeastern
      European Russia, 1725–1887   85

Maps

1   Major ecological zones of Russian Eurasia   4
2   The Muscovite tsardom in the 1680s   46
3   The steppe region of European Russia, c. 1900   82
4   The Russian empire, c. 1914   110
5   The USSR, c. 1950   240

Contributors

Brian J. Boeck is Assistant Professor of History at DePaul University. He is revising the manuscript "Shifting Boundaries on the Don Steppe Frontier: Cossacks, Empires, and Nomads to 1739" on the integration of the Don region into the Russian empire.

Nicholas B. Breyfogle is Associate Professor of History at The Ohio State University. He is the author of *Heretics and Colonizers: Forging Russia's Empire in the South Caucasus* and is currently working on an environmental history of the Lake Baikal region of Siberia.

Cassandra Cavanaugh is Regional Director for Central Asia and the Caucasus of the Open Society Institute's Eurasia Project. She holds a Ph.D. in Russian history from Columbia University, and has written on the role of public health in Russian and Soviet colonization of Central Asia.

Valerie Kivelson is Professor of History at the University of Michigan, Ann Arbor. She is the author of *Cartographies of Tsardom: The Land and Its Meanings in Seventeenth-Century Russia*, as well as works on Muscovite witchcraft, politics, and religion.

David Moon is Professor of Russian History at the University of Durham, England. His current research on the steppes grew out of earlier work on the Russian peasantry. His publications include: *The Russian Peasantry 1600–1930: The World the Peasants Made*; "Peasant migration and the settlement of Russia's frontiers 1550–1897," *Historical Journal* 30 (1997); and "The environmental history of the Russian steppes: Vasilii Dokuchaev and the harvest failure of 1891," *Transactions of the Royal Historical Society*, 6th series, 15 (2005).

Michaela Pohl teaches Russian and European history at Vassar College. Her research focuses on Kazakhstan after Stalin, and on diasporas in the borderlands of the former Soviet Union (Soviet Germans and Chechens in Kazakhstan).

Alfred J. Rieber is Professor of History at the Central European University. Among other books, he is author of *Merchants and Entrepreneurs in Imperial Russia*, and editor of *Forced Migration in Central and Eastern Europe, 1939–50* and *Imperial Rule*. He is completing "Struggle over the Borderlands" on the origins of the Cold War.

Matthew P. Romaniello is Assistant Professor of History at the University of Hawaii. He is currently completing a study of Muscovite colonialism following the conquest of the Khanate of Kazan.

Jeff Sahadeo is Assistant Professor of Political Science and European and Russian Studies and Associate Director of the Institute of European, Russian and Eurasian Studies at Carleton University. He is the author of *Russian Colonial Society in Tashkent, 1865–1923* and co-editor of *Everyday Life in Central Asia*.

Abby Schrader is Associate Professor and Chair of History at Franklin and Marshall College. She is the author of *The Languages of the Lash: Corporal Punishment and Identity in Imperial Russia* and is currently working on a project that explores gender and social identity in the settlement of Siberia.

Elena Shulman is Assistant Professor of History at Texas Tech University. She is the author of *Stalinism on the Frontiers of Empire: Women and State Formation in the Soviet Far East*.

Charles Steinwedel is Associate Professor of History at Northeastern Illinois University in Chicago. He has published articles on documenting identity in the Russian empire and on nationality and empire in the Volga-Urals region. He is currently completing a book on the Russian empire in Bashkiria from 1550 to 1917.

Willard Sunderland is Associate Professor of History at the University of Cincinnati. He is the author of *Taming the Wild Field: Colonization and Empire on the Russian Steppe*. He is currently completing a microhistory of the Russian empire centered on the life of Baron von Ungern-Sternberg, the "Mad Baron" of Mongolia.

Lynne Viola is Professor of History at the University of Toronto. She is the author of *Peasant Rebels under Stalin* and *The Unknown Gulag*.

Andrei A. Znamenski is Associate Professor of History at Alabama State University. He is the author of *Shamanism and Christianity: Native Encounters with Russian Orthodox Missions in Siberia and Alaska, 1820–1917* and *Shamanism in Siberia: Russian Records of Indigenous Spirituality*, and editor of *Shamanism: Critical Concepts in Sociology*

Preface

This volume originated at the conference "Peopling the Periphery: Russian Settlers in Eurasia from Muscovy to Recent Times," held at The Ohio State University, Columbus, OH, 29–30 September 2001. This multidisciplinary workshop explored the policies, practices, cultural representations, and daily-life experiences of Slavic settlement in non-Russian regions of Eurasia over the past 500 years, ending with a roundtable discussion of the current status of ethnic Russians living in former Soviet republics. We would like to thank all the participants of the conference for what was an extremely productive and engaging meeting devoted to this central theme of Russian and Eurasian history. In addition to the people whose work appears here, others who made the conference such a success include Sergei Zhuk, Frank Wcislo, Kira Stevens, Charles King, Natalya Kosmarskaya, Eve Levin, David Hoffmann, Aaron Retish, John Wilson, and Kristin Collins.

The volume also includes two essays that were not presented at the conference, those of Valerie Kivelson and Lynne Viola. Viola's essay originally appeared in *Kritika: Explorations in Russian and Eurasian History* 4, no. 1 (Winter 2003): 101–28, and we thank the journal for permission to reprint a slightly revised version of the article here. Portions of the chapters in this volume by Kivelson and Jeff Sahadeo have since appeared in revised form in their published monographs, respectively *Cartographies of Tsardom: The Land and Its Meanings in Seventeenth-Century Russia* (Ithaca: Cornell University Press, 2006) and *Russian Colonial Society in Tashkent, 1865–1923* (Bloomington and Indianapolis: Indiana University Press, 2007). We thank Cornell University Press and Indiana University Press for permission to reproduce this material here. We also thank the Russian National Library for permission to publish the Remezov map in Kivelson's article, the Anahita Gallery, Inc. (Santa Fe, New Mexico) for their kind permission to publish "Tashkent horseracing track (1900)," and cartographer Bill Nelson for his excellent maps. The publishers have made every effort to contact authors/copyright holders of works reprinted in *Peopling the Russian Periphery*. This has not been possible in every case, however, and the publishers would welcome correspondence from those individuals/companies whom they have been unable to trace.

For their generous financial support of the conference, we would like to express our appreciation to the following institutions and departments at Ohio State: the

Mershon Center, the Center for Slavic and East European Studies, the Office of International Affairs, the College of Humanities, and the Department of History. For their further financial support that made possible the publication of this volume, we would again like to thank the Center for Slavic and East European Studies, the College of Humanities, and the Department of History at Ohio State. The Taft Research Center at the University of Cincinnati also provided important financial assistance at the publication stage.

We offer a special thank you to Victoria Clement, Kristin Collins, Maryann Keisel, Wynn Kimble, and William Wolf, who provided invaluable help in organizing the conference and in preparing the volume. The sage advice of the anonymous readers who critiqued the manuscript in its various stages greatly improved the volume, and we are especially appreciative of the extensive comments of two now not-so-anonymous referees, Robert Geraci and David McDonald. Finally, we would like to express our appreciation to Peter Sowden, Tom Bates, and the editorial staff at Routledge (and Bookcraft) for their great assistance in bringing the book to life, to Christopher Feeney for his copyediting, and to Richard Sakwa, series editor, for including the volume in the BASEES/Routledge series on Russian and East European Studies.

Archives and abbreviations

Archives

Kazakhstan

AOM	Akmolinskii oblastnoi istoriko-kraevedcheskii muzei (Astana)
APRK	Arkhiv Presidenta Respubliki Kazakhstana (Almaty)
GAAkO	Gosudarstvennyi arkhiv Akmolinskoi oblasti (Astana)
OPDAO	Otdelenie partiinoi dokumentatsii Akmolinskoi oblasti (Astana)

Russia

GAAO	Gosudarstvennyi arkhiv Arkhangel'skoi oblasti (Archangel)
GAKhK	Gosudarstvennyi arkhiv Khabarovskogo kraia (Khabarovsk)
GAOO	Gosudarstvennyi arkhiv Orenburgskoi oblasti (Orenburg)
GAOPDFAO	Gosudarstvennyi arkhiv obshchestvenno-politicheskikh dvizhenii i formirovanii Arkhangel'skoi oblasti (Archangel)
GARF	Gosudarstvennyi Arkhiv Rossiiskoi Federatsii (Moscow)
GARO	Gosudarstvennyi arkhiv Rostovskoi oblasti (Rostov-on-Don),
GASK	Gosudarstvennyi arkhiv Stavropol'skogo kraia (Stavropol')
GASO	Gosudarstvennyi arkhiv Samarskoi oblasti (Samara)
GAVO	Gosudarstvennyi arkhiv Vologodskoi oblasti (Vologda),
RGADA	Rossiiskii gosudarstvennyi arkhiv drevnikh aktov (Moscow)
RGAE	Rossiiskii gosudarstvennyi arkhiv ekonomiki (Moscow)
RGALI	Rossiiskii gosudarstvennyi arkhiv literatury i iskusstva (Moscow)
RGASPI	Rossiiskii gosudarstvennyi arkhiv sotsial'no-politicheskoi istorii (Moscow)
RGAVMF	Rossiiskii gosudarstvennyi arkhiv Voenno-Morskogo Flota (St Petersburg)
RGB	Rossiiskaia gosudarstvennaia biblioteka, otdel rukopisei (Moscow)
RGIA	Rossiiskii gosudarstvennyi istoricheskii arkhiv (St Petersburg)
RGO	Nauchno-otrazlevoi arkhiv Russkogo geograficheskogo obshchestva (St Petersburg)
RGVIA	Rossiiskii gosudarstvennyi voenno-istoricheskii arkhiv (Moscow)

RNB	Rossiiskaia natsional'naia biblioteka (St Petersburg)
TsAFSB	Tsentral'nyi arkhiv federal'noi sluzhby bezopasnosti (Moscow)
TsGIARB	Tsentral'nyi gosudarstvennyi istoricheskii arkhiv Respubliki Bashkortostan (Ufa)
TsKhAD	Tsentr khranenia arkhivnikh dokumentov administratsii Altaiskogo kraia (Barnaul)
TsKhDMO	Tsentr khraneniia dokumentov molodezhnykh organizatsii (Moscow, part of RGASPI since 1999)
VOANPI	Vologodskii oblastnoi arkhiv noveishei politicheskoi istorii (Vologda),

United States

HIL	Hilandar Research Library (Columbus, OH)
HUHL	Harvard University, Houghton Library (Cambridge, MA)
LLC	Law Library of Congress, Russian Manuscript Scrolls (Washington, DC)

Uzbekistan

| TsGANTMD | Tsentral'nyi gosudarstvennyi arkhiv nauchno-tekhnicheskikh i meditsinskikh dokumentov Respubliki Uzbeskistan (Tashkent) |
| TsGARUz | Tsentral'nyi gosudarstvennyi arkhiv Respubliki Uzbekistan (Tashkent) |

Abbreviations

art.(s)	article(s)
ch.	chast'
chp.	chapter
d (dd.)	delo (dela)
f.	fond
ff.	folia
kn.	kniga
l. (ll.)	list, listy
no.	number
ob.	oborot
op.	opis'
p. (pp.)	page(s)
pt.	point
t.	tom
v.	volume
vyp.	vypusk

Russian colonizations

An introduction

Nicholas B. Breyfogle, Abby Schrader, and
Willard Sunderland

According to the foundation tale of the Maidu tribe of California, after the great Earthmaker spirit created the world, he pointed to one small corner and told the tribe's ancestors: "You will live here ... Living in a country that is little, not big, you will be content."[1] It is hard to know what the Earthmaker spirit said to the first Russians, but their arrangement turned out to be just the opposite. The corner they ultimately received was huge, and they do not seem to have been especially content – at least not content enough to stay in one place. According to the Primary Chronicle, the earliest Slavs of what would become western Russia and Ukraine were migrants with a penchant for moving. Members of ancient tribes from plains near the Danube, they migrated north to the forest zone where they proceeded to clear the land, build towns, organize a state, and migrate further, eventually spreading themselves and their culture across all of what became known as "the Rus' land," a massive territory stretching, roughly, from the Baltic and White seas in the north to the edges of the Pontic steppe in the south.[2] Over subsequent centuries, the original Rus' land changed names and became even bigger, while the Rus' diversified and turned into Russians, Ukrainians, and Belorussians. But the migration continued, and it unfolded in multiple directions, transforming the eastern Slavs collectively – and the Russians especially – into the most dispersed Europeans of the Old World. Today the Russians, together with their language, shops, culinary habits, and worldviews, inhabit all the corners of northern Eurasia, from Kaliningrad to Vladivostok and Anadyr to Chisinau.

How and why did this colonization unfold? And what were the consequences – for the Russians, for the other peoples and cultures of Eurasia, and for Eurasia itself? Our volume explores these questions by examining the problem of colonization in Russian life from the Muscovite to the Soviet era. Given the emphasis on colonization, the essays focus, naturally enough, on the history of settlers and settlement. But they branch inevitably into other topics as well – the history of interethnic relations, political culture, imperial governance, economic development, demography, environmental management and science, and the social politics of class and gender. It is not surprising that research on Russian colonization leads in such diverse directions because colonization in Russia was never just a matter of people moving and settling. As the historian Vasilii Kliuchevskii (1841–1911) famously put it, colonization should be seen as the "basic fact" of Russian history, and as such, it relates to all the key structures, processes, and events of Russian life.[3] Study the history of Russian colonization and you find, in effect, Russia itself – in all its imposing scale and complexity. The essays here evoke this interrelationship. They offer new perspectives on the meanings and practices of Russian settlement, while at the same time exposing the deep interconnections between the subject and some of the most important questions and themes of the Russian experience.

The historiography of Russian colonization

Because of its importance, colonization has a long presence in Russian historical writing, going back as far as the Primary Chronicle. As a rule, however, the early chroniclers, whether in Kiev, Moscow, or elsewhere, did little more than record the fact that a given town or village was settled with settlers, soldiers, monks, or lords. No special explanations or meanings were attached to the process. In fact, the idea that colonization represented a special process as such did not exist. Colonization in the Rus' chronicles amounted to "settlement," and settlement was a prosaic fact implying the physical occupation of land, nothing more. Town-building was an attribute of Russian princes. Muscovite documents made note of the clearing of land, and unsettled and unfarmed spaces were indicated as "empty lands" or "wastes." But there is nothing in the sources of early Russia to suggest that Russians at the time invested the enterprises of migration and settlement with larger meaning.

This lack of interest in greater significance began to change in the early eighteenth century. In the age of Peter the Great, Russia's newly Europeanized "learned men" developed a fonder – or at least more self-consciously curious – view of colonization. It was now an important lever of the political economy as well as, depending on circumstances, a worthy symbol of royal and national glory and progress – the kind of endeavor that deserved to be described and explained, in the past as well as the present. The full impact of this important intellectual shift came a few decades later with the reign of Catherine II (1762–96), when the Russian state conquered the Black Sea steppes and became engaged for the first time in managing colonization on a large scale. Catherine's scholars did not write thick tomes on the history of Russian settlement, but they did at least acknowledge that Russia had a colonizing history, which was itself an important development.

The first historians to build on this breakthrough were the scholars and *intelligenty* of the mid-nineteenth century. S.M. Solov'ev, the "state school" historian, K.D. Kavelin, the "liberal," and A.P. Shchapov, the "regionalist," differed on many things, but they all agreed that colonization represented a dominant leitmotif of Russian history. In fact, by the era of the Great Reforms just about everyone agreed that colonization deserved special attention, and it was not long before the subject became a field of research in its own right. In the late nineteenth and early twentieth centuries, against the backdrop of mass migrations in Russia and abroad, a new generation of scholars argued that colonization stood at the very center of Russia's national narrative. And to prove it, they dutifully churned out monographs and articles on colonization for thick journals and regional historical societies. The result: colonization became a bona fide historical subject with its own questions, categories, heroes, recognized sources, and dueling approaches and interpretations.[4] Some scholars emphasized the role of the state, others the contributions of the "common man" (though rarely the common woman). Some criticized the government's stewardship of the process, others defended it. Most cheered the good things Russian settlement had done for non-Russian "nations, peoples, and tribes." But by 1917, regardless of how one interpreted the phenomenon, writing on colonization had become a thoroughly respectable pursuit within the Russian academy.

The coming of the Soviet order did not change this. Research on colonization remained important and in fact increased markedly over the Soviet years as successive generations of specialists busily rewrote the history of Russian colonization Soviet-style, offering changing interpretations over time. In the literature of the 1920s, when Russian chauvinism was out and class critique was in, plebeian Russian colonists became the obvious heroes of the drama, the tsars and the landlords the obvious villains, but all Russian colonizers – plebeian colonists included – were chastised for exploiting non-Russian peoples. By the mid-1930s, a new Stalinist line cleansed most Russian colonists of their sins (even some landlords got gentle treatment), and Russian colonization was turned into a "positive force" that had brought "economic development" and "cultural improvement" to the borderlands. After the Stalin years, the line then shifted again, becoming more evenhanded in its assessments of "progressive Russian influence," though by far the most striking change was less a matter of interpretation than of scale. Between the 1950s and the end of the Soviet era, writing on colonization exploded in size. Every Soviet republic, region, town, and locality seemed to deserve an account of its colonizing history, and each history deserved to stand on a solid bedrock of socio-economic and demographic data, mined in copious detail from central and regional archives and packed, neo-Stakhanovite style, into imposing graphs and footnotes.[5] By the Perestroika period, some historians of colonization had begun to apologize for the ideological excesses of earlier scholarship, but the high empirical style continued through to the end of the USSR and still appears in much contemporary Russian writing on the subject.

Western research on Russian colonization during the Cold War years, by comparison, was less exhaustive and voluminous. Influenced by Kliuchevskii and his students such as Pavel Miliukov (1859–1943) and Matvei Liubavskii (1860–1936), Western historians accepted the centrality of colonization as a given and focused on providing a less obviously ideological rendition of the subject for Western readers. Among other things, Stalinist (and Brezhnevian) overstatements about pure Russian pioneers and visionary Soviet planners were challenged, tsarist colonial policy on the Kazakh steppe was both praised and chided, and Catherine the Great's fondness for foreign colonists was defended as a good idea at the time. There was no single school of views or approaches. Instead Western research on colonization reflected the shifting trends of Western academic scholarship between the 1950s and the early 1990s, with the history of policy surrendering by

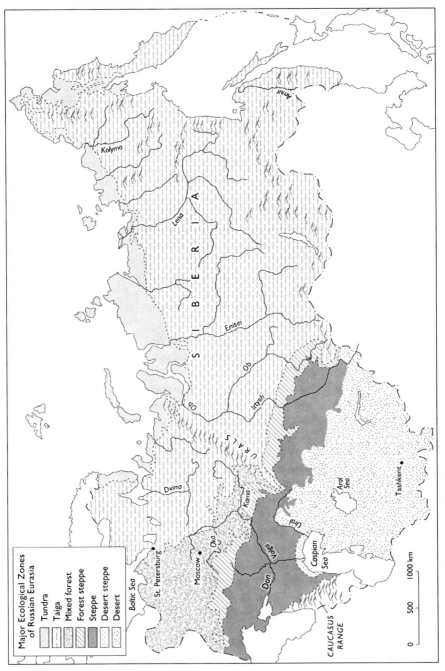

Map 1 Major ecological zones of Russian Eurasia

and large to social history, though demographic and economic history as well as historical geography remained important throughout.[6] As a result, by the early 1990s, in the West, as in the USSR, the study of colonization had become an identifiable historical subfield with its own specialized historiography, conference panels, questions, and concentrations. Together, Russian/Soviet and Western historiography placed the subject on the map and filled it with facts, figures, and notable interpretations.

There were, however, some limitations. For one, much of the scholarship on colonization prior to the mid-1990s – Western as well as Russian/Soviet – stressed the late imperial period at the expense of other eras, both earlier and later. As a result, the Great Siberian Migration tended to appear as a remarkable exception rather than as simply a phase within a longer colonizing history. Also, despite the detailed focus, especially by Soviet historians, on the social experience of migration, whole categories of migrants – women, religious dissenters, exiles, "repressed persons" – went unnoticed, while other aspects of the social history of migration, such as the cross-cultural encounters that came with borderland settlement, were treated mechanically, usually as little more than the sum of concrete exchanges and borrowings between ethnic groups. Environmental history was also mostly absent, and the Russian case was studied on its own rather than within a comparative framework. Even state policy, the most scrutinized aspect of colonization, tended to be approached almost exclusively in terms of discrete settlement initiatives in particular periods, with a heavy emphasis on juxtaposing intentions and outcomes rather than exploring what state plans revealed about deeper issues of governance and ideology. In other words, colonization scholarship in the Cold War decades was at once rich in information yet restricted in its scope and methodology. It tended to be empirical rather than conceptual, insular rather than comparative.

Since the 1990s research on colonization has changed considerably, and the shift reflects broader changes in the Russian field and in the study of history more generally. Archives today are much more open to both Western and Russian researchers than they ever were during the Soviet period, which means that there are new materials to study. With the collapse of the USSR and the diminished ideological significance of 1917, there are also new reasons to see continuities of colonization across the divides of the Russian past, and to recognize similarities between Russian colonization and colonizations elsewhere. Like Russian history more broadly, the study of Russian colonization met "the linguistic turn," "the new social history," "the new cultural history," and "the new imperial history," and changed in the process. The Russian frontier, for example, used to be a unidimensional line of Russian settlement. Now it is a multicultural zone of interaction between Russians and non-Russians, "strangers" and "natives." In a similar way, the once narrow study of colonization policy has started giving way to interest in the political culture of colonization – that is, the deeper ideological presuppositions about territory, population, class, gender, enlightenment, progress, and power that shaped the government's evolving approach to colonization as a state project.[7]

The essays in this volume reflect these developments. Our principal goal is to showcase the recent scholarship on colonization that is pushing the field in new directions. Consequently, we emphasize breadth and diversity, both of methods and themes and across regions and periods. The articles here range from the mid-sixteenth century to the mid-twentieth. Within this long span, neither the Muscovite, Imperial, nor Soviet era of colonization is excluded – nor, for that matter, is any one period prioritized as more emblematic than the others. The sources supporting the essays are also diverse, ranging from the institutional to the personal, the literary to the statistical, and they appear in revealing combinations, with regional archives cited as readily as metropolitan ones and the oral testimonies and personal letters of migrants interwoven with the revelations of government dispatches and protocols. The disciplinary range of the articles – from the history of medicine to environmental history and women's history – is similarly broad and reflects the new sensibilities that are shaping the study of Russian history in general. Our authors are also comfortable with the literature on colonization beyond the Russian case, which suggests not only the influence that comparative studies of colonization are having on the Russian field but also the influence that the Russian field *should* have on comparative studies.[8] Our hope is that this volume will contribute to movement in this direction, bringing Russia into a broader international view.

At the same time, we have had to make choices. Our volume does not address all possible topics or geographical regions. The focus of the essays falls mainly on Eastern Slavic – and in particular, Russian – migrants rather than on the foreigners or "domestic" "others" who joined Slavs in Russia's historical migrant pool, and, with the exception of one essay, we stress rural rather than urban settlement and permanent movement rather than seasonal migration. The role of religious dissenters, and of religious forces more generally, is for the most part absent here.[9] The articles likewise concentrate much more on the southern and eastern borderlands of the tsarist and Soviet states than on other peripheries, and some important periods are omitted – the resettlements of the Catherinian years, for example, do not appear in the volume, nor does Slavic settlement in the Baltic region after World War II.[10] The rich and fascinating history of Russian migrations to the New World, from Alaska to Brooklyn, are also unexplored here. These limits and gaps reflect the discrete research interests of our authors, but achieving total coverage in colonization would be daunting in any case, even with twice as many essays. The subject is too big and too complex for complete inclusion and single interpretations. Knowing this, we make no claim to offer a total view. Instead, our goal is to highlight how current research is changing Russian colonization studies, enhancing our picture of how colonization "worked" and what it meant to the actors and observers involved, colonists and colonized, high and low, Russian and "other."

Themes of the volume

A central motif of this new picture is the recognition of the essential diversity of colonization. Kliuchevskii was right: colonization *is* the "basic fact" of Russian history. But "basic" was neither simple nor uniform. Colonization was carried out by a stunningly diverse panorama of settlers (Russians, non-Russians, foreigners, traders, peasants, military servitors, urban workers, religious dissenters, political dissidents, criminals, witches, women, men, and families) who moved under varied circumstances (as exiles, runaways, or voluntary "resettlers"), established themselves in diverse environments, and were observed, extolled, condemned, and controlled by varied sorts of non-colonists from the government and "the public" alike. In fact, Russian colonization unfolded with such splendid diversity that it is more accurate to talk of Russian *colonizations* in the plural than the singular. Ever evolving and multifaceted, Russian borderland settlement was a process in which outsider colonists, native peoples, the natural environment, and the world of the state and its representatives influenced one another in ever shifting combinations. Differences of time and place could and did create different colonizations. As these essays make clear, there were watershed moments in which colonization changed qualitatively and quantitatively: the relatively restrained colonization of Muscovite Russia contrasts with the ever expanding waves of settlement that appeared under Catherine the Great, intensified and transformed in the late Imperial period along with the Great Migration to Siberia, and became a central component of Soviet social, economic, and security agendas in the twentieth century. The meanings of ethnic and religious affiliation in the context of colonization also changed considerably, as they did throughout the globe, from the Muscovite to the Soviet eras, from a relative indifference to such human identity categories to an overpowering fixation.

Yet for all the diversity, colonization was also constant. That is, even as the particulars of the process varied from period to period and region to region, the process itself stayed the same, shaped by "persistent factors" such as Russia's "permeable frontiers," enormous distances, small numbers of officials, and much vaster numbers of plebs and peasants.[11] In other words, when viewed in its broadest scope, the history of Russian colonization is a history of diversity *within* continuity. The intertwined processes of movement and settlement had myriad regional, local, even individual inflections, yet they were also coherent. Dramatic changes occurred in material culture, ideology, social life, and the urge and power of government to act on society between the sixteenth century and the age of Sputnik, but these changes modified Russian colonization – they did not completely reorder it.

The twists and turns of Russian colonization also never diverted the Russian state and people onto their own separate *Sonderweg*. Russian migration did indeed have distinguishing characteristics, even important ones, such as a long-running and heavy state involvement in managing the colonization enterprise, a colonist pool composed overwhelmingly of rural people, fuzzy or non-existent geographical boundaries separating "Russia proper" from its imperial territories, which created a generally myopic view among educated Russians of the colonial dimensions of the settlement process, and the striking mixture of repression and popular enthusiasm that characterized migration to the periphery in the Soviet era. And these are just a few of the factors that could be considered special about the Russian case. But this distinctiveness should not be overstated. Echoes of each of the seemingly uniquely Russian or Soviet characteristics that we have just listed can be found elsewhere, and, in fact, the closer one looks into Russian colonization the more one sees how its practices and patterns formed part of a broader international story of migration, state-building, the projection of power over non-metropolitan peoples, and the transformation and exploitation of "empty" or "underutilized" territories. The methods, terminologies, and mentalities of settlement in Russian Eurasia carried their own inflections, shaped by the particulars of the country's history and geography, which is what one would expect, but they did not result in the creation of a uniquely "Russian" approach to colonization.

Convict settlement, for example, was a tsarist and Soviet practice but it was also a British and French one. The settlement of religious sectarians to new frontiers was similarly international – the Dukhobors and Molokans in the South Caucasus in the nineteenth century, the Puritans in Plymouth Colony in the seventeenth, for example. *Pomest'e* grants to military servitors on Muscovy's marchlands resembled *timar* grants to *sipahis* in the Ottoman Balkans. The Russian government's settlement and incorporation of its steppe territories resembled the operations of the Qing empire on grasslands further east, as well as Dutch and British settlement of the Eastern Cape and the American agriculturalization of the Great Plains. The frontier identities and cross-cultural adaptations of early Cossack communities have much in common with the "middle ground" worlds of the North American *métis* and the gauchos of the Argentine pampas. And borrowed terms such as "pioneer" (*pioner*), "squatter" (*skvater*), and "colonization" (*kolonizatsiia*), not to mention references to the Amur River as a "Russian Mississippi" and the Caucasus as "our Algeria," were easy to find in official Russian writing by the late nineteenth century, proving that the Russians in charge of colonization at the time were self-consciously comparing and contrasting Russian settlement and colonial power to what they observed in other states.[12] Borderland migration and settlement were clearly widely occurring phenomena and, to a point, everywhere they unfolded they were shaped by common concerns and expressed through comparable idioms. As a result, determining what exactly made Russian colonization "Russian" is more a question of subtle emphasis than of drawing distinct lines between Russian ways and the ways of other colonizing states and societies. Russian colonization was, in effect, Russian *and* international at the same time.

A changing yet near-continuous process, unfolding over centuries and playing itself out within an international continuum of migration – this is the basic frame that shapes the three principal ways that our authors approach Russian colonization in this volume: as a state project, as a set of social experiences, and as an encounter between colonizers and the natural world. From the state's perspective, colonization was consistently linked to basic issues of security, economic development, and social change and control. Of these, security was most basic of all. The

princes of Moscow, who cut their way to power through the rubble of the Golden
Horde, feared nomadic raids and frontier rebellions. As a result, as we see in the
essays by Brian Boeck and Matthew Romaniello, military matters were paramount. The Riurikids and early Romanovs needed to settle their defensive lines
along the edges of the southern steppe and their garrison towns in places like the
Middle Volga. But at the same time, they could not settle them too much. Too
many settlers on the frontier meant too few serfs in the interior (not to mention too
many irate and laborless boyars). Therefore, as Boeck shows, after the mid-seventeenth century, Muscovite rulers *discouraged* the sort of large-scale population
movement to the south that would have been necessary to reinforce the steppe
lines.

The tension between the needs of movement and stasis persisted throughout the
Imperial and Soviet periods, and the government's recurring (if imperfect) solution was to organize the sort of migration that would serve both objectives at once.
Some people were to be moved for security purposes, by force if necessary, while
others had to be kept in place to ensure proper social and economic order in the
interior. Elena Shulman's essay on the Khetagurovite movement, a Stalinist initiative to settle the Russian Far East in the 1930s, exposes this dynamic clearly. The
Soviet government encouraged young, patriotic, single Slavic women to go east in
order to reinforce the state's security position in the face of the perceived Japanese
threat. At the same time, it banned the movement of seemingly less useful migrants
and forcefully "cleansed" the area of "suspect groups," especially Japanese,
Chinese, and Korean laborers. The suspect groups did not appreciate this, of
course, but the Khetagurovites did. Many of the new settlers moved right into the
homes of the "cleansed," taking over their former jobs. As Shulman shows, the
young enthusiasts who answered the party's call enthusiastically supported the
program, embracing it as the central basis of their patriotic Soviet identity.[13]

In addition to security, state agents were also preoccupied with colonization's
economic implications. As Romaniello and Valerie Kivelson show, Muscovite
leaders wanted to ensure that land and other natural resources in Siberia and the
Middle Volga were put to productive use. Andrei Znamenski highlights that this
concern remained paramount for administrators in the Altai in the eighteenth and
nineteenth centuries. And Charles Steinwedel's essay demonstrates that early
twentieth-century statesmen like Petr Stolypin and Aleksandr Krivoshein focused
on much the same thing: maximizing the economic potential of Siberia for the
benefit of the state (albeit through private landholding and greater reliance on individual initiative). Not surprisingly, the goal of economic expansion through colonization if anything only intensified during the Soviet era. As Michaela Pohl
makes clear, the mass resettlements to the Virgin Lands of Kazakhstan in the
1950s were inextricably linked to Nikita Khrushchev's desire to increase overall
agricultural and industrial production.

A similar continuity shows in the arena of social reform – indeed the state's aims
to increase economic productivity and "improve" society were often intertwined.
Through the centuries, government types saw resettlement as a means to purge the
central provinces of unwanted elements such as religious dissenters, political

opponents, and criminals – creating in the process the image of Siberia as a vast, frozen penal colony – while at the same time using it as a tool to create new types of communities on the frontier that would contribute to the state's goals of economic expansion. The Stolypin-era migration plan and the Khetagurovite project in the Russian Far East again come to mind here as examples, as does Lynne Viola's examination of the utopian social ambitions of the "special settlements" of the north during the Stalin period. Aspirations towards social engineering were also apparent in the Russian elite's embrace, beginning in the eighteenth century, of a European-style civilizing mission in which ordinary Russian colonists – even backward peasants who did not appear inspiring at all in Tula or Tambov – were imagined as *Kulturträger* for even more "backward" peoples on the state's undeveloped frontiers.

Of course, just as there were striking continuities in the government's efforts to deploy colonization as a strategic, economic, and social tool, there were also enduring challenges – most importantly the sheer vastness and diversity of the country, the state's limited fiscal, military, administrative, and logistical resources, and the overwhelming peasant or lower-class origin of its settlers. A number of the essays comment on these recurring obstacles. Viola's article on the "special villages" exposes the shortcomings of state aspirations quite clearly. As she demonstrates, Soviet efforts to re-educate "hostile elements" from the center by expelling them to the north and incarcerating them in penal colonies fell far short of their utopian goal. In fact, rather than conforming to the elaborate modernist plans devised for them in the center, the colonies ended up largely beyond the center's control, plagued by intractable problems of disease, hunger, alcoholism, corruption, and drastic mismanagement. Jeff Sahadeo's essay on the "elusive quest for modernity" in late tsarist Tashkent emphasizes a similar point. As he shows, Russian elites (both official and public) in late imperial Tashkent agreed so wholeheartedly with St Petersburg's stated mission to spread enlightenment in Central Asia that they hindered some of the center's other objectives, notably St Petersburg's colonialist economic goals and the hesitant shift towards broadening political participation after 1905. Furthermore, these same local elites found themselves stymied in pursuing their "progressive" mission by the influx to the city of thousands of "dirty," "backward," and ultimately threatening lower-class Russian migrants. The official tsarist vision of progress through migration in Central Asia was thus sabotaged by migration itself.

Sahadeo's essay is also a useful reminder that not all Russian colonization was agricultural. In an overwhelmingly peasant country, rural settlement predominated, which is why this volume stresses colonization in the countryside. But numerous rural colonists drifted – or were drafted – into settling towns, and town-building was long a concern of Russian colonization planners. Siberian fortress towns – like Tobol'sk, Tomsk, and Irkutsk – became the essential linkage points of Russian power in the region in the mid-seventeenth century, and empire-builders of later times such as Peter the Great, Ivan Kirilov, Catherine the Great, Grigorii Potemkin, Nikolai Murav'ev, and Joseph Stalin likewise stamped the state's presence on sparsely inhabited frontiers through the building of cities. (St Petersburg,

Orenburg, Vladikavkaz, Ekaterinoslav, Odessa, Khabarovsk, Komsomol'sk on Amur, and Magadan are just a few examples.) The city of Tashkent was founded long before the Russians transformed it into the capital of their Turkestan. But, as Sahadeo suggests, this very old town became the focus of new construction and expansion under the tsarist authorities, which itself required the influx of new migrants, all of which only underscores the key role envisioned for towns by the Russian government as both the material and symbolic strongholds of Russian power in the periphery.

Another challenge faced by the state was the problem of violence. While Russia's rulers planned for borderland settlement that would bring security, economic progress, and social order, outside the boardrooms and command centers things could be much more volatile. Outsider settlement all too often provoked anger and rebellion among indigenous peoples, just as it sparked conflict between settler communities. Pohl's examination of the chaotic conse-quences of the Virgin Lands campaign in Kazakhstan in the 1950s exposes this aspect of the colonization dynamic in vivid detail. Massive, rapid state-spon-sored migration to the Kazakh steppe produced not only brawls but large-scale riots and fights between incoming "Virgin Landers," indigenous Kazakhs, and members of those previously deported communities of Volga Germans and Caucasian peoples who had been unceremoniously dumped in Kazakhstan in the 1940s. This violence plagued the work of authorities on the Kazakh steppe for the duration of the resettlement campaign, and the dislocations of the period then cast long shadows over the way the campaign was remembered thereafter. Pohl's description of these social explosions is a reminder of the costly and tragic gap that often separated colonization in practice from colonization by design. Simi-larly, examining a much earlier period, Kivelson notes how, despite official prohibitions against maltreatment of indigenous Siberians, Russian state repre-sentatives, Cossacks, and peasant settlers alike engaged in savage, frequent, and unrepentant violence against native inhabitants. Sahadeo, too, underscores the widespread and disruptive violence between settlers and Central Asians in pre-revolutionary Turkestan.

The essays also point out that colonization was very much a gendered process, and that the politics of gender represented yet another variety of challenge for state authorities. Under both the tsars and the commissars, the settlement zones, espe-cially zones of predominantly military-oriented settlement, often suffered striking gender imbalances, producing government efforts to increase the number and types of female settlers – as the Khetagurovite campaign underscores. The mate-rial and social realities of settlement also created new forms of sexual and family dynamics within settler communities, and between settlers and the indigenous people who lived near them – as Kivelson notes in regard to the taking of native women as hostages, wives, and slaves by Russian male settlers in Siberia.

Migration and settlement – the act of leaving old places and creating new ones on distant frontiers – held the potential, at least in theory, to overturn or reshape gender norms. It is little surprise, then, that political and social authorities, either consciously or unconsciously, attempted to reinforce them. Sometimes this reassertion of gender structures was the result of the demands of frontier life, as Romaniello underscores in his discussion of the relationship between dowries, marriage patterns, and colonial land holding among Russian military servitors in the Kazan region in the sixteenth century. Sahadeo too examines how the status of women became a litmus test for the successes and failures of Russian civilization. In order to elevate themselves in comparison to Central Asians, Russian elites in Tashkent touted their purportedly respectful treatment of women, and expressed alarm at the begging or prostitution of Russian female settlers because it overturned their notions of the imperial hierarchy. In other cases, the reinforcement of gender codes was clearly imposed from the center. As Shulman notes, for example, prospective Khetagurovites were invited by Stalinist propaganda to sign up as seemingly equal partners in a common patriotic cause, yet they were also reminded by Khetagurova herself that it was the "lads" who would be building roads and cutting down trees on the far eastern frontier, while women were needed to provide "caring hands," "cheerful laughter," and traditional feminine contributions.

The state's challenges in organizing, controlling, and gendering settlement were echoed, in their way, by the challenges faced by settlers themselves. As a number of our authors make clear, relocating to the borderlands, even for the most favored and best-equipped migrants, was a difficult undertaking. For runaways and convicts, it was usually fraught with special uncertainty, deprivation, and abuse, as Viola's essay on the "special settlers" of the early 1930s clearly shows. At the same time, it is also true that the very fact of moving to the frontier could provide newcomers with promising opportunities. For example, colonists utilized the social spaces opened up to them in frontier regions to challenge and manipulate state categories and demands. Thus, as Romaniello reveals, military servitors in the Middle Volga, in order to satisfy familial needs for land, challenged and reformulated the structures of *pomest'e* land tenure to

Figure I.1   Settlers traveling to their land allotments in Siberia, late nineteenth century. From *Aziatskaia Rossiia*, v. 1 (St Petersburg, 1914), 479.

serve their purposes. Some of the Russian Old Believers in the Altai region – the "rock people" – who appear in Znamenski's essay likewise took full advantage of the tsarist government's decision to define them not as Russian peasants but as "settled aliens" in order to obtain the legal and economic benefits that flowed from this status.

In colonization, there was often room to serve the common good and one's own good at the same time. Shulman's essay, for example, reveals how the young Khetagurovite migrants who responded so enthusiastically to the state's ideological messages in the 1930s were also not averse to taking advantage of the practical material incentives provided by the migration program. Even where colonization produced violence and turmoil, it also generated possibility. Indeed, while Pohl exposes the horrible turbulence and dislocation of the Virgin Lands campaign, she also stresses how Khrushchev's initiative nonetheless provided hundreds of thousands of varied people – both newcomers and prior residents, Russians, Kazakhs, Germans, and others – with the chance to build a new region, new lives, and new self-definitions.

Cross-cultural interaction was another near constant feature of the migrant experience in the borderlands. Russian and Slavic settlers frequently had to contend with neighbors who looked different, prayed differently, and spoke a different language. They also had to contend with officialdom's shifting approaches to these differences. Kivelson, Romaniello, and Znamenski, for instance, all suggest that authorities in the Muscovite and early imperial periods were less concerned with the ethnic and religious belonging of their colonists than with effective political and economic management in the borderlands. The tsar's servitors and pioneers could be ethnically and religiously diverse as long as they were politically reliable – that is, as long as they paid their taxes or tribute, ensured peace and social order, and defended the realm when necessary from external attack or internal rebellion. Yet by the late imperial and Soviet periods, considerations of nationality loomed far larger in the minds of colonization planners, as Steinwedel and Shulman suggest, and as Cassandra Cavanaugh highlights in her discussion of the links between ethnicity, acclimatization theory, and Russian colonization in Central Asia.

At the same time, the state's notions of who was who in ethnic or religious terms were at best only part of the picture. In the local settlement worlds of the borderlands, identities were more fluid than fixed, and official perceptions of ethnoconfessional separateness did not always coincide with the lived realities of hybridity and synthesis. As we see in Kivelson's article, for example, Muscovite mapping in Siberia helped codify ethnocultural groups in the Russian mind, yet in the settlements themselves settlers and native peoples were mixing and merging through economic, sexual, and familial ties. In certain cases, relations between ethnicities were structured in accordance with clear hierarchies of power that privileged Orthodox and/or ethnically Russian communities. In other encounters, power relations between settlers and natives were more amorphous, generating more equitable fields of interaction and even ones that placed Slavic settlers at a disadvantage. Interethnic tension and conflict were certainly a part of the story of Russian colonization, but so too were friendship, intermarriage, and mutually beneficial economic relations.

Like state aspirations and social experiences, the interplay between colonizers and the natural environment was a similarly enduring feature of Slavic colonization – it unfolded as an essential dynamic wherever and whenever colonization occurred. Russian settlers shaped the environment just as the environment shaped them, and state officials and non-state students of colonization made recurrent attempts of their own to mold the natural landscapes of the colonizing zones, both physically and conceptually. As Kivelson makes clear, mapping land holdings in Siberia emerged as a significant activity as early as the seventeenth century and carried important implications for the articulation of state power in the region. Boeck notes how the southern steppe represented a disease frontier that both hindered and defined the character of Muscovite settlement (or lack thereof) in that region. Cassandra Cavanaugh likewise demonstrates how Russian students of climate developed their own climatological science in order to understand and assist Russian colonization efforts in Central Asia in the late imperial and early Soviet periods. Here, the inability of Russian settlers to conquer the climate threatened to undermine Russian notions of the superiority of European people over natives. In the process, the sufferings of Russian settlers in the new environment made more concrete and permanent the concept of ethnic difference between the northern Slavs and the southern Central Asians. Colonists and their relations with the native peoples and local ecology became focal topics in scientific debates over the place of race and biology in the building of socialism and, less overtly, the general imperialist-civilizational endeavor.

Of course, regardless of what strategies were employed to "know the territory," the process of bringing peripheral regions under cultivation and of introducing new crops and agrarian and industrial practices had serious and often destructive environmental consequences for local populations, outsider migrants, and the larger ecosystems they inhabited. While much research remains to be done in this area, David Moon's article provides a suggestive introduction to the complex impact that settlement could produce within a given natural environment – in his case, the environment of the European steppe. As Moon shows, the overall degradation of the steppe seemed severe enough by the late nineteenth century that it prompted Russian scientists to express alarm over the long-term viability of the steppe's ecology – concerns which then made their way into the intense debates over colonization that defined the late imperial "colonization question." These concerns were notably absent in the 1930s, however, when the Khetagurovites set out to "tame" and "rule" for socialism the "empty" and "savage" natural world of the Far East. Colonization was thus always as much an environmental issue as it was a political and social one. Indeed, these three crucial dimensions of the colonization story were often closely intertwined.

Conclusions

Since 1991, Slavic colonization has entered yet a new phase. In response to the uncertainties, material hardships, and social tensions that flowed from the collapse of the USSR, tens of thousands of Russian families in the newly independent states, many of them the descendants of earlier generations of settlers, left their homes in the 1990s and early 2000s – some voluntarily, some forcibly – and relocated to a "Mother Russia" that was never quite their own. (The same holds true for the thousands of Ukrainians and Belorussians who returned after 1991 to their equally unfamiliar "motherlands.") Those Slavs who remained in the "near abroad" have had varied fates. Some have adjusted to new norms and emerging opportunities, overcoming, in certain contexts, clear abuses and restrictions on their rights. Others have stood still, trapped in a bitter nostalgia for the old USSR and clamoring for the return of privileges they once took for granted. Meanwhile, politicians in Moscow continue to engage, some frivolously, others seriously, with the Gordian knot of what to do about the millions of ethnic Russians who now live in assertively non-Russian countries, some of whom would like to become Russian citizens, many of whom do not, but all of whom represent at once a potential help and a potential hindrance to "Russian state interests." For now at least, Russia's Federal Migration Service seems to be committed to an initiative that would sponsor the long-term return migration to Russia of hundreds of thousands of Russians from the "near abroad," bringing the history of Russian out-migration around full circle.[14]

Russian colonization, in other words, has turned into Russian *decolonization*, with predictably complicated consequences. In fact, today's post-colonial landscape is the direct result of a long history of Slavic borderland migration whose net effect was to mix and refashion the peoples and territories of Eurasia on a truly continental (indeed, transcontinental) scale. The history of this migration was both state-directed and driven from below. It was characterized by social cooperation and popular enthusiasm as well as by state repression and intercommunal violence. It changed over time yet remained also strikingly constant, even over the course of centuries, reflecting the persistent facts of Russia's distinctive geography and social and political structures. The essays that follow offer the latest roadmap to this enduring and important terrain of the modern Russian experience, revealing a new appreciation of its fascinating variety and complexity.

Notes

1 Brian Fagan, *Before California: An Archeologist Looks at Our Earliest Inhabitants* (Lanham, 2003), 3.
2 *Povest' vremennykh let* (St Petersburg, 1996), 144.
3 V.O. Kliuchevskii, *Sochineniia v deviati tomakh* (Moscow, 1987), v. 1, 49.
4 For a representative sample, see S.V. Ezhevskii, "Russkaia kolonizatsiia severo-vostochnogo kraia," *Vestnik Evropy*, no. 1 (1866): 211–63; N. Serpovskii, *Pereseleniia v Rossii v drevnee i novoe vremia i ikh znacheniia dlia khoziaistva strany* (Iaroslavl', 1885); P.A. Sokolovskii, *Ekonomicheskii byt zemledel'cheskogo naseleniia Rossii i kolonizatsiia iugo-vostochnykh stepei pered krepostnym pravom* (St Petersburg, 1878);

P.N. Miliukov, *Ocherki po istorii russkoi kul'tury* (reprinted: Moscow, 1983), v. 1; A.A. Kaufman, *Pereselenie i kolonizatsiia* (St Petersburg, 1905); M.K. Liubavskii, *Istoricheskaia geografiia Rossii v sviazi s kolonizatsiei* (Moscow, 1908); N. Firsov, *Inorodcheskoe naselenie prezhnego Kazanskogo tsarstva v Novoi Rossii do 1762 goda i kolonizatsii Zakamskikh zemel' v eto vremia* (Kazan, 1869); G.I. Peretiatkovich, *Povolzh'e v xv i xvi vekakh: ocherki iz istorii kraia i ego kolonizatsii* (Moscow, 1877); I. Bentkovskii, *Zaselenie Chernomorii s 1792 po 1825 god* (Ekaterinodar, 1880); G.I. Peretiatkovich, *Povolzh'e v xvii i nachale xviii veka (ocherki iz istorii kraia)* (Odessa, 1882); N. Serpovskii, *Pereseleniia v Rossii v drevnee i novoe vremia i ikh znachenie v khoziaistve strany* (Iaroslavl', 1885); D.I. Bagalei, *Materialy dlia istorii kolonizatsii i byta stepnoi okrainy Moskovskogo gosudarstva (Khar'kovskoi i otchasti Kurskoi i Voronezhskoi gubernii) v xvi–xviii stoletii* (Khar'kov, 1886–90), 2 vols; D.I. Bagalei, *Ocherki po istorii kolonizatsii stepnoi okrainy Moskovskogo gosudarstva* (Moscow, 1887); P.N. Butsinskii, *Zaselenie Sibiri i byt ee pervykh nasel'nikov* (Khar'kov, 1889); and the journal *Voprosy kolonizatsii* (1907–14).

5   For a suggestive range of this literature, see A.V. Fadeev, *Ocherki ekonomicheskogo razvitiia stepnogo predkavkaz'ia v doreformennyi period* (Moscow, 1957); L.F. Skliarov, *Pereselenie i zemleustroistvo v Sibiri v gody Stolypinskoi agrarnoi reformy* (Leningrad, 1962); E.M. Brusnikin, Pereselencheskaia politika tsarizma v kontse xix veka, *Voprosy istorii* (1965): 28–38; E.I. Druzhinina, *Iuzhnaia Ukraina v 1800–25 gg.* (Moscow, 1970); M.S. Simonova, "Pereselencheskii vopros v agrarnoi politike samoderzhaviia v kontse xix–nachale xx v.," in *Ezhegodnik po agrarnoi istorii Vostochnoi Evropy 1965 g.* (Moscow, 1970), 424–34; V.M. Kabuzan, *Izmeneniia v razmeshchenii naseleniia Rossii v xviii–pervoi polovine xix vv. (po materialam revizii)* (Moscow, 1971); B.V. Tikhonov, *Pereseleniia v Rossii vo vtoroi polovine xix v.: po materialam perepisi 1897 g. i pasportnoi statistike* (Moscow, 1978); S.B. Bernshtein, "Osnovnye etapy pereseleniia Bolgar v Rossiiu v xvii–xix vekakh," *Sovetskoe slavianovedenie*, no. 1 (1980): 48–50; S.I. Bruk i V.M. Kabuzan, "Migratsiia naseleniia v Rossii v xviii–nachale xx veka (chislennost', struktura, geografiia)," *Istoriia SSSR*, no. 4 (1984): 41–59; A.P. Fomchenko, *Russkie poseleniia v Turkestanskom krae v kontse xix–nachale xx v. (sotsial'no-ekonomicheskii aspect)* (Tashkent, 1983); and Iu.M. Tarasov, *Russkaia krest'ianskaia kolonizatsiia iuzhnogo Urala: vtoraia polovina xviii–pervaia polovina xix v.* (Moscow, 1984), 91–118.

6   See, for example, Donald Treadgold, *The Great Siberian Migration: Government and Peasant in Resettlement from Emancipation to the First World War* (Princeton, 1957); Carsten Goehrke, *Die Wüstungen in der Moskauer Rus': Studien zur Siedlungs-, Bevölkerungs- und Sozialgeschichte* (Wiesbaden, 1968); George J. Demko, *The Russian Colonization of Kazakhstan, 1896–1916* (Bloomington, 1969); François-Xavier Coquin, *La Sibérie: peuplement et immigration paysanne au xixème siècle* (Paris, 1969); Roger P. Bartlett, *Human Capital: The Settlement of Foreigners in Russia, 1762–1804* (New York, 1979); Barbara Anderson, *Internal Migration during Modernization in Late Nineteenth-Century Russia* (Princeton, 1980); Judith Pallot and Denis J.B. Shaw, *Landscape and Settlement in Romanov Russia, 1613–1917* (Oxford, 1990); Edward H. Judge, "Peasant resettlement and social control in late Imperial Russia," in *Modernization and Revolution: Dilemmas of Progress in Late Imperial Russia; Essays in Honor of Arthur P. Mendel*, eds Edward H. Judge and James Y. Simms, Jr. (New York, 1992), 75–93.

7   See, for example, Thomas Barrett, *At the Edge of Empire: The Terek Cossacks and the North Caucasus Frontier, 1700–1860* (Boulder, 1999); Michael Khodarkovsky, *Russia's Steppe Frontier: The Making of a Colonial Empire, 1500–1800* (Bloomington, 2002); Daniel Brower, *Turkestan and the Fate of the Russian Empire* (London, 2003), esp. 126–51; Nicholas B. Breyfogle, *Heretics and Colonizers: Forging Russia's Empire in the South Caucasus* (Ithaca, 2005); Steven G. Marks, "Conquering the Great East: Kulomzin, peasant resettlement, and the creation of Modern Siberia," in *Rediscovering*

Russia in Asia: Siberia and the Russian Far East, eds Stephen Kotkin and David Wolff (Armonk, 1995), 23–39; Detlef Brandes, *Von den Zaren adoptiert: die deutschen Kolonisten und die Balkansiedler in Neurußland und Bessarabien 1751–1914* (Munich, 1993); Mark Bassin, "Turner, Solov'ev, and the 'Frontier Hypothesis': the nationalist signification of open spaces," *Journal of Modern History* 65, no. 3 (1993): 473–511; Alberto Masoero, "Autorità e territorio nella colonizzazione siberiana," *Rivista storica italiana* 65, no. 2 (2003): 439–86; David Moon, "Peasant migration and the settlement of Russia's frontiers, 1550–1897," *Historical Journal* 40, no. 4 (1997): 859–93; Marc Ferro, *Histoire des colonisations: des conquêtes aux indépendences, xiiième–xxème siècle* (Paris, 1994); A.V. Remnev, "Sdelat' Sibir' i Dal'nyi Vostok russkimi: k voprosu o politicheskoi motivatsiiakh kolonizatsionnykh voprosov xix–nachala xx vekov," *Elektronnyi zhurnal Sibirskaia zaimka*, no. 3 (2002),www.zaimka.ru/03_2002/ remnev_motivation; Svetlana Lur'e, "Geopoliticheskaia organizatsiia prostranstva ekspansii i narodnaia kolonizatsiia," *Tsivilizatsiia i kul'tury*, no. 3 (1996): 175–89; John R. Staples, *Cross-Cultural Encounters on the Ukrainian Steppe: Settling the Molochna Basin, 1783–1861* (Toronto, 2003); Willard Sunderland, *Taming the Wild Field: Colonization and Empire on the Russian Steppe* (Ithaca, 2004); idem, "Empire without imperialism? Ambiguities of colonization in Tsarist Russia," *Ab Imperio*, no. 2 (2003): 101–15; Jonathan Andrew Bone, "Socialism in a far country: Stalinist population politics and the making of the Soviet Far East, 1929–1939," (Ph.D. diss., University of Chicago, 2003); Jonathan L. Dekel-Chen, *Farming the Red Land: Jewish Agricultural Colonization and Local Soviet Power, 1924–41* (New Haven, 2005); and Francine Hirsch, *Empire of Nations: Ethnographic Knowledge and the Making of the Soviet Union* (Ithaca, 2005).

8 For recent studies that stress Russia's historical influence and entanglement with foreign empires and societies, see, for example, Marshall Poe, *The Russian Moment in World History* (Princeton, 2003); Steven G. Marks, *How Russia Shaped the Modern World: From Art to Anti-Semitism, Ballet to Bolshevism* (Princeton, 2003); Dominic Lieven, *Empire: The Russian Empire and its Rivals* (New Haven, 2001).

9 On this, see, for example, Breyfogle, *Heretics and Colonizers*; Staples, *Cross-Cultural Encounters*; and Sergei Zhuk *Russia's Lost Reformation: Peasants, Millennialism, and Radical Sects in Southern Russia and Ukraine, 1830–1917* (Washington, 2004).

10 On the latter, see David Laitin, *Identity in Formation: The Russian-Speaking Populations in the Near Abroad* (Ithaca, 1998).

11 The ideas of "persistent factors" and "permeable frontiers" are taken from Alfred Rieber, "Persistent factors in Russian foreign policy: an interpretive essay," in *Imperial Russian Foreign Policy*, ed. Hugh Ragsdale (New York, 1993), 315–59.

12 For a brief list of works to support these references and comparisons, see Andrew Gentes, "Katorga: penal labour and tsarist Siberia," *Australian Slavonic and East European Studies* 18, no. 1–2 (2004): 41–61; Robert Hughes, *The Fatal Shore: The Epic of Australia's Founding* (New York, 1988); Breyfogle, *Heretics and Colonizers*; Alice Bullard, *Exile to Paradise: Savagery and Civilization in Paris and the South Pacific, 1790–1900* (Stanford, 2000); Leonard Thompson and Howard Lamar, eds *The Frontier in History: North America and South Africa Compared* (New Haven, 1981); Dane Kennedy, *Islands of White: Settler Society and Culture in Kenya and Southern Rhodesia, 1890–1939* (Durham, 1987); Sunderland, *Taming the Wild Field*; Khodarkovsky, *Russia's Steppe Frontier*; Peter C. Perdue, *China Marches West: The Qing Conquest of Central Eurasia* (Cambridge, MA, 2005); James A. Millward, *Beyond the Pass: Economy, Ethnicity, and Empire in Qing Central Asia, 1759–1864* (Stanford, 1998); Barrett, *At the Edge of Empire*; C. Patterson Giersch, *Asian Borderlands: The Transformation of Qing China's Yunnan Frontier* (Cambridge, MA, 2006); Richard White, *The Middle Ground: Indians, Empires, and Republics in the Great Lakes Region, 1650–1815* (New York, 1991); Daniel H. Usner, Jr., *Indians, Settlers, and Slaves in a Frontier Exchange Economy: The Lower Mississippi Valley Before 1783* (Chapel Hill,

1992); William Cronon, *Changes in the Land: Indians, Colonists, and the Ecology of New England* (New York, 1983); Richard W. Slatta, *Cowboys of the Americas* (New Haven, 1990); and Willard Sunderland, "The 'colonization question': visions of colonization in late imperial Russia," *Jahrbücher für Geschichte Osteuropas* 48, no. 2 (2000): 210–32.

13 In addition to her article in this volume, see also Elena Shulman, "Soviet maidens for the socialist fortress: the Khetagurovite campaign to settle the Soviet Far East, 1937–39," *Russian Review* 62 (July 2003): 387–410.

14 Interfax (Russia), July 25, 2007.

Part I

Muscovy, expansion, and the limits of migration

1 Claiming Siberia

Colonial possession and property holding in the seventeenth and early eighteenth centuries

Valerie Kivelson

When west European conquistadors and colonists staked their claims to territories in the vast New Worlds they discovered across the Ocean-Sea, they took great pains to establish the legality, morality, and philosophical legitimacy of their possession and occupation of the new lands, and their subjugation of the indigenous populations. Critical to these European discussions was the relationship of the native peoples to their lands prior to European conquest, a relationship that had to be in some way devalued or invalidated in order to justify colonial appropriation. In righteous tracts and heated debates, in decrees, laws, and ceremonies of possession, Englishmen, Frenchmen, and, most vehemently, Spaniards weighed the competing interests of indigenous peoples and the colonists. In a series of exchanges epitomized by the famous debates between Juan Ginés de Sepúlveda and Bartolomé de Las Casas, the Spanish explored the moral obligations and pitfalls involved in their seizure of land in the New World, while the English, less conflicted on the issue, confidently composed apologetics under such titles as "The Lawfulness of Removing out of England into the Parts of America."[1]

The agonizing problem of justifying the domination and dispossession of the American peoples produced fierce internal critiques of European colonialism, critiques so powerful that rumors spread in the sixteenth century to the effect that Charles V meant to salve his conscience by renouncing his American holdings.[2] In Spain, the Las Casas view won the day. Papal assurances that Indians were fully human and had salvageable immortal souls worked in tandem with monarchical interests in preserving the lives and labor of colonial subjects, gaining the residents of the New World some modicum of recognition and legal protection from their Iberian overlords. Particularly in their governance of organized societies in Mexico and Peru, the Spanish colonial regime relied on extant administrative divisions and economic structures, and maintained an interest in preserving them.[3] Spanish thinkers and policy makers, along with colonizers from Portugal, Holland, and France, conceded that Indians might have legitimate claims to land deriving from the right of first possession as well as from natural law, which granted them rights to sustenance.

However, conveniently, early modern discourse also provided a wide and convincing array of arguments for legitimizing imperial claims. Europeans could refer baldly to the right of conquest, or they could enact elaborate ceremonies to convince themselves and anyone else who might pay attention that the lands had been voluntarily ceded or sold to them. The English, and to a lesser extent the Spanish, invoked their right to the land by dint of labor, arguing that as the Indians had failed to cultivate and enclose fields and pastures in any proper, recognizable way, they had abnegated any rights or claims they might have to those properties. Through lassitude and neglect, they had yielded to the stronger, clearer claims of honest European farmers who would sink profitable labor into the land. Or they could refer to higher Christian morality, which obligated them to propagate the faith among the benighted, and entitled them to seize heathen lands in recompense for various and sundry violations of God's law and natural law.[4] Relying on sources as varied as Aristotle, Augustine, and Hobbes, building on Roman law, English common law, and even Muslim *aljama* law, Europeans fretted over imagining ways to justify their blatant seizure of land from the inhabitants of the "Indies."[5]

To anyone familiar with the famous "silence of Muscovy," it will come as no surprise to learn that when Muscovite Russians conquered Siberia in the late sixteenth and seventeenth centuries, they appear, by contrast, to have lost not a wink of sleep over this issue. They wasted no ink in attempting to justify their conquest and colonization of the Siberian steppes, and even the most thoughtful commentators appear to have enjoyed untroubled consciences on the subject. Studies of the Siberian conquest have devoted correspondingly little attention to understanding how the Muscovites themselves conceived of and justified their actions in Siberia, how they imagined their relationship to the land and its prior residents. Following seventeenth-century sources, most scholarship has assumed that the Russians saw the indigenous population as at best incidental and at worst an obstacle to be removed and destroyed.

This apparent indifference to the niceties of conquest fits well with general ideas about Muscovy. Why would any Muscovite bother to investigate the legalities of appropriation and forcible removal when no such legality protected even Russians at home, in the heartlands? The era of Siberian expansion coincided with the period in which the peasantry was reduced to the condition of serfdom, and townspeople were locked into their towns. It corresponded with the state's arbitrary distribution of huge tracts of land in the north of Russia, along with the previously free peasants who had worked them. What kind of legal culture could emerge from such a society, and why would one expect it to translate into concern for the rights and claims of Siberian reindeer herders and walrus hunters?

It is the argument of this chapter that Muscovite conquerors and colonists, and more particularly Muscovite rulers and administrators, did in fact develop a carefully nuanced set of ideas about the property and possession claims of prior inhabitants of the Siberian lands and about their on-going role in constituting a Muscovite imperial space. Just as Englishmen, Frenchmen, and Spaniards played out their own cultures' preconceptions about proper ways of making and justifying claims to land in the New World, so Muscovite adventurers and administrators reenacted their particularly Russian understandings of property and possession in the Siberian expanses. Far from revealing an absence or suspension of legal culture or thinking, Muscovite imperial practices demonstrate a deep and consistent commitment to the kinds of legal and political claim-making that were operative in Russia at the time. The particular understandings of what makes a claim legitimate in a given situation have important implications for the way that colonial practices affected indigenous life. In a rather surprising twist, despite the brutality and violence of its implementation, Muscovite patterns of imperial claim-making allowed for a broad sphere of entitlement and an inclusive incorporation of non-Russian subjects, perhaps more inclusive than the imperial visions and practices of most of the contemporary western European colonial powers.

As they attempted to explore, control, and imagine their growing Siberian holdings, Muscovites had to figure out the role that indigenous peoples would play on two primary levels: as economic actors and possessors of property; and as political subjects.[6] In each of these areas, the mental categories and approaches brought to bear derived from the ideas and practices familiar from Muscovite politics and culture. Let us examine each of these realms in turn, beginning with property rights and human economies.

Imperial subjects and possession of property

Primarily an agricultural society during the early centuries of tsarist rule, Muscovy had necessarily elaborated a finely tuned system of landholding and a body of property law by the sixteenth and seventeenth centuries. The various legal bases for claims of possession that would hold up in court were familiar to anyone who might need to protect or contest such a claim. The courts were filled to overflowing with suits devoted to sorting out property rights. Privileged landlords and servitors in the tsar's army and administration sued each other constantly, lodging claims that their rivals had forcibly occupied their land and deprived them of revenues, that their rivals' peasants were poaching in their woods, chopping down their forests, harvesting their grain, and generally trespassing on their private property. Neighbors sued each other for falsely registering sales of land that never took place and thus swindling the original owner out of legitimate property rights. Widows and orphans sued their legal guardians for cheating them out of their legitimate holdings. Absentee landlords complained that their properties had been appropriated in their absence.

When contesting abuses, landlords rested their claims on a variety of evidence. They explained that they held their land by inheritance, by purchase or dowry, or by the gracious grant of the merciful sovereign tsar as documented in deeds, registers, and grants. Most convincingly, they referred to local witnesses who could testify to their ownership of the land in question. For ultimate proof, they would refer to tax registers that showed their serfs had paid hard cash to the tsar's treasury in past years, proving beyond doubt that the land – and the peasants who farmed it – belonged to the claimant and acknowledged that relationship. In 1698, the Tikhonov Monastery asserted that it owned a certain piece of land "with the monastic peasants," and could provide registers of the dues it had collected over the years to prove it. Since people rarely pay taxes on other people's land, this kind of evidence of compliance from below appears to have been particularly convincing.[7]

The landed elite were not alone in laying legal claim to pieces of property. In spite of their insistence that they held their land "as mine alone" (*svoeiu odnoiu*), landlords held only one of several simultaneous stakes in particular pieces of property.[8] Property claims were always layered and overlapping.[9] Above the individual landlord, claiming ownership on an altogether different plane, was the tsar, the ultimate property holder in Muscovy. Landholders gratefully referred to their property as their "grants from the sovereign," and landless servicemen knew to address their supplications to the tsar, as ultimate distributor of property, when they hoped to gain some real estate. Most property was held in conditional tenure at the pleasure of the tsar, revocable for cause at any moment (although in practice estates were rarely reappropriated). Knowledge that the tsar stood behind the scenes as ultimate owner of the land may have made the individual landlords' sense of title to their property more precarious, but it did nothing to diminish their eagerness to expand their holdings or willingness to fight for their claims in street brawls or in court.

These two strata of simultaneous ownership did not exhaust the multiplicity of claims on any given piece of property. Another set of entitlements arose from below. As the Tikhonov Monastery case suggests, landlords held property "with their peasants," and peasants asserted their own rights in court as vociferously as their proprietors did. Very frequently peasant witnesses identified both the "legal" and "actual" holders of the land. For instance, the peasants who undermined Lukian Novokshchenov's claim to a field in Iur'ev Pol'skoi Province insisted that: "the peasants of the Pokrov Convent estate village Dubenki own the field called Tiapkovo."[10] The convent owned the property officially, and for that matter could be said to own the peasants, but in the minds of the peasant witnesses, the convent's peasants owned the land too. Similarly, a 1703 case from Mozhaisk notes: "The witnesses [said that] the peasants of the Kolotskoi Monastery own that land, and their land is entirely encircled by the lands and woods belonging to the Kolotskoi Monastery's peasants."[11] In their testimony, peasants articulated a concept of multiple degrees of ownership, and the courts listened seriously to their interpretations, referring to peasant testimony in verdicts that favored peasant claimants over outsiders of various degrees. In upholding peasant claims, the courts at the same time supported the claims of their masters, so the system undoubtedly served the interests of the landlords. Nonetheless, given competing interests, the testimony of the peasants on the ground weighed heavily in tipping the scales of justice toward their own, and their own masters', interests and desired outcomes.

Serfs by definition occupied a position of restricted mobility and reduced autonomy within Muscovite society, but by the same token they benefited from an insoluble connection to a given piece of land. This mutually constituting relationship between serf and landed property gave peasant claims significant weight in the eyes of the law, a weight that proved useful in sorting out the claims of competing landlords. The power of peasant claims magnified rather than constricted the strength of landlords' claims, and the reverse held true as well. In these ways, multiple, simultaneous, overlapping claims were the norm in Muscovy, and presented no conceptual difficulty for anyone concerned. To the question whether a given piece of property belonged to the tsar, the landlord, or the peasant community, the obvious answer would have been "all of the above."

Western societies, too, maintained their own variously complex and layered relationships of tenancy, usage rights, and commons. Still, most European law was at least familiar with the notion of identifying one clear, ultimate owner, whether a singular or collective entity, whose claims could not be encroached upon by either crown or tenants.[12] Nested claims to ownership, as natural as breathing to Muscovites long accustomed to them, and to Spanish and Portuguese cultures as well, proved far more nettlesome in an English tradition, where simple, outright title to land provided one of the most important foundations of rights and of the law itself.

Comparative economics and demographics may offer some explanations for these very different systems. In England, an island, and in Western Europe to a somewhat lesser degree, land itself stood at a premium. Finding willing renters and tenants who would put the land under the plow and into active use presented no problem, particularly in the population-rich sixteenth and seventeenth centuries. Neither crown nor landed elite needed to worry too much about finding laborers to work the fields and pastures of their realms. In Muscovy, the ratio of acreage to people was quite different; a vast land with ever-receding frontiers, the tsarist empire valued property according to its productive population as much or more than its latent potential, a theme noted also by Matthew Romaniello in this volume. The tsar could not sit by passively and allow Russian real estate to languish unworked. The great 1649 law code stipulated in one article after another that estates that fell out of use were to be immediately granted to someone engaged in active service who would put it back under the plow.[13] The economic interests of the individual landholder recapitulated the meta-interests of the tsar: gentry landholders and servicemen agitated throughout the seventeenth century to secure their labor force by enserfing the peasantry and binding them to their estates. The peasants, in turn, made the most of their connection to the land, rooting claims to fields and pastures in their holding and working particular plots. Tied in a circular network of economic interests, tsar, landlord, and peasant came to accept, enact, and enforce a set of superimposed, mutually reinforcing claims and entitlements in specific pieces of land and specific locations.

How are these insights into Muscovite conceptions of property and ownership and Muscovite human economics relevant to the conquest and absorption of Siberia? Like the heartlands of Muscovy, Siberia offered latent but elusive promise. Rich in the luxurious and valuable furs for which Europe provided a seemingly insatiable market, and also blessed with an attractive if secondary bounty of intriguing stones, walrus tusks, fish, and salt, Siberia lay inaccessible and distant, described by the late seventeenth-century cartographer Semen Remezov as a "waterless and scarcely passable rocky steppe."[14] Without the labor of the native population, the skill of indigenous hunters and trappers, the tantalizing "soft gold" pelts would remain out of Russian reach.

Grigorii Anikievich Stroganov, the first Russian to hold an official grant from the tsar for territory in the Urals, edging into Siberia, set a precedent for Muscovite appropriation of Siberian lands. In 1558, two decades before the Cossack Ermak defeated the Siberian khan Kuchium and opened western Siberia to Russian settlement, Tsar Ivan IV issued a charter to Stroganov, granting him great tracts of land in the Perm region, which he airily described as "in our patrimonial holding." Concerned about alienating the resident non-Russians, Zyrians and Ostiaks, who occupied the region, the tsar restricted his grant to "empty places, with black forests and wild rivers and lakes, empty islands and inlets." "Prior to this, no one has plowed fields in that place, nor built houses, and from that place no one has paid any kind of taxes whatsoever to my grand princely and tsarist treasury. And at this present moment, it is not granted to anyone and not recorded in any cadastral books nor deeds of purchase." Guaranteed empty, the land should be promptly filled and put to productive use, like any land in the Muscovite realm. "Grigorii should build an outpost and arm it with cannon and guns and fill it with soldiers to defend it, and chop the woods and clear the fields and plow them and build houses. And he should summon people who are not officially registered anywhere and are not taxpayers to seek out salt deposits and set up salt works."[15] Land grants to these settlers presumably followed some of the same guidelines as those established farther into Siberia later in the century, where newcomers were granted land "where appropriate for plow and pasture," and given seed grain to get themselves started and a ten-year tax exemption. In return, after the ten-year grace period ended, half of their product was to be earmarked for the tsar's grain storehouses. In spite of what looks like a rental agreement, the settlers were entitled to sell their houses and farm structures to anyone willing to assume the obligations to the state.[16]

The Stroganov holdings in Perm were a transitional case, closer to home and more tentative than later colonizing efforts, but they provided a blueprint for future inroads in Siberia. Where the land was seen as empty, and no resources were accruing to the treasury, Siberian administrators followed Stroganov's example in importing carefully screened settlers from Russia. Stroganov, like later Siberian administrators, had to promise to check all newcomers' credentials. Only "wanderers," "unregistered people," and, importantly, "non-taxpayers" qualified to settle the new territories. Those who did not fit the bill found themselves promptly deported to their former residences and, in the case of serfs, their former owners. This stipulation was meant to prevent leakage of taxpayers from the central tax rolls and to maintain the integrity of Russia's enserfed labor force, issues which also played an important role on the Ukrainian frontier, as discussed by Brian Boeck in this volume.[17] As Muscovite colonial rule advanced more deeply into Siberia, the same policies of importing only unaffiliated wanderers and exiles from Russia continued. Men without bonds to break back home were welcomed into the rough frontier service, set up with land, and registered among the gunners and Cossacks who guarded Russian outposts and explored frozen river routes.[18]

In its effort to possess and exploit the riches of Siberia, Moscow supplemented its colonial settlement with a policy of recognition and incorporation of the indigenous population, drawing new subjects into its lucrative web of revenue generation. In 1592, an order issued in the name of Tsar Fedor Ivanovich commanded Prince Petr Gorchakov to build a new outpost at Pelym, just beyond the Urals. In the course of his work, Gorchakov was told to register the local Voguls in the sovereign's service and send them along with Russian servicemen to build the fortifications. In return, he should promise to lighten their tribute obligations and give them rewards from the tsar, both in cash and in grain. He should assure them that they were in no danger and that the sovereign would extend his kindness and favor to them and protect them in all matters. Moreover, he should assign them land around the fort where they could settle and farm, but they should be kept out of the outpost itself and separate from the Russians.[19] In 1594, the tsar granted, "from his patrimony, the Siberian lands," a small bit to an Ostiak prince and his brother, in reward for his loyal service. The grant bestowed two districts on the princes "together with all benefits and with the fur revenues ..., so the brothers can hold (*vladet'*) those districts with all profits and with the eleven people who live there, and can collect the tribute for themselves."[20]

In recognition of Russia's economic self-interest, Muscovites designated the conquered populations as "*iasak* people," that is, people subject to tribute in fur (*iasak*) rather than tax in money. Just as the laws of the seventeenth century harp on the need to keep Muscovite land in active use, so Siberian decrees and regulations of the same period emphasize the importance of maintaining good relations with the iasak people in order to secure a constant flow of furs. Clearly fighting an uphill battle against the violence of the men at the vanguard of imperial expansion, Muscovite chancelleries continually instructed their officials and servicemen to "protect the iasak people" and "treat them tenderly." Already at the end of the sixteenth century, just a decade after the first major conquests in western Siberia, Tsar Fedor ordered the lowering of iasak payments for the Tatars of Pelym, because so many of their people had been killed or had died, and so many of the fur-bearing animals had been trapped, that they were unable to pay their full load. The order demanded that iasak be collected "in moderation, so that they will not be driven away."[21] In 1599, the new tsar, Boris Godunov, specified that his Siberian officials assure the Siberians of his good wishes, earnest protection, and his desire that they should suffer no want or oppression. The tsar and his son promised "that they should live in peace, without fees, in towns or yurts, in provinces and districts."[22] True to his vows, shortly thereafter Tsar Boris upheld the plea of a Siberian Tatar named Epancha, who complained that his land was being overtaxed and his property violated. In response, the tsar confirmed Tatar possession of any land that they plowed and worked. Such lands were not to be given to anyone else, not to Russian peasants or servicemen:

Order them to plow their land for us and for themselves, so that our treasury will profit and, to the extent that they plow their fields, the farmers will live in plenty (*sytnym byti*).

And if the Tatar Epancha or any other Tatar complains that we are building this fort to oppress them, and that we should not distribute land to [Russian] plowmen and trappers, you tell them that we had reports of the great losses they were suffering and we, by our custom of tsarist mercy, pitying them, ordered [Russian] trappers and plowmen placed on empty land and that their land should not be appropriated.

With these assurances, "they should live in peace and quiet ... and joyously, and their fields will bring profit to us."[23]

The tsar recognized that his territories served his interests and benefited his treasury only if they were in active use, held or owned by laboring people, whether those people were plowing fields or trapping sables. The following year, Godunov ordered iasak collection to resume as previously, but worried that the poor and sick should be exempted, "so the Siberians do not suffer hardship and so they will not be driven off." After the collection was complete, the officials were required to "question the iasak payers to make sure they had not been insulted, mistreated, or oppressed" during the process. His heartwarming concern had its limits. From the able-bodied, the iasak should be checked for quality as well as quantity: "Get the best quality furs, not poor, shabby, raggedy furs of sable, fox, beaver, squirrel or ermine, and don't keep the best ones for yourselves!"[24]

To keep track of the various tax- and tribute-paying people and the lands assigned to them for farming or trapping, successive tsars ordered the keeping of elaborate "iasak books," registers of the names of each individual head of household, sometimes with astonishing detail about his dependents and what tribute he owed:

Kurmancha's yurt (household): Kurmancha Katyev is old. He hasn't paid iasak for a long time. Betiuk Kurmanchin, also called Nikitka, is married. Five sables were collected, but he still owes five more sables in this collection. Kazarin Kokurman is married. 10 sables were taken. Of that same yurt, Synchika Kurmanchin is listed on the Tiumen' register for the year 107 (1598–9), when five sables were collected, but he died in the year 108 (1599–1600).[25]

Each individual subject mattered, whether in Moscow or Verkhotur'e, as did their economic and marital status and their location. Individual Siberians may have longed to have mattered less, and to have remained invisible to the tsar and the iasak-collector, but Muscovite techniques for recording and keeping track of each and every subject effectively incorporated them into the realm. Once registered, iasak payers would have a difficult time evading their tribute payments, but, on the other hand, they would have documentary support for claiming territory, whether for trapping, grazing, or farming.

Muscovite ideological armature supported a course of incorporation that did not require dispossession of the natives. They could stay more or less where they were, under the overlay of tsarist and other Russian claims. Like the serfs and other subordinated landholders in the Russian heartlands, native claimants were forced to accept new limits and conditions on land that had once been theirs alone. They found themselves restricted in movement, and portions of their lands parceled out to the constantly arriving Russian settlers. Significantly, however, their claims to lands were never categorically erased and their form of land use never ideologically invalidated with a stroke of a philosophical or cartographical pen.

Compare the maps produced in Muscovy with those produced by Western powers charting their colonial holdings in the same period. Muscovite maps invariably defined Siberian spaces by the names of the people who dwelled there. The first surviving map of all of Siberia, the so-called Godunov map of 1667 (named after a Siberian governor, not the tsar), divides the territory with thin, snaking lines or branching rivers that delineate the lands of the Samoedy, Urliukovy, Bashkirtsy, Kalmyki, Mugaly, Saiantsy, Ablaev's people, Kontashchiny, and Ostiaki, who people the expanse between the Urals and the Great Wall. Most subsequent seventeenth-century efforts to map the Siberian vastness rely on the Godunov model, dividing the continent into the same indigenous ethnographic-political units.[26]

Muscovite cosmographies attribute the names of Siberian lands and regions to their nomadic progenitors, proudly incorporating themselves into the line of khans of the steppe rather than erasing that heritage. Working in this tradition, Semen Remezov, the great cartographer and booster of Siberia who worked at

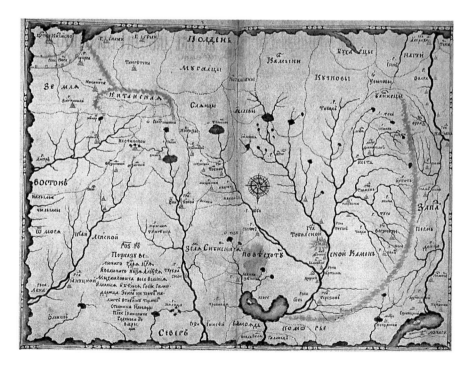

Figure 1.1 Semen Remezov's copy from the early eighteenth century of the Godunov Map of all Siberia (1666/67). RNB, Ermitazhnoe sobranie 237, *Sluzhebnaia chertezhnaia kniga*, ll. 30–1. By permission of the Russian National Library.

the very end of the century and into the beginning of the next, wrote "They say Vizantiia (Byzantium) took its name from Tsar Viza; Moscow from the name of the great forefather Mosokh; Kazan from the Tsar Kazan; Siberia from Tsar Sibir'."[27] Remezov included his own copies of the Godunov map, with its divisions of Siberia into indigenous geo-political units, in each of his three magnificent atlases of Siberia (see Figure 1.1). Further, he illustrated his more detailed regional maps with ethnographic detail, sketching in tiny yurts, tents, mosques, and settlements to depict the localized presence and something of the customs of the indigenous peoples of mountain and steppe.[28] Along with the occasional town with a clearly Russian name – Berezov, Krasnoiarsk – Siberian maps display a plethora of places retaining their indigenous names: Tobol'sk, Irkutsk, Surgut, Omsk.

Of course, imperial expansion being an inherently ugly process, not all encounters proceeded in the gentle spirit imagined on paper. A friendly invitation from Tsar Ivan IV to the Iugor princelings in 1556–7 offered them the option of continuing to hold their own lands, described with typical arrogance as lying within the tsar's "patrimony," and paying tribute from those lands. The less cordial correlate followed: "And if you do not pay tribute, troops will come with sharp blades and you will be in disgrace."[29] Evidence of horrific, violent treatment of Siberians at the hands of the Russians abounds. Although multiple ownership of land was normal and easily assimilated in more abstract contexts, agrarian Russians and nomadic, pastoral Siberians with their very different uses of land found it harder to coexist peaceably. In a skirmish between Russian peasant farmers and pastoral Iakuts in the far north-east, the Iakuts petitioned the local Russian governor, explaining that they desperately needed their traditional pastures for their livestock, and that two newly settled Russian farmers had occupied those meadows, squeezing them out and beating them badly to boot. Trying to balance all interests, the governor worked out a compromise, which may still have looked less like a compromise than a loss from the point of view of the indigenous population whose lands were being parceled out. He reaffirmed the Russian peasants' claim to their fields but limited their access to pasture land. "Tell the Iakuts to keep their livestock five or 10 versts from the fields, so they don't trample the grain, and give each peasant three desiatins of hayfield, no more. Give the rest to the Iakuts. Let Russians no further offend Iakuts nor Iakuts Russians."[30]

In stronger terms, in response to a grievance filed by a group of Bratskie people, a 1684 decree expressly forbade the settlement of Russian agriculturalists on the land of "nomadic foreigners."[31] Here official policy echoed the categorical stand of the 1649 law code, which affirmed the separate, distinct, and inviolable rights of various groups of people to particular kinds of land:

> Do not grant foreigners' service landholdings to anyone besides foreigners.
> Do not grant Russians' service landholdings to foreigners.
>   In the future do not grant the service lands of Russians to Tatars, or Tatar lands to Russians as service landholdings.[32]

Clear though official policy was, clashes between Russians and natives erupted continually. Not only peasant plowmen but also official representatives of the crown engaged in vicious assaults on the indigenous people. Cossacks, soldiers, and iasak collectors readily wielded their "sharp blades" and firearms against the populations they had been ordered to treat gently and protect from all harm and oppression. Using the excuse that the natives were becoming restive, refusing to pay iasak, or acting defiantly, troops brutalized the locals. The Russians' own reports describe burning yurts along with their residents, beating old women to death, shooting entire villages, tying men down and kicking them, stealing everything in sight, and seizing women and children as slaves. Taking hostages and keeping them prisoner for years in the Russian forts and outposts formed a routine staple of Muscovy's pacification policy.[33] The Cossack explorer Vladimir Atlasov sent in a detailed report of his treatment of recalcitrant natives he encountered in his adventures in the Siberian Far East. "The Kamchadaly refused to submit to the Great Sovereign or to pay iasak. So he, Vladimir, with his service men smashed them and beat some of them and burned their settlements, so that they would fear the Great Sovereign and submit to him."[34] He apparently felt no compunction in reporting his actions in unexpurgated form.

In spite of the raw honesty of his report, even more of the horror of his behavior comes across in yet greater detail in an extraordinary document from 1688 that records a Iakut perspective on these encounters. The Iakut petition describes an assault by two Cossacks, Mikhail Grebenshchikov and Vladimir Atlasov. "They came to my family's yurt," wrote an aggrieved victim, "and beat my father and my brothers and my relatives, and maimed them. They tortured them. They tied their hands behind their backs and tied them to the woodpile and out of insatiable greed stamped on their chests and beat them and stole everything possible by force." Further testimony revealed that Grebenshchikov "did not know the Iakut language and he was peaceful and quiet, but Volod'ka Atlasov beat and tortured and violently robbed them." He beat women and old men, not pausing even when his victims included respected shamans of the tribe.[35]

Aside from its excruciating descriptions of violence, the document is remarkable for several reasons. First, Atlasov himself is a giant figure in Russian history, a Lewis and Clark equivalent who explored the frozen and inhospitable lands of the far north-east and established that Kamchatka was a peninsula. His valiant and noble reputation rests on his discoveries as well as on the idea that he was "oriented toward peaceful union of the people of Kamchatka with Russia." According to his own account, he "called them [to serve the tsar] peacefully and tenderly."[36] Encountering this vivid description of his actual conduct allows us to see a hero of Russian arctic exploration fully exposed. The voices of the victims depict in wrenching detail the ugly underside of Muscovite imperial conquest.

Second, the context in which the document was produced, and the fact that this record of the view from below was produced at all, are worth considering. The Iakuts' testimony survives, preserved in colonial archives, because the Iakuts felt entitled to bring charges in the tsar's court of justice, where the case was heard, its evidence duly recorded, verdict passed, and sentence carried out on the offenders.

"By ukaz of the great sovereign and in accordance with the natives' petitions, Cossacks Volod'ka and Mishka will be punished for their criminality and troublemaking and violence and injury and destruction. Tie Volod'ka to the stocks and beat him mercilessly with a knout. Beat Mishka with a wooden switch [a lesser punishment] because he does not know the Iakut language. Take signed security documents for both of them, guaranteeing that they won't make trouble and rebellious mischief in the future."[37] The great Atlasov, arctic explorer, was sharply brought to task for his misconduct. In other words, within an inequitable, hierarchical, autocrat system, in which notions of natural rights or civil liberties were nonexistent, the Russian sovereign and his judicial-administrative system were nonetheless committed to taking seriously the petitions of Siberian natives and to dispensing justice to natives and Russians alike.

Incorporating imperial subjects

This approach to the Siberian population is, in itself, an extraordinary finding and moves us from the first aspect of our analysis, of native Siberians as economic actors, confirmed at least partially in their rights as possessors of territory, to the second aspect, their incorporation as political subjects. Muscovite administrators routinely heard cases brought by native Siberians, sometimes against their fellow tribesmen, sometimes against Russians, and the verdicts appear to have striven for fair resolution, wherever that lay. For instance, when a Iakut man sued in the Iakutsk governor's office, protesting the abduction of his wife by a Russian serviceman, the court ordained that the Russian, along with a Iakut co-conspirator, should be beaten with a wooden switch without mercy.[38] They sued in court not only to protest against Russian violence, seizure of land, occupation of meadows, destruction of woods and habitats for fur-bearing animals, and exploitive iasak collection, but also against each other for breach of promise, domestic violence, fraud, insufficient dowry payment, murder, and a host of other, quotidian and seemingly internal disputes.[39] For example, a Iakut brought suit in the Russian district office in Iakutsk against a shaman who had bewitched his relative.[40] Another set of Iakuts complained in the same court about a brawl that had broken out during a wedding and about a shaman's threat to bewitch the lot of them.[41] In the trial of a Iakut who had murdered another member of his tribe, the guilty party was sentenced to merciless beating and then was given to the son of the victim in "perpetual slavery." The litigants signed the back of the case report with their marks, a set of line drawings of reindeer and boats.[42] Each case was heard, recorded, and resolved. Although the resolutions of many cases have been lost, those cases that survive with the relevant verdict show that the plaintiff, whatever his or her "ethnicity," tended to win the desired result, at least until the other side lodged a counter-suit.

Siberian petitioners inserted themselves into the broader categories used by all subjects of the tsar, and Muscovite officials acknowledged them using that common vocabulary of subjecthood in the realm. They adopted the same language of supplication that their Russian counterparts would have used. Native leaders, called "princelings," or *murzas* in Russian, referred to themselves as "your slave" when addressing the tsar, using the same terminology that members of the privileged Russian elite would employ. Lesser folk, whether Russian or native, opened their requests to the tsar with the same stock invocation: "I, your orphan, petition you." Of course, many of their petitions reached the courts through the intermediary pens of official or unofficial scribes and of translators, as the occasional document reveals. "Translated by Ontiushka Odintsov," says a note at the bottom of a young Iakut woman's testimony.[43] It is perhaps all the more remarkable, then, that the Russian translators chose to employ the same terminology for Siberians as for themselves. As we have seen, Muscovites were prone to making distinctions by type. Tatar land should remain in Tatar hands; Russian land should go to Russians. Members of the elite used one set of terms to describe themselves and were subject to one set of legal fines and punishments; members of the lower orders used another set of terms and were subject to another, harsher set of fines and punishments. And yet, strikingly, the distinctions between colonized and colonizing subjects evaporated when addressing the tsar and representatives of his judicial system. Colonial subjects, once incorporated into the empire and accepting the protection of the tsar's great hand, became full members of the polity, with all the burdens and obligations, entitlements, and protections that entailed.

Burdens and impositions they certainly bore, and those have been well described elsewhere. Crushed by their obligation to produce furs from animals rapidly disappearing because of overtrapping, attacked by Cossacks and their troops, pushed from their grazing lands by Russian settlers, humiliated and brutalized by the Russian custom of holding hostages and taking women as domestic slaves and sexual partners, the indigenous people endured more than enough abuse to drive them to flight and violent resistance. However, on the flip side, as subjects of the Russian tsar, they could and did exercise a legitimate claim on the mercy, protection, and justice of that monarch. Chief among these entitlements was the right to redress in court, which, as we have seen, they used actively and effectively. Next on the list was an entitlement to define themselves in spatial terms, by a powerful, legally guaranteed connection to a particular piece of land, which held true as much for settled agrarian populations as for hunters, pastoralists, or fishing communities. As we have seen, Muscovite peasants, by dint of their legal enserfment, enjoyed an effective claim on particular plots of land, from which they could not be dislodged. For nomadic tribesmen in Siberia, the benefits must have been less readily apparent, as the complaints about the encroachment of Russian farmers on their grazing lands illustrate. Nonetheless, the Muscovite habit of thinking in spatial terms, of linking people irrevocably with particular places, redounded in some ways to the natives' advantage.

Muscovite cartographers incorporated this grounded sense of geopolitical positioning in their efforts to depict the layout of Siberia as an expansive sequence of bounded tribal nations. This way of imagining imperial space emerges most dramatically in Remezov's richly colored "ethnographic map," which divides the sweep of the continent into a variegated patchwork of contrasting blobs, each depicting the land of a particular people. It is an extraordinary production, painted in bright orange, brown, yellow, ochre, and ivory, annotated in black ink. Enclosed in a cartouche vibrant with flowers and greenery, a text announces itself as "Inscription about the lands of the hordes."

> This map shows the lands inscribed between rivers and landmarks and boundaries, and the boundaries among all adjoining Siberian towns as they come together along rivers, of towns and foreign districts and nomadic hordes of whatever kind and tongue, and shows the landmarks that mark them off from their neighbors. They hold their ancestral lands, and they do not cross the boundaries of their native homelands and they do not enter their neighbors' [lands] with their cattle or for any enterprise whatsoever, because if they enter [another's territory] to hunt animals, conflict and banditry will break out among them.[44]

Rather than erase the presence of indigenous peoples and turn the land into empty, virgin territory the way European mapmakers were wont to do in their depictions of the opulent reaches of the New World, Remezov and his comrades in the Muscovite imperial vanguard adopted exactly the opposite stance: they exaggerated both the geographic stability and political identity of the native peoples. Most of the population of northern Siberia was nomadic, following reindeer herds on foot, on dogsled, or on reindeer back. Slightly more to the south, they rode on Bactrian camels. The boundaries that Remezov describes with such clarity and paints with heavy black lines were a figment of an outsider's political imagination. Moreover, where Western maps and descriptions of New World societies insistently harped on the Indians' lack of social and political organization, the polities illustrated so clearly on Remezov's maps – Tsardom of the Giliaks, Land of the Koriaks, Land of the Unpacified Samoyeds – were not only presented in visual terms as political units on a par with Muscovy and China, but were granted that stature even in the face of evidence to the contrary. The on-the-ground descriptions of nomadic organization provide a very different picture, in which people were organized into functional units of households or small social units, comprising eight or ten households, or into looser uluses, followers of a given leader. The 1652 report from one of Atlasov's expeditions describes the scale on which Koriaks were brought into submission to the tsar: "Just before we reached the Kamchatka River, we came upon two yurts of non-iasak-paying reindeer-riding Koriaks, and tenderly called them to come under the tsar's hand." (The passage continues to record the startling violence that often followed such "tender" invitations.[45]) Small clusters of households like this – two yurts, a handful of people – provided a far more practical form of social organization for wanderers in the frozen tundra than would the conventional ethno-polities that Remezov's maps create.

The ethno-political language of Muscovite imperial mapping, so different from Western imperial maps in its attention to fixing the geographic location and political identity of the colonized, served no less immediate and utilitarian a purpose. The rest of Remezov's inscription makes the Russian agenda clear: "Following the reports about [the foreign hordes] and the map, we will incorporate them and impose tribute upon them." Why, then, did bald imperial ambition assume such very different form in Muscovy? Again, to interpret Muscovite conduct in Siberia, one must look back to Muscovite understandings of title to property and how it could be established.

Back home in Riazan or Kostroma or Pskov, disputes over possession of property were most convincingly decided by the evidence of local residents, neighboring serfs and the serfs of the estate in question, who could testify convincingly to the ownership history of each plot of land in the region. When court officials trekked out to the provinces to try to figure out who owned which piece of swamp or meadow, they turned to local expertise. Rounding up hundreds of peasant witnesses, they would walk around the borders of an estate, marking out the boundaries in accordance with the wisdom of long-time residents. Particularly in wilderness areas, where property merged into untamed forest or steppe, peasants' local knowledge proved crucial in establishing boundaries. Peasant testimony served to affirm possession in a mute landscape, where no other means could provide any clarity.

If land tenure proved confusing and proprietary claims elusive in the Muscovite heartlands, the problem was magnified a hundredfold in the underpopulated steppe lands and tundra of Siberia. If a tsar claimed sovereignty in a wasteland, who was to know the difference? Only with the affirming testimony of the indigenous population, preferably a population marked with the dignifying status of a full-fledged polity with an identifiable people and leader, could the tsar make effective, plausible claims to sovereignty. To this purpose, when Cossack bands wheedled or coerced tribes and uluses to "come under the mighty arm of the tsar," they made their new conquests swear a fearsome oath of loyalty and submission to his sovereign majesty by the power of their own faith and their own gods. Seizing hostages to force the Tungus people around the Sea of Okhotsk to accept Muscovite overlordship, Andrei Buturlin ordered them to "take an oath according to their faith that henceforth they would submit (*byli pokorny*) to the sovereign in eternal servitude (*v vechnom kholopstve*)."[46] In the early 1640s, Russian officials administered an oath to the Bratsk people, who swore allegiance to the tsar "on our faith, by the sun, by the earth, by fire, by the Russian sword and by guns." If they somehow were to break their oath, "then, in accordance with my faith, the sun will not shine on me, ... I will not walk on the earth, I will not eat bread, the Russian sword will cut me down, the gun will kill me, and fire will destroy all our uluses [settlements] and our lands."[47]

These staged rituals recall the Spanish Requirement, a set of threats and conditions that Spanish conquistadors were required to read aloud to uncomprehending audiences of mystified Indians. Muscovites enjoyed an advantage over their Spanish counterparts in that their conquest was overland and contiguous, which made it easier to collect skilled translators and interpreters en route. Nonetheless, even though the participants presumably understood more of the content in the Siberian case, these rituals of possession had meaning not only, perhaps not even primarily, for those forced to participate in them, but also for those who orchestrated the sad charades.[48] Like the proverbial tree in the forest, Muscovite imperial gains in the steppe had to be witnessed and authenticated to take on any reality. They had to be substantiated by actual people, lands, and nations, who could perform submission and give demonstrable reality to Muscovite imperial dominion. With no other major power in the region, no competing empire to bump up against borders and harden the edges of their claims, Muscovites needed the participation of their conquered peoples to enact and substantiate the fact of their empire.[49] Muscovite conquerors needed to assert and reify native polities with definable geographic borders, even invent bounded nations when necessary, so they could assert and testify to Muscovite sovereignty.

For conquered peoples in Siberia as for serfs in central Russia, political dominion and possession of property were integrally interconnected. Serfs and townspeople assumed a given position in the tsardom based on their spatial location, which gave them in turn claims on the tsar's protection and secured to their rights to land. As Russia extended its reach across the continent, the link between possession and politics took on new relevance. While they were devastated by unprecedented taxation levels and fierce brutality, as well as by the loss of some of their grazing lands to the colonizing Russians, the tsar's newly adopted "orphans" were nonetheless granted recognition and acknowledgement of their spatial position and their local affiliation. They found themselves able to exercise an effective claim on the protective mercy of their new "guardian," the mighty tsar, and his courts of justice. Muscovite imperial policies drew colonial subjects into the tsar's crushing but protective embrace both as political units and as needy supplicants.

Politically and economically, Muscovites built their imperial vision on particularist building blocks. Their empire, like Remezov's map, could stand only as the sum of its individual, distinct, and clearly demarcated constituent parts. Integrated into a tsarist realm through a common relationship of submission and supplication, the subjects of the empire retained and were even fortified in their state of difference from the whole. Muscovite political imagination required the presence of religiously distinct *inovertsy* (people of different faith), linguistically distinct *inoiazychnye* (people of different tongues), and geographically distinct *inozemtsy* (people of different lands) in order to create a meaningful empire that would provide plausible, convincing testimony to the might of the tsar.

The impulses underlying New World and Siberian colonial conquest shared many of the same economic motives and political-logistical determinants. Violence and disease took a fearsome toll among the Siberian peoples, just as they decimated the indigenous populations of the Americas. Nonetheless, Muscovite attitudes toward people and property, geography and typology, created a fundamental belief that the indigenous population had to be geographically fixed and reified in its difference, rather than assimilated or eradicated. The long-term results suggest that differences between Russian attitudes toward imperial conquest and the various views worked out by European colonizing states, each deriving from particular cultural understandings of possession and dominion, were significant ones and had real-world implications for the colonized peoples. Muscovite policies militated for the preservation of indigenous populations and polities, for retaining the people on the periphery. Muscovites envisioned the creation of an empire of states, an empire in the truest sense, of a collection of formerly sovereign polities, retaining their political and cultural difference under a distant, resource-extracting tsar.

A recent swell in scholarly investigations of the fate of nations under Soviet rule has solidified the idea that the Soviet Union, while crushing some nations, actively forged others where they had not existed before.[50] Muscovite imperial policies may be said to have anticipated this movement by several centuries, creating identifiable nations with ethnic epithets and clear boundaries, in an attempt to make sense of the amorphous, mobile, nomadic populations and frighteningly empty, undefined spaces of the Siberian landmass. In so doing, they were able, ideologically, to fill that largely empty landmass with subject nations that would gratefully testify to the suzerainty of the great tsar over all the empire's constituent pieces. When his subject nations acknowledged his overlordship, the tsar in turn acknowledged them as his subjects and foster children, to tax, protect, and count like gold and treasure. Reveling in the taxonomy of nations under his powerful scepter, the tsar reminded himself and others that he was no less than "sovereign tsar and grand prince, by grace of God, of all Russia, Vladimir, Moscow, Novgorod, tsar of Kazan, tsar of Astrakhan, sovereign of Pskov, and grand prince of Smolensk, Tver, Iurgorsk, Perm, Viat'ka, Bolgar, and others, sovereign and grand prince of the Nizhnii Novgorodian lands, of Chernigov, Riazan, Polotsk, Rostov, Iaroslavl, Belozero, Liefland, Udorsk, Obdorsk, Kondinsk, and ruler of all the Siberian lands and of the great River Ob, and ruler of the Northern lands and sovereign of many other lands."[51] Accreted onto the already lengthy list of Russian principalities that Muscovy had absorbed through time, Siberia, with its variegated and scrupulously catalogued population, figured as yet another separate but integral part of the Muscovite tsardom.

Notes

1   On English apologists and this work in particular, see William Cronon, *Changes in the Land: Indians, Colonists, and the Ecology of New England* (New York, 1983), 56–9. On the Spanish and other European views, see Anthony Pagden, "Dispossessing the barbarian: the language of Spanish Thomism and the debate over the property rights of the American Indians," in *The Languages of Political Theory in Early–Modern Europe*, ed. idem (New York, 1987), 79–98; idem, *Lords of All the World: Ideologies of Empire in Spain, Britain and France, c. 1500–1800* (New Haven, 1995); and Stephen Greenblatt, *Marvelous Possessions: The Wonder of the New World* (Chicago, 1991), 55–64, 168–71.

2   Pagden, "Dispossessing," 95.

3   James Lockhart and Stuart B. Schwartz, *Early Latin America: A History of Colonial Spanish America and Brazil* (Cambridge, 1983); François Chevalier, *Land and Society in Colonial Mexico: The Great Hacienda* (Berkeley, 1963); Steve J. Stern, "Paradigms of conquest: history, historiography and politics," *Journal of Latin American Studies* 24, Quincentenary Supplement: "The colonial and post-colonial experience. Five centuries of Spanish and Portuguese America" (1992): 1–34.

4   There is a rich and fascinating literature on claim-making and possession in European tradition in general and in New World colonial contexts in particular. See Greenblatt,

Marvelous Possessions; Patricia Seed, *Ceremonies of Possession in Europe's Conquest of the New World, 1492–1640* (Cambridge, 1995); Virginia DeJohn Anderson, "King Philip's herds: Indians, colonists, and the problem of livestock in early new England," *William and Mary Quarterly*, 3rd series, 51:4 (1994): 601–24; and Cronon, *Changes in the Land*. On property claims, see interesting exchanges in Richard Epstein, "Possession as the root of title," *Georgia Law Review* 13 (1979): 1221–43; Carol M. Rose, "Possession as the origin of property," *University of Chicago Law Review* 52 (1985): 73–88; John Brewer and Susan Staves, eds, *Early Modern Conceptions of Property* (London, 1996).

5 Each conquering power drew on its own traditions of claim-making. According to Patricia Seed, the Portuguese charted lands and the heavens, the Dutch relied on written forms – deeds, authorizations, descriptions, and maps full of newly coined Dutch place names – and the French cajoled or compelled their native conquests to perform rituals of voluntary consent and submission. The Spanish read out formal declarations of conquest and spelled out the terms of native submission. The English preferred to establish claims through action; they fenced in fields and sowed seeds to prove their title. *Ceremonies of Possession*, 71–97.

6 Actually, there is a third important level that should be considered, that is Muscovite understanding of Siberians as souls in the great drama of salvation, but that is outside the parameters of this chapter.

7 Quotation from RGADA, f. 1209, stlb. Kaluga, 26646, ch. II, l. 139. Other cases of possession claims through history of peasant *obrok* payments: RGADA, f. 1209, stlb. 36717; stlb. Torzhok, 27491, l. 183; Nizhnii Novgorod, stlb. 20886, l. 487. On the argument to possession because of history of paying taxes, see Rose, "Possession."

8 RGADA, f. 210, Prikaznyi stol, stlb. 2239, ll. 25–9.

9 Compare Max Gluckman's discussion of what he calls nested regimes of hierarchy, in his *Essays on Lozi Land and Royal Property* (Livingstone, Northern Rhodesia, 1943).

10 RGADA, f. 1209, Iur'ev Pol'skoi, stlb. 34253, l. 67 (pagination unclear); stlb. Murom, 36201, l. 381. All of these cases use the same verb (*vladet'*) for owning/holding land, whether peasants, gentrymen, or monasteries were exercising that claim. For an intriguing discussion of multiple, overlapping claims to land in the very different context of post-emancipation Cuba, see Rebecca J. Scott and Michael Zeuske, "Property in writing, property on the ground: pigs, horses, land, and citizenship in the aftermath of slavery, Cuba, 1880–1909," *Comparative Studies in Society and History* 44 (2002): 669–99.

11 RGADA, f. 1209, Viaz'ma i Mozhaisk, stlb. 29680, l. 180.

12 Spanish and Portuguese property regimes displayed many similar features. Land was granted by the king to landlords, and in the new world *donatarios* and *encomiendas* granted regional magnates control of the labor of Indian populations, conditional upon maintaining the productivity of the land. Like Russian peasants, Indians in the Spanish colonies often litigated successfully to defend their property rights. Many thanks to Sueann Caulfield, David Frye, and Rebecca Scott for helping me on these comparative issues. Lockhart and Schwartz, *Early Latin America*; Chevalier, *Land and Society*; James Lockhart, "Encomienda and hacienda: the evolution of the great estate in the Spanish Indies," *Hispanic American Historical Review* 49:3 (1969): 411–29.

13 *Muscovite Law Code (Ulozhenie) of 1649*, Part I: *Text and Translation*, trans. and ed. Richard Hellie (Irvine, CA, 1988), chp. 17, art. 41, 135; arts 45–6, 137–8.

14 RGB, f. 256, Rumiantsev, no. 346, l. 22; reproduced in S.U. Remezov, *Chertezhnaia kniga Sibiri, sostavlennaia tobol'skim synom boiarskim S. Remezovym v 1701 godu*, v. 1 (Moscow, 2003).

15 G.F. Miller, *Istoriia Sibiri*, 2 vols (Moscow-Leningrad, 1941), v. 1, Prilozheniia, no. 2, 332–5.

16 Ia.P. Al'kor and B.D. Grekov, eds, *Kolonial'naia politika Moskovskogo gosudarstva v Iakutii XVII v. Sbornik dokumentov* (Leningrad, 1936), no. 95.

17 Tsarist reluctance to allow settlement across the Urals in many ways parallels Boeck's discussion of the Ukrainian frontier: fear of irritating powerful neighbors and fear of draining the center of laborers and taxpayers restrained Muscovite imperialist ambitions.

18 Petition from exiled Cherkasy to be granted arable land near the River Cherpanikh: RGADA, f. 1177, op. 1, no. 28, l. 43. Registration of peasants on arable land near Tobol'sk (1677): RGADA, f. 924, Tobol'skaia prikaznaia palata, nos. 4 and 5 (1693). Registration of wanderer (*guliashchii chelovek*) with peasants, ibid., no. 6. Agreement of wanderer to be in service of Berezov Cossack: RGADA, f. 833, Berezovskaia prikaznaia izba, no. 1. Exiles enrolled in Cossack regiments: RGADA, f. 1177, Iakutskaia prikaznaia izba, op. 1, no. 21, l. 14. Invitation to wanderers and trappers to settle on land near Ilim: RGADA, f. 1177, Iakutskaia prikaznaia izba, no. 5, ll. 141–52.

19 Miller, *Istoriia Sibiri*, v. 1, Prilozheniia, no. 11, 346–54.

20 Ibid., no. 14, 361. The verb is the same as that used by landlords and peasants in the Russian agricultural lands. Arable land granted to iasak-paying Iakuts: RGADA, f. 1177, op. 1, d. 28, ll. 86–8.

21 Miller, *Istoriia Sibiri*, v. 1, Prilozheniia, no. 23, 372–3.

22 Ibid., no. 31, 381–2.

23 Ibid., no. 33, 383–4. Similar issues are discussed in S.V. Bakhrushin, "Sibirskie slobodchiki (iz istorii kolonizatsii Sibiri)," in his *Nauchnye trudy*, v. 3, pt. 2 (Moscow, 1955), 216–17.

24 Miller, *Istoriia Sibiri*, v. 1, Prilozheniia, no. 39, 390–2.

25 Ibid., no. 47, 405–6. Another such list: RGADA, f. 1177, no. 21, ll. 1–16.

26 HUHL, Bagrow Collection, Remezov's copy of Godunov map, 1667, MS Russ 72 (1); and Semen U. Remezov, Map of Siberia; RNB, Erm. Sob. 237, Sluzhebnaia chertezhnaia kniga Remezova, ll. 30ob–31.

27 RNB, Erm. Sob. 237, Sluzhebnaia chertezhnaia kniga, l. 12; *Sibirskiia letopisi* (St Petersburg, 1907); *Kosmografiia 1670* (St Petersburg, 1878–81); HIL microfilm, Krakow, Chartoriski Library nos. 1273, 1417, "Kosmografiia v 76 glavakh" (without beginning); HIL microfilm, St Petersburg State University Library, St Petersburg, reel 76, ms. 22, "Sbornik smeshannogo soderzhaniia," ff. 13r–41v.; "Izbranie vkrattse ot knigi glagolemyia Kosmografiia," in *Izbornik slavianskikh i russkikh sochinenii i statei, vnesennykh v khronografy russkoi redaktsii (Prilozhenie k Obzory Khronografov russkoi redaktsii)*, comp. and ed. Andrei Popov (Moscow, 1869), 398, 508–17.

28 Yurts: RNB, Erm. Sob. 237, Sluzhebnaia chertezhnaia kniga Remezova, ll. 47ob–48. Tents: HUHL, Khorograficheskaia kniga, MS Russ 72 (6): 147.

29 Miller, *Istoriia Sibiri*, v. 1, Prilozheniia, no. 1, 331–2.

30 Al'kor and Grekov, *Kolonial'naia politika*, no. 117. Similar clashes over land usage occurred in colonial New England. See Anderson, "King Philip's herds"; and Cronon, *Changes in the Land*, 54–81.

31 Al'kor and Grekov, *Kolonial'naia politika*, no. 134.

32 *Muscovite Law Code (Ulozhenie) of 1649*, chp. 16, arts 13, 14, 41.

33 N.I. Prokof'ev and L.I. Alekhina, eds, *Zapiski russkikh puteshestvennikov XVI–XVII vv.*, in series "Sokrovishcha drevnerusskoi literatury" (Moscow, 1988); Al'kor and Grekov, *Kolonial'naia politika*; and Yuri Slezkine, *Arctic Mirrors: Russia and the Small Peoples of the North* (Ithaca, 1994), 1–46.

34 *Zapiski russkikh puteshestvennikov*, 418, 428.

35 Al'kor and Grekov, *Kolonial'naia politika*, no. 138.

36 N.I. Prokof'ev, "Literatura puteshestvii XVI–XVII vekov," in *Zapiski russkikh puteshestvennikov XVI–XVII vv.*, 13. On Atlasov and the mapping of Kamchatka, see D.M. Lebedev, *Geografiia v Rossii XVII veka* (Moscow-Leningrad, 1949), 32–4.

37 Al'kor and Grekov, *Kolonial'naia politika*, no. 138, p. 197.

38 RGADA, f. 1177, Iakutskaia prikazanaia izba, no. 12, ll. 253–4.

39 There is a wonderful assortment of such cases in Al'kor and Grekov, *Kolonial'naia politika*.

40 RGADA, f. 1177, Iakutskaia prikazanaia izba, no. 2, l. 152.

41 Ibid., no. 7, l. 67. Another charge against a shaman for bewitchment: no. 16, ll. 78–80.

42 Ibid., no. 12, ll. 183–6.

43 Al'kor and Grekov, *Kolonial'naia politika*, no. 110, p. 163.

44 RGB, F. 256, Rumiantser Collection, no. 346, Remezov, Chertezhaia kniga, 1.25.

45 *Zapiski russkikh puteshestvennikov XVI–XVII vv.*

46 *Zapiski russkikh puteshestvennikov XVI–XVII vv.*, 413. Even after their incorporation into the empire, indigenous people continued to swear by their own faith in important legal contexts. For instance, when testifying that they were too poor to pay the full iasak assigned to them, a group of Iakuts swore "by their faith." RGADA, f. 1177, no. 21.

47 Al'kor and Grekov, *Kolonial'naia politika*, 10–11; available in translation in Basil Dmytryshyn, E.A.P. Crownhart-Vaughan, and Thomas Vaughn, eds, *Russia's Conquest of Siberia, 1558–1700: To Siberia and Russian America: Three Centuries of Russian Eastward Expansion*, v. 1, *A Documentary Record* (Portland, 1985), no. 63, 198–9. The bit about Russian guns and fire was meant to be taken seriously. When the Bratsk people violated the terms of the oath a few years later, the Russian governor of the region, Vasilii Pushkin, accordingly threatened not only to kill the men and "your wives and children and ulus people" but also "your livestock are to be destroyed and your iurts are to be burned relentlessly." Al'kor and Grekov, *Kolonial'naia politika*, 129–31; Dmytryshyn et al., *Russia's Conquest*, no. 65, 202–5. See also *Zapiski russkikh puteshestvennikov XVI–XVII vv.*, 352.

48 On the Spanish Requirement, Seed, *Ceremonies of Possession*, 69–99, text of the Requirement on 69. Also Greenblatt, *Marvelous Possessions*, 97–8.

49 The French, too, required ritual performances of consent from their colonial conquests, although they tended more often to enter into trading relations rather than colonial relations in the New World in this period. L. Blussé and F. Gaastra, eds, *Companies and Trade: Essays on Overseas Trading Companies during the Ancien Régime* (Leiden, 1981); Seed, *Ceremonies of Possession*; Peter Moogk, *La Nouvelle France: The Making of French Canada – A Cultural History* (East Lansing, 2000). On the significance of imperial competition, see James D. Tracy, "*Iasak* in Siberia vs. competition among the colonizers in Canada: a note on comparisons between fur trades," *Russian History/Histoire Russe* 28:1–4 (2001): 403–10.

50 Ronald Suny, "The empire strikes out: Russia, the Soviet Union, and theories of empire," in *A State of Nations: Empire and Nation-making in the Age of Lenin and Stalin*, eds, Ronald Grigor Suny and Terry Martin (Oxford, 2001), 23–66; Ronald Suny, "Nationalities in the Russian empire," *Russian Review* 59:4 (2000): 487–92; and his *The Revenge of the Past: Nationalism, Revolution, and the Collapse of the Soviet Union* (Stanford, 1993); Rogers Brubaker, *Nationalism Reframed* (Cambridge, 1996); Francine Hirsch, *Empire of Nations: Ethnographic Knowledge and the Making of the Soviet Union* (Ithaca, 2005); Terry Martin, *The Affirmative Action Empire: Nations and Nationalism in the Soviet Union, 1923–39* (Ithaca, 2001); Yuri Slezkine, "The USSR as a communal apartment, or how a socialist state promoted ethnic particularism," *Slavic Review* 53:2 (1994).

51 Miller, *Istoriia Sibiri*, v. 1, Prilozheniia, no. 9, 344; discussed in Miller text, 207–8. Other instances of similarly elongated titles, on the great seal of Aleksei Mikhailovich, reproduced in *Zapiski russkikh puteshestvennikov*, 351. A Dutch account by Isaac Massa includes in the tsar's titles also sovereignty over the Nogais, Severia, Livonia, and the Samoyeds: Isaac Massa, *A Short History of the Beginnings and Origins of these Present Wars in Moscow under the Reign of Various Sovereigns down to the Year 1610*, trans. and with an introduction by G. Edward Orchard (Toronto, 1982), 23. Dmytryshyn et al., *Russia's Conquest*, provides a slightly different version, p. 400. Other impressive lists are provided in *Kosmografiia 1670*, 34, 265.

2 Containment vs. colonization

Muscovite approaches to settling the steppe

Brian J. Boeck[1]

Since the nineteenth century, the pervasive view of the northern Black Sea steppes in the Russian imagination has been that of agricultural lands of abundance. Right away thoughts come to mind of huge prairies full of radiant sunflowers and seas of amber grain stretching as far as the eye can see. But before the steppe could become the black-soil "breadbasket of Europe," it had first to be culturally reimagined as a place of opportunity for the Russian state, rather than a threat to its existence. Only the defeat and decimation of the nomads in the late eighteenth century finally transformed the Pontic steppes into "virgin lands" suitable for colonization and hospitable for agriculture. This study focuses on the seventeenth century, when the steppe presented multiple dangers for the Russian state. The aim here is to explain why the Muscovite government was primarily interested in cordoning off the steppe, not colonizing it.[2]

The nomadic threat was the single most compelling reason for Muscovy's lack of enthusiasm for southern colonization schemes.[3] Although the Tatars disappear from most Russian history texts around 1380, they steadfastly maintained a presence on the ground in the northern Black Sea steppes until the late eighteenth century. In the sixteenth and early seventeenth centuries, the Crimean Khanate, the only major power of the early modern period to be consistently conspicuously absent from the mental radar screens of most historians, was capable of spewing thousands of raiders into the Muscovite state while remaining shielded from Russian counter-attack by a sea of steppe. Though it is impossible to calculate the cumulative impact of Tatar raids on Russia, one estimate puts the number of Russians captured by Tatars at over one hundred thousand in the early seventeenth century.[4] In the early decades of the seventeenth century, centuries after Russia was "liberated" from the Tatar yoke, the amount paid by the Muscovite state to the Crimean Khanate in gifts – interpreted as tribute by the Tatars – totaled almost one million rubles.[5]

Long considered by the Crimean Khan as part of his domain, in actuality the steppes north of the Black Sea remained outside of the effective jurisdiction of any state. With the exception of a few forts such as Voronezh and Kursk located in the forest-steppe zone, the southern frontiers of the Muscovite state hugged the forests from Tula to Riazan.[6] The territory controlled and administered by the Crimean Khan was largely limited to the Crimean peninsula and a few forts/towns on its steppe periphery from the Dniester to the Kuban.[7] Although the Khan's forces could mount punitive raids into the steppe and his nomadic subjects seasonally utilized portions of the steppe, in effect the steppe was a huge, largely unpoliced no man's land.

Like the open seas, the steppe became a haven for bandits, raiders, and men who acknowledged no masters. Its lawless nature made it a place to avoid. Even with hired guns, journeys into the open grassland prairies were hair-raising. For example, in 1681 after hearing that they would soon arrive in Perekop, the fort which controlled the entrance to the Crimean peninsula and marked the end of the steppe, a Russian diplomatic delegation could not suppress its jubilation:

> We became overjoyed and gave great thanks to our almighty Savior, our God, and to his most pure Mother, that they guided us safely through such a terrifying (*strashnyi*) trip and did not send against us our enemies with devouring swords, who day and night pursued us from all sides, desiring to annihilate us, because of their bandit rapacity.[8]

In 1685 soldiers from the recently created Khar'kov regiment explained to Muscovite officials why they could not pursue a group of renegade Don Cossacks and Kalmyks into the open steppe: "Those places are huge steppe lands, without water and forest, and it is impossible to conceal ourselves ... Also there are Tatars in those places, and we fear that reconnaissance parties would disappear."[9]

Aside from the dangers posed by outlaws, the steppe also presented an epidemiological danger to the Muscovite state. It served as a conduit through which epidemics from the southern disease environment could enter Muscovy. In order to prevent the spread of infectious diseases, termed the plague (*morovoe povetrie*) in Muscovite documents, the government[10] ordered officials to constantly interrogate travelers and traders about the presence of plague in the Don region, the lower Volga, and Crimea. A document of 1625 from Voronezh outlines what the governor (*voevoda*) was to do if he received reports of the plague in the Don region:

> you are ordered to set up strong checkpoints (*krepkie zastavy*) in the direction of the Don [region] so that no one can by any means ride or walk through or around those checkpoints into the steppe towns (*polskie gorody*) and districts, so that they do not introduce the plague from the Don.[11]

Although its resources were limited, the state sought to quarantine pestilence at the edge of the steppe before it could reach the heartland of the state.

In view of the fact that for several centuries the balance of power in the steppe had not favored sedentary powers, Muscovite rulers took little interest in acquiring or colonizing steppe lands. The rich soils of the Eurasian steppes, which in later periods of Russian history would yield ample opportunities for colonization, were worthless without sufficient security against nomadic raiders intent on harvesting human fodder for the Ottoman slave trade. The state's entire southern perimeter lacked convenient "natural" boundaries, making frontier defense costly and complicated. Agriculture in Muscovy was risky enough without having to factor in the possibility that one nomadic raid could forever deprive a whole district of peasant labor and bankrupt dozens of military men. The risks of settling subjects in southern steppes still far outweighed possible rewards, making it prudent for Muscovy to plant its colonies elsewhere.

Because of the danger posed by Tatar raids, however, Russia could not completely turn its back on the steppe. From the late fifteenth century, the Muscovite state began to employ groups of steppe mercenaries, called Cossacks, to perform services such as providing armed escorts for Muscovite diplomats and merchants in the steppe region. By the mid-sixteenth century the Muscovite state began to send regular payments of cash, weapons and gunpowder to the Cossacks of the Don region, employing them as a ready source of supplementary military manpower and rewarding them for diplomatic and information-gathering services they rendered.[12] These stipendiary Cossacks arranged themselves into a military brotherhood called the Don Cossack Host. Although the first Cossacks were of Turkic origins, gradually over the course of the sixteenth century Slavs from both Muscovy and the Polish-Lithuanian Commonwealth increasingly entered the Cossack ranks.[13]

Until the middle of the seventeenth century, dealing with Cossack clients provided a cheap and effective alternative to colonization. The Don Cossacks acknowledged an allegiance to the tsar and performed services for him in the steppe in exchange for an annual subsidy and the right to trade tax-free in Russia. At the same time, they lived outside of the Muscovite state, governed themselves democratically without outside interference, and conducted independent relations with other frontier communities.[14] The cornerstone of their deal with the Muscovite state was the so-called right to refuge. No one accepted into Don Cossack society was to be considered subject to the jurisdiction of Muscovite officials.[15] In essence, a Russian who joined the Don Cossacks, even if he was a fugitive from justice, was no longer subject to Muscovite laws and his past identity as a tax-paying subject of the tsar was erased. The precise origin of this unique arrangement is unknown, but its perpetuation until the last decades of the seventeenth century indicates that the services that the Cossacks provided as clients outweighed the disadvantages of allowing groups of Russians to slip out from under the state's direct administrative control.

For roughly half the cost of maintaining a single government garrison on the edge of the steppe, it was possible to contract with the Don Cossacks to conduct raids and serve as the eyes and ears of the Muscovite government in the south.[16] This enabled Muscovy to assert military pressure upon Crimea, and, if necessary, the Ottoman forts in the northeast Black Sea region, without committing its forces to any form of action that would involve the Muscovite state in a direct confrontation with the Ottoman empire. The absence of direct subordination of the Don Cossacks to the Russian state allowed the Muscovite government to disavow any responsibility for their actions. When Ottoman or Crimean officials complained about Cossack raids, the standard response from Moscow was that "the Don is inhabited by outlaws, and fugitive slaves of Boyars and all kinds of transient free people and they make ... attacks of their own volition and not by orders of our Grand Sovereign, and the Grand Sovereign does not stand up for such bandits."[17]

The fact that the Muscovite state generally pursued a risk-averse policy towards the steppe, preferring for most of the seventeenth century to contract with clients rather than plant colonies, demonstrates the absurdity of the one-size-fits-all approach to Russian expansion over several centuries. Nothing could be further from the case than Norman Davies' suggestion that:

> Russia and its rulers were addicted to territorial conquest ... Here, if ever, was an extreme case of *bulimia politica*, of the so-called "canine hunger," of gross territorial obesity in an organism which could only survive by consuming more and more of its neighbors' flesh and blood.[18]

Analysis of the steps taken by the Muscovite state in the mid-seventeenth century suggests that rather than unlimited expansion, cautious consolidation was the prevailing objective in the south.

The Muscovite state's weakness in the steppe region forced it to avoid aggressive actions. When the Don Cossacks unexpectedly captured the Ottoman fort of Azov in 1637, the Muscovite government had to decide whether to accept or decline the Cossack invitation for Muscovite forces to occupy and annex it.[19] A group of bureaucrats and boyars prepared a report for the tsar estimating the cost of garrisoning and provisioning Azov at over 120,000 rubles per year – a sum which would have depleted the government's budget and represented an exponential increase in expenditure over the 2,000 to 3,000 rubles annually paid to the Don Cossacks.[20] The doubts expressed by participants in an Assembly of the Land called to discuss the issue, the tremendous costs, and a healthy respect for Ottoman power, convinced Mikhail Fedorovich in 1642 that Muscovy could live without a steppe fort on the edge of the Black Sea.

The Muscovite appetite for new colonization was also tempered by the demands of mobilizing and controlling a limited labor pool in a large territory. Populating the peripheries ranked considerably lower in the Muscovite list of priorities than preventing unauthorized migration. The existence of "free lands" along the southern and eastern frontiers of the Muscovite state, combined with the fact that there was virtually no way for a few hundred government migration checkpoints (*zastavy*) distributed over thousands of kilometers of territory to stop unauthorized migration, contributed to the emergence of a system of state-regulated migration control that came to be known as serfdom.

The government's original objective was to keep peasants from moving, not to make them chattel slaves. Under the traditional Muscovite land system, rather than cash payments, military men were awarded *pomest'e* grants (a revocable allotment of lands, village(er)s and revenues) for their upkeep.[21] Without labor, however, these holdings were not economically viable. Increasingly the government had to confront the problem of peasant flight or risk the disruption of its military capability, especially in the south. As Richard Hellie has demonstrated, the group he calls the "middle service class" played a significant role in the development of serfdom through its countless petitions to the tsar and participation in the *Zemskii Sobor* (Assembly of the Land) of 1649.[22] The interests of the state and military servitors coincided and were codified in the *Ulozhenie* (Law Code) of 1649, the legal document that permanently bound peasants to the residences recorded in the most recent tax-rolls.

It is often overlooked, however, that the Law Code of 1649 not only bound peasants to their masters and/or the state, but also severely restricted the mobility of military men and townspeople.[23] The ascription of virtually the entire Russian population to places of residence recorded in state record books marked the culmination of government efforts to harness and utilize its limited human resources to the fullest. Rather than actively promote migration, the state preferred its subjects to stay where they were.[24]

Vulnerability, not *bulimia politica*, explains the only significant government experiment with people-moving to the southern steppe frontier in the seventeenth century. Devastating Tatar raids during the Smolensk War (1632–4) revealed that when forces were diverted to fight in the west, the entire southern flank of the Muscovite state was exposed to Tatar attack. Large-scale raids (*tatarskie velikie voyny*) caused whole districts to become "depopulated" and caused servitors to become impoverished and "without people, horses, and guns."[25] In response to the devastation, the state began construction of an 800-kilometer-long system of defensive works incorporating forts, wooden and earthen ramparts, ditches, watchtowers, and steppe patrols.[26] Inaugurated in 1635, the system of fortifications which became known as the Belgorod line was designed to close off the lands between the Vorksla, Donets, Oskol, Tikhaia Sosna, upper Don, Voronezh and Tsna Rivers so as to make the advance of large groups of Tatar cavalry impossible.

This unprecedented move to the south advanced Muscovite frontiers to the edge of the open steppe. The line itself was positioned in the transitional forest-steppe zone and was constructed in areas where significant stands of forest were available.[27] The southern boundaries of the Muscovite state, which earlier ranged from 150–250 kilometers south and southeast of Moscow, were in some places pushed an additional 100–200 kilometers to the south between 1635 and 1653.

The high priority assigned to completing what was probably the largest public works project ever undertaken by the Muscovite state is indicated by the fact that the state for a time chose to open the boundaries of its service class. At first the line was settled through recruitment from the rapidly dwindling pool of free people (*vol'nye liudi*).[28] Later the government had to resort to moving servitors from other areas.[29] During the early years of building the line, the need for manpower was so great that even peasants and former contract soldiers who had become enserfed were permitted to enroll as servitors on the frontier.[30] Brian Davies has noted that the state was forced "to subordinate the interests of serf owners to its goal of rapid military colonization of the frontier."[31] Soon, however, the Law Code was enacted and the government found itself embroiled in controversies over whether these newly recruited servitors could or should be returned to their former masters.[32]

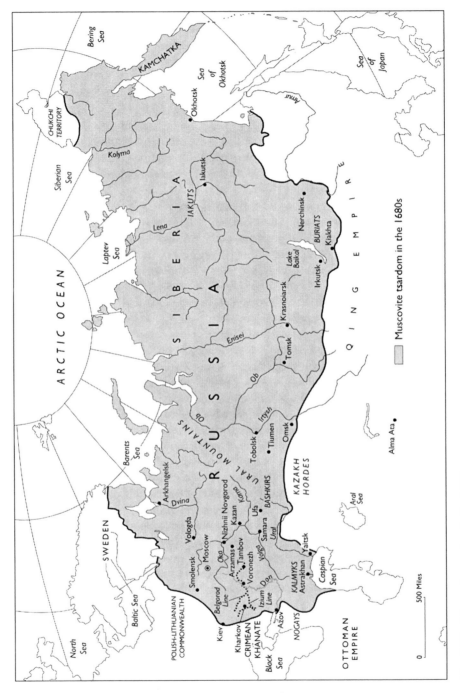

ARCTIC OCEAN

Bering
Sea

KAMCHATKA

CHUKCHI
TERRITORY

Siberian
Sea

Kolyma

Okhotsk
Sea
of
Okhotsk

Sea
of
Japan

Amur

Laptev
Sea

Lena

IAKUTS

Iakutsk

S I B E R I A

Nerchinsk

BURIATS

Kiakhta

Lake
Baikal

Irkutsk

Q I N G   E M P I R E

Krasnoiarsk

Enisei

Tomsk

Ob

Irtysh

Omsk

Alma Ata

Tiumen

Tobolsk

U R A L   M O U N T A I N S

Ob

R U S S I A

Barents
Sea

Arkhangelsk

Dvina

Vologda

Nizhnii Novgorod

Kama

Kazan

Ufa

BASHKIRS

KAZAKH
HORDES

Aral
Sea

Moscow

Oka

Arzamas

Tambov

Voronezh

Volga

Samara

Ural

Yaitsk

Belgorod
Line

Smolensk

Izium
Line

Don

KALMYKS

Astrakhan

Caspian
Sea

SWEDEN

Baltic
Sea

North
Sea

POLISH-LITHUANIAN
COMMONWEALTH

Kiev

Kharkov

CRIMEAN
KHANATE

Black
Sea

Azov

NOGAYS

OTTOMAN
EMPIRE

Muscovite tsardom in the 1680s

0   500 Miles

Map 2 The Muscovite tsardom in the 1680s

The overwhelming need for manpower, however, forced the government to temporarily retreat from its enforcement of the articles in the Law Code mandating the return of all fugitives. In March 1653, rather than return fugitives who had enrolled in government service on the southern frontier, it was decided to leave them in place and monetarily compensate those who petitioned the tsar "in order not to devastate the [Belgorod] line."[33] In March 1656, a decree issued by the tsar ordered that all fugitives who had settled along the line after 1653 would be returned to their masters.[34] As a result, the first massive fugitive manhunts, or "dragnets" as Brian Davies calls them, were initiated. These investigations involved government officials who would visit a district, often along with representatives of landowners, in order to find, record, and return fugitives.[35] In some cases several thousand serfs could be returned as a result of these investigations.[36]

The lesson learned from the Belgorod line was that new colonization, even when strategically necessary or desirable, caused considerable logistical problems for the government. Settling new territories required manpower. But with military men, and the agricultural laborers upon which they depended for sustenance, bound to specific lands in the core territories of the state, the traditional Muscovite land-holding system could not replicate or relocate itself conveniently. Professional new formation regiments were an expensive alternative, but they could not be easily sustained without some kind of provisioning system on the local level. In the early stages of constructing the Belgorod line the effort to recruit free people revealed that their numbers had dwindled to the point that they could no longer be recruited in large numbers.

The greatest obstacle to new southern colonization, however, was the state's commitment to enforcing the migration restrictions characteristic of the early evolution of serfdom. The brief suspension of these restrictions during the construction of the Belgorod line caused decades of bureaucratic headaches. The creation of new settlements, combined with the admission of large numbers of new people into state service, created a strong migration pull that disrupted other districts. In settling the steppe there was no conceivable way for state officials to ascertain the true identities of potential settlers. It would have taken months to verify each name against the cadastral surveys kept in Moscow, and, in the age before identity cards and fingerprints, nothing hindered potential settlers from inventing identities for themselves. The state quickly began to regret its decision to settle first and ask questions later, as petitions from destitute military men began to demand the return of agricultural laborers.

The settlements created along the Belgorod line, long after they had been officially closed to newcomers, continued to act as magnets for agricultural laborers who were attracted by the promise of a better deal. By advancing fortified lines and creating security, the Russian settlement frontier also advanced, in spite of efforts by the government and landlords to keep agricultural laborers bound to the core lands of the old southern defense perimeter south of Moscow. The Belgorod episode demonstrated that the state could either enforce serfdom, in order to preserve the traditional Muscovite land-holding and administrative systems, or expand settlement in the south. The inability of officials to weed fugitives out of the dwindling pool of potential colonists made it extremely difficult to do both simultaneously.

During the course of the second half of the seventeenth century no additional attempts were made to expand Muscovite state structures into the steppe.[37] Although we are not privy to the decision-making process, the Belgorod line became a stopping point for Russian settlement, serfdom, and the expansion of the Muscovite administrative system. To stand Norman Davies' appetite analogy on its head, the Muscovite state, upon experiencing a case of indigestion after its first serious southern meal in nearly a century, refrained from consuming again.

For the first time in its history, after building a great *val* (rampart) along its southern perimeter, the Muscovite state acquired a sense of security from Tatar raids. Owen Lattimore, who focused on the motives that moved China to construct great walls, describes the establishment of limits as an essential aspect of imperial frontier policy:

> It is the regular practice, whether dealing with the Roman, the Chinese, or the British-Indian imperial boundaries, to state the historical problem, in a one-sided manner. It is assumed that an imperial border policy is concerned solely with keeping out the barbarians ... This obscures the fact that such a boundary is equally important in another respect: it represents the limit of growth of an imperial system.[38]

After building and populating the Belgorod line, the Muscovite government settled upon an *ukraina* – the general Russian word for a limit or frontier – that it could live with.

Beyond the Belgorod line, the government ceded settlement initiative to Ukrainians (*Cherkasy*) and Don Cossacks (*Donskie kazaki*).[39] Both groups were classified as juridically distinct from Russians (*russkie liudi*).[40] Unlike the tsar's subjects in Rus', who were directly subordinated to the Muscovite administrative, legal, and tax systems, the Ukrainians and Don Cossacks beyond the Belgorod line lived under separate deals with the tsar. The multiethnic brotherhood of Don Cossacks acknowledged allegiance to the tsar, but maintained autonomy in all spheres. The Ukrainians settled in the steppe by the tsar were placed under the command of the Muscovite military, but were given broad latitude in governing themselves through elected colonels, lived according to their own laws and traditions, and were not incorporated into the Russian land-holding system.[41] By sub-contracting settlement in the steppe to two communities that were outsiders from the point of view of the Muscovite legal system, the government could enhance the security of the state in the south without uprooting or seriously disturbing the serfdom-dependent social structure of the metropole.

In contrast to the practice in certain later periods of Russian history, the Muscovite government made clear distinctions between core and periphery. The limit of the Belgorod line came to be considered the boundary of Rus'. The towns on the line were conceived of by Muscovites as *ukrainnye gorody* (frontier towns) and the line itself marked the zone of transition between the steppe and Rus'.[42] Both government and Cossack documents consistently speak of people coming and going to the Don from the "Russian towns," referring to the territories enclosed behind the Belgorod line.[43] Moreover, contemporary usage of the term Rus' suggests that it referred only to the metropole – the core lands of the Muscovite state that were under direct administration – and did not extend to frontiers such as the Don and Siberia.[44] This evidence completely dispels the notion promoted by Richard Pipes, and repeated in recent studies of the Russian empire by Geoffrey Hosking and Dominic Lieven, that Russians recognized no clear distinctions between the Rus' metropole and the other territories of *Rossiia*, the empire.[45]

Policies that discouraged Russians from settling in the steppe after 1653 resulted in the allocation of lands south of the Belgorod line to Ukrainian settlers.[46] Over time the government directed Ukrainians, whose migration east of the Dnieper was accelerated by the events associated with the Khmelnyts'ky uprising and his eventual alliance with the tsar in 1654, to settle beyond the fortified line.[47] The subsequent establishment of four *Cherkas* regiments beyond the line gave Ukrainians a firm foothold in the lands south of Kursk, Belgorod and Voronezh. When the government decided in the 1670s to construct a new line of fortifications further to the south, which would come to be called the Izium line, Ukrainians were brought in to settle the territory in order to prevent the dissipation of servitors from the Belgorod line and to avoid conflicts with Russian landowners. The settlement of Russians in the area was actually forbidden by government decree.[48] By the 1680s, Ukrainians, whose right to movement was not circumscribed, composed more than 80 percent of the population of the four regiments beyond the original Belgorod line.[49] While the military organization of the area termed by historians as the "Slobodskaia Ukraina" would only persist into the eighteenth century, its lasting effects are evident in the fact that Russian colonization south of the Belgorod line was forestalled for over a century – the Ukrainian small-holders had no incentive to share their lands with fugitives – giving the territory a Ukrainian majority. Thus, by giving the green light to Ukrainian colonization, while impeding Russian settlement, the imperial limit, or *ukraina*, played no small role in shaping the settlement frontier between Russians and Ukrainians. In many substantial ways the central section of the modern international border between Russia and northern Ukraine mirrors the administrative boundaries established by Muscovite policy makers.

Russian peasant settlement was successfully contained in the vicinity of the Belgorod line. A conservative estimate would suggest that between 1637 and 1710 at least 150,000 Russians settled behind the line and 30,000 Russians established themselves along its eastern edges in government-controlled lands between Tambov and Penza.[50] Very rough estimates would suggest that in the same years around 3,000 Russians settled in the Sloboda Ukraine (as compared to around 40,000 Ukrainians) and about 10,000 Russians migrated to the Don region.[51]

Although Russians could continue to migrate clandestinely to the Don region, they could not continue to behave as Russian villagers. This migration did not lead to colonization, the creation of new, self-sustaining agricultural communities or the replication of Russian social structures.[52] Russians who relocated to the Don region had to live according to Cossack customary law, which shunned agriculture and regulated relations between the Cossack fraternity and outsiders. Prior to the early eighteenth century, many Don Cossack *gorodki* (fortified settlements) were predominantly populated by males.[53] Correspondingly, the migration of Russian peasant families intent on pursuing agriculture was hampered by the cultural and political geography of the lands beyond the line and was primarily channeled in the direction of territories of the Middle Volga River.

After the construction of the Belgorod line, the government's primary objective was to prevent Russian migration to the steppe, not to promote it. In May 1666, the first decree was sent from the tsar ordering the Don Cossacks not to harbor fugitives.[54] Although the Cossacks ignored the decree, it initiated a drawn-out struggle of wills between the Muscovite government, the population of southern districts, and the Cossacks. In order to stem unauthorized migration, the government decided to employ the system of fortifications created to defend against Tatar raids to limit the outward movement of its own population.

The Stenka Razin rebellion (1670–1), which revealed the explosive potential of fugitives to the frontier, represented a major turning-point in the government's attitude towards the problem of southern boundaries. Previously, the frontier towns were given relatively free rein to trade and interact with the Don region. Interference from the central government was minimal. When reports reached Moscow in May 1670 that Razin had successfully returned to the Don after raiding on the Volga, the government took measures to enforce a total economic blockade of the region. In an order sent from the Military Chancellery (*razriad*) to G. Romodanovskii, the governor of the Belgorod regiment, the government outlined its new policy:

> Additionally, no traders whatsoever are to travel to the Don, with any goods, or grain or food supplies, or with anything else, until the Don is purified of Stenka's banditry. And ... if any traders attempt to go to him with any goods or [food] supplies or anything else, and if someone catches some of them or if by someone's informing on them they are caught, you our boyar and *voevoda*, are to order those outlaws to be put to death without any mercy in the towns of the Belgorod regiment, wherever someone is caught ...[55]

In an associated move, the government, in this case the Military Chancellery, ordered the entire border with the Don region to be sealed off. In July 1670, an order was sent to over 50 southern towns (as close to the Don as Korotiak and as far away as Tula) forbidding travel to and from the Don. The governor of the Belgorod regiment was ordered to announce and enforce a ban against travel to the Don region under penalty of death.

After Razin was captured and the disorders subsided, the government had to decide whether the borders with the Don would be reopened. In July 1671, after the Don Cossack atamans had triumphantly brought Razin to the tsar, the governor of Voronezh was instructed to allow traders through his checkpoints, but to make sure that they had firm surety bonds (*krepkie poruky*) to guarantee their return.[56]

This caused some minor confusion, since he interpreted the instruction to mean that they had to obtain surety bonds in Voronezh. The subsequent clarification of policy from the Military Chancellery established the policy that would be followed in later decades:

> And whatsoever traders arrive in Voronezh from the interior (*verkhnye*) and frontier towns, they are to be recorded: which towns they are from, what rank of people they are, what their names are. Upon recording them, they are to be released to go to the Don with their goods without requiring new surety bonds. And command them sternly, that they are to return this spring and not to winter in the Don. When they return, they must present themselves in Korotiak or Voronezh, and without presenting themselves they should not pass by, in order that from this point forward it will be known who has returned and who has not.[57]

The resolution also prescribed that orders be sent to the governors of all towns (*v gorody vo vse*) informing them of the new rules concerning surety bonds. These rules were spelled out as follows:

> Whichever people from the towns desire to go to the Don for the business of trade or for any other affairs, they should bring petitions to the governor and chancery officials signed by themselves or their spiritual fathers, or whoever they trust in such matters. In their petitions they should record by name (*imianno*) who is going to the Don for what purpose, and for how many months or weeks. Correspondingly the governor is to record their petitions in a book and verify their surety bonds, that they will return to their homes in the specified period of time, and give them travel documents signed by [the officials] themselves and not [simply] stamped with a seal. In these documents it should be recorded specifically the person's name and rank, and for what reason the person has been given leave to the Don, so that in Voronezh and Korotiak they will not be detained. In those documents it should also be recorded that they, when traveling to the Don, present themselves in Voronezh and in Korotiak, and without presenting themselves they should not pass by, since it has been ordered that such people must be recorded in those towns and their travel documents are to be inspected to find out for how long they have been given leave.[58]

Thus, by 1671, the Russian authorities had implemented a boundary regime with the Don region that was in many ways as rigorous as many border regimes between separate states in the nineteenth century. This document demonstrates that Muscovy was an early pioneer in what John Torpey sees as a trend by modern states to claim "the legitimate authority to permit movement within and across their jurisdictions."[59] Customs duties were assessed, travel documents were issued and examined, and government officials monitored entry and exit.[60]

In spite of state efforts to prevent an exodus from Rus' to the Don region, in the decades after the construction of the Belgorod line several thousand of the tsar's subjects elected to relocate from certain servitude to risky freedom. According to a 1685 petition to the tsar from landlords in Tambov, "the Khoper and Medveditsa Rivers [the northern extensions of the Don River basin] had become filled with people and in those fortified settlements where in former times there were twenty or fifteen people now there are two hundred or three hundred ...."[61] Although precise population figures for the Cossack lands are not available, since Cossacks required neither bureaucrats nor tax-registers, existing evidence suggests that the number of settlements doubled, or possibly even tripled, between 1650 and 1700: in the 1630s there were at least 35 Cossack settlements, by 1682 there were more than 70, and by 1700 the number had exceeded one hundred.[62] As the flow of Russian migration to the Don increased, it became difficult for the government to justify the legal loophole that was created long before it had solidified its presence in the steppe. Russians who bribed, outwitted, or outran border officials were still becoming Cossacks and thus forever slipping out from under the government's fiscal and administrative yoke.

Deluged by petitions from landlords demanding the return of fugitives, the government had few options. It could revoke the Don Cossack Host's separate deal with the tsar and attempt to introduce direct administrative control over the whole Don region, a move which was likely to provoke a new rebellion and upset the strategic balance in the south exactly at a time when the Russian government was pursuing a forward policy in the Dnieper basin (the Chihirin wars and Crimean campaigns). The only other option was to put more obstacles in the way of migration and attempt to convince the Cossacks not to accept fugitives. The government chose the latter.

The administration of Vasilii Vasilievich Golitsyn took an active role in formulating a new boundary policy.[63] In 1684–6 further consolidation of boundaries between Russia and the Don region took place. An order was sent to the governors of Belgorod regiment towns along the Don, Severskii Donets, Sosna, and Oskol Rivers instituting new checkpoints. The order required local officials "to station in those towns and districts servitors at checkpoints and guard posts (*storozhakh*), so that no fugitives ... pass into the Don region."[64] A repeat order issued a few months later further suggested that checkpoint captains (*zastavnye golovy*) send patrols into places far from the checkpoints, which would suggest that a second tier of mobile patrols was intended to supplement the stationary checkpoints.[65] It is clear that this was a blanket order for the capture of all fugitives, since undocumented travelers were to be interrogated to find out who they were, where they were coming from, and why they were "fleeing" to the Don.

The decision to keep subjects out of lands set aside for clients forced the government to turn the Belgorod line into a boundary of territorial sovereignty in its modern sense. According to Ladis Kristof, a true boundary is not a "legal fiction" but "the outer line of effective control exercised by the central government" that is necessarily "coordinated with an empirical force actually present and asserting itself in the terrain."[66] Kristof suggests that states establish such lines of effective control not just to keep their enemies out, but also to keep in their own citizens and resources.[67] A petition from Ivan Sas(ov), who was responsible for boundary enforcement between Korotiak and Ostrogozhsk, in the 1690s illustrates this trend. The description of his responsibilities almost reads like those of a modern border guard:

> I was ordered to be on guard (*berezhenie derzhat'*) along the fords and places where the Tatars cross rivers between Korotiak and Ostrogozhsk to prevent the approach of armed outlaws, Tatars and Kalmyks, and bandit Cossacks from the Don and against [the exodus] of fugitive outlaws from your Grand Sovereign's towns. ... And [I am] to allow traders with travel documents to pass after recording where they are going, for what purpose, and for how many months and weeks.[68]

The boundary-making state attempted to cordon off the steppe in order to protect itself from nomadic raids, bandits, and the illegal migration of its subjects, who became "outlaws" from the moment they left their legal residences.

It is difficult to evaluate Muscovite boundary policy from a comparative perspective, since the comparative history of state borders and their role in enforcing migration control have not been explored in any detail.[69] "The regular maintenance of immigration control," write the authors of a handbook on international migration law, "made its debut in the western world at a remarkably recent date."[70] According to the same source, most European states implemented migration control only in the aftermath of the French Revolution.[71] Although the boundary between Spain and France is often considered the first modern border, it emerged gradually over several centuries, involved significant input from local populations, and was rarely patrolled before the nineteenth century.[72]

In contrast, during the second half of the seventeenth century, the administrative boundary between Russia and the Don acquired all the trappings of modern international boundaries: identity documents, checkpoints, patrols, inspections, etc. The evolution of Russian southern boundaries in the direction of the Don region in the second half of the seventeenth century suggests that the state was searching for a compromise between its geopolitical interests, served by its Cossack clients in the steppe, and its sovereignty over its Russian subjects, whom it prohibited from settling in the steppe. Instead of integrating the Don region into the empire, the Russian government created and policed administrative boundaries between Russian provinces and the Don. Though modified on various occasions to suit the state, the Don Cossacks' separate deal with the tsars would last until the end of the monarchy itself.

The soundness of the Muscovite policy of cordoning off the steppe is best measured against the results of the first important attempt to deviate from that policy. Although the young Tsar Peter I confronted a geopolitical environment created by his ancestors, he saw the world very differently. His first action upon becoming sole ruler was to campaign against the Ottoman Black Sea fort of Azov, the very town his grandfather refused to annex in 1642. For him the steppe was merely an annoying obstacle on the way to something of real value: the sea. In order to attain his Azov aspirations, in 1695–6 the tsar willed a navy into existence and put most of the population of the Belgorod line – an auspicious resource inherited from his father – to work building boats.[73]

With assistance from Don Cossacks – they, not the tsar's navy, engaged the Ottoman fleet at a critical moment in the second military campaign – the tsar succeeded in taking Azov. Capturing Azov, however, proved to be more simple than colonizing it.[74] By Petrine decree, in 1698, 2,750 military men and over 6,500 members of their families were transferred from other garrisons (primarily in the lower Volga region) to Azov. The colony, however, was an abysmal failure. Herded to Azov and plunked down in half-ruined, half-built settlements, they quickly began to do what most unwilling pioneers did: they died and dispersed. A report produced for the Admiralty in 1702 revealed an extraordinarily bleak assessment of the fate of the transfers: out of 2,750 military men and 6,546 members of their families sent to Azov after 1698, 1,482 military men (54 percent) and 4,200 of their relatives (64 percent) had died in Azov.[75] Unfortunately for government planners, but luckily for them, 706 servitors and 845 of their relatives had managed to flee. After about four years of "service" in Azov, only 562 stalwarts (20 percent) remained at their posts.[76] The tsar's haste to plant colonies in the open steppe had crossed the ecological (open steppe) and epidemiological boundaries his ancestors had sought to avoid.

Azov's problems were compounded by the fact that the tsar's enthusiasm for southern ports disregarded the realities of steppe colonization. The settlements were separated from the metropole by hundreds of kilometers of steppe, making them dependent upon long supply lines. Because Tatar raids made growing grain virtually impossible, the Azov colonists had to deal with perpetual shortages and inflated prices. A 1706 petition from a group of soldiers provides a cogent diagnosis of Azov's problems:

> At present we cannot subsist on our bread rations because the town of Azov is peripheral (*ukrainnoi*) and far removed from our old places of residence. [In Azov] We buy grain, clothing, firewood and lumber for two and three time more than in those old towns. In those towns [where the petitioners formerly resided] grain is sown nearby, and clothes are made at home, and there is enough firewood for everyone, and other needs are [satisfied] at home (*inoe chto trebno est' v domakh*). Whatever cannot [be made at home] is purchased much cheaper than in Azov and it is possible to travel freely [to trade] from town to town. For us, it is impossible to travel in small groups to satisfy our needs, and we cannot even go out a half *versta* without being attacked by the Kuban *murzas* and Tatars who, by their bandit attacks, cause great destruction to people, take people captive, and rob cattle. Because of all this, we have become impoverished and have incurred significant debts (*oskudali i odolzhalis*).[77]

Peter's soldiers had come to understand what Muscovite rulers had taken for granted. Colonies planted in the open steppe were economically and militarily vulnerable. Only continuous infusions of resources and labor could keep them alive.

In its short existence Azov never learned to live without life-support from the metropole. Because the settlements did not even possess enough security to enable them to feed themselves, it is not likely that Azov could have soon severed the umbilical cord of supply shipments that sustained it. The imperial ambitions that inspired the birth of Peter's colonies in the Black Sea steppes led to their sacrifice in 1711, when miscalculations in battle at Pruth forced the Russian tsar to hand back to the Ottomans everything he had gained in the south.[78] Russia retreated from the Black Sea to the security of the Belgorod line.

The failure of a different settlement scheme also attempted under Peter I further dampened enthusiasm for agricultural experiments in the steppe. In the late 1690s, possibly as a result of a more secure situation in the northern areas of the steppe following the conquest of Azov, several Russian peasant settlements spontaneously arose in the region of the Bitiug River (a branch of the Don River south of Voronezh). The illegal settlements, inhabited by fugitives from districts behind the Belgorod line, were discovered by government officials in 1698.[79] In order to prevent others from following the example of the Bitiug pioneers, a detachment of soldiers was sent in 1699 to destroy the settlement. Over 1,500 dwellings (*dvory*) were burned and the inhabitants were deported to their previous places of residence. The message was clear. The government's objective was to preserve the *status quo*. The unauthorized settlements had to be annihilated, because they could only siphon off serfs and set a precedent for other would-be pioneers.

The story of the Bitiug settlements does not end, however, with the destruction of the illegal colony. A decision was made to replace self-motivated, but fugitive, peasant pioneers with unwilling pioneers who answered directly to the tsar. The virgin soil would be turned, but on the state's terms by people it controlled. In 1701 nearly 5,000 state peasants were forcibly relocated from districts north of Moscow (such as Kostroma, Rostov, and Iaroslavl) and ordered to till the southern steppes along the Bitiug River.[80] The countless ordeals of these strangers in a strange land, one of the first contingents of peasants to fall victim to state experiments in colonization, cannot be adequately reconstructed from existing accounts, but a statistical appraisal of the settlement speaks for itself. After two years of tilling, only 369 peasants were still at work, while 3,409 (69 percent) had died and 1,141 (23 percent) had managed to run away.[81]

The failure of two important attempts to establish self-sufficient government-sponsored settlements in the steppe during the Petrine period confirms the wisdom of Muscovite restraint. Containment, directed at keeping the insiders in and the outsiders out, required massive investments in boundary infrastructures, but in the long run maximized benefits. Colonization without containment came at a high human and material cost. The Muscovite investments in the Belgorod line and the Don Cossack alliance established a permanent presence in the steppe and facilitated the conquest of Azov. In contrast, the Petrine settlements were poorly planned and easily uprooted. Until the nomads were deprived of their mobility, common sense dictated that steppe settlements were wasteful investments of precious resources. The immediate successors of Peter I went back to the tried and true method of advancing fortified lines. The administration of Catherine II was able to settle the steppe, but only after systematically subjugating nomads from the Dniester to Dagestan. Security enabled the portions of the steppe *ukraina* not reserved for the Cossacks to be reimagined and repackaged as a *Novorossiia* (New Russia) of limitless possibilities.

This study has argued that the Muscovite appetite for expansion was far more modest than some have imagined. Because serfdom served as a constraint on colonization, the government preferred its subjects to stay stationary. It resorted to colonization when necessary for security, but it favored containment and cautious consolidation. This was an empire that rejected an invitation to annex Azov in 1642 because its bureaucrats calculated that the cost in men, material, and money was prohibitive, and that deployed its soldiers to impede colonization without authorization. State officials cultivated juridical double standards that placed Russians in an underprivileged position relative to the tsar's Cossack clients, and they cut a separate deal with Ukrainian settlers to enhance security in the south. Russian rulers pioneered policies of migration control and border patrol in an effort to maintain boundaries between the privileged military communities in the steppe beyond the Belgorod line and the weaponless, enserfed masses of the Rus' metropole. All of these developments demonstrate that Russian rulers of the seventeenth century preferred a menu of pragmatic approaches to empire-building over *bulimia politica* and obesity in the body politic.

Notes

1 I would like to thank the International Research & Exchanges Board (IREX) and the Social Science Research Council for generous support of my research in Russia. Brian L. Davies provided valuable insights and encouragement at critical points in my work.
2 The focus here is on the steppe lands between the Dnieper and the Volga, with primary emphasis on the Don River basin. For a more extensive survey of Russia's historical relationship with the entire steppe over centuries, see the groundbreaking study by Willard Sunderland, *Taming the Wild Field: Colonization and Empire on the Russian Steppe* (Ithaca, 2004).
3 For an overview of Russia's relations with the nomadic peoples of the steppe, consult Michael Khodarkovsky, *Russia's Steppe Frontier: The Making of a Colonial Empire, 1500–1800* (Bloomington, 2002).
4 A.A. Novosel'skii, *Bor'ba Moskovskogo gosudarstva s tatarami v pervoi polovine XVII veka* (Moscow, 1948), 436.
5 The statistics cited here are available in the appendix to the above. No indication of the size of the state budget for the early seventeenth century exists. In the 1680s the annual budget of the Muscovite state was around a million rubles. See *Ocherki istorii SSSR. Period Feodalizma XVII vek* (Moscow, 1955), 438.
6 For a general treatment of the Muscovite southern defense perimeter, see Denis B. Shaw, "Southern frontiers of Muscovy, 1550–1700", in *Studies in Russian Historical Geography*, eds James H. Bater and R.A. French, v. 1 (London, 1983).

7 No adequate study of Crimean state structures exists. I base the conclusions here on my reading of the primary sources. For a basic account based upon published sources, see Iu. V. Priimak, *K khronologii osmanskogo prisutstviia v severo-vostochnom prichernomor'e konets XV- pervaia tret' XIX vv.* (Armavir, 1997).

8 *Stateinyi spisok stol'nika Vasiliia Tiapkina i d'iaka Nikity Zotova posol'stva v Krym v 1680 godu* (Odessa, 1850), 26.

9 RGADA, f. 111, donskie dela, kn. 12, l. 57ob.

10 The term government is used here and throughout for the sake of convenience to refer to the system of *prikazy* (administrative bureaus) that were responsible for most routine administration in Muscovy. Although all orders were issued in the name of the tsar, in actuality the bulk of decision-making was carried out by clerks in Moscow under the supervision of senior clerks and boyars. Since it is not always possible to determine the level of personal participation in decision-making by Muscovite tsars, I employ the term "government" here to refer to the administration as a whole.

11 N. Vtorov and K. Aleksandrov-Dol'nik, *Drevniia gramoty i drugie pis'mennye pamiatniki, kasaiushchiesia Voronezhskoi gubernii i chastiiu Azova*, vyp. 2 (Voronezh, 1851), 32.

12 Although almost all Don Cossack records before the Time of Troubles have been lost, the Nikonian Chronicle preserves several references to the Don Cossacks. See for example *Polnoe sobranie russkikh letopisei*, v. 13: 271, 326.

13 For a detailed treatment of the earliest period of Cossack history, see Günter Stöckl, *Die Entstehung des Kosakentums* (München, 1953).

14 For a classic account see S.G. Svatikov, *Rossiia i Don, 1549–1917: issledovanie po istorii gosudarstvennogo i administrativnogo prava i politicheskikh dvizhenii na Donu* (Belgrade, 1924). For a comprehensive survey of these topics, see N. A. Mininkov, *Donskoe kazachestvo v epokhu pozdnego srednevekov'ia (do 1671g.)* (Rostov on Don, 1998).

15 G.K. Kotoshikhin, *O Rossii v tsarstvovanie Alekseia Mikhailovicha* (St Petersburg, 1906), 135; Patrick Gordon, *Diary*, in RGVIA, f. 846, op. 15, d. 5, l. 472 ob.

16 In most years, the government sent 3,000 rubles or less to the Cossacks. Brian Davies estimates the cash entitlements of the Kozlov garrison in 1639 as ca. 6,000 rubles. See Brian L. Davies, *State Power and Community in Early Modern Russia: The Case of Kozlov, 1635–49* (New York, 2004), 117. On the subsidy sent to the Don Cossacks, see V.P. Zagorovskii, "Donskoe kazachestvo i razmery donskikh otpuskov v xvii veke," *Trudy Voronezhskogo universiteta* v. LIII (1960): 131–46.

17 [V. D. Sukhorukov], *Istoricheskoe opisanie zemli voiska donskogo* (Novocherkassk, 1869), 170; RGADA, f. 89, turetskie dela, 1637, d. 1, l. 401. It is interesting to note that the Muscovite use of the doctrine of "plausible deniability" is similar to contemporary practice in Western Europe. See Janice E. Thomson, *Mercenaries, Pirates, and Sovereigns: State-Building and Extraterritorial Violence in Early Modern Europe* (Princeton, 1994).

18 Norman Davies, *Europe: A History* (Oxford, 1996), 655. For an earlier assertion of Russia's "appetite for land" and "obsession" with expansion, see Richard Pipes, *Russia under the Old Regime* (New York, 1974), 118.

19 The relevant documentation is contained in RGADA, f. 89, turetskie dela, 1642, d. 1. Estimates are on ll. 14–15.

20 Ibid., ll. 14–15. Budget figures for the period are not available, but the sum would have represented over 10 percent of the entire state budget in the 1680s.

21 On *pomest'e*, see also Matthew Romaniello in this volume.

22 Richard Hellie, *Enserfment and Military Change in Muscovy* (Chicago, 1971).

23 A.G. Man'kov, *Razvitie krepostnogo prava v Rossii vo vtoroi polovine XVII veka* (Moscow, 1962), 248–323. Also see A.G. Man'kov, *Ulozhenie 1649 goda: kodeks feodal'nogo prava Rossii* (Leningrad, 1980) and *Sobornoe Ulozhenie. Tektst. Kommentarii* (Leningrad, 1987).

24 By the late sixteenth century, all travelers were expected to obtain travel documents (*proezzhie gramoty*) from local officials. By the seventeenth century, unauthorized migration had become a criminal offense (see works of Man'kov cited above). No adequate study of these policies exists, but hints of them are scattered throughout the documentary record. For a very brief account, see F.A. Brokgauz and I.A. Efron, *Entsiklopedicheskii slovar'* XXII, s.v. "pasport," 924. Numerous examples of such travel documents are preserved in the *Donskie dela*.

25 *Akty sobrannye v bibliotekakh i arkhivakh Rossiiskoi imperii* III (St Petersburg, 1836), 143.

26 For a full account of the construction of the Belgorod line see V.P. Zagorovskii, *Belgorodskaia cherta* (Voronezh, 1969). For a more extensive treatment of the logistics of southern settlement, see Carol Belkin Stevens, *Soldiers on the Steppe: Army Reform and Social Change in Early Modern Russia* (DeKalb, 1995). For a comprehensive account of community and governance along the Belgorod line, see Davies, *State Power and Community*.

27 Zagorovskii, *Belgorodskaia cherta*, 17–18.

28 It is interesting to note the Muscovite definition of those who were free: "those who are not in [government] service, not [urban] tax payers, and not tillers of the soil, and who are not serving as the bondsmen of any one ..." *Akty sobrannye*, 430. Such a definition obviously did not leave a large pool of potential settlers.

29 V.M. Vazhinskii, *Zemlevladenie i skladyvanie obshchiny odnodvortsov v XVII veke (po materialam iuzhnykh uezdov Rossii)* (Voronezh, 1974), 58.

30 Ibid., 58–9.

31 Brian Davies, "The recovery of fugitive peasants from Muscovy's southern frontier: the case of Kozlov 1636–40," *Russian History* 19, nos. 1–4 (1992): 32.

32 Ibid., 29–56; Man'kov, *Razvitie*, 122–8. For an internal memo on policy to 1676, see also N.I. Pavlenko, ed., *Dvorianstvo i krepostnoi stroi v Rossii XVI–XVII vv.* (Moscow, 1975), 342.

33 Pavlenko, *Dvorianstvo*, 342; Man'kov, *Razvitie*, 124–5.

34 Pavlenko, *Dvorianstvo*, 342; Man'kov, *Razvitie*, 125–6.

35 A.A. Novosel'skii, "Otdatochnye knigi beglykh kak istochnik dlia izucheniia narodnoi kolonizatsii na Rusi v XVII v," *Trudy istoriko-arkhivnogo instituta* II (Moscow, 1946): 127–52.

36 Ibid., 144–5.

37 V.V. Golitsyn's Crimean campaigns were conducted as part of the Holy Alliance and, as far as I can tell, did not involve any serious plans for settlement. Moreover, their failure revealed that the Russian military could not yet operate effectively and efficiently in the steppe. For a general discussion of settlement, see V.P. Zagorovskii, "Obshchii ocherk istorii zaseleniia i khoziaistvennogo osvoeniia iuzhnykh okrain Rossii v epokhu zrelogo feodalizma (XVI – nachalo XVIII veka)," in *Istoriia zaseleniia i khoziaistvennogo osvoeniia voronezhskogo kraia v epokhu feodalizma* (Voronezh, 1986).

38 Owen Lattimore, *Inner Asian Frontiers of China* (New York, 1951), 239.

39 Don Cossack identity originally developed as an overarching category that united people of diverse backgrounds, Turkic and Slavic. Cossack identity and Russian identity, regardless of what the latter precisely constituted, were never coterminous. A Cossack could be of Russian background, but not all Cossacks were Russians. On *Cherkas* as the commonly used term for Ukrainians in Muscovite documents, see Mykhailo Hrushevsky, *History of Ukraine-Rus'*, ed. Frank E. Sysyn, v. 8, *The Cossack Age, 1626–50* (Edmonton, 2002), xxviii, 303–9.

40 Because each group possessed a different set of legal rights, the government took care not to mix categories. For example, a bureaucrat sent to settle a territorial dispute near the Bakhmut River in 1704 was ordered to establish: "At present in those places how many, and in which precise locations, are there settlements of Russians, or Cherkasy, or Don Cossacks." RGADA, f. 111, donskie dela, kniga 20, l. 342ob.

41 D.I. Bahalii, *Istoriia slobids'koi ukraini* (Kharkiv, 1993), 63–88; Shaw, "Southern frontiers," 130–1; and Vazhinskii, *Zemlevladenie*, 149–57, 214–15.

42 The following quotation provides an illustrative example of the Belgorod line as the point where Rus' begins and ends: "... those outlaw Cossacks headed north along the Don ... it was reported that they are heading towards Rus' to Korotiaka and Voronezh and the vicinity of other towns of the Great Sovereign ...." See *Krestianskaia voina pod predvoditel'stvom Stepana Razina: sbornik dokumentov* (hereafter *KVSR*) (Moscow, 1959), 2: 69.

43 Numerous examples are published in *Dopolneniia k aktam istoricheskim, sobrannyia i izdannyia Arkheograficheskoiu kommisseiu* (hereafter *DAI*). (St Petersburg, 1846–72). *DAI*, 17: 167, "Savatii ... came to the Don from the Russian towns." See also *DAI*, 17: 136, 183, 185, 195.

44 A comprehensive study of the Muscovite understanding of Rus' and its frontiers (*ukrainy*) needs to be conducted. Prior to its privatization by the Ukrainian national movement in the nineteenth century, the term *ukraina* was used by Russians to refer to various frontiers. Examples indicating that Siberia was not considered Rus' are available in *Akty istoricheskie* IV (St Petersburg, 1842). A document from 1671 reads: "how many ... fugitive peasants have gone from Rus' to Siberia ...," 475.

45 Pipes, *Russia under the Old Regime*, 79; Geoffrey Hosking, *Russia: People and Empire* (Cambridge, 1997), 40; and Dominic Lieven, *Empire: The Russian Empire and Its Rivals* (New Haven, 2000), 226, 229. None of these studies discusses the Belgorod line.

46 This article is not the proper forum to examine the fascinating issue of Ukrainian identity. For a more extensive consideration of Ukrainian identity, see my "What's in a name? Semantic separation and the rise of the Ukrainian national name," *Harvard Ukrainian Studies* 27 (forthcoming).

47 V.P. Zagorovskii, *Iziumskaia cherta* (Voronezh, 1980), 50.

48 Vazhinskii, *Zemlevladenie*, 48; and Zagorovskii, *Iziumskaia cherta*, 50–1.

49 Vazhinskii, *Zemlevladenie*, 57.

50 For the difficulties in estimating population see Ia.E. Vodarskii, *Naselenie Rossii v kontse XVII–nachale XVIII veka* (Moscow, 1977), 172, 180. It is very difficult to distinguish between population increase as a result of migration and as a result of natural increase, especially since cadastral surveys were updated irregularly and women were not counted. For the population of the Belgorod line see Davies, *State Power and Community*, 115, 247. My estimate is 30,000, based on I. Tikhomirov, "K istorii kolonizatsii Penzenskogo kraia v nachale XVIII veka," *Zhurnal ministerstva narodnogo prosveshcheniia (novaia seriia)* XXX (1910): 64, 67; Iu.A. Mizis, *Zaselenie Tambovskogo kraia* (Tambov, 1990), 75; and Vodarskii, *Naselenie*, 180–4.

51 The approximate figure for migration to the Don region is derived from my archival work on that region. See the appendix on demography in my doctoral dissertation, Brian J. Boeck, "Shifting boundaries on the Don Steppe frontier: cossacks, empires and nomads to 1739" (Ph.D. diss., Harvard University, 2002), 583–6. For Sloboda Ukraine, consult Bahalii, *Istoriia*, 97–100.

52 The notion of colonization as it emerged in early modern Europe involved organized or planned settlement within a legal framework that usually provided for agricultural allocation of land. See D.W. Meinig, *The Shaping of America: A Geographic Perspective on 500 Years of History*, v. 1, *Atlantic America* (New Haven, 1986), 7, 31, 66, 221, 239, 240. For Russian concepts of colonization, see Sunderland, *Taming the Wild Field*, 88–9, 209–12.

53 In the 1690s, Patrick Gordon recorded concerning the Don Cossacks that "at first they suffered no women to live among them, but did worse by making use of boys, but of late they live with their wives and families." Patrick Gordon, *Diary*, in RGVIA, f. 846, op. 15, d. 5, l. 539. Local oral tradition also preserved memory of the era before the reign of Peter I when women were rare. See Evlampii Kotel'nikov, "Istoricheskoe svedenie Voiska Donskogo o verkhnei kurmoiarskoi stanitse," *Chteniia v obshchestve istorii i drevnostei rossiiskikh* kn. 3 (1863): 6–7.

54 RGADA, f. 111, donskie dela, 1666, d. 1, ll. 45–6.

55 *KVSR*, 1: 163.

56 *KVSR*, 4: 90.

57 *KVSR*, 4: 81.

58 RGADA, f. 210, belgorod stol, d. 715, ll. 244–6ob; and *KVSR*, 4: 90–1.

59 John Torpey, *The Invention of the Passport: Surveillance, Citizenship and the State* (Cambridge, 2000), 9.

60 The fact that this policy did not simply remain a dead letter is demonstrated by several forms of related documentation. See Davies, *State Power and Community*, 179–80; L.B. Veinberg, *Materialy po istorii voronezhskoi i sosednikh gubernii* (Voronezh, 1885), 681.

61 RGADA, f. 111, donskie dela, kn. 13, l. 53ob.

62 S.I. Riabov, *Donskaia zemlia v XVII veke* (Volgograd, 1992), 34–41.

63 On Golitsyn, see Lindsey A.J. Hughes, *Russia and the West: The Life of a Seventeenth-Century Westernizer, Prince Vasily Vasil'evich Golitsyn (1643–1714)* (Newtonville, 1984). Collective petitions from landowners seem to have played a key role in this decision. See RGADA, f. 210, belgorod stol, d. 1525, ll. 345–8.

64 RGADA, f. 210, belgorod stol, d. 1525, l. 336.

65 Ibid., 337–9.

66 Ladis Kristof, "The nature of frontiers and boundaries," in *Systematic Political Geography*, 2nd edn, ed. Harm J. de Blij (New York, 1959), 137.

67 Ibid., 137–8.

68 RGADA, f. 210, belgorodskii stol, d. 1391, 635–6.

69 The most recent survey, Malcolm Anderson, *Frontiers. Territory and State Formation in the Modern World* (Cambridge, 1996), devotes little coverage to events before the nineteenth century.

70 Richard Plender and Martinus Nighoff, *International Migration Law* (Dordrecht, 1988), 62.

71 Ibid., 64–5.

72 Peter Sahlins, *Boundaries: The Making of France and Spain in the Pyrenees* (Berkeley, 1989).

73 For the most recent account, see Edward Phillips, *The Founding of Russia's Navy* (Westport, 1998), 39–42.

74 For a more detailed treatment of the Azov enterprise see Boeck, "Shifting boundaries," Chapter 7.

75 RGAVMF, f. 177, op. 1, d. 22, l. 291ob.

76 Ibid., l. 327.

77 RGAVMF, f. 177, op. 1, d. 88, 676–7.

78 See Svetlana Filippovna Oreshkova, *Russko-turetskie otnosheniia v nachale vosemnadtsatogo veka* (Moscow, 1971).

79 The incident narrated here is described in RGADA, f. 210, belgorod stol, d. 1720, l. 256–60.

80 V.P. Zagorovskii, Obshchii ocherk, 19.

81 Ibid.

3 Grant, settle, negotiate

Military servitors in the Middle Volga region

Matthew P. Romaniello

And with God's grace, and because of the great faith of the Orthodox Tsar Ivan Vasil'evich, and on account of his heartfelt desire, God turned over to him the godless Tatars of Kazan, and on account of his faith, desiring the love of God, our pious sovereign destroyed their Muslim faith, and he ruined and demolished their mosque.[1]

Tsar Ivan IV's conquest of the Khanate of Kazan in 1552 ushered in a new era of Muscovite expansion south along the Volga River and east into Siberia, and soon confronted the Russian state with the problem of how to govern these newly incorporated lands and peoples. Almost immediately, Muscovite authorities replaced the Khanate's political and religious administrative structures with their Russian equivalents, such as a *voevoda* (regional governor) and a new Orthodox bishopric, justifying the triumphant rhetoric of the Russian Orthodox Church. Moscow hoped to secure the region from nearby nomadic raiders, pacify its indigenous population, and thus successfully extend its borders. Control over the former Khanate's lands and people, however, was a project that had only begun.[2]

Security was the pivotal issue for the Muscovite government in its new territory, the Middle Volga region. Dangers came from without and within as steppe nomads threatened the region, and rebellions by the tsar's new multiethnic and multiconfessional subjects continued.[3] The only solution to these threats was a strong military presence. At the time of the conquest, the Muscovite army was undergoing a change toward supplying its cavalry (*pomeshchiki*) through land grants (*pomest'ia*) to support their service. These new military servitors became the leading force of Muscovite control over the former Khanate territory.[4] However, in order to obtain the large number of troops required, the Muscovite government willingly utilized some of its newly conquered non-Russians as military servitors alongside Russian settlers from the interior provinces. Accompanying these former enemies of the tsar were newly arrived Russian political exiles from the central provinces. As a result, the Middle Volga region was secured by a blended military force of questionable origins, with Russians and non-Russians, Orthodox and non-Orthodox. Controlling the Middle Volga region became a joint project between elite Russian settlers and the indigenous population, each with the goal of redeeming their status inside Muscovy's borders. At the same time, the relatively high social standing of Russian migrants to the former Khanate makes Muscovite expansion into the Middle Volga a unique moment in the history of Russian colonialism, standing in sharp contrast to those portions of the empire that relied upon an influx of Russian peasants, such as the southern frontier or Siberia.[5] Small numbers of Russian peasants arrived as runaways from the interior provinces of Muscovy, but failed to alter the demographic composition in a significant way.

Having been empowered by the central government's need for their presence on the frontier, the Middle Volga region's *pomeshchiki* persistently negotiated with the government for concessions to improve their social position or wealth. Demanding increased land grants, decreased military service obligations, or arranging for their sons' inheritance or their daughters' dowries were all grounds for negotiation with the government. It was not remarkable in Muscovy to petition the government for any or all of these privileges, but the Middle Volga's military servitors were notably successful. In fact, individual negotiations with the central authorities affected the ability of the Muscovite government to control its new lands.

In the end, military servitors enjoyed a limited period in which they could shape the nature of Muscovite authority. By the end of the seventeenth century, the role of the cavalry in the armed forces had diminished in favor of gun-wielding infantry. As *pomeshchiki* lost their privileged status in the Muscovite army, they also lost the ability to extract concessions from the Muscovite government. This change corresponded with the increased security of the lands of the former Khanate, as Muscovy's border had continued to move to the south and west. Between 1552 and the end of the seventeenth century, however, Muscovite expansion was shaped by a diverse group of military servitors who exploited the state as much as the state exploited them.

Granting *pomest'e*

To govern the Middle Volga region effectively, the central chancelleries needed to secure the region against nomadic invaders and potential uprisings of the local population, and so turned toward *pomeshchiki* to resolve these frontier concerns. Creating a *pomeshchik* was simple in principle: in exchange for a grant of land, the state required military service. While the process of granting land for military service had been utilized in Muscovy since the fifteenth century, the *pomest'e* system in the Middle Volga differed from the earlier version in the interior. *Pomeshchiki* served as cavalry in the tsar's army. In order to cover the expense of providing the required arms, supplies, and horses, a *pomest'e* grant needed to produce sufficient revenue from its agricultural productivity. Generally, this goal was achieved through the labor of peasants. Using the large non-Russian peasant population in the Middle Volga region allowed Muscovy to export the *pomest'e* system to this territory without requiring any resettlement of Russian peasants.

As the central authorities integrated the labor of non-Russian peasants into their frontier security plan, Moscow also utilized the specialized military capabilities of the region's non-Russian elites. The Khanate of Kazan was a successor state to the Mongol Golden Horde; the Khanate's army maintained the tradition of Mongol cavalry as much as the Muscovites themselves did. While the highest nobles of the Khanate – the Tatar *mirzas* – blended with the highest nobles of Muscovy, the remaining Tatar and Chuvash cavalry found themselves re-employed in the tsar's army in their traditional capacity, becoming the frontier's new *pomeshchiki*. Surprisingly, while the *mirzas* may have converted to Russian Orthodoxy to maintain their elite status, many of the new Tatar and Chuvash *pomeshchiki* kept their original faith without pressure from Moscow. The value of these non-Russian *pomeshchiki* in securing the region far outweighed any possible concerns about their individual faiths.

In addition to enlisting Tatar and Chuvash former enemies as the tsar's new *pomeshchiki* in the region, Muscovy also drew on another unusual choice for defenders of the tsar's authority: Russian political exiles. The use of banished princes and nobles as *pomeshchiki* in the Middle Volga was a direct result of the massive political upheaval known as the *oprichnina*, begun by Ivan the Terrible shortly after his successful conquest of Kazan. It is outside the scope of this chapter to discuss the causes, processes, or results of the *oprichnina* in depth,[6]

Figure 3.1 "Casan Tatarorium" [Tatar Kazan]. From Adam Olearius, *Vermehrte Newe Beschreibung Der Muscowitischen und Persischen Reyse* (Schleswig, 1656; reprinted Tübingen: Max Niemeyer Verlag, 1971), 347–8. By permission of Max Niemeyer Verlag.

however, among the *oprichnina*'s first victims were many of princely rank who were forcibly relocated to Kazan. R.G. Skrynnikov has identified approximately 180 princes and nobles exiled to the region in 1565, dislocated primarily from the interior provinces of Iaroslavl, Rostov, Starodub, and Obolensk. Furthermore, Ivan's government seized the hereditary lands of these exiled nobles and turned them into *pomeshchiki*, granting smaller portions of *pomest'e* than their original possessions.[7] While the reliability of this group in defending the interests of the kingdom would certainly have been in question, loyal service to the tsar was the only option for reclaiming their lost status.

As a result, the Muscovite government relied on two groups of questionable merit to defend its new territory: conquered former enemies (non-Russians) and exiled enemies of the tsar (Russians). Both groups needed to demonstrate loyal service, though most non-Russian servitors received *pomest'e* only after completing some time in the tsar's army. Both Iangil'd Enandarov and Bakrach Ianchurin received their *pomest'e* in 1595, but each Tatar had previously enlisted in the tsar's service. For his longer period in the army, Enandarov ultimately obtained more land than Ianchurin, who was a more recent entry into the tsar's ranks.[8] If more than one generation of a family provided military service, or if the servitor had been injured in the tsar's service, the reward of land could increase.[9] Dmitrev Grigorev syn Azter'ev, for example, was provided with a house in addition to his *pomest'e* in recognition of his injuries during service.[10] Some unfortunates were not as lucky: Andrei Vasil'ev syn Davydov, who served the tsar in both Kazan and Alatyr in the 1660s, was left wounded and with nothing by the early 1670s.[11] More than a century after the initial conquest of the Khanate of Kazan, loyal military service remained the most frequent explanation for the award of *pomest'e* to an individual servitor.[12]

Loyalty demonstrated through service, especially in successive generations of a single family, overrode any consideration of a servitor's religious faith. Both converts to Russian Orthodoxy and Muslims received extensive land grants in the Middle Volga region – a fact that truly distinguished frontier service from the interior regions of Moscow, where religious noncomformity was highly undesirable.[13] Iakov Vasil'ev syn Asanov, a converted Tatar in service to the tsar and former Tatar *mirza*, received extensive lands in Kazan province along the road to Samara in the 1590s. This included the village of Bimer, settled with both Orthodox Russians and converted Tatar peasants. His son maintained possession over the land, received the right to build a mill, and even received more land, taken from the Spaso-Preobrazhenskii Monastery's lands in Kazan in 1616.[14] The family retained possession over all of their lands throughout the seventeenth century, successfully defeating claims made on their land by Kazan's Bogoroditsii Convent, and later by a fellow *mirza* family, as well as resisting two attempted tax increases.[15] Unsurprisingly for an important landowner, the local governor supported the Asanov family during a Russian and Tatar peasant protest against the Asanovs.[16]

The Khoziashev family were another Tatar family of Kazan with extensive landholdings in the province; however, the Khoziashevs remained Muslim. Their *pomest'e* included two villages, Isheevskoe and Taveleva, and a tavern.[17] Another

Tatar family, the Enmametevs, repeatedly attempted to claim the Khoziashev's land in the 1630s, which would have dispossessed the original servitor's three children, but without success.[18] The central authorities rewarded the loyalty of the Khoziashev family, who successfully defeated at least two more claims on their family's estates later in the seventeenth century.[19]

The Begishevs were a Muslim Chuvash family with lands in both Iadrin and Sviiazhsk provinces. In 1619, a grant confirmed Ekbulat Begishev's right to his father's land, and subsequent grants maintained his rights despite the governor of Kazan's attempt to seize their land in Sviiazhsk.[20] The Begishevs' village in Sviiazhsk province, Chirkina, was populated by Muslim Tatars. Iambulat Atkeev, an Orthodox Tatar servitor, made at least two attempts to claim the village, but each time the central authorities sided with the Muslim Begishevs because of their long history of loyal service to the tsar.[21]

In the end, there was unquestionably a mixed ethnic military force securing the territory of the former Khanate of Kazan, but it is difficult to establish the specific percentage of each group. The number of Russians waxed and waned across the period, but non-Russians remained more numerous. In general, there was a shift toward increasing the size of the infantry, especially around the end of the seventeenth century, as the number of military servitors diminished. This pattern corresponds with the ongoing process of military reforms, in which the infantry played an increased role, beginning with the Smolensk War with Poland in 1632–4 and continuing up to Peter the Great's overhaul of the Russian army at the beginning of the eighteenth century.[22] For example, in Sviiazhsk, one of the region's first Muscovite settlements, there were 220 *pomeshchiki* in 1613–4, of whom only 10 were Russian. By 1637, the military servitors had grown to 386, of whom 161 were Russian. In 1669, the military servitors had declined to 149, but non-Russians had returned to their numerical dominance, with 82 Muslim Tatars and 28 other non-Russians outnumbering 39 Russian servitors.[23]

The influence and prominence of non-Russian and non-Orthodox families among the servitor ranks, equivalent in social rank with all other members of the provincial nobility, demonstrates the colonial context for Muscovite governance in the Middle Volga region. Some elite Tatars converted to Russian Orthodoxy in the sixteenth century and so enjoyed high status, but conversion never became a prerequisite for Muscovite service in the century following the conquest of Kazan because of the continuing defensive needs of an exposed frontier. There was no other region in Muscovy where non-Orthodox *pomeshchiki* served in greater numbers than their Orthodox equivalents.[24]

In addition to the ethnic and confessional differences between the Volga's *pomeshchiki* and those in the central provinces, *pomeshchiki* in the Middle Volga were expected actually to settle on the frontier. This is not surprising, since both the Russians and non-Russians in the region had been considered enemies of the tsar in the recent past. Yet, these residence requirements were a distinctive feature of the territory, since such requirements for *pomeshchiki* were not enacted elsewhere in Muscovy until 1649, when the Law Code (*Ulozhenie*) specified that all service Tatars in Muscovy reside on their lands.[25] Even then, however, the Law

Code did not extend this principle to Russian servitors throughout Muscovy, although those Russians settled in the region continued to face this restriction. Warnings from the *Prikaz Kazanskogo dvortsa* (the region's governing office) to Russian servitors to continue their residence on their *pomest'e* remained one of the most common forms of communication between the central chancelleries and the frontier for the remainder of the century.[26]

In order to reinforce frontier residence, the central government followed a set of procedures to restrict the activities of the military servitors even when not performing required military duties. By clustering the land of the Middle Volga's *pomeshchiki* on the frontier to ensure their availability for service, the Muscovite government changed its traditional patterns in granting *pomest'e*. Military servitors with *pomest'ia* in the central provinces frequently found themselves with several small grants distributed across a geographically diverse area. That pattern of land grants prevented *pomeshchiki* from developing close connections or strong power bases in one particular district, whereas in the Middle Volga region the servitors' continuing presence on their lands was highly desirable.[27] Furthermore, this process reinforced the continuing exile of servitors in the Middle Volga from the central provinces. If a servitor received more than one land grant, all of this land was located on the frontier in order to avoid military servitors abandoning frontier land for the safety of the central provinces. To ensure the proximity to the region of those multiple-grant *pomeshchiki*, their land was either in more than one district of the Middle Volga region or in the form of a combination of land inside it and some in the near north – a roughly triangular region defined by Vladimir and Nizhnii Novogorod at its base and Vologda as its apex. Iakov Matiunin, for example, possessed land in Nizhegorod, Alatyr, Kurmysh, and Arzamas districts.[28] Andrei Vasilev syn Elagin accepted land in Arzamas in addition to his possessions in Kazan in 1676.[29] Andrei Vel'iamov received land in Alatyr in July 1687 not far from his earlier grants in Vologda and Galich, even if outside the Volga region.[30]

These isolated examples are representative of the Middle Volga region. The muster records of the *voevoda* of Saransk in 1670 recorded military servitors from a wide section of the Volga, specifically those in Alatyr, Arzamas, Kadom, Kurmysh, Murom, Nizhnii Novgorod, Saransk, Shuia, and Temnikov.[31] This report covers only those *pomeshchiki* responsible for providing some service to the *voevoda* of Saransk, but provides a general overview of the situation. The report covered a total of 66 *pomeshchiki* with land in those districts; 40 possessed land in more than one district, and 27 of those possessed land outside of the eight districts covered in the report. The amount of land in a single person's possession ranged from Prokofei Ivanov syn Stupishii with a combined 1,000 acres of land in Nizhnii Novgorod and Kostroma, to Ivan Volodimer syn Volyskov with only 30 acres in Arzamas and Alatyr. The land granted outside of the original eight districts of the report was all located within the northern triangular region. No one in the Saransk report possessed land in any other place than the original eight districts and the northern region. Therefore, even those with extensive lands could still be described as "frontier *pomeshchiki*," because they lacked holdings in the interior provinces.

When military servitors resisted the state's plans for keeping them on the frontier or failed to provide their required military service, the central chancelleries resorted to more coercive measures in order to achieve their goal. Initially, *pomeshchiki* were issued a warning that threatened the revocation of the land grant.[32] If the warning failed, then the land was seized and granted to another servitor, usually one with the same ethnic background. This maintained the ethnic composition of the tsarist military forces in the region. The service-Tatar Tolubaik Tonashev received the village of Beteman as his *pomest'e* in Kazan district in April 1622 under such circumstances; the land originally had been assigned to a different service-Tatar, Isennaleevskii.[33] Maintaining the association between certain lands and designated ethnicities in the Middle Volga predated the Law Code of 1649, which established the principle for all of Muscovy.[34]

From the conquest of Kazan until the end of the seventeenth century, *pomeshchiki* remained the guiding force of Muscovite security policy for its new territory. Unable to control the region without *pomeshchiki,* the central authorities found themselves forced into a series of compromises, slowly altering the nature of military service in Muscovy. This all occurred despite the potentially questionable loyalty of these *pomeshchiki*. The great numbers of non-Russians and non-Orthodox servitors was a notable break from policies in the interior; requiring residence on the servitor's *pomest'e* was another. It is impossible to know what further changes might have ensued if the state's reliance on this population continued, but the shift toward infantry instead of cavalry for security resulted in the *pomeshchiki*'s diminishing importance in Muscovy. In the end, the use of multi-ethnic military servitors in the Middle Volga region was a pivotal moment in the history of the Russian empire, when the indigenous population played a greater role than Russian colonists did in the establishment of Muscovite control.

Grounds for negotiation

Much of the power of the military servitors in guiding frontier policies is not revealed in the state's grants and demands, but rather in the ongoing, often protracted negotiations among the servitors and the central and local authorities that every grant of *pomest'e* could produce. The central chancelleries planned on maintaining the ethnic division among the grants (keeping "Russian" *pomest'ia* separate from "Tatar" *pomest'ia*) and preventing the servitors from abandoning their frontier lands. Local administrators, however, were concerned primarily with maintaining or increasing the number of potential *pomeshchiki* in their territory, and willingly neglected the central chancelleries' two concerns in order to achieve their goals. For their part, servitors challenged the size of the grant, its location, and their service obligations, and also worried about the possible seizure of the land following their death, removing their children's inheritance. These conflicting interests meant that the negotiation process, rather than the interests of the central state, ultimately determined the nature, composition, and number of military servitors on the frontier.

The adversarial nature of granting *pomest'e* to a potential *pomeshchik* was such that even a first grant to a loyal servitor could produce drawn-out negotiations. Many servitors began their negotiations with outright rejections of land grants. As local authorities preferred any servitor to unclaimed land, regional *voevody* frequently attempted to entice reluctant servitors, potentially increasing the burden on those already in their territory. For example, the *voevoda* of Alatyr granted land to Kozan Pushechnikov in the 1620s, which originally had been offered to Grigor Nekliudov. The *voevoda* attempted to convince Pushechnikov to accept the land, because his current *pomest'e* shared a border with the rejected land. The *voevoda* suggested Pushechnikov would surely want the rejected land "for his family."[35]

The *voevoda*'s interference with this rejected land grant was a fairly typical occurrence. If a Russian servitor could not be found for *pomest'e*, local officials might offer that land to a non-Russian servitor in violation of the central authorities' principles, demonstrating their commitment to full enlistment over ethnic separation of property. For example, the Chuvash Men'shov syn Andreianov accepted as his *pomest'e* land that the Russians Ivan and Kalin Esipov rejected in 1613.[36] While not illegal at that time (as it would be after the Law Code of 1649), it was unusual. Furthermore, crossing ethnic land divisions continued even after 1649, a clear demonstration of the different priorities of the local and central authorities. When a Russian servitor, Fedor Stilenev, died without an heir in 1690, the central authorities offered his land to another Russian, Lov Zhukov. Once Zhukov rejected the land as "untrustworthy," the local *voevoda* successfully enticed a local Tatar servitor, Elbno Fedorovshii, to take the land, though as Fedorovshii was an Orthodox convert the grant at least respected a religious divide, if not an ethnic one.[37]

While the given reasons for rejecting *pomest'e* varied, most servitors chose to reject an initial offer in order to improve their bargaining position. Possibly the servitor would be offered more land, fewer days of required military service, or lowered tax obligations as incentives for accepting his *pomest'e*. The central chancelleries, knowingly or unknowingly, supported this tactic by responding to one rejection with an offer for other lands. Boris Matveev and Fedor Sychov first rejected land in Arzamas, and then later in Alatyr, as the *Pomestnyi Prikaz* (Land-grant Chancellery) attempted to find land suitable for them in this new frontier.[38] Many non-Russians, who often benefited from Russian rejections, employed the same negotiating tactic. Mikhail Petrov and Ivan Semenov deti Beklemeshev, converted Tatars, first rejected land in Alatyr and then again in Nizhegorod district in 1687/88, in an attempt to find suitable land for themselves.[39]

While an outright rejection of a grant was possible before a servitor received any land, there was no reason to stop negotiating with the state after *pomest'e* had been accepted, especially because the viability of the new estates was often questionable. Frequently, claiming that the land was of poor quality was a plausible excuse for achieving personal goals, such as exchanging, expanding, or even selling a land grant. By relying on the region's environmental strengths in beekeeping, trapping, and fishing, servitors could avoid deteriorating soil quality. However, reliance on traditional peasant slash-and-burn agriculture would quickly exhaust the soil. Complaints about non-arable soil became increasingly common during the seventeenth century, even reaching the Metropolitan of Kazan, one of the wealthiest landowners in the region.[40] Servitors were no less likely to protest. Ivan Romadinovskii of Atemar wrote a particularly plaintive petition in 1652, when he begged the tsar to allow him to sell his *pomest'e* to a nearby monastery, because "nothing grows" on his land and "there is certain death from hunger."[41]

Both the rejection of land grants and claims of the soil's depletion were possible strategies to acquire different or better quality lands, but the most common approach to changing the size or quality of the land under a *pomeshchik*'s control was to challenge the current boundaries of the *pomest'e*. Many servitors petitioned the tsar to have the tax records for their boundaries adjusted, in the hope of reducing their tax obligation. Kondratei Filimonov, for example, managed to lower the yearly tax payments for his fields in Simbirsk district in December 1682.[42] Nikita Semenov syn Bolkovskii wrote several petitions in the 1690s to persuade the central authorities that he should keep his *pomest'e* in Arzamas without fulfilling his military service obligations.[43]

When not attempting to limit their obligations to the state, servitors frequently sought to increase their position by acquiring a portion of their neighbors' land. In most cases, the current *pomeshchik* of the land in question was victorious against claims for it. However, infrequent successes by those attempting to dispossess the current *pomeshchik* likely encouraged more petitions and litigation. In 1691, for example, Lev Dmitrev syn Ermolaev lost control over his *pomest'e* in Nizhegorod district to Stepan Romanov syn Kolitsov. Ermolaev possessed a small amount of *pomest'e* land next to Kolitsov's hereditary estate. When Kolitsov petitioned the tsar for more land, he received Ermolaev's plots. His success was potentially a result of his higher status in Muscovite society, demonstrated by his possession of hereditary lands as well as *pomest'e*. Ermolaev was compensated with new *pomest'e* along the Kama River, though it was much further to the east than his original land.[44]

Not all land disputes between servitors were resolved by a state agency. On rare occasions, *pomeshchiki* resorted to violence in order to settle their land disputes. In 1685, the *voevoda* of Saransk investigated the accusations of Timofei Iachont'ev syn Karazulov against Matvei Erlov, a local *pomeshchik* who resided on his *pomest'e* in Saransk district. Karazulov accused Erlov of arriving on Karazulov's *pomest'e* in Murom district, "breaking him," and seizing his land, and then forcing Karazulov to live on a small portion of his *pomest'e* in Simbirsk. Karazulov's complaint led to an investigation, with Erlov denying that there had not been any violence. Instead, Erlov explained, Karazulov willingly made this land deal in order to be summoned to Moscow to meet with the tsar, which could happen if he made a poor land deal. As amusing as Erlov's explanation was, the *Pomestnyi Prikaz* rejected it, fining Erlov for the attack. Interestingly, while Erlov was found at fault and fined, he was allowed to keep possession of the land he had seized.[45]

The *pomeshchiki*'s familial concerns also drove negotiations between the frontier and the central chancelleries after the initial land grant. As *pomest'e* remained the property of the tsar, a *pomeshchik*'s rights to that property lasted only for the time in which he could provide military service. Guaranteeing his son's claim to his *pomest'e* and being able to divide *pomest'e* to provide a dowry for his daughter forced each servitor to negotiate with the central chancelleries to achieve his personal goals. In general, a son's inheritance guaranteed the continuing presence of a single family of the appropriate ethnic background settled on the frontier; this fact encouraged acceptance for patrilineal inheritance among all of the parties. Dowries, however, remained an area of contention throughout the early modern period.

When arranging the inheritance of *pomest'e* from a servitor to his son, there was widespread agreement at all levels. The servitor provided for his family, and the local and central authorities benefited from continual military service from the *pomest'e*. Both Russian and non-Russian families passed lands from one generation to the next; the Asanovs, Khoziashevs, and Begishevs demonstrated that neither ethnicity nor religion affected this outcome. Russian examples are as common. In 1646, for example, the *Pomestnyi Prikaz* granted Aleksei Bogdanov syn Dubrovskii the land in Arzamas district that his father had been given in 1626/7, and Bogdan Iakovlev syn Solovtsov became the third generation of his family to receive their *pomest'e* in Arzamas in 1674.[46]

The commitment to maintaining the connections of single families to their *pomest'e* even extended to awarding the land to minors, after the practice had become less common elsewhere in Muscovy.[47] For example, Ivan Alekseevich Alenin, a minor, received the land of his recently departed father in Saransk district on 18 April 1654, because "it was necessary" for the city to keep its residents.[48] The youngest children in the Alferov family, *pomeshchiki* of Saransk and Penza districts, received all of the family's *pomest'ia* despite the claims of their elder cousins, Dmitrii and Vasilii, who had left the Middle Volga region.[49] This grant kept the land with the members of the family who offered evidence of continuing residence on the frontier.

Partible inheritance among all the heirs was common in Muscovy, but exceptions were possible. If there was only one heir, inheritance followed a direct line. However, if multiple heirs succeeded their father, there was no single pattern for inheritance.[50] For example, the eldest of three Kozlov brothers, Nikita, had inherited all the *pomest'e* of his father in 1666, which included several villages in both Nizhegorod and Alatyr districts. His brothers attempted unsuccessfully to claim a portion of land for themselves.[51] Conversely, the next year in Kerensk, one family's estate was divided into three to provide for two brothers, Bekbulat and Uraz Makmametev, and their cousin, Shmamet Lasaev syn Shukinchev.[52]

Since the central authorities required residence for the Middle Volga's *pomeshchiki*, current residence on the *pomest'e* would assist any possible heir. If no family members remained in the region, then a non-related servitor from the region would become the beneficiary. Liubim Besson syn Mekishin, a resident of Simbirsk, had to petition for his father's land in Arzamas in 1677, because he had lost the grant to his cousin Ivan Mekishin, a resident of Arzamas.[53] Semen Ivanov syn Bogtachevskii lost the village of Kamenii Brod in Simbirsk district to Savva Timofeev syn Voronkov, living then in Simbirsk, even though the village had been the *pomest'e* of Bogtachevskii's family for two previous generations. Bogtachevskii, however, had left Simbirsk.[54]

If there was a dispute among potential recipients for *pomest'e*, any claimant with both familial connections to the land and current residence in the region would typically win out over unrelated petitioners. In July 1681, Mikhail Ruzhevskii and one of his neighbors, Aleksei Stepanovich Khlopov, both filed claims for Ruzhevskii's father's large estate in Simbirsk district. Khlopov failed to prevent Ruzhevskii from receiving his father's land.[55] In 1692, Kazan's *voevoda* Dmitrii Vasil'evich Urakov tried to seize the *pomest'e* of Stepan and Fedia Levashev for himself. The Levashevs presented eight deeds to demonstrate their claim to their estate, beginning with the family's original grant from 1646. With this evidence and proof that they had paid their taxes, the Levashevs defeated the *voevoda*.[56]

On rare occasions when familial connections failed to win these inheritance disputes, the social rank of the unrelated petitioner had to be significantly higher than that of the family. High rank carried with it better access to influence in the central chancelleries. In 1676, Andrei Vasilev syn Elagin bequeathed his father's land in Arzamas to his nephew, Fedor Petrov of Sviiazhsk. Petrov was a relative and lived within the Volga region, which was normally sufficient claim to support inheritance rights. However, when the *voevoda* of Arzamas was asked to approve this exchange, he notified Elagin and Petrov that a boyar, Iakov Nikitich Odoevskii, already had rights for the land.[57] Odoevskii's elite rank in Muscovite society trumped the Elagin family's connection to their *pomest'e*, bypassing the standard criteria for land inheritance in the Middle Volga region.

When social rank influenced inheritance rights, it was a notable exception to standard practices. Rank in Muscovite society, however, was the largest determining factor for success in dividing *pomest'e* to provide a dowry for a servitor's daughter. Although the passing of *pomest'e* from father to son resembled patrilineal inheritance, *pomest'e* never became the legal property of a *pomeshchik*. This created a new reason for negotiations with the central authorities, as a *pomeshchik* was often required to try to win official approval for the illegal action of providing a dowry for his daughter with land.[58]

A servitor's need to rely on his only source of wealth – his *pomest'e* – to provide his daughter a dowry led many to attempt to extend their rights over the disposition of the land. For both Russians and non-Russians of high social rank, arranging dowries was relatively easy, because of their ability to influence the highest levels of the Muscovite government. A Chuvash *syn boiarskii*, Smirnoi Petrov syn Andreianov, gave his daughter Marfa an extensive dowry including bolts of cloth, various dresses, and the village of Voskresenskova in Kazan district from his *pomest'e* upon her marriage to Mikita Ivanov syn Brekhov in 1636.[59] Some wealthier nobles managed to avoid the trouble of transferring *pomest'e* by buying the land. This was the case for Boyar Boris Ivanovich Morozov, who bought the village of Seriatinoe in Arzamas district for his daughter's dowry from a local monastery in May 1640.[60]

Without the same ability to access the central chancelleries, some *pomeshchiki* still succeeded in receiving approval for using their service land as a dowry. Fedor Prokof'ev Derevii gave the village, Zhrikhinoi (along the Volga), to Vasilii Nikoforov syn Kokorin as a dowry for his daughter's marriage in 1654, and Boris Gavrilov syn Ostrovskii's daughter received the village of Levasheva in Arzamas district and peasants from his estates in Vologda to marry Leontii Aleksov syn Kopnin in 1683.[61] Success stories such as these were the result of the *pomeshchiki*'s ability to exploit the conflicting authority of individual chancelleries. Even if one chancellery denied the first request, another might assent. While decisions from the *Pomestnyi Prikaz* were the most common, other chancelleries could grant permission as well. Though the *pomeshchiki* without elite rank were at a disadvantage in dowry negotiations, the nature of the Muscovite government provided an opportunity for success.[62]

Unsurprisingly, while there was success, many petitions for the division of *pomest'e* for a dowry resulted in failure. Mikhail Mikhailov syn Oshcherin had already given his son-in-law, Vania Netesev, a small portion of his *pomest'e* in Arzamas district in 1675/6. The *Pomestnyi Prikaz* rejected the petition to approve the dowry, and instructed the *voevoda* of Arzamas to seize the land.[63] While land seizure was not the usual result of a dowry request, Oshcherin did receive a notable lesson that *pomest'e* was clearly the property of the state. For overstepping his claim to the land, Oshcherin and his family were punished. As always, seizure of *pomest'e* remained the best tool of the central authorities for imposing their plans upon the frontier.

Understanding the variety of negotiation among the three parties – central and local authorities, and the *pomeshchiki* – does not provide any clear indication of which was the most successful in shaping frontier policy. In various ways, each group had a limited ability to shape the conditions under which *pomest'e* was received. *Pomeshchiki* rejected *pomest'e*, petitioned for lesser service obligations, and attempted to provide for the future generations, all of which attenuated the central and local authorities' ability to control the number and ethnic composition of the military servitors. Undoubtedly the residence requirement for frontier *pomeshchiki* and maintaining the ethnic division of service land were the chancelleries' guiding principles, but the ongoing negotiations between the frontier and the center limited the chancelleries to guiding rather than imposing. Negotiations over land grants demonstrated the limitation of the state's autocratic power on its borders.

Conclusions

Even with limitations, using *pomest'ia* grants in the Middle Volga region allowed the central chancelleries to fortify and defend the frontier against both internal and external threats, achieving the state's goal, if not fulfilling their principles. As the frontier expanded, the external threats diminished, but the internal threats continued to be a real danger for Muscovite control. The Stenka Razin revolt, for example, was the most widespread and devastating rebellion in the region during the seventeenth century. In the fall of 1670, rebels laid siege to Simbirsk, burned Alatyr, killed several *voevody*, and seized Penza along with many of the region's southernmost towns. Within two months, regiments of local *pomeshchiki* defeated the rebel forces at Simbirsk, Koz'modem'iansk, and the southern towns of the Middle Volga region. If there had been any question concerning the effectiveness of the *pomeshchiki*, their success in re-establishing state control during the Razin revolt answered it, at least momentarily.[64]

As successful as the regional *pomeshchiki* were in restoring Muscovite control over the Middle Volga region, this could not disguise the recent innovations in military technology that slowly but surely eroded the importance of cavalry inside the tsar's army. The tsar's army began to experiment with new formations and the composition of its troops, increasing the use of infantry as early as the Smolensk War (1632–4). This drove the composition of the military toward increased reliance upon infantry rather than cavalry, lessening the need to support the Volga region's large number of military servitors, especially of non-Russian origins. Shortly after the Razin Revolt, Muscovy even hired the nearby Kalmyk nomads to suppress a minor rebellion in Simbirsk.[65] This established a precedent of relying upon the formerly hostile steppe nomads as Muscovite auxiliaries, which signaled the end of the reliance upon non-Russian *pomeshchiki* for security. While Muscovite control over the former Khanate of Kazan had been a joint project between Russians and non-Russians for more than a century, by the end of the seventeenth century that era was over.

The *pomest'e* system provided capable defense for the Middle Volga when the ability of Muscovy to defend the territory had been very much in question. Military servitors became the state's best method of control and protection, and, as a result, *pomeshchiki* in the Middle Volga gained unique opportunities. Russian and non-Russian, Orthodox and non-Orthodox, all served together as the tsar's army, and all attempted to exploit the state's need for their own agendas. While many of their interests were purely local and focused on caring for their own families, these frontier *pomeshchiki* influenced the government's policies and gradually forced changes. Although changes such as requiring residence on *pomest'e* or dividing *pomest'e* by ethnic group might seem insignificant, they ultimately affected all of Muscovy and not merely its frontier.

The settlement of the Middle Volga region, therefore, was not so much a process of colonization as a military occupation, at least initially. Military servitors provided a useful solution to the difficulties created with Muscovy's conquest of the multiethnic and multiconfessional population, in an area that had not yet been secured from even greater dangers posed by the steppe nomads. The need for *pomeshchiki* created unique opportunities for non-Russians to find a role within Muscovy that allowed them to maintain, or even gain, a relatively high social status. Unfortunately for their future, as *pomeshchiki* became less essential to the defense of the region, compromises with the non-Russians also diminished. Russian peasants began to migrate to the Middle Volga region in increasing numbers during the seventeenth century, which further decreased the state's willingness to compromise with the indigenous population. Non-Russian military servitors were replaced either by infantry or by hired mercenaries from among the steppe nomads. By the eighteenth century, an aggressive campaign to convert and control the non-Russian population began, finalizing their lost value to the Russian government.[66]

The conquest of the Khanate of Kazan created an unusual moment in time, when the Russian imperial project of expansion was defended by Russians and non-Russians, who increasingly exploited their important role for personal gain. In this early form of colonial rule, central and local authorities, Russian colonists, and the indigenous population could all benefit from the negotiations among them. While *pomeshchiki* would not guide the Russian empire outside the Middle Volga region, this was a successful demonstration to the central authorities that while governing practices from the interior could be replicated on the frontier, these policies would have to adjust to reflect their new circumstances. In the end, the entire empire would be transformed in the process.

Notes

1 *Polnoe sobranie russkikh letopisei* v. 13:1 (St Petersburg, 1862), 251.
2 For a general discussion of Muscovite expansion, see Andreas Kappeler, *The Russian Empire: A Multiethnic History* (London, 2001); and Michael Khodarkovsky, *Russia's Steppe Frontier: The Making of a Colonial Empire, 1500–1800* (Bloomington, 2002). For Muscovite governance over the former Khanate, see N.N. Firsov, *Kolonizatsiia Volzhsko-Kamskogo kraia i sviazannaia s nei politika: Obshchii obzor* (Kazan, 1930); and I.P. Ermolaev, *Srednee Povolzh'e vo vtoroi polovine XVI–XVII vv. (Upravlenie Kazanskim kraem)* (Kazan, 1982).
3 The Middle Volga region was multiethnic before and after the Muscovite conquest, with Turkic Tatars and Chuvashes and Finno-Ugric Maris, Mordvins, and Udmurts living throughout the region in large numbers.
4 Concerning *pomest'e* and *pomeshchiki* on the frontier, see: A.V. Vasil'ev, "K istorii zemlevladeniia v Sviiazhskom uezde," *Izvestiia obshchestva arkeologii, istorii i etnografii pri Imperatorskom Kazanskom universitete* 12 (1894): 602–12; S.V. Rozhdestvenskii, *Sluzhiloe zemlevladenie v Moskovskom gosudarstve XVI veka* (St Petersburg, 1897); I.M. Pokrovskii, *K istorii pomestnogo i ekonomicheskogo byta v Kazanskom krae v pervoi polovine XVII* (Kazan, 1909); and Valerie Kivelson, *Autocracy in the Provinces: The Muscovite Gentry and Political Culture in the Seventeenth Century* (Stanford, 1997).
5 For the south, see Carol B. Stevens, *Soldiers on the Steppe: Reform and Social Change in Early Modern Russia* (DeKalb, 1995); and Brian Davies, *State Power and Community in Early Modern Russia: The Case of Kozlov, 1635–49* (New York, 2004). For Siberia, see L.P. Shorokhov, "Vozniknovennie monastyrkikh votchin v Vostochnoi Sibiri," in *Russkoe naselenie pomor'ia Sibiri (period feodalizma)* (Moscow, 1973), 148–63; Basil Dmytryshyn, "The administrative apparatus of the Russian colony in Siberia and Northern Asia, 1581–1700," in *The History of Siberia: From Russian Conquest to Revolution*, ed. Alan Wood (New York, 1991), 17–36; I.L. Man'kova, "Gosudarstvennaia politika v otnoshenii zemlevladeniia uralo-sibirskikh monastyrei v XVII–nachale XVIII vv.," *Religiia i tserkov v Sibiri* 4 (1992): 12–24.
6 For an accessible recent account, see Andrei Pavlov and Maureen Perrie, *Ivan the Terrible: Profiles in Power* (London, 2003), 107–203.

7 R.G. Skrynnikov, *Tsartsvo terrora* (St Petersburg, 1992), 238–65.

8 I.P. Ermolaev and D.A. Mustafina, eds, *Dokumenty po istorii Kazanskogo kraia: Iz arkhivokhranilits Tatarskogo ASSR (vtoraia polovina XVI–seredina XVII): Tektsy i komment* (Kazan, 1990), no. 16 (18 July 1595), 49–51.

9 Nurmamet Nurkeev was awarded hereditary land in addition to his *pomest'e* in acknowledgment of his loyal service following his father's. Ibid., no. 31 (13 April 1622), 72–4.

10 RGADA, f. 1156, Saranskaia prikaznaia izba, op. 1, d. 9, ll. 4–5, after 27 June 1680.

11 RGADA, f. 159, Prikaznye dela novoi razborki, op. 2, Posol'skii prikaz, d. 1171, l. 1, between 1671 and 1676.

12 As late as 1675, when the Russian Leontii Luk'ianov syn Chufarov received his *pomest'e* in Simbirsk *uezd*, loyal service was cited as the reason for the grant. P. Martynov, comp., *Seleniia Simbirskogo uezda (Materialy dlia istoriia Simbirskogo dvorianstva i chastnogo zemlevladeniia v Simbirskom uezde)* (Simbirsk, 1903), 120.

13 For a discussion of foreign mercenaries' conversion, see W.M. Reger, "Baptizing Mars: the conversion to Russian orthodoxy of European mercenaries during the mid-seventeenth century," in *The Military and Society in Russia, 1450–1917*, eds Eric Lohr and Marshall Poe (Leiden, 2002), 389-412.

14 Ermolaev and Mustafina, *Dokumenty*, no. 17 (11 April 1597), 51–2; no. 21 (no earlier than September 1602), 56–7; no. 23 (18 November 1604), 58–9; no. 32 (after 16 February 1616), 74–5; and no. 33 (22 February 1616), 76–8.

15 Ibid., no. 47 (March 1632), 107–9; no. 51 (no earlier than 1636), 113–14; no. 36 (10 June 1620), 82; and no. 66 (no earlier than 1645), 146–7.

16 Ibid., no. 58 (16 September 1640), 133–4.

17 Ibid., no. 43 (7 June 1623), 99–101; and Evfimii Malov, comp., *Drevniia gramoty i raznye dokumenty (Materialy dlia istorii Kazanskoi eparkhii)* (Kazan, 1902), 8–9 (5 October 1633).

18 Ermolaev and Mustafina, *Dokumenty*, no. 48 (no earlier than 1633), 109–11; and Malov, *Drevniia gramoty*, 10–11 (14 December 1638).

19 Ermolaev and Mustafina, *Dokumenty*, no. 61 (20 April 1641), 136–7; and Malov, *Drevniia gramoty*, 12–15 (16 July 1653).

20 Begishev was identified as a Chuvash in the earliest documents, though later records identify his family as "service Tatars." However, it was common in the seventeenth century for Muscovite sources to label any Muslim as "Tatar." Stepanov Mel'nikov, ed., *Akty istoricheskie i iuridicheskie i drevniia tsarskiia gramoty Kazanskoi i drugikh sosedstvennykh gubernii* (Kazan, 1859), no. 4 (26 June 19), 8–9; no. 6 (1621), 11–12; no. 7 (9 July 1621), 13–14.

21 Ibid., no. 9 (8 February 1624), 15–16; no. 15 (5 February 1636), 28–9; and no. 16 (after 16 February 1636), 29–30.

22 For a discussion of military reforms, see Thomas Esper, "Military self-sufficiency and weapons technology in Muscovite Russia," *Slavic Review* 28 (1969): 185–208; and Robert I. Frost, *The Northern Wars: War, State and Society in Northeastern Europe, 1558–1721* (Harlow, Essex, 2000).

23 V.I. Buganov and L.F. Kuz'mina, comp., *Razriadnye knigi, 1598–1638 gg* (Moscow, 1974), 264; S.I. Porfir'ev, "Rospis' sluzhilym liudiam po oblasti Kazanskogo dvortsa na 7146 (1637) goda," *Izvestiia obshchestva arkheologii, istorii i etnografii pri Kazanskom universitet* 28 (1912): 462–3; RGADA, f. 210, Razriadnyi prikaz, op. 21, d. 228, ll. 1–7ob, 1669.

24 For the history of Tatars in the tsar's army in the sixteenth century, see the work of Janet Martin: "The *Novokreshcheny* of Novgorod: assimilation in the sixteenth century," *Central Asian Survey* 9 (1990): 13–38; "Multiethnicity in Muscovy: a consideration of Christian and Muslim tatars in the 1550s–80s," *Journal of Early Modern History* 5 (2001): 1–23; and "Tatars in the Muscovite army during the Livonian War," in Lohr and Poe, eds, *The Military and Society in Russia*, 365–87.

25 Richard Hellie, trans. and ed., *The Muscovite Law Code (*Ulozhenie*) of 1649,* Part 1, *Text and Translation,* The Law of Russia: series 1: v. 3 (Irvine, 1988), chp. XVI, art. 45, 112.

26 Some examples include, RGADA, f. 1209, Pomestnyi prikaz, op. 78, d. 2753, 1654; op. 78, d. 2749, ll. 1 and 2, 1688; and d. 2750, 20 May 1694, all for Saransk.

27 In the Saransk muster roll for 1670, 39.4 percent of the servitors had single-district *pomest'e,* and the remainder had possessions in nearby districts. RGADA, f. 210, op. 21, d. 245, 22 June 1670. Earlier scholars argued single-district landholdings were a rare exception by 1700, but the single-district landholdings found in cases like Saransk correspond with Valerie Kivelson's study of provincial landholding. For a complete historiographic discussion as well as Kivelson's findings, see her *Autocracy,* 84–92.

28 RGADA, f. 1209, op. 78, d. 33, no earlier than 1686/87.

29 RGADA, f. 1209, op. 78, d. 147, ll. 2–4, 25 September 1676.

30 RGADA, f. 1209, op. 78, d. 35.

31 RGADA, f. 210, op. 21, d. 245.

32 For example, Kazan's *voevoda* attempted to seize the *pomest'e* of the Iaushev family of service-Tatars in Kazan district in 1650. The *Prikaz Kazanskogo dvortsa* sided with the Iaushevs, though the *voevoda* warned them to pay their taxes and provide service in order to keep the *pomest'e.* Ermolaev and Mustafina, *Dokumenty,* no. 76 (9 April 1650), 163–7.

33 Isennaleevskii had died, and his children abandoned the *pomest'e,* leaving it unclaimed. Ibid., no. 40, 95–7. This replacement system by ethnicity was obviously true for Russians as well. For example, after being warned as early as 1671 of his failure to fulfill his duties, Savva Fedorovich Lukin's *pomest'e* in Simbirsk *uezd* was seized by the central authorities in 1675 and awarded to the brothers, Zomin and Petr Popov. RGADA, f. 1209, op. 78, d. 2782, March 1675.

34 Hellie, *The Muscovite Law Code* XVI: 41, 105.

35 RGADA, f. 1209, op. 78, d. 4, no earlier than 1622/23.

36 Ermolaev and Mustafina, *Dokumenty,* no. 28, 66–7, 26 June 1613.

37 RGADA, f. 1455, op. 1, d. 1330, 23 September 1690.

38 RGADA, f. 1209, op. 78, d. 18, 1672/73.

39 RGADA, f. 1209, op. 78, d. 36, 1687/88.

40 Metropolitan Mafeia was awarded new lands in Kazan *uezd* after protesting that the metropolitanate's old land had been "used up." RGADA, f. 281, Gramoty kollegi ekonomii, op. 4, d. 6451, August 1616.

41 RGADA, f. 1209, op. 78, d. 176, March 1652.

42 Martynov, *Seleniia Simbirskogo uezda,* 168.

43 Bolkovskii petitioned the *voevoda* of Arzamas in 1690/91 without success, resulting in a petition to the tsar. RGADA, f. 210, op. 20, d. 70, November 1692.

44 RGADA, f. 1455, op. 1, d. 1163, after April 1691.

45 The case is contained in a series of documents, RGADA, f. 1156, op. 1, d. 6, ll. 1–3, 15 October 1685; l. 4, 1686, and l. 5, 18 August 1686.

46 RGADA, f. 1455, op. 3, d. 251, 27 October 1646; and d. 482, 21 September 1674.

47 For the most recent discussion of inheritance rights, see Janet Martin, "Widows, welfare, and the *pomest'e* system in the sixteenth century," *Harvard Ukrainian Studies* 19 (1995): 375–88.

48 RGADA, f. 1209, op. 78, d. 2746.

49 RGADA, f. 1455, op. 3, d. 493, 22 June 1675.

50 For an extensive discussion of partible inheritance, see Kivelson, *Autocracy,* 101–16.

51 RGADA, f. 1209, op. 78, d. 13, no earlier than 1666.

52 RGADA, f. 1455, op. 3, d. 393, 28 January 1667.

53 RGADA, f. 1209, op. 78, d. 150, 12 February 1677. Many petitions exist from sons trying to reclaim their father's *pomest'e.* For another example, see N.I. Zagoskin, *Materialy istoricheskie i iuridicheskie raiona byvshago Prikaza Kazanskogo dvortsa,* t. I, *Arkhiv Kniazia V. I. Baiusheva* (Kazan, 1882), no. 8, 9–10, and no. 10, 11–12.

54 Martynov, *Seleniia Simbirskogo uezda*, 94-5, 20 March 1686.

55 Ruzhevskii sent the *voevoda* a long letter explaining his father's service to the tsar; on the basis on this service, he asked to keep his father's land. Khlopov sent a petition to the *voevoda* as well, acknowledging that the land had been granted to Ruzhevskii but that the land of that *pomest'e* was better than the *pomest'e* he already possessed. Both are contained in RGADA, f. 1209, op. 78, d. 2783. Ruzhevskii's letter is ll. 1–4; Khlopov's petition is l. 5.

56 RGADA, f. 1455, op. 3, d. 831, 1692. For an insight into the Levashev family's relationship with their peasants, see N. Novombergskii, ed., *Koldovstvo v Moskovskom Rusi XVII-go stoletiia (Materialy po istorii meditsiny v Rossii t. III ch. I)* (St Petersburg, 1896), no. 4, 14–25. Thanks to Eve Levin for bringing this case to my attention.

57 RGADA, f. 1209, op. 78, d. 147, ll. 2–4, 25 September 1676.

58 For a discussion of *pomeshchiki*'s dowries, see Kivelson, *Autocracy*, 101–28; and Ann Kleimola, "'In accordance with canons of the Holy Apostles': Muscovite dowries and women's property rights," *Russian Review* 51 (1992): 204–29.

59 Ermolaev and Mustafina, *Dokumenty*, no. 50, 112–13.

60 RGADA, f. 281, op. 1, d. 286, 9 July 1636.

61 RGADA, f. 1455, op. 3, d. 296, 6 July 1654; and op. 2, d. 6450, 18 March 1683.

62 The *Pomestnyi Prikaz*, for example, endorsed Petr Gavrilov syn Domozhirov's petition to the tsar to give a portion of his *pomest'e* in Nizhegorod district to Ivan Rodinov syn Zheriskii, his current son-in-law, and resident of Alatyr. RGADA, f. 1209, op. 78, d. 39, l. 1, 1685/86. The *Prikaz Bol'shogo dvortsa* approved *stolnik* Petr Grigor'evich Ramodanovskii's petition for creating a dowry from his land in Arzamas. RGADA, f. 1209, op. 78, d. 39, ll. 2–4, 1685/86. The *Prikaz Kazanskogo dvortsa* approved the petition of Fedor Maksimov syn Dement'ev for using his *pomest'e* as a dowry in Alatyr district. RGADA, f. 281, op. 1, d. 290, 1646/47.

63 RGADA, f. 1209, op. 78, d. 144, ll. 1–2, 1675/76.

64 Recent studies of Razin include: A.G. Man'kov, ed., *Inostrannye izvestiia o vosstanii Stepana Razina: Materialy i issledovaniia* (Leningrad, 1975); V.I. Buganov, *Krest'ianskie voiny v Rossii XVII–XVIII vv.* (Moscow, 1976), 51–112; E.V. Chistiakova and V.M. Solov'ev, *Stepan Razin i ego soratniki* (Moscow, 1988); Vladimir Solov'ev, *Anatomiia russkogo bunta: Stepan Razin: Mify i real'nost'* (Moscow, 1994); and V.I. Buganov, *Razin i Razintsy* (Moscow, 1995).

65 A brief description of the events of Simbirsk revolt and its suppression is contained in LLC, Scroll I-19, no earlier than June 1674. The details of the payment to the Kalmyks for their military service are found in RGADA, f. 159, op. 2, d. 1349, 15 June 1674.

66 F. G. Islaev, *Pravoslavnye missionery v Povolzh'e* (Kazan, 1999); and Paul W. Werth, "Coercion and conversion: violence and mass baptism of the Volga peoples, 1740–55," *Kritika: Explorations in Russian and Eurasian History*, New Series, 4 (2003): 543–69.

Part II

Colonization on the Imperial Russian frontier

4 Agriculture and the environment on the steppes in the nineteenth century

David Moon

By the end of the nineteenth century, the open steppes of southeastern Russia had been transformed from a region that had been relatively sparsely inhabited, largely by Tatar and Kalmyk nomadic pastoralists and communities of Cossacks, into the home of around 10 million settled farmers. Most of the farmers were migrants, or the descendants of migrants, from central Russia, Ukraine, and also from Germany. The peopling of this peripheral region of the Russian empire by agricultural settlers led to considerable changes in the economy and land use. Steppes that for centuries had been used by nomads as pastures for their herds were plowed up by farmers, who sowed grain in the very fertile black earth (*chernozem*). The nomads either moved away or gave up their nomadic way of life. The transformation of the steppe region also had an impact on the natural environment. Over the course of the nineteenth century, educated Russians, in particular government officials and natural scientists, put forward differing views on the prospects for agriculture in the steppe environment. Some viewed the steppe environment as ideal for growing grain and were generally optimistic about the prospects for the continued development of arable farming. Others were more cautious, however, and expressed concerns that arable farming and related activities were doing serious damage to the environment with adverse consequences for agriculture and its future prospects. By the end of the nineteenth century, the most pessimistic commentators were worried that the steppes were turning into a desert. To some extent, the two strands – optimistic and pessimistic – came together towards the end of the century in a confidence that, armed with statistical and scientific knowledge, the degradation of the environment could be reversed and nature "improved" for the benefit of the human population.

I

The open, or treeless, steppes of southeastern Russia comprised the basins of the Volga and Don Rivers below the cities of Samara and Voronezh, and the plains to the north of the Caucasus Mountains and to the southwest of the Urals. Administrative boundaries did not coincide with environmental regions. The open steppe region made up most or large parts of the provinces of Saratov, Astrakhan, Orenburg and Stavropol, and the Don Cossack territory. Boundary changes within

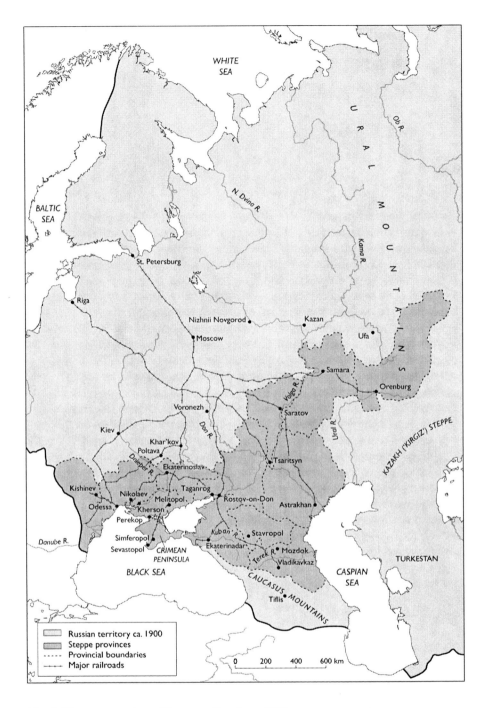

WHITE SEA

BALTIC SEA

U R A L M O U N T A I N S

N. Dvina R.

Ob R.

Kama R.

St. Petersburg

Riga

Nizhnii Novgorod

Kazan

Ufa

Moscow

Samara

Orenburg

Volga R.

Voronezh

Saratov

Ural R.

KAZAKH ('KIRGIZ') STEPPE

Kiev

Don R.

Khar'kov

Poltava

Dnepr R.

Ekaterinoslav

Tsaritsyn

Kishinev

Taganrog

Nikolaev

Melitopol

Rostov-on-Don

Astrakhan

Odessa

Kherson

Perekop

Kuban R.

Stavropol

TURKESTAN

Danube R.

Simferopol

Ekaterinadar

Sevastopol

CRIMEAN PENINSULA

Terek R.

Mozdok

Vladikavkaz

CASPIAN SEA

BLACK SEA

CAUCASUS MOUNTAINS

Tiflis

	Russian territory ca. 1900
	Steppe provinces
- - -	Provincial boundaries
-·-·-	Major railroads

0   200   400   600 km

Map 3 The steppe region of European Russia, *c.* 1900

the region from 1850 resulted in the creation of Samara and Ufa provinces and the Terek territory. These administrative regions also contained areas with different environments. The northern parts of Saratov and Samara provinces had tracts of forested steppe (*lesostep'*). Orenburg and Ufa provinces included the southern end of the heavily forested Ural Mountains. Stavropol province extended as far south as the foothills of the Caucasus Mountains, which were also covered in woodland. Open steppes were to be found, moreover, in adjoining regions of the Russian empire. To the north and west open grasslands began at the edge of the forested steppe in Voronezh and Khar'kov provinces. Other open steppe regions of the Russian empire are largely outside the scope of this chapter: Ekaterinoslav, Kherson and Tauride provinces ("New Russia" or southern Ukraine), and southern Siberia and the "Kirgiz" steppe (northern Kazakhstan).[1]

The open steppes of southeastern Russia share similar environments with some diversity. The following brief survey draws on a multi-volume geographical description of the Russian empire, published between 1899 and 1914, that was based on statistical and scientific studies carried out over the previous decades. Throughout the steppe region the climate was continental and semi-arid. Mean January temperatures fell from -5° C in Stavropol to -16° C in Orenburg. Average temperatures in July were over 20° C throughout the region, and exceeded 25° C in Astrakhan. Mean rainfall declined from around 380 mm a year in Samara and Orenburg to only 150 mm in Astrakhan. In stark contrast to the rest of the region, including the eastern part of Stavropol province, the city of Stavropol, which was located in hill country, received 720 mm of rainfall a year. The average figures for rainfall concealed considerable year-by-year fluctuations, and periodic droughts, especially in the spring and summer months. The heat and aridity in the summer were exacerbated by hot, dry winds (*sukhovei*) from the east. In general, therefore, the climate of the region was more severe in the east and southeast than in the west and northwest. The soil in most of the open steppe region was very fertile, as it formed part of the belt of black earth that stretched across the southern half of Russia and Ukraine. In the far southeast, less fertile chestnut (*kashtanovye*) soils prevailed. There were also large stretches of sand, especially in Astrakhan province, but also elsewhere in the steppe region. Before they were plowed up, the flora of the open steppes consisted of wild grasses, herbs, flowers, and shrubs. There were areas of woodland, but they were confined mostly to river valleys and ravines. The fauna had once included large herds of wild horses and steppe antelopes (*saigaki*). Larger mammals shared the fate of the nomads as their habitats were transformed into farmland. The smaller fauna, such as rodents and locusts, however, remained to plague farmers.[2]

The transformation of the environment followed the Russian conquest of the open steppes, which began in the 1550s as the tsars "gathered the lands of the Golden Horde" (the westernmost part of the former Mongol empire).[3] But large-scale agricultural settlement of the open steppes did not start until the eighteenth century. For a long time, colonization was hindered by raids by the indigenous nomads and by environmental conditions that differed from those the settlers were used to in their homelands, as Brian Boeck highlights in his essay in this volume.[4] Over the eighteenth and nineteenth centuries, however, the peasant population of the region grew rapidly as the government encouraged the settlement of the steppes, and countless Russian and Ukrainian peasants moved southeast and east on their own accord. The settler population also grew as a result of relatively fast natural increase.[5] The numbers of male peasants in the region grew from under 20,000 in the early eighteenth century to 1.85 million in the 1850s, and almost 4.9 million in 1897. These included German settlers who had moved to the Volga basin in response to an invitation from Catherine the Great in the 1760s. After difficult early years, their numbers grew steadily from the original 27,000 colonists (male and female), reaching 55,000 in 1811 and 390,000 in 1897.[6] The peasant migrants from central Russia and Ukraine were not the first Slavs to settle on the open steppes since the Mongol invasion of the thirteenth century. The pioneers had been the Cossacks, who had lived along the rivers of the region since at least the sixteenth century. The largest Cossack host lived along the lower Don. There were around 30,000 male Don Cossacks in the early eighteenth century, but their numbers grew quickly, reaching 290,000 in 1859, and almost half a million in 1897. There were also Cossack communities in the North Caucasus and Orenburg province.[7] (See Table 4.1.) The permanent agricultural population of the steppes was augmented by hundreds of thousands of seasonal migrant laborers from central Russia and northern Ukraine.[8]

Table 4.1 The male peasant and Cossack populations of the open steppes of southeastern European Russia, eighteenth and ninteenth centuries

	c. 1720	*1850s*	*1897*
Peasants (*soslovie*)	17.90	1,845.10	4,851.10
Don Cossacks	30.00	290.00	498.00
N Caucacus Cossacks (excl. Kuban)	?	86.50	82.70
Orenburg Cossacks	?	104.90	176.00
Total	47.90	2,326.50	5,607.80

Sources: David Moon, "Peasant migration and the settlement of Russia's frontiers, 1550–1897," *Historical Journal* 40 (1997): 863;

A.P. Pronshtein. ed., *Don i stepnoe Predkavkaz'e: XVIII-pervaia polovina XIX v. Zaselenie i khoziaistvo* (Rostov on Don, 1977), 32, 51, 55;

Thomas M. Barrett, *At the Edge of Empire: The Terek Cossacks and the North Caucasus Frontier, 1700–1860* (Boulder, 1999), 47;

N.A. Troinitskii, ed., *Obshchii svod po imperii rezul'tatov razrabotki dannykh pervoi vseobshchei perepisi naseleniia, proizvedennoi 28 Ianvaria 1897 goda,* 2 vols (St Petersburg, 1905), 1: 164–5, 168–9.

P. Semenov, comp., *Geografichesko-statisticheskii slovar' Rossiiskoi imperii,* 5 vols (St Petersburg, 1863–85), 3: 688.

Notes
1   All figures are in thousands.
2   All figures are approximate.
3   For the territory covered, see text.

The peasant settlers and German colonists began to plow up the steppes and sow grain in the eighteenth century. The Cossacks were slower to take up arable farming. Only gradually over the nineteenth century did grain assume greater importance in their economy than livestock husbandry, fishing, and other activities as they struggled to support themselves and meet their military service obligations.[9] The Russian government tried to encourage the indigenous nomadic pastoralists to settle and take up arable farming, but with fairly limited results.[10] The agricultural settlers faced the problem of growing grain in areas with fertile soil, but low and unreliable rainfall. The problem was exacerbated as many of the settlers had moved from regions with higher rainfall where retaining moisture in the soil was less crucial. It took time for settlers to adapt their agricultural techniques, implements, and crops to the environment of the open steppes.[11] The region, moreover, suffered from regular bad harvests that were usually caused by the periodic droughts. In the nineteenth century, serious drought-induced crop failures occurred in 1822, 1832–3, 1840, the late 1840s, 1855, 1873–4, 1885 and 1891.[12]

The growing numbers of settled agriculturalists and the development of arable farming entailed considerable changes in land use. Although grain had been grown in the region before Russian conquest and peasant settlement, it had been far less important than pastoralism.[13] In the 1950s, the geographer M.A. Tsvetkov calculated figures on changes in land use from a variety of contemporary sources.[14] There were problems with his sources, but his figures can be used to show general trends in land use. (See Table 4.2.) According to his data, there was a 500 percent increase in the area of arable land in the open steppe region between 1725 and 1887. Since Tsvetkov's data did not include the North Caucasus, where cereal farming developed rapidly over the nineteenth century,[15] the increase in the area of arable land in the region as a whole was far greater. The growth was achieved at the expense of pasture and meadow, i.e. steppe, much of the relatively small area of woodland, and "waste" land.

Table 4.2 Changes in land use in the open steppe region of southeastern European Russia, 1725–1887

Year	Total area	Arable area	%	Pasture, etc. area	%	Forest area	%	Waste area	%
1725	112,144	6,721	6	48,445	43.2	23,026	20.5	33,952	30.3
1861	112,144	13,485	12	36,018	32	16,593	15	46,048	41
1887	112,144	34,309	30.6	36,631	32.7	13,118	11.7	28,086	25

Source: M. A. Tsvetkov, *Izmeneniia lesistosti evropeiskoi Rossii: s kontsa XVII stoletiia po 1914 goda* (Moscow, 1957), 111, 115, 117.

Notes
1 All areas in thousands of hectares.
2 "Pasture, etc." includes meadows, vegetable gardens, orchards, and hempfields.
3 Data for provinces/territories of Saratov, Samara, Simbirsk, Astrakhan, Stavropol, Orenburg, Ufa, and Don inside borders of late nineteenth century.

II

The debate over the prospects for arable farming in the environment on the open steppes in the nineteenth century can be placed in wider political, scientific, and cultural contexts. The imperial Russian state had a long-standing interest in the expansion of its territory. It sought to settle its peripheral regions with a predominantly Slav and agricultural population in order to secure control over them and promote economic development. The gradual implementation of the abolition of serfdom after 1861 removed a major constraint to peasant movement to outlying parts of the empire, and from the 1880s encouraging peasant migration – to southeastern European Russia, southern Siberia, the Russian Far East, and northern Kazakhstan – was a key part of government policy.[16] For some officials and educated Russians, moreover, the settlement of the empire's peripheral regions entailed wider ideas, such as Russian nationalism and imperial destiny, the "civilization" of the empire's borderlands.[17] These were all seen as practical goals to be achieved on the basis of detailed analysis of the empire's natural, material, and human resources. This was the science of "statistics." In the early 1850s a group of reform-minded "enlightened bureaucrats," including the Miliutin brothers Dmitrii and Nikolai, virtually took over the Imperial Russian Geographical Society (founded in 1845) to enable them to gather statistics on demography and social and economic conditions to support their efforts to promote reform.[18] The Imperial General Staff also took a great interest in statistics in order to give them information about the empire's resources, which could be mobilized, and the territories the armed forces were responsible for defending. Between the late 1840s and 1860s the general staff compiled two series of surveys of the empire's central and outlying provinces and regions. A key figure in the development of "military statistics" was Dmitrii Miliutin.[19] Thus, the successful colonization and cultivation of the steppes was an important political issue, and politics would influence attitudes to the issue of the prospects for agricultural development in the steppe environment.

There is also a very important scientific context to the debates. Over the nineteenth century, natural scientists decisively challenged notions that the earth and its inhabitants had been created by God a few thousand years earlier and had been largely unchanged since the Deluge. The new theories, in particular the works of Charles Lyell on geology and Charles Darwin on evolution, presented a much older earth, whose environment had changed considerably over the eons, and in which humans had evolved only relatively recently. Furthermore, some argued that humans had an impact on the environment. In an influential book published in the USA in 1864, George Perkins Marsh argued that "human action" had harmful and sometimes irreversible effects on nature. Among his concerns were deforestation and desertification. He urged caution in human use of natural resources.[20] For much of the period between 1815 and 1855, however, the Russian authorities had severely restricted the dissemination of the new scientific ideas, as they saw them as a threat to the established political and religious order.[21] The relaxation of censorship after 1855 allowed the translation of older works, such as Lyell's, and of new works by Darwin, Marsh, and others. As a result, the readership for foreign scientific works in Russia was greatly increased.[22] The Russian intelligentsia did not simply passively absorb the new theories from the West, but placed them in the contexts of their own concerns. Moreover, Russian scientists engaged with the findings of Western scientists.[23] The number of scientists in the Russian empire carrying out work of international importance grew considerably in the second half of the nineteenth century. This was due not just to the work of talented individuals, but to the government policy of expanding and developing scientific education and research. Both the government and scientists were concerned, moreover, to use science to tackle problems facing Russia. As will be seen, scientists applied their growing knowledge to the development of agriculture on the steppes and the question of human impact on the environment.[24]

The debates concerning the prospects for agriculture on the steppes can also be placed in a broader cultural context involving ideas about the identity and future of Russia. For Russians in the "westernizing" tradition, Russia was part of Europe; Western Europe was the model for Russia to follow; and Russia could assert its European identity by "civilizing" "Asia." In contrast, Slavophiles rejected the idea that Russia should take the path of Western Europe, and argued that Russia had its own special destiny.[25] While Slavophiles stressed the cultural and religious differences between Russia and Western Europe, some educated Russians also paid attention to geographical and environmental differences. Echoing the "geographical determinism" popular among intellectuals around the world at the time, many Russian intellectuals believed that geography had had a decisive influence on Russia's history and explained many of the differences between Russia and Western Europe. In the mid-nineteenth century, the historian Sergei Solov'ev asserted: "Nature for Western Europe, for her peoples, was a mother, for Eastern Europe [Russia], for the peoples who were fated to exist there, [it was a] stepmother."[26] Educated Russians also looked east, and paid increasing attention to the relationship between Russia and Asia. In the late nineteenth century a small but influential group of Orientalists (*Vostochniki*) asserted that the roots of Russia's identity and its destiny lay in Asia. For others, however, the East – from where the Mongols had conquered Russia in the thirteenth century – was hostile.[27]

These cultural issues are relevant to the debate concerning the prospects for agriculture in the steppe environment since the open steppes of southeastern "European" Russia lay on one of the crossroads between Europe and Asia. The idea of dividing the Russian empire into "European" and "Asian" parts along the line of the Ural Mountains and Iaik/Ural River was proposed in the early eighteenth century, but was not universally accepted. In the early and middle decades of the nineteenth century it was common to locate the more arid steppes to the east of the lower Volga and to the southeast of the lower Don in "Asia." In the absence of a clear and indisputable geographical boundary between Europe and Asia, the location of the border – or, indeed, the existence of a border at all – was, in Mark

Bassin's words, "the ideological construction of geographical space."[28] Among the determinants of "European" or "Asiatic" identity for contemporaries were: "race" (Slav and German or Tatar and Mongol); religion (Christianity or Islam and paganism); economic activities (arable farming or nomadic pastoralism); and environment (fertile soil or arid, sandy steppes).[29] Thus, the settlement of the steppes by Slav (and German), Christian arable farmers was linked with wider cultural issues concerning the identity of the steppe region and the empire as a whole, and these issues would influence attitudes to the development of agriculture and the question of environmental change in the region.

III

Educated Russians had differing views on the prospects for arable farming in the environment of the steppes. From at least the eighteenth century, there were optimistic perceptions of the ability of agricultural settlers to transform the "empty" steppes into populated, prosperous agricultural land.[30] In the 1760s, the Imperial Academy of Sciences organised an expedition to the steppes. Samuel Georg Gmelin, a German scientist who took part, noted the fertility of the soil in the Don and Volga river basins, and was very positive about the prospects for various forms of agriculture in parts of the region that had sufficient rainfall.[31]

Such optimistic views were echoed by a number of government officials, for example Konstantin Veselovskii (1818–1901). He worked in the Ministry of State Domains between 1838 and 1857, serving as head of the Agricultural Department's Statistical Section and assistant editor of the Ministry's journal. In addition, he was a member of the Geographical Society and Academy of Sciences, and was associated with the "enlightened bureaucrats" Nikolai and Dmitrii Miliutin.[32] Veselovskii used his positions to promote the development of agriculture, including on the steppes. In the *Journal of the Ministry of State Domains* he published articles which argued that, contrary to some assertions, the open steppes were not an infertile, arid land unsuitable for settlement.[33] He was an advocate of the schools and model farms (including two on the open steppes) set up by the Ministry to train agricultural specialists.[34] In 1851 he summed up his optimistic views about the prospects for agricultural development on the open steppes:

> The sparsity of the settlement of the south and southeast is explained partly by historical reasons, [and] partly by the physical conditions of the region. These lands, which were ... freed from the Tatars ... later than others, were for a long time boundless, unpopulated steppes, and they began to be settled ... only in recent memory. ... The extent of settlement is determined as much by physical conditions as the industrial development (*promyshlennym razvitiem*) and level of activity of the inhabitants. Russia inside its boundaries includes huge areas which, due to the severity of the climate, are almost uninhabitable; it also includes ... areas with better climates, which are sparsely settled due to shortages of forests and water. But, there is no doubt that in time, with greater development of the spirit of diligence (*promyshlennogo dukha*), when the

forces of the mind will be partly victorious over the unfavorable influence of nature, these lands will also be better settled.[35]

In his 1857 book on the climate of Russia,[36] Veselovskii presented data on heat, wind, and moisture, and discussed their impact on agriculture (but not the other way round). He restated his optimistic view for the prospects for growing grain on the steppes. His optimism was based not just on his confidence in the ability of Russian settlers to adapt to the environmental conditions, but on an argument that these conditions were entirely appropriate for grain cultivation. In the chapter on heat, he emphatically argued against the notion that, because of the climate, the "treeless steppes" were a "land of pastures, i.e. a land which was destined mainly for animal husbandry." Rather, he believed that the hot and dry climate made the steppes better suited to growing grain than fodder grass. He argued that livestock husbandry was the easiest and simplest way of using the land given the low level of "civilization" (*grazhdanskogo razvitiia*) of the nomadic peoples who still lived on the Caspian steppe. Moreover, he argued that grain cultivation had been widely practiced on the steppes before the Mongol invasion. Above all, he was optimistic that, with the continued increase in population of the steppes and the favourable climatic conditions, arable farming would prevail over animal husbandry as the main economic activity.[37] He was less sanguine about the prospects for grain cultivation on the steppes in the chapter on moisture, however, where he acknowledged the relatively low rainfall and frequency of droughts. He would have been aware, moreover, of a recent series of droughts and bad harvests in the steppe region from articles published in his Ministry's journal.[38] He pointed out, however, that wheat – the main grain crop on the steppes – needed less rainfall than other cereals, and went so far as to claim that wheat had been grown successfully in eastern Crimea "without a drop of rainfall."[39]

Veselovskii's optimism was based in part on a belief that human activity had little negative impact on the environment. At the start of the book (p.vii), Veselovskii used the telling term "external nature" (*vneshnaia priroda*), in which he included climate, making clear his belief that the environment was outside, and largely beyond, the influence of humans. He argued that the climate was mostly a result of global factors, such as the distribution of the continents and oceans, and the position of the earth in relation to the sun, and that local factors, such as the existence or absence of forests, played at most a very small role. He took issue with the growing body of opinion that the climate of the steppes was becoming more severe, and drier, as a result of deforestation (see below). He argued emphatically that there had not been significant changes in the climate in historical time, and doubted the veracity of evidence – often the recollections of old people – used to support such arguments.[40]

Veselovskii's optimistic views concerning the settlement and cultivation of the steppes and the limited impact of humans on the environment were shared by others; for example, some of the army officers who compiled the provincial surveys for the Imperial General Staff in the 1850s and 1860s. Captain Mochul'skii, who compiled the survey of Khar'kov province, also argued against the idea that deforestation of the steppe region was adversely affecting the climate.[41] Lieutenant-Colonel Beznosikov, who surveyed the newly formed province of Samara on the left bank of the Volga in the early 1850s, was very optimistic about the prospects for arable farming. He drew attention to the abundance of land, the climate, which he considered not severe, and the abundant harvests that covered shortages in bad years. He called the region the "bread basket" of Russia, and added that the "harvest of wheat ... and other types of grain ... was so good that, in time, a great development of cereal cultivation in the southern part of the province must be expected."[42] Captain Krasnov, who surveyed the Land of the Don Cossack Host, stated that the steppe climate of the region was conducive to the growth of cereal crops. He asserted that the main cause of the frequent harvest failures was not aridity and heat, as farmers complained, but "poor farming, lazy and careless labor." (He cited Veselovskii's example of wheat growing in the Crimea without rainfall.) Furthermore, he argued that the dryness of the summer and autumn in the Don region "greatly assisted the threshing and winnowing of grain."[43]

Other specialists who took an optimistic view of the Russian settlement and cultivation of the open steppes were prepared to admit that the shortage of moisture was more of a problem, albeit a problem that could be overcome by artificial irrigation. Addressing the Geographical Society in March 1889, army engineer M.N. Annenkov acclaimed the transformation of the steppes of southern Russia from land that had earlier been considered suitable only for the nomadic way of life into a region with populated, productive arable land and flourishing cities. He argued that the productivity of the region would be higher if the land was irrigated to overcome the periodic droughts. Annenkov's main interest at this time, however, lay further east: the more arid land in Central Asia. He was optimistic that the Russian people could transform and make fertile these "vast and until now barren tracts."[44]

Thus, such optimistic statements were made by government officials, army officers, and others who shared the imperial government's aim of settling and promoting the development of agriculture on the steppes. Applying knowledge derived from statistical and scientific studies, such as the need for good farming techniques and irrigation, moreover, would make the steppes even more fruitful. Some of the views about the appropriateness of the steppe environment for arable farming by Slav settlers and on nomadic pastoralism as an activity for "less civilized" peoples clearly reflected notions of "cultural superiority" of the Slavs over the nomads, and the Russians' "rightful" appropriation of their land.

IV

This optimism and indeed confidence in the prosperous future of the steppes inhabited by Slav farmers was not shared by all educated Russians. From at least the early nineteenth century there were growing anxieties that human activities were harming the steppe environment and, crucially, were making it less suitable for the cultivation of grain. The doubters argued that, within living memory, the climate had become more severe. The summers had become hotter and the winters colder. Summer droughts were becoming more frequent and lasting for longer. On the other hand, more rainfall fell in thunderstorms and torrential downpours. Observers also felt that the hot, dry winds from the east in the summer were increasing in intensity. The downpours and winds had a further consequence: they caused erosion, removing the fertile black earth and inundating fields with sand. To blame was deforestation, caused by the settlers felling the relatively small areas of woodland on the steppes for timber for construction, firewood, and other purposes. The serious droughts and harvest failures of the 1830s and 1840s were part of the spur to such views.[45] These were the views that Veselovskii was arguing against, and proponents of this more pessimistic view included his colleague in the Ministry of State Domains, A.P. Zablotskii-Desiatovskii.[46]

A strong advocate of such concerns was Ivan Palimpsestov (1818–1901). A member of the clerical estate, he was educated in the seminary in Saratov, but also studied agriculture. He went on to teach agriculture and natural sciences in seminaries, and then in the Richelieu lycée and University of New Russia in Odessa. He was very active, moreover, in the Imperial Society for Agriculture of Southern Russia, devoting great efforts to the work of the Society and the development of agriculture on the steppes.[47] Thus, he very much shared the government's aim of settling and cultivating the steppes. He disagreed sharply with Veselovskii, however, on the impact on the environment of the peopling and plowing up of the steppes. Palimpsestov was one of those whose work Veselovskii had criticized in 1857 for drawing on the memories of old men rather than scientific evidence to support arguments about climatic change on the steppes.[48] He responded in a speech at the Richelieu lycée in 1864. He admitted that some of his evidence was the recollections of older inhabitants, but stated that he also drew on scientific observations made over the preceding 30 years. At the heart of his argument was that – contrary to Veselovskii's contention – there was a close connection between the atmosphere and the land. Thus, any change in the face of the land would lead to a change in the climate. The previous flora of the steppes – trees[49] and rich, dense grasses – had been replaced by pasture for livestock, arable land under grain, long fallow, or even land with no vegetation. He argued that rainfall had been higher over the previous richer vegetation for a number of reasons. It had reduced the reflection of the sun's rays onto clouds, and there had been greater evaporation as a result of the respiration of the plants. The lower rainfall after deforestation meant that the levels of rivers and seas were lower, reducing evaporation from them, and thus leading to less rainfall. The destruction of woodland on the steppes had had another consequence: it had removed a barrier to the hot, dry winds from the east, which were exacerbating the droughts. Palimpsestov raised the specter that, unless the deforestation of the steppes was stopped, the climate would become more severe, like that of the steppe regions of Asia.[50] In order to prevent this, he advocated protecting the remaining woodland and planting trees.[51] In fearing that the steppes were in danger of becoming like the arid, Asiatic steppes, however, Palimpsestov was not just concerned about the consequences for agricultural development. It could be argued that he was also concerned about the cultural identity of the steppes, which, he asserted, were "our blood inheritance," that had been "returned to us" by Catherine the Great in the eighteenth century.[52] Palimpsestov was a transitional figure in the development of scientific education and research in the Russian empire. His rich imagination could not compensate for his lack of a formal scientific education outside of seminaries, his work was criticized by the new generation of scientists,[53] and in spite of his efforts, farmers on the steppes still struggled in years of drought.

Palimpsestov's views were shared by a number of his contemporaries from a variety of backgrounds writing about different parts of the steppe region. Vasilii Cherniaev, a university-educated botanist, expressed deep concerns about the environmental consequences of the deforestation of the Russian and Ukrainian steppes in a speech delivered at Khar'kov University in 1858.[54] Prince Viktor Vasil'chikov published an article in *Otechestvennye zapiski* in 1876 putting forward his worries for the future of agriculture in the black-earth region, which he felt was threatened by deforestation, droughts, and soil exhaustion. He was writing on the basis of his experience of farming in the forest-steppe province of Tambov.[55] In 1884, S. Nomikosov of the Don Statistical Committee put forward similar concerns in a "statistical description" of the Don territory. Deforestation, he claimed, had altered the climate such that old folks did not recognize their homeland, and had turned the territory into one that was short of moisture. The alleged changes, he asserted, were harmful for agriculture, including livestock husbandry as well as arable farming.[56] Back in 1873, moreover, the Valuev commission on the state of agriculture had included in its report concerns that deforestation in the steppe regions was causing climate change and soil erosion.[57] Thus, from the 1850s to the 1880s, the central and local authorities, natural scientists, and the wider educated public in the Russian empire became increasingly aware of the issue of harmful human impact on the environment of the steppe region and its implications for the future development of arable farming.

The government in St Petersburg and provincial administrations responded to the growing concerns by supporting scientific studies of the steppe environment. In 1885, on the request of the governor of Stavropol in the North Caucasus, the Ministry of State Domains sent mining engineer D.L. Ivanov to investigate whether the steppe in the eastern part of the province was suitable for settlement. He was to pay particular attention to groundwater resources.[58] His arrival, however, coincided with a serious drought. Ivanov made a direct connection between the drought, and other environmental problems he encountered, and the peopling and plowing up of the region. He concluded that "agricultural colonization had weakened the natural resources of the land [as a result] of their excessive and irrational utilization." The "destruction of the forests and vegetation, the despoilation of the soil ..., the irrational use of water," excessive cultivation and development of livestock husbandry, together with disregard for the value of indigenous agriculture and rapid restriction of nomadic pastoralism had infringed the natural equilibrium. All these had led to the drying up of the land and unfavorable changes to the climate. "In general," he concluded, "a rich agricultural region" was being transformed into an "unappealing, dry steppe." His findings were so negative that he felt it necessary to defend himself in advance in the conclusion to his article by emphasizing the seriousness of the matter.[59]

Russian scientists were concerned to draw practical conclusions from such studies and the wider experience of the settlement and plowing up of the steppe. It was widely agreed that planting trees and protecting existing woodland would help in preventing climate change, as trees were thought to have a moderating influence on the climate. Trees could also act as windbreaks and so prevent soil erosion, and trees planted in gullies could reinforce them and prevent further erosion. Existing legislation protecting woodland was reinforced, and trees were planted on parts of the steppes.[60] A further measure to deal with the environmental problems of developing arable farming in an environment with unreliable rainfall was artificial irrigation. Many schemes were proposed and some, usually smaller scale, were implemented.[61] A third strand in applying science to improve the prospects for agriculture on the steppes was agronomy. There were many proposals for the expansion of education for peasants in the best ways to farm in the steppe environment.[62]

In spite of the growing concerns that human activity was harming the environment of the steppes, however, as Veselovskii and others pointed out, there was simply not sufficient evidence acceptable to scientists to prove the case.[63] Increasingly, however, the issue was taken up by Russian scientists who had had the opportunity of a fuller and higher standard of scientific education than had been available to Palimpsestov and many of his contemporaries. There was, thus, a direct link between the government policy of promoting the settlement and cultivation of the steppes and the development of science in the empire in the latter part of the nineteenth century. The work of two scientists is worth singling out as examples: the climatologist Aleksandr Voeikov (1842–1916) and soil scientist Vasilii Dokuchaev (1846–1903).

Voeikov was educated at St Petersburg University, where he later held the chair in physical geography, and in Germany. He was also an important member of the Geographical Society.[64] He made his name with his major book on climate published in 1884. In contrast to Veselovskii's book on the climate (see above), Voeikov treated his subject not as an external phenomenon, but as an integral part of the entire natural environment. Thus, the climate influenced vegetation, and vegetation – in particular forests – influenced the climate. Forests increased the amount of moisture in the atmosphere, especially in the summer, and thus forested areas received more rainfall than steppes or fields. Trees, moreover, contributed to the retention of moisture in the soil. He pointed to studies that indicated that forests had a moderating influence on temperature and weakened the force of the wind. Forests were particularly important in this regard, he argued, on the steppes of southern Russia, where the summers were hot and dry as a result of the prevailing winds from the interior of Asia. To emphasize this point, he contrasted the steppes with Great Britain and Norway, where the proximity of the sea and the prevalence of maritime winds made the summers temperate and wet.[65]

Thus, Voeikov took very seriously arguments that forests, and their removal, had a considerable influence on the climate and other aspects of the environment.

But he was not fully satisfied with theories that had been put forward, or the data and methodology on which they were based. Returning to the question of the influence of forests on the climate in 1892, he wrote:

> Even after meteorological instruments had been invented and many observations had already been accumulated, [people] still did not know how to approach the question being investigated. Many books were written on the influence of forests on the climate, water and such like, but for a long time there were no quantitative, comparative measurements. Opinions were divided to the extent that some were prepared to attribute all possible benefits to forests, and to see in [their] destruction the source of all calamities afflicting humankind; others denied forests had any influence on the climate and river water, saying that forests have the same influence on the climate as an unfurled umbrella, i.e. both protect from the sun and nothing more.[66]

In a similar vein, writing about the question of climate change in 1894, he stated:

> When ... have we not had occasion to hear discussions or read articles in which opinions are expressed that such weather is not recalled [even] by extremely old people. After investigations, however, it turns out that in the majority of cases not only very old people, but even the young had experienced something similar, but had forgotten. People carrying out meteorological observations, or using the observations of others, assist their memories and do not fall into such mistakes.[67]

Voeikov was making the point that scientific questions needed scientific answers based on a sufficiently large body of data, which had been gathered in the appropriate, scientific manner. Voeikov and his colleagues worked hard to achieve these. They set up networks of meteorological stations and encouraged the collection of data to support further studies. Voeikov set up a specialist journal, *Meteorologicheskii vestnik*, under the auspices of the Geographical Society in 1890. Their concerns were motivated by practical needs, and they established a special branch of their discipline – agricultural meteorology – to provide data to assist in the development of agriculture.[68]

Vasilii Dokuchaev, who was also educated and worked at St Petersburg University, became the leading specialist on another key part of the steppe environment from the point of view of agriculture – the black earth.[69] The work that made his reputation was his study of the Russian black earth (*Russkii chernozem*), published in 1883. Dokuchaev carried out extensive fieldwork on expeditions to various parts of the black-earth region.[70] He examined the geographical distribution and origins of the fertile soil of the steppes. He argued that the black earth had been formed over time as a result of the weathering of the parent rock and the decomposition of steppe grasses. Thus, for Dokuchaev, soil was a substance that changed, and continued to change, in processes of interaction with the physical and organic worlds of which it was a part.[71] His study of the black earth had immense importance in practice. It had been commissioned in 1876 by the Imperial Free Economic Society in the interests of aiding the improvement of agricultural productivity in the aftermath of two poor harvests in the black-earth region in 1873 and 1875.[72] Dokuchaev's work was also supported by the Department of Agriculture of the Ministry of State Domains. In the introduction to a soil map of Russia, sponsored by the Department and published in 1879, Dokuchaev wrote: "the improvement in agriculture, [which is] unavoidable with the growth in the population, can proceed along correct and dependable lines only with a comprehensive familiarity with soils: only solid, scientific study of present and previous soils can definitely tell us what they will be like in the future."[73] Dokuchaev put his work on the black earth to practical use. In the 1880s and 1890s, the *zemstva* of Nizhnii Novgorod and Poltava provinces commissioned him to lead scientific studies to provide them with a "correct," scientifically based evaluation of the soil for purposes of taxation and improving agriculture.[74] Dokuchaev was thus committed to studying the black earth and applying his findings for the benefit of agricultural development.

It took a natural disaster, however, to bring the issues of the development of agriculture and human impact on the steppe environment to a head.

V

In 1891–2 large parts of black-earth Russia were struck by a catastrophic drought, harvest failure, and famine.[75] The crisis provoked an outburst of anxiety among the intelligentsia, in which the issue of the cultural identity of the steppes was raised. One of the most pessimistic responses was that of Vladimir Solov'ev. In October 1891, he wrote:

> Since the start of the last decade, some writers have persistently pointed out that Russia, with the existing order, or disorder, of its national economy, is threatened with being transformed into an uninhabited desert. Indeed, for whom could it be a secret that the primitive economy, appropriate only in virgin (*devstvennye*) lands, has already exhausted our land; that the black earth is being more and more depleted by plowing; that at the same time, as a result of the felling of the forests and especially the draining of marshes, the rivers are becoming shallower and permanent repositories of land and atmospheric moisture are being destroyed. This process is being carried out before our very eyes, and in order to see where it will finally lead, there is no need to go beyond the present borders of the Russian Empire: our Turkestan – a desert with a few oases – was once a flourishing, well populated country with one of the main centers of Islamic education.[76]

A number of influences can be detected in this dramatic response. It is possible to discern a development of the views of his father (the historian Sergei) on the negative influence of "stepmother nature" on the Russian people mentioned earlier. Vladimir Solov'ev, moreover, was one of the intellectuals who feared the malevolent influence of Asia (see above). In 1892 he wrote a longer article, entitled "The Enemy from the East," in which he developed his ideas. The enemy was the "desert which is advancing on us from the East."[77] He was well aware of the growing concerns about the impact of human activity on the environment of the steppes that had been put forward by scientists over the preceding years, and had first written on the subject back in 1884.[78]

The unfolding disaster prompted the Free Economic Society to invite a number of natural scientists, government officials, and noble landowners to take part in two lengthy discussions in November and December 1891. The participants were asked to consider whether the harvest failure was due exclusively to meteorological conditions, or whether the agricultural technology employed had meant that farmers were less able to deal with the conditions.[79] The majority of speakers, including Voeikov, agreed that the drought in the summer of 1891 – which lasted for as long as 92 days in Tsaritsyn – was the main or sole cause of the harvest failure. (Incidentally, no one claimed – as Veselovskii had done in 1857 – that wheat could be grown without any rainfall.) Voeikov also noted the effects of the dry, easterly wind.[80] Several speakers, for example future Minister of Agriculture A.S. Ermolov, stated that the drought in 1891 had been so severe that no matter what techniques had been used or crops sown the outcome would have been the same.

Ermolov did suggest, however, that it might be possible to develop new farming methods that would be more successful in drought conditions.[81] Some speakers argued that crops had fared better on nobles' than peasants' land as a result of the better techniques employed by the former. This prompted lengthy discussion of a variety of technical matters, for example: plows and plowing techniques (in particular deep and shallow plowing); crops and varieties, e.g. corn (*kukuruza*), that were more resistant to drought; the timing of sowing; the use of fertilizers; crop rotations; whether fallow land should be left bare or sown with root vegetable or fodder grasses.[82] At the heart of the discussions was the key issue of how best to ensure moisture retention in the soil. Several participants, for example I.S. Ikonnikov of Saratov province, drew on their experience of farming on the open steppes.[83] A.E. Filipenko argued that they needed to look to agricultural techniques and crops in Asia, not Europe, as they were more appropriate to the conditions on the steppes.[84]

Some speakers went further, and argued that the ways in which the land was cultivated were damaging the environment and threatening to turn Russia, and not just the steppes, into a desert. Thus, the discussions in the Free Economic Society turned to the issue of environmental change. Attention focused on the soil and the climate. The agronomist Valerian Cherniaev (the son of Vasilii, see above[85]) reported that he had never seen "the steppe in such a bezotvradnyi condition as he had observed in Saratov and Samara provinces," where there were wide cracks in the land caused by the drought. The drought was not the sole cause of the harvest failure in his opinion. He also attributed it, in part, to "poor cultivation of the soil and the absence of correct approaches to cultivation." He noted that the harvest had failed completely in Samara, Orenburg, and parts of Ufa provinces (on the trans-

Volga steppe), where farmers "plowed up and sowed as much land as possible" without much care to improve the way they cultivated the land.[86] Filipenko argued that plowing up the steppe had changed the soil, making it drier and less able to retain moisture, and so it drained away rapidly through gullies. Moreover, water tables were falling.[87] In contrast, the soil scientist P.A. Kostychev argued that the steppe became wetter, not drier, after plowing.[88]

There was less agreement on the question of whether the climate was changing and, if it was, whether this was due to human activity. Ikonnikov believed that it was the land, not the climate, that had changed. Kostychev also doubted that droughts were more frequent. In the tradition of debates on this issue, N.A. Khvostov drew on his personal recollections of the balmy weather of his youth, prior to massive deforestation. Voeikov (whose reaction to Khvostov's remarks was not recorded) stated that the available data showed that, although no big difference had been observed in the total level of precipitation, droughts had become more frequent as a result of the "reduction in vegetation cover." This, he argued, had led to an increase in the force of the wind, which was drying out the land. He stressed, however, that more resources were needed to aid the development of agricultural meteorology.[89]

Analysis of the causes of the harvest failure and the question of environmental change filled the pages of the scientific and more general periodical press after 1891.[90] Several leading specialists, including Dokuchaev, Ermolov, Voeikov, and the geographer D.N. Anuchin, wrote, contributed to, or edited pamphlets sold for the benefit of famine victims, which included discussion of some of the key issues. Dokuchaev, who did not take part in the debate in the Free Economic Society, put forward his views in a book entitled *Our Steppes: Past and Present* published in 1892. He argued against the notion that the climate was changing as a result of deforestation. Instead, he put forward the view that the cause of the disaster was that the land was drying out because of the plowing up of the steppe and the removal of most of the original vegetation. Dokuchaev and other specialists proposed numerous measures to avert future disasters and counteract the harmful influence that some Russians believed people were having on the environment of the steppes. Most proposals were not new; for example, the protection of woodland and reforestation, soil conservation and reinforcement of gullies, the development of dry farming techniques, and calls for further scientific studies.[91] Kostychev and others strongly advocated the dissemination of farming techniques that were appropriate for an environment with relatively low rainfall.[92] There was an expansion of agronomical advice to peasants in the years after 1892.[93] Another measure to which more attention was given after 1891 was irrigation. In 1892, under the overall direction of army engineer Annenkov, large-scale public works to create irrigation schemes were carried out in the basin of the river Don and in the trans-Volga steppes of Samara province. Among the scientific advisers for the project were Voeikov and Dokuchaev.[94]

Dokuchaev went on to play a larger role. In the spring of 1892 he was invited by the Forestry Department of the Ministry of State Domains to head a "special expedition" to develop various means to overcome the problem of droughts on the steppes. Three research plots of around 5,000 hectares were set up and detailed studies were conducted into the natural environment. Experiments were then carried out into the effectiveness of various measures, such as tree planting, regulation of the water supply, and different crops, among others, to make agriculture more viable on the steppes. At the heart of Dokuchaev's ideas was the need to learn from the natural environment the best ways to cultivate the steppes by working with nature. Thus, crops should be selected that were closest to the natural vegetation of the region. He was also interested, however, in "improving" nature for the benefit of agriculture on the steppes. Practical and financial constraints, however, prevented him from implementing larger plans for planting shelterbelts of trees and regulating and damming rivers.[95] In a similar manner, Voeikov steered a middle course between exploitation and conservation of the natural environment in order to promote careful use of Russia's natural resources. He summarized his attitudes on the influence of people on nature in an article published in 1894. Human activity, he argued, had both destructive and constructive influences on the earth's crust. While careless and rapacious activity could cause gulleying, soil erosion, and affect the climate, it was possible to take measures to regulate human influences. Thus, while acknowledging that human activity could have a harmful impact on the environment, Voeikov was not opposed to the idea of humans changing the environment. Rather, in an attitude similar to that of George Perkins Marsh, he believed that people ought to transform the earth for their own purposes, but that they needed to be careful in the ways they did so. Voeikov went on to advocate ways in which the arid steppes of Asiatic Russia, suitably irrigated, could be exploited by Slav settlers.[96] Thus, the main response to the harvest failure of 1891 by geographers, scientists, and officials was to seek ways to allow the continued agricultural development of the steppes by intervening in the environment to try to avert the threat of future disasters. Indeed, Dokuchaev, Voeikov, and their colleagues were among the pioneers of "sustainable development."[97]

The harvest failure of 1891 did not put a stop to the settlement of the open steppe regions in the southeast of the Russian empire by peasant migrants, nor to the government's policy of encouraging migration. The more optimistic view of the prospects for Slav, agricultural settlement of the open steppes quickly resurfaced among government officials. Around the turn of the century, the central government and *zemstva* began to produce manuals for migrants. They contained information about the regions being settled, including natural environments, indigenous populations, and local economies and crops that differed from those the settlers were familiar with in central European Russia. Migration was presented as "difficult but potentially rewarding." But, in the words of Willard Sunderland: "the overarching impression was that these were territories of possibility where Russian peasants could overcome the challenges of nature, get along with native peoples, and do well."[98] The prevailing view at the turn of the century was also more cautious, and stressed the extent to which the development of arable farming on the steppes had altered the environment, and the urgent necessity of taking further measures to overcome the problems.[99]

VI

Thus, over the nineteenth century, geographers, natural scientists, government officials and other members of educated society in the Russian empire put forward differing views of the prospects for arable farming in the environment of the open steppes. Some expressed optimism, and in the process argued that humans had little negative impact on the environment; others were more cautious, or deeply pessimistic, and believed that, as a result of human activity, the climate had changed and the region faced desertification. How can these differing views be explained? The political, scientific, and cultural contexts outlined earlier provide some clues. Government officials, influenced by what they saw as the interests of the state in promoting the agricultural settlement of the empire's steppe peripheries, especially prior to the late nineteenth century, tended to be more optimistic about the prospects for settlement and to downplay the environmental impact. Veselovskii is a good example of such an attitude. The development of science and scientific research into the question of environmental change had an undoubted influence on a change towards more cautious or pessimistic attitudes. By the end of the century, the work of such scientists as Voeikov and Dokuchaev seemed to give hard, scientific proof to some of the less well-grounded concerns expressed earlier in the century, and were making strides towards a greater understanding of the interaction between human activity and the environment. The growing anxiety in Russian culture over the latter part of the nineteenth century seems to have exerted an influence on the changing mood. Deforestation, desertification, the "threat from the East", and their meanings were developing themes in Russian culture. Vladimir Solov'ev gave clear expression to such ideas.

These contexts do not provide a complete explanation for the differing attitudes, however. Not all government officials were optimistic. Zablotskii-Desiatovskii did not share Veselovskii's optimism. Ermolov was deeply concerned by the disaster of 1891–2. Moreover, not all scientists were in agreement, and some of those who did detect human impact on the environment, in particular Voeikov, were appropriately skeptical about the findings of scientific studies. In any case, a clear distinction cannot be made between the two worlds, scientific and official, as they were closely intertwined, and overlapped in such institutions as the Geographical Society, Academy of Sciences, and the Free Economic Society. And the official and scientific worlds overlapped with the broader world of Russian culture in the wider, periodical press. To some extent, a change towards more cautious attitudes took place over the course of the nineteenth century, which reflected prevailing views and attitudes among officials, scientists, and cultural figures.[100] The gradual change in attitudes was already underway before 1891, but the crisis played a major role in bringing the debate to a head, and to a wider public, and in prompting serious action by officials working with leading scientists to try to address the problems of environmental change and to try to put the agricultural settlement of steppe regions on a more sustainable basis.

Notes

1 P. Semenov, *Geografichesko-statisticheskii slovar' Rossiiskoi imperii*, 5 vols (St Petersburg, 1863–85), 1: 148–53; 2: 111–16; 3: 673–81; 4: 408–18, 472–83, 723–9; 5: 399–406; V.P. Semenov, ed., *Rossiia: Polnoe geograficheskoe opisanie nashego otechestva*, 11 vols (St Petersburg, 1899–1914), 2, *Sredne-russkaia chernozemnaia oblast'*, Map facing 32, 57; 7, *Malorossiia*, Map facing 24; 14, *Novorossiia i Krym*, Map facing 48, 72–7. In 1870, the Land (*Zemlia*) of the Don Cossacks was renamed the Don territory (*oblast'*).

2 Semenov, *Rossiia*: 5, *Ural i Priural'e*, 64–5, 78–83, 91–3, 105–8; 6, *Srednee i nizhnee Povol'ze i Zavol'zhe*, 50–2, 53–4, 64–6, 69–86; 14, *Novorossiia i Krym*, 39, 51–2, 57, 60–4, 72–89. See also A.V. Dulov, *Geograficheskaia sreda i istoriia Rossii: konets XV–seredina XIX v.* (Moscow, 1983), 10–11.

3 Andreas Kappeler, *The Russian Empire: A Multiethnic History* (Harlow, Essex, 2001), 22.

4 See Dulov, *Geograficheskaia sreda*, 63–6; Michael Khodarkovsky, *Russia's Steppe Frontier: The Making of a Colonial Empire, 1500–1800* (Bloomington, 2002); Willard Sunderland, *Taming the Wild Field: Colonization and Empire on the Russian Steppe* (Ithaca, 2004).

5 For general studies, see S.I. Bruk and V.M. Kabuzan, "Migratsiia naseleniia v Rossii v XVIII-nachale XX veka (chislennost', struktura, geografiia)," *Istoriia SSSR* no.4 (1984): 41–59; David Moon, "Peasant migration and the settlement of Russia's frontiers 1550–1897," *Historical Journal* 30 (1997): 859–93. For a case study of the North Caucasus, see V.P. Gromov, "Sootnoshenie narodnoi i pravitel'stvennoi kolonizatsii Predkavkav'ia v poslednei chetverti XVIII-pervoi polovine XIX v.," *Izvestiia Severo-kazkazskogo nauchnogo tsentra vysshei shkoly. Obshchestvennye nauki* no.4 (1983): 34–8; idem, "Rol' migratsii i estestvennogo prirosta naseleniia v zaselenii stepnogo predkavkaz'ia v pervoi polovine XIX veka," ibid., no.2 (1985): 76–80.

6 Fred C. Koch, *The Volga Germans in Russia and the Americas, from 1763 to the Present* (University Park, 1977), 22, 39, 69, 102–8, 307–13; N.A. Troinitskii, ed., *Obshchii svod po imperii rezul'tatov razrabotki dannykh pervoi vseobshchei perepisi naseleniia, proizvedennoi 28 Ianvaria 1897 goda*, 2 vols (St Petersburg, 1905), 2: 22. See also Roger P. Bartlett, *Human Capital: The Settlement of Foreigners in Russia, 1762–1804* (Cambridge, 1979); Judith Pallot and Denis J.B. Shaw, *Landscape and Settlement in Romanov Russia, 1613–1917* (Oxford, 1990), 79–111.

7 The Cossacks were not exclusively Slav, but of mixed ethnic origins. Thomas M. Barrett, *At the Edge of Empire: The Terek Cossacks and the North Caucasus Frontier, 1700–1860* (Boulder, 1999), 23; Shane O'Rourke, *Warriors and Peasants: The Don Cossacks in Late Imperial Russia* (New York, 2000), 61–2; A.P. Pronshtein, *Zemlia Donskaia v XVIII veke* (Rostov on Don, 1961).

8 B.G. Pliushchevskii, "Krest'ianskie otzhozhie promysly na territorii evropeiskoi Rossii v poslednie predreformennye desiatiletiia (1830–1850 gg.)," (doctoral diss., Institut Istorii, AN SSSR, Leningrad, 1974), 70–87, 98–113; Timothy Mixter, "The hiring market as workers' turf: migrant agricultural laborers and the mobilization of collective action in the steppe grainbelt of European Russia, 1853–1913," in Esther Kingston-Mann and Timothy Mixter, eds, *Peasant Economy, Culture, and Politics of European Russia, 1800–1921* (Princeton, 1991), 294–340.

9 See Pronshtein, *Zemlia Donskaia*, 75–86; idem, ed., *Don i stepnoe Predkavkaz'e: XVIII-pervaia polovina XIX v.: Zaselenie i khoziaistvo* (Rostov on Don, 1977), 72–89, 100–26; O'Rourke, *Warriors and Peasants*, 64–9; Barrett, *Edge of Empire*, 89–108.

10 See Michael Khodarkovsky, *Where Two Worlds Met: The Russian State and the Kalmyk Nomads, 1600–1771* (Ithaca, 1992), esp. 208–9; P. Nevol'sin, "Otchet o puteshestvii v Orenburgskii i Astrakhanskii krai," *Vestnik Imperatorskogo Russkogo Geograficheskogo Obshchestva* [hereafter *Vestnik IRGO*] no.4 (1852): 1–34 [5th pagn], here 21, 25–9; RGIA, f. 379, op.1, 1824, d.619; GASK, f. 146, op. 1, d. 38, 1871–5.

11 See L.V. Milov, *Velikorusskii pakhar' i osobennosti rossiiskogo istoricheskogo protsessa* (Moscow, 1998), 66–73, 81–90, 120–2; David Kerans, *Mind and Labor on the Farm in Black-Earth Russia, 1861–1914* (Budapest, 2001), 23–5, 38–9, 40–1, 133–4, 185; V.V. Kogitin, "Sistemy zemledeliia u russkogo naseleniia nizhnego povolzh'ia vtoroi poloviny XVIII-nachalo XX veka," in A.G. Seleznev and N.A. Tomilov, eds, *Material'naia kul'tura narodov Rossii: Kultura narodov Rossii*, 1 (Novosibirsk, 1995), 112–22; Koch, *Volga Germans*, 52–7.

12 See Arcadius Kahan, "Natural calamities and their effect on the food supply in Russia," *Jahrbücher für Geschichte Osteuropas* 16 (1968): 353–77; [A. Ermolov], *Neurozhai i narodnoe bedstvie* (St Petersburg, 1892).

13 N.A. Gorskaia, ed., *Krest'ianstvo v periody rannego i razvitogo feodalizma* (Moscow, 1990), 462–8.

14 M.A. Tsvetkov, *Izmenenie lesistosti evropeiskoi Rossii: s kontsa XVII stoletiia po 1914 god* (Moscow, 1957). See also V.K. Iatsunskii, "Izmeneniia v razmeshchenii zemledeliia v Evropeiskoi Rossii s kontsa XVIII v. do pervoi mirovoi voiny," in idem, ed., *Voprosy istorii sel'skogo khoziaistva, krest'ianstva i revoliutsionnogo dvizheniia v Rossii* (Moscow, 1961), 113–48.

15 See Pronshtein, *Don i stepnoe Predkavkaz'e*, 111–17; P.A. Shatskii, "Sel'skoe khoziaistvo Predkavkaz'ia v 1861–1905 gg.," in S.A. Chekmenev, ed., *Nekotorye voprosy sotsial'no-ekonomicheskogo razvitiia iugo-vostochnoi Rossii* (Stavropol, 1970), 3–320.

16 See David Moon, "Peasant migration, the abolition of serfdom and the internal passport system in the Russian empire, c.1800–1914," in *Free and Coerced Migration: Global Perspectives,* ed. David Eltis (Stanford, 2002): 324–57; Donald W. Treadgold, *The Great Siberian Migration* (Princeton, 1957).

17 See Mark Bassin, *Imperial Visions: Nationalist Imagination and Geographical Expansion in the Russian Far East, 1840–1865* (Cambridge, 1999); Willard Sunderland, "The 'colonization question': visions of colonization in late imperial Russia," *Jahrbücher für Geschichte Osteuropas* 48 (2000): 210–32.

18 W. Bruce Lincoln, *In the Vanguard of Reform: Russia's Enlightened Bureaucrats, 1825–1861* (De Kalb, 1982), 91–100, 102–3, 122–3; Bassin, *Imperial Visions*, 94–101, 123–7.

19 See David Rich, *The Tsar's Colonels: Professionalism, Strategy, and Subversion in Late Imperial Russia* (Cambridge, MA, 1998).

20 George Perkins Marsh, *Man and Nature or Physical Geography as Modified by Human Action*, ed. David Lowenthal (Cambridge, MA, 1965) [reprint of 1864 edition].

21 Alexander Vucinich, *Science in Russian Culture: A History to 1860* (London, 1965), 231–6, 248–50, 343.

22 Charl'z Liaiell', *Osnovnye nachala geologii ili noveishie izmeneniia zemli i ee obitatelei*, 2 vols (Moscow, 1866) (first published in Britain in 1830–3); Georg Marsh, *Chelovek i priroda, ili o vliianii cheloveka na izmenenie fiziko-geografiskikh uslovii prirody* (St Petersburg, 1866); Alexander Vucinich, *Science in Russian Culture, 1861–1917* (Stanford, 1970), 56–7, 118.

23 For example, in Ia. Veinberg, *Les: znachenie ego v prirode i mery k ego sokhraneniiu* (Moscow, 1884) there are citations to the works of Marsh (many times), Lyell, and a number of French and German scholars; A.I. Voeikov was very widely read in Western European and North American scientific literature, see his *Klimaty zemnogo shara v osobennosti Rossii* (St Petersburg, 1884), and his critical review of Christy Miller, "Why are the prairies treeless [sic]?", *Proceedings of the Royal Geographical Society* (1892) in *Izvestiia Imperatorskogo Russkogo Geograficheskogo Obshchestva* [hereafter *Izvestiia IRGO*] 28, no. 4 (1892): 418–19; and V.V. Dokuchaev cited and engaged with the works of Lyell, Murchison, and other Western European geologists, see, e.g., V.V. Dokuchaev, *Sochineniia*, 9 vols (Moscow-Leningrad, 1949–61), 3: 533, 534, 537–8. Historians of science have paid most attention to the Russian reception of Darwin's

work. See Loren Graham, *Science in Russia and the Soviet Union* (Cambridge, 1993), 56–72.

24 See Graham, *Science*; Vucinich, *Science ... to 1860*; and idem, *Science ... 1861–1917*.

25 See Bassin, *Imperial Visions*, 37–68.

26 S.M. Solov'ev, *Istoriia Rossii s drevneishikh vremen*, 2nd edn (St Petersburg, n.d.), 3: 625. See also Mark Bassin, "Turner, Solov'ev, and the 'Frontier Hypothesis': the nationalist significance of open spaces," *Journal of Modern History* 65 (1993): 473–511. Russian geographers, in contrast, paid little attention to the impact of the environment on humans. D.J.M. Hooson, "The development of geography in pre-Soviet Russia," *Annals of the Association of American Geographers* 58 (1968): 250–72.

27 See David Schimmelpenninck van der Oye, *Toward the Rising Sun: Russian Ideologies of Empire and the Path to War with Japan* (DeKalb, 2001), 3–117.

28 Mark Bassin, "Russia between Europe and Asia: the ideological construction of geographical space," *Slavic Review* 50 (1991): 1–17.

29 See A. Maksheev, *Voenno-statisticheskoe obozrenie Rossiiskoi imperii* (St Petersburg, 1867), 27–8.

30 See Willard Sunderland, "An empire of peasants: empire-building, interethnic interaction, and ethnic stereotyping in the rural world of the Russian empire, 1800–1850s," in *Imperial Russia: New Histories for the Empire*, eds Jane Burbank and David L. Ransel (Bloomington, 1998), 174–98. See also Bassin, *Imperial Visions*, 186–9, 275; Robert F. Byrnes, "Kliuchevskii's view of the flow of Russian history," in *Historiography in Imperial Russia*, ed. Thomas Sanders (Armonk, 1999), 239–61.

31 Samuel Georg Gmelin, *Puteshestvie po Rossii dlia issledovaniia trekh tsarstv estestva, perevedena s nemetskogo*, 2 parts (St Petersburg, 1771–7), 1, *Puteshestvie iz Sanktpeterburga do Cherkaska, glavnogo goroda Donskikh kozakov v 1768 i 1769*, 269–70; 2, *Puteshestvie ot Cherkaska do Astrakhani i prebyvanie v sem gorode s nachala Avgusta 1769 po piatoe Iiulia 1770 goda*, 15–16, 30. See also Peter Simon Pallas, *Travels through the Southern Provinces of the Russian Empire, in the years 1793 and 1794*, trans. from the German, 2 vols (London, 1802), 1: 498–9.

32 On his life and career, see *Entsiklopedicheskii slovar'*, 82 vols (St Petersburg, 1891–1904) [hereafter *ES*], 6 (1892): 100; K.S. Veselovskii, "Vospominaniia", *Russkaia starina* 116 (October-December 1903): 5–42; Lincoln, *Vanguard*, 82, 95, 230–1.

33 E.g. I.G. Rekk, "Otchet o stepnom khoziaistva v Saratovskom zavol'zhe," *Zhurnal ministerstva gosudarstvennykh imushchestv* [hereafter *ZhMGI*] 7, no.2 (1843): 39–49.

34 Lincoln, *Vanguard*, 127, 238.

35 K.S. Veselovskii, "Prostranstvo i stepen' naselennosti Evropeiskoi Rossii," *Sbornik statisticheskikh svedenii o Rossii* I (St Petersburg, 1851): 1–29.

36 K. Veselovskii, *O klimate Rossii* (St Petersburg, 1857).

37 Ibid., 49–52.

38 For example, I.G., "Khoziaistvennoe obozrenie ekaterinoslavskoi gubernii, za poslednie piat' let (1847–1851g.)," *ZhMGI* 43, no. 2 (1852) [3rd pagn]: 30–5.

39 Veselovskii, *O klimate Rossii*, 332–8.

40 Ibid., 234–7, 317–20, 385–400.

41 *Voenno-statisticheskoe obozrenie Rossiiskoi imperii*, 17 vols (St Petersburg, 1848–58), 12, part 1, *Khar'kovskaia guberniia*, comp. Mochul'skii, 55.

42 *Voenno-statisticheskoe obozrenie* 5, part 3, *Samarskaia guberniia*, comp. Beznosikov, 105–11.

43 *Materialy dlia geografii i statistiki Rossii, sobrannye ofitserami general'nogo shtaba: Zemlia voiska donskogo*, comp. N. Krasnov, (St Petersburg, 1863), 167–8, 250–5.

44 M.N. Annenkov, "Sredniaia Aziia i ee prigodnost' dlia vodvoreniia v nei Russkoi kolonizatsii," *Izvestiia IRGO* 25, no. 4 (1889): 277–93.

45 See, for example, Andreevskii, "Zamechaniia o lesovodstve i o neobkhodimosti razvedeniia lesov v iuzhnykh guberniiakh Rossii," *Lesnoi zhurnal* (1834), ch. 3, kn. 1, 1–31; V. Passek, "Istoriko-statisticheskoe opisanie Khar'kovskoi gubernii 1836 goda,"

Materialy dlia statistiki Rossiiskoi Imperii (St Petersburg, 1839), 125–68, here 140–2; I. Palimpsestov, "Vzgliad na sel'skoe khoziaistvo i byt zhitelei pravogo priberezh'ia Volgi ot Saratova do Tsaritsyna," *ZhMGI* 34, no. 3 (March 1850): 199–235, here 204; A.P. Zablotskii, "Khoziaistvennye zamechaniia o nekotorykh guberniiakh iuzhnogo kraia Rossii," *ZhMGI*, part 1 (1841), book 1 [2nd pagn]: 11–55.

46 Veselovskii, *O klimate*, 317, 385–6; and Zablotskii, "Khoziaistvennye zamechaniia."

47 On his life and work, see *ES*, 22a (1897): 631; I.U. Palimpsestov, *Moi vospominaniia* (Moscow, 1879).

48 Veselovskii, *O klimate*, 385–6.

49 Palimpsestov believed that the steppes had once been forested. I. Palimpsestov, "Peremenilsia li klimat iuga Rossii?," in *Sbornik statei o sel'skom khoziaistve iuga Rossii, izvlechennikh iz Zapisok Imperatorskogo Obshchestva sel'skogo khoziaistva iuzhnoi Rossii s 1830 po 1868 god*, ed. idem (Odessa, 1868), 1–51, here 8.

50 Palimpsestov, "Peremenilsia."

51 P[alimpsestov], "Lesovodstvo. Nechto v rode 'Vvedeniia' v uroki lesovodstva dlia Novorossiiskogo kraia," *Zapiski Imperatorskogo Obshchestva Sel'skogo Khoziaistva Iuzhnoi Rossii* (1852) no. 1: 15–80.

52 Palimpsestov, *Stepi iuga Rossii byli-li iskoni vekov stepami i vozmozhno-li oblesit' ikh?*, rev. edn (Odessa, 1890), 264.

53 V.V. Dokuchaev, "Otzyv o trude Iv. Palimpsestova: 'Stepi iuga Rossii byli-li iskoni vekov stepami i vozmozhno-li oblesit' ikh?','" in Dokuchaev, *Sochineniia*, 6: 239–45 (first published in 1895).

54 V.M. Cherniaev, *O lesakh Ukrainy: rech', proiznesennaia v torzhestvennoi sobranii imperatorskogo khar'kovskogo Universiteta, 1-go sentiabria 1858 g.* (Moscow, 1858). On the author see *Russkii biograficheskii slovar'* [hereafter *RBS*] XI, 337–8.

55 Viktor Vasil'chikov, "Chernozem i ego budushchnost'," *Otechestvennye zapiski* (1876) no. 2 [2nd pagn], 167–82. See also *Novyi Entsiklopedicheskii Slovar'*, 10 (St Petersburg, n.d.), 681–2.

56 S. Nomikosov, *Statisticheskoe opisanie Oblasti voiska Donskogo* (Novocherkassk, 1884), 93, 96–7, 122, 148, 199–217.

57 [Valuev], *Doklad vysochaishe uchrezhdennoi komissii dlia issledovaniia nyneshnego polozheniia sel'skogo khoziaistva i sel'skoi proizvoditel'nosti v Rossii* (St Petersburg, 1873), 7, 41.

58 "Mestnaia khronika," *Severnyi Kavkaz* no. 55 (18 June 1885).

59 D.L. Ivanov, "Vliianie Russkoi kolonizatsii na prirodu Stavropol'skogo kraia," *Izvestiia IRGO* 22, no. 3 (1886): 225–54, quotations from 252. A summary of his report to the governor was published as: "O khode geologicheskikh issledovanii v Stavropol'skoi gubernii," *Stavropol'skie gubernskie vedomosti, chast' neoffitsial'naia* no. 45 (9 November 1885). See also Barrett, *Edge of Empire*, 66–7. Ivanov's article was very influential on scientists, for example Alexander Voeikov, who conducted his own study of the 1885 drought. RGO, f. 17, op. 1, no. 127; A. I. Voeikov, "Zasukha 1885 goda po svedeniiam poluchennym imperatorskim russkim geograficheskim obshchestvom," *Zapiski IRGO po obshchei geografii* 17, no. 2 (1887): 1–22.

60 See Veinberg, *Les*; Tsvetkov, *Izmenenie*, 29–60, 162–200. For an overview of tsarist forest legislation, see Brian Bonhomme, *Forests, Peasants, and Revolutionaries: Forest Conservation and Organization in Soviet Russia, 1917–29* (Boulder, 2005), 14–59.

61 For examples, see A. Bode, "O dobyvanii vody v stepnykh mestakh iuzhnoi i iugo-vostochnoi chasti Evropeiskoi Rossii," *ZhMGI* [4th pagn]: 141–5; I.I. Filipenko, *Vopros obvodneniia stepei: na osnovanii issledovanii proizvedenykh v 1881 godu, po porucheniiu Novouzenskogo Zemskogo Sobraniia* (St Petersburg, 1882); GASO, f. 43, op. 8, d. 33 1889–91; GARO, f. 46, op. 1, d. 780; I. Palimpsestov, *Ob ustroistve vodokhranilishch v stepiakh iuga Rossii* (Odessa, 1867); "Iskustvennoe oroshenie polei (irrigatsiia)," *Stavropol'skie gubernskie vedomosti, chast' neoffitsial'naia* (1881), nos. 7–9.

62 For examples from Samara province and the Don region, see: I. Lishin, *Ocherk Nikolaevskogo uezda (Samarskaia guberniia) v statisticheskom i sel'sko-khoziaistvom otnosheniiakh* (St Petersburg, 1880), 26, 28, 39, 64; GARO, f. 55, op. 1, d. 1409.

63 See above and N. Danielevskii, review of K. Veselovskii, *O klimate Rossii*, in *Vestnik IRGO* 25 (1859) [4th pagn]: 1–13, here 10.

64 On his life and work, see *ES* 4a: 830–1; Pokshishevskii, "Aleksandr Ivanovich Voeikov i ego raboty o cheloveke i prirode," in A.I. Voeikov, *Vozdeistvie cheloveka na prirodu: izbrannye stat'i*, ed. V.V. Pokshishevskii (Moscow, 1949), 3–39. For a select bibliography, see ibid., 251–5.

65 Voeikov, *Klimaty*, esp. 291–324, 583. See also A.I. Voeikov, "O vliianii lesov na klimat," *Zasedaniia Peterburgskogo Sobraniia sel'skikh khoziaev* no. 5 (1878): 1–13.

66 A.I. Voeikov, "Po voprosu lesnoi meteorologii," *Meteorologicheskii vestnik* [hereafter *MV*] no 2 (1892): 51–60.

67 A.I. Voeikov, "Kolebanie i izmenenie klimata," *Izvestiia IRGO* 30, no. 5 (1894): 543–78.

68 A. Klossovskii, "Otvety sovremennoi meteorologii na zaprosy prakticheskoi zhizn'," *MV* no. 1 (1891): 5–13; no. 2: 53–62; G.L. "Meteorologicheskie nabliudeniia," *ES* 19 (1896), 175–9; idem, "Meteorologicheskie stantsii," ibid., 179.

69 On his life and career, see L.A. Chebotareva, "Vasilii Vasil'evich Dokuchaev (1846–1903). Biograficheskii ocherk," in Dokuchaev, *Sochineniia*, 9: 49–153.

70 I. Krupenikov and L. Krupenikov, *Puteshestviia i ekspeditsii V.V. Dokuchaeva* (Moscow, 1949), 31–54.

71 V.V. Dokuchaev, *Russkii chernozem* (St Petersburg, 1883) (and *Sochineniia*, 3).

72 Chebotareva, "Dokuchaev," 60.

73 V.V. Dokuchaev, "Kartografiia russkikh pochv: Ob"iasnitel'nyi tekst k pochvennoi karte evropeiskoi Rossii," in idem, *Sochineniia* 2: 69–241, here 73.

74 See S.S. Sobolev, "Razvitie idei V.V. Dokuchaeva," in Dokuchaev, *Sochineniia*, 9: 30–3.

75 See M.N. Raevskii, "Neurozhai 1891 goda v sviazi s obshchei kharakteristikoi nashei khlebnoi proizvoditel'nosti a takzhe vyvoza khlebov zagranitsu za pred"idushchie gody," *Izvestiia IRGO* 28, no. 1 (1892): 1–29.

76 Vladimir Solov'ev, "Narodnaia beda i obshchestvennaia pomosh'," *Vestnik Evropy*, 10 (October 1891): 780–93, here 781.

77 V.S. Solov'ev, "Vrag s Vostoka," in *Sochineniia v dvukh tomakh*, ed. A.V. Gulyga and A.F. Losev, 2 vols (Moscow, 1988), 2: 480–92 (first published July 1892). For similar views, see N.V. Vereshchagin, "Po povodu neurozhaia tekushchego goda," *Trudy Imperatorskogo Vol'nogo Ekonomicheskogo Obshchestva* [hereafter *Trudy IVEO*] 2, no. 5 (1891): 178–196.

78 V.S. Solov'ev, "Evreistvo i Khristianskii vopros," *Pravoslavnoe obozrenie* (August 1884): 755–72; (September 1884): 76–114.

79 "Besedy v I Otdelenii Imperatorskogo Vol'nogo Ekonomicheskogo Obshchestva po voprosu o prichinakh neurozhaia 1891 goda i merakh protiv povtoreniia podobykh urozhaev v budushchem," *Trudy IVEO* no. 1 (1892): 67–144.

80 Ibid., 71, 82.

81 Ibid., 85, 88.

82 These had long been discussed in the steppe regions. I. Palimpsestov, "Glubokaia pashnia," in *Sbornik statei*, 150–9; idem, "O chernom pare," ibid., 160–2 (first published in the 1850s).

83 "Besedy," 93–5.

84 Ibid., 119–20. See also 92.

85 *RBS* 11: 335–7.

86 "Besedy," 95–8. Raevskii made a similar point in December 1891. "Neurozhai," 13.

87 Ibid., 118–19, 124. See also 128.

88 Ibid., 125. Kostychev had carried out research on the steppes. *ES* 16: 414–15.

89 "Besedy," 110, 121–2, 124. See also A. Voeikov, review of A.N. Baranovskii, *Glavnye cherty klimata chenozemnykh oblastei Rossii*, in *MV* no. 6 (1892): 242–6.

90 See, for example, I.I. Bok, "Neskol'ko slov po voprosu lesorazvendenii," *Izvestiia IRGO* 28, no. 2 (1892): 204–12; P.A. Kostychev, "O prichinakh osobennogo sil'nogo deistviia zasukha na chernozeme," *Trudy IVEO* no. 4 (1893): 1–16; A.A. Izmail'skii, "Kak vysokhla nasha step'. Issledovaniia otnositel'no vlazhnosti pochvy i podpochvy," *Sel'skoe khoziaistvo i lesovodstvo: Zhurnal Ministerstva Gosudarstvennikh Imushchestv* 173, no. 8 (August 1893): 267–89; 173, no. 9 (September 1893): 1–27. See also James Y. Simms, "The crop failure of 1891: soil exhaustion, technological backwardness, and Russia's 'agrarian crisis'," *Slavic Review* 41 (1982): 236–50

91 Dokuchaev, *Nashi Stepi prezhde i teper'* (St Petersburg, 1892) (and in idem, *Sochineniia*, 6: 13–102); [Ermolov], *Neurozhai i narodnoe bedstvie*; A.I. Voeikov, "Klimat i narodnoe khoziaistvo," in *'Pomoshch' golodaiushchim': Nauchno-literaturnyi sbornik*, ed. D.N. Anuchin (Moscow, 1892), 485–98; P. Barakov, *O vozmozhnykh merakh bor'by s zasukhami* (Odessa, 1892); I.A. Lishin, *K voprosu obvodneniia i obleseniia stepnoi polosy Samarskoi gubernii* (Moscow, 1892).

92 P. Kostychev, *O bor'be s zasukhoi v chernozemnoi oblasti postredstvom obrabotki polei i nakopleniia na nikh snega* (St Petersburg, 1893). N. Tulaikov, "'Sukhoe' zemledelie (sistema Kembellia)," *Polnaia entsiklopediia russkogo sel'skogo khoziaistva i soprikasaiushchikhsia s nimi nauk*, 12 vols (St Petersburg, 1900–10), XII, 1262–7.

93 M. Vonzblein, "Agronomiia obshchestvennaia," *Polnaia entsiklopediia* XII, 10–15. For contrasting interpretations of agronomy, see Kerans, *Mind and Labor*; Yanni Kotsonis, *Making Peasants Backward: Agricultural Cooperatives and the Agrarian Question in Russia, 1861–1914* (Basingstoke and London, 1999).

94 A.P. Perepelkin, ed., *Stenograficheskii otchet o soveshchaniiakh pri [Imperatorskom Moskovskom] Obshchestve [Sel'skogo Khoziaistva], s 18-go po 22-e Dekabria 1892 goda, po obshchestvennym rabotam po obvodeniiu iugo-vostochnoi chasti Rossii, proizvennym v 1892 g. rasporiazheniem Zaveduiushchego Obshchestvennymi rabotami Generala M.N. Annenkova* (Moscow, 1893); A. Voeikov, "S"ezd v Moskve po voprosu obvodneniia stepnoi i chernozemnoi polosy Evropeiskoi Rossii," *MV* no. 1 (1893): 21–3; Dokuchaev, *Sochineniia*, 6: 87, 95–6; Chebotareva, "Dokuchaev," 99, 103–4.

95 Dokuchaev, *Sochineniia*, 6: 105–204. See also David Moon, "The environmental history of the Russian steppes: Vasilii Dokuchaev and the harvest failure of 1891," *Transactions of the Royal Historical Society*, 6th series, 15 (2005), 166–71.

96 Voeikov, "Vozdeistvie cheloveka na prirodu," [1894], in idem, *Vozdeistvie cheloveka na prirodu*, 40–90. See also Hooson, "Development," 261. On Marsh, see above.

97 See J.D. Oldfield, "Russia, systemic transformation and the concept of sustainable development," *Environmental Politics* 10 (2001): 94–110; Douglas Weiner, *Models of Nature: Ecology, Conservation and Cultural Revolution in Soviet Russia* (Pittsburgh, 1988), 10–11, 230–1.

98 Willard Sunderland, "Peasant pioneering: Russian peasant settlers describe colonization and the eastern frontier, 1880s–1910s," *Journal of Social History* 34 (2001): 895–922, here 898–9.

99 See A.P. Engel'gardt, *Chernozemnaia Rossiia* (Saratov, 1903).

100 The more dramatic development and evaporation of the euphoria around the Amur basin in the Far East in mid-century has been described in Bassin, *Imperial Visions*.

5   The "ethic of empire" on the Siberian borderland

The peculiar case of the "rock people," 1791–1878

Andrei A. Znamenski[1]

Rereading the famous 1822 Speranskii Statute on Alien (*Inorodsty*) Administration, which defined the place of the Siberian natives within the Russian Empire, I ran across the name of a group called "Bukhtarmintsy" who numbered no more than 600 people and resided in the Bukhtarma and Uimon valleys of the Altai, southwestern Siberia, and were related to the category of "settled aliens."[2] This fact did not attract my attention until I found out that the "Bukhtarmintsy," also known as the "rock people" (*kamenshchiki*), were not Siberian natives at all, but pure Russian settlers. Not only were they Russians, but also predominantly Old Believers, whom the empire had relegated to the category of tribute (*iasak*) payers. Although this status granted in 1791 was eventually taken away in 1878, the fact that for almost 90 years a group of Russian settlers officially lived as "aliens" (*inorodtsy*) appeared to me to be unusual.

As exceptional and peculiar as it may appear, the case of the "rock people" sheds light on the general development of the Russian eastern borderlands in the eighteenth and nineteenth centuries. Obviously, historians might approach this case as an example of shifting identity or the interplay of social estate and ethnic categories in a loosely controlled frontier environment.[3] There is also much interesting material here for insights into the history of Russian religious dissent, specifically Old Believers.[4] However, I intend to approach this case from a different angle, as I am interested in searching for possible factors that prompted tsarist authorities to relegate and then maintain the "rock people" in a tribute-paying category (a status that they did not initially request but eventually strove to continue). This essay places the case of the "rock people" in the general context of Russian imperial governance of the Siberian borderland in the eighteenth and nineteenth centuries. My intention is not to make a comprehensive examination of the ethnohistory of the "rock" community, but to "unpack" this interesting case in order to illuminate the attitudes of the Russian government toward natives and non-natives in Siberia. I am especially concerned with the period before the 1880s, at which point mass colonization and the ideas and practices of "modernity" – with its concepts of ethnicity, race, and administrative unity – gradually started to erode traditional "Muscovite" approaches to subject populations in this part of the empire.

I would like to argue that, on the Siberian borderland, the empire practiced elements of pre-industrial imperial paternalism[5] in its relations with its subject population until at least the 1880s, and in some respects, such as population and land policies, well beyond the nineteenth century. After Jeremy Adelman and Aron Stephen, who discussed analogous policies in Spain's Latin American possessions, I call these rudiments of pre-industrial paternalism the "ethic of empire."[6] Although with the intensive colonization of the Siberian frontier in the second half of the nineteenth century, the trappings of modernity increasingly penetrated this frontier area, the fact that the government was ready to maintain a group of Russians in a tributary category irrespective of their ethnic origin or Christian confessional affiliation suggests the resilience of this ethic. Moreover, the very status of Siberian natives as tribute payers, which the authorities partially undermined in 1913 but did not totally eliminate until 1917, points in the same direction.

In addition, I would like to note that, at least until 1906, free settlement on the eastern frontier was restricted by numerous bureaucratic regulations.[7] Both the government and existing tradition also sought to lock all settlers, both those who practiced individual land seizures and those who ascribed themselves to existing communities, within peasant communes. Most importantly, in Siberia such an important "modern" tool of colonization as individual ownership of land as private property never even became an issue. It is true that by the turn of the twentieth century Siberia absorbed hundreds of thousands of settlers from European Russia. Yet these people only worked on their land plots, and never owned the land; Siberian land belonged either to the state or, as in the case of the Altai, directly to the crown (the so-called *Kabinet* administration). Although from the 1860s Russian peasant colonization increasingly streamed to the east – overcoming and overwhelming the many bureaucratic obstacles – even as late as the end of the nineteenth century, authorities still could not make up their minds if they should encourage broad independent colonization or regulate and restrict the movement of the subject population.[8]

Of the three major interactive elements one finds on the Russian frontier – the state, indigenous people, and settlers[9] – this essay centers on the first one: Russian borderland policies. One might certainly view this approach as an attempt to return to the "old tradition" of the macro-level analysis of the frontier in broad political, social, and economic dimensions. Yet it is not my intention to stray away from currently prevailing cultural and ethnohistorical "frontier" methodologies.[10] Incorporation of recent techniques developed by the students of North American borderlands[11] into Russian frontier studies has helped scholars to revisit both the old simplistic vision of the frontier as the advance of civilization into wilderness and also the more recent one that portrays the borderland exclusively as a battleground between colonizers and native victims. As a result, now we have a more nuanced approach to the frontier as a process of cultural interactions, reciprocal exchanges, and contests that affected all of the participants in these encounters. More importantly, these new approaches bring to light the voices of such neglected groups as settlers and indigenous people and help to reconstruct their visions of settlement and colonization.[12]

From the viewpoint of this new scholarship, it is clear, for example, that the Siberian frontier hardly resembled either a "classic" Anglo-American "civilization march" described by Frederick Jackson Turner in his famous impressionistic essay or, no less an impressionistic picture, an endemic conflict of Euroamericans and natives, which Patricia Nelson Limerick grimly portrayed as the "legacy of conquest."[13] Compared to these approaches, the metaphor of the "middle ground" offered by one of the "new Western historians," Richard White, successfully captures the fluid nature of the frontier as a place of contest, cultural exchange, and reciprocity.[14] This concept is very useful for research on the cultural and ethnohistorical aspects of frontier encounters, especially in situations of temporary equilibrium of power. Yet, taken to the extreme, as in the work of Colin Calloway on American-Spanish-French and Indian relationships in North America or, for that matter, in my own earlier article on Chukchi-Russian-American encounters,[15] this metaphor easily turns into the "new worlds for all," where all agents of a frontier encounter, including empires, tribes, and individuals act as equal partners. This, as I now see, was not the case in Siberia.

It appears that one of the reasons for the temporary existence of the "middle ground" on the North American frontier was the established practice of English, American, and, to some extent, French representatives, to treat their own populations and native communities as sovereigns in their own right.[16] We do not find, for example, such attitudes on Russian Siberian or Spanish frontiers, where authorities treated borderland people, both natives and non-natives, as subject populations and where many of these subjects subscribed to this type of relationship.[17] If we were to search for metaphors to grasp the context of the Siberian borderland encounters, the best one that comes to my mind is the Spanish "closed" borderland in North and South America, which was similarly loaded with a pre-modern paternalistic ethic and institutions.[18] In my view, an examination of Russian imperial policies on the Siberian frontier will help to probe into the frontier histories of other empires that carried a similar burden of "archaic" paternalist attitudes toward their borderlands as, for example, Spain in North and South America.

In applying methodologies developed for the analysis of the Anglo-American frontier to the study of borderlands elsewhere, it is essential not to lose the sight of the different political, economic, and cultural contexts of frontier encounters. I realize that one cannot totally avoid juxtaposing Russian and other borderlands against the American frontier simply because frontier studies originated in the realm of American historiography. As a matter of fact, the practice of casting the eastern Russian frontier against its Anglo-American "analogy" has a long tradition started by the writings of Siberian regionalists and continued by the post-war Western scholarship.[19]

The story that unfolds below is not so much the history of the "rock people" per se as an outline of the enduring imperial paternalism and social estate categorization operative on the Siberian borderland. I argue that that this minor particular case illuminates the resilience of these pre-modern attitudes in this part of the Russian empire, which, especially as applied to the second half of the nineteenth century, points to paradoxes of Russian modernity. Since the majority of the "rock people" originated from runaway state peasants and miners ascribed to south Siberian plants, I am first of all interested in examining the status of these groups, primarily before the beginning of the mass colonization in the 1860s. Second, since the government attached the runaway "rock" communities to the rank of tribute payers, I explore the status of the indigenous population in Siberia, who traditionally also belonged to this category. Finally, the essay probes into the mythology that nineteenth-century regionalist observers constructed around the case of the "rock people", portraying them as agents of modernity.

To situate the "rock people" historically and geographically, one needs to remember that until the beginning of the nineteenth century, they resided in a "middle ground" zone contested by Russia, the Western Mongol (Zunghar) tribal federation, and China, which sought to turn local populations into their tribute payers.[20] Until the 1760s, Russia formally governed the northern steppe Altai, while the Western Mongol federation, which represented a loosely connected tribal alliance, ruled over its southern mountain part. The region was populated by the Altaians, native nomads who were known in old Russia under the name of the "mountain Kalmyks" and who until the middle of the 1750s constantly drifted between Zungharia, China, and Russia. In the second half of the eighteenth century, after the advancing Chinese physically and politically eliminated the Zunghar "empire," the area continued to be a contested ground between China and Russia. Seeking protection from a genocidal warfare unleashed by the Chinese troops, the Altaian tribes sought and eventually received permission to enter the Russian empire as her subjects.[21] Eventually, Russia absorbed the entire Altai region, which acquired the status of *Kabinet* land, i.e. the direct possession of the imperial crown. Still, until the 1860s, the Russian-Chinese border in the southernmost part of the Altai remained undefined, and a few native Altaian clans in this area even paid a complimentary tribute both to the Chinese and Russian empires.[22]

The mountain area of the Altai populated by the new subjects was officially known as the "Kalmyk nomadic encampments," while the local Russians nicknamed it the "Rock." Because of the geopolitical situation, colonization of the Altai and especially its southern "rocky" part began relatively late compared to the rest of Siberian areas. In contrast to central and eastern Siberia where Russian exploratory parties set their feet as early as the first half of the seventeenth century, the Altai saw large-scale Russian advances only in the second half of the eighteenth century. The eventual attention of the Russian government to this area could be explained both by a desire to capitalize on the Chinese-Zunghar rivalry by taking tributary territories of the crumbling Zunghar "empire" and by a desire to take hold of local mineral resources (silver, copper, gold). The latter was a reflection of the general shift in colonization priorities in Siberia toward mining that was to supplement the extraction of fur tribute.

The making of the "rock people"

Between 1726 and 1739 Akinfii Demidov, the famous monopolist developer of mining and iron works in Siberia, established a few mines and processing plants in

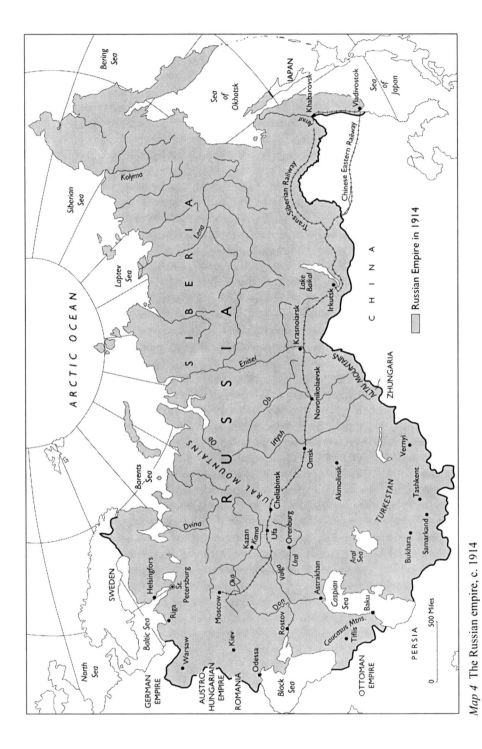

Map 4 The Russian empire, c. 1914

Russian Empire in 1914

the northern Altai (the so-called Kolyvan-Voskresensk plants). Having discovered that Demidov routinely underreported the amount of extracted silver, and realizing the potential riches of the Altai's natural resources, in 1747 the authorities confiscated his property along with all surrounding lands and populations and turned them into *Kabinet* domain.[23] Until 1917, all incomes derived from the Altaian land were delivered directly to the imperial family treasury.

In thinly populated Siberia, rapidly developing mining and processing works faced a constant shortage of labor: at first, in the 1730s, the *Kabinet* plants had only 144 workers.[24] In the 1740s and 1750s, the government wanted to resolve the problem by temporarily drafting soldiers and state peasants. By the middle of the eighteenth century, all non-tribute paying populations of the Altai became ascribed to the mines and plants either as workers (*bergaly*) or as "ascribed peasants" (*pripisnie krest'iane*). The latter had to labor in arbitrarily defined auxiliary capacities, and the amount of service required of each peasant to fulfill his levy of tribute was fixed only in 1779.[25] At first, the administration of the mines and plants did not draw any distinction between the ascribed peasants and soldiers, freely reshuffling them. It was only in 1828 that the two groups of people were separated and their status and the amount of duties were finally specified. Still, those two groups could not prove a stable source of labor. Soldiers had to carry out their regular military duties, while peasants had to work the land. Exiles, whose labor was widely used in the rest of Siberia, were forbidden from entering the area owned by the *Kabinet* because of its proximity to the Chinese border.

In 1761, authorities found a solution by using a system of a military draft (*rekrutchina*) to "recruit" workers from the ranks of the Siberian state peasants. Those who were drafted (57 persons per thousand) were relegated to the category of permanent *bergaly* workers. Working from 12 to 14 hours per day, the *bergaly* were subjected to military discipline and stayed "on duty" in the mines for the rest of their lives. The children of these workers were automatically included in the same category of life-long workers who could be "released" only in case of death or serious injury.[26] Being recruited through a military draft and subjected to a military discipline (*voennii ustav*), the *bergaly* were entitled to fixed food rations; they were also separated in various ranks and obliged to live in barracks or in their own cabins located on the territory of the works. Relief for these workers came in 1849 and 1851 when the term of their life-long service was at first lowered to 35 years and then reduced to 25 years, as for the regular Russian military – changes that helped to reduce the number of runaways. In 1864, all *bergaly* were finally released from their obligatory labor.[27]

At the same time, the government maintained the category of the ascribed peasants. Like the majority of Siberians (about 90 percent of the population[28]), the Russian peasant settlers in the Altai belonged to the category of state peasants. This meant that in addition to their agricultural duties, they had to pay common monetary dues (*obrok*), which in 1828 reached eight rubles per person, and the so-called four-ruble poll tax (*podushnaia podat'*). Moreover, state peasants had to pay local (*zemskie* and *mirskie*) taxes, which supported the police, postal system, schools, governmental buildings, and peasant administration. Furthermore, they had to carry "in-kind" responsibilities: road maintenance, delivery of mail and governmental cargoes, repairing government buildings and prisons, and providing food supplies to the clergy. On top of everything, like all Russian peasants, they were subjected to the military draft (57 draftees per thousand peasants).[29] Worse yet, these "ascribed peasants" carried even more duties than regular state peasants, also performing auxiliary tasks for mines and plants. The latter included cutting firewood, sorting coal ore collected in piles, delivering the coal and iron ore, and finally maintaining dams.[30] Although in 1807, in the rest of Siberia, the government released the majority of state peasants living in the vicinity of mines and plants from performing obligatory non-agricultural duties, this reform did not touch the Altai. The *Kabinet* administration concluded that freeing this region might be harmful to its business.[31] The system established by the *Kabinet* in the Altai to regulate the life and administration of the "ascribed peasants" (like the *bergaly*) survived until 1864 and represented essentially the same serfdom.[32]

These harsh labor conditions, coupled with the allure of the mountain ranges of the Altai in the eighteenth century as a geopolitical buffer zone, provoked mining workers and peasants to escape. Blessed with a relatively mild climate for Siberia, the mountainous Altai served as a natural hideout where runaways could establish themselves under weak or virtually absent governmental supervision. By the end of the eighteenth century in the remote locations of the "Rock," Altai runaways erected cabins and built villages.[33] The fact that until the early nineteenth century many ascribed peasants and miners were affiliated with Old Believers, who nourished escapist ideals, increased this population movement southward. Roy Robson draws our attention to a remarkable inclination of Old Believers for flight and emigration toward the borderlands, which created a popular impression of them as "pioneers of the Russian wilderness."[34]

After Catherine the Great ascended to power, persecutions of the Old Believers subsided. They were allowed to live and worship openly as long as they did not challenge established rules.[35] A few of the "rock" runaway communities – who experienced repeated crop failures, had to rely on hunting, and faced a pressure from the Kazakhs, "native colonizers," who penetrated the Altai from the south – decided to capitalize on this situation. Using the management of the *Kabinet* works as their intermediaries, they appealed to the Russian government to accept them back as the tsarina's subjects. Moreover, the "rock people" sent a delegation to St Petersburg, which resulted in the empress's edict of 15 September 1791, to forgive the "stray children" of the empire.[36] As a matter of fact, this act reflected the general lenient stance of the Catherinean administration, which issued various decrees "forgiving" runaway Old Believers and ordinary fugitives.

The edict ordered the Siberian governor-general to admit residents of eight "rock" villages located in the Bukhtarma valley (Bykova, Fykalka, Belaia, Upper Bukhtarma, Iazovaia, Korovikha, Malo-Narymka, Sennaia)[37] to the empire by assigning them a status of tribute payers (*iasachnie*). The "forgiven" people were allowed to expand their crops to the foothills of the Altai Mountains, to the Uimon Valley, and were automatically exempt from those burdensome obligations carried by the rest of the peasantry.[38] As tribute payers, the new subjects at first were even placed in the same tributary unit along with the Kazakhs, "native newcomers" to the Altai, and for a short while they were administratively subordinated to the Kazakh chiefs.[39] In 1824, the commission sent to Siberian indigenous tribes to fix the amount of the tribute confirmed the "rock" villages in their tributary status and assigned them to the category of "settled aliens," which officially made them *inorodtsy*. By the end of the nineteenth century, the population of the "rock people" increased and the number of their villages expanded to 23.[40]

There is no exact information on why the government came to a decision to endow the "rock people" with the tributary status. Although it might be tempting to view this measure as an intentional effort of authorities to strike a compromise with the runaway community by turning it into the spearhead of Russian colonization in this borderland area, apparently this was not the only motive. It also appears that in admitting the "rock people" to Russia as tribute paying subjects, the empire followed an already established procedure of trying to expand its tributary territory. In the Altai, this policy started in the 1750s with the incorporation of the nomadic "mountain Kalmyks" of the central and southern Altai and ended in 1864 with the admission of their southernmost bands, who stopped paying double tribute both to China and Russia and began to forward their *iasak* to the Russian empire. In addition, there might also be a practical consideration such as the heavy reliance of the "rock" communities on hunting, which the authorities viewed as a potential source of furs.[41] One may also speculate that it was easy for the government to relegate the "rock people" to the category of tribute paying "others" because the majority of them belonged to the Old Believers. Still, in the long run, the ethnic origin and the religious affiliation of the "rock people" did not matter. Interested in expanding its tributary population, the empire turned them into her subjects anyway.

Status of "alien" tribute payers

What made the status of tribute payers so special that, later, both Siberian natives and the "rock" communities worked hard to maintain themselves in this status? From the seventeenth century, when Russia began to incorporate indigenous Siberians as subjects, to the end of the empire in 1917, the native population of Siberia belonged to the category of tribute payers (*iasachnie*), whose major obligation was to deliver fur tribute (*iasak*) to the imperial *Kabinet*. Tribute payments were not something new introduced by the Russian empire at this borderland area. As a matter of fact, the majority of Siberian natives were very familiar with the *iasak* system, which had been routinely imposed by strong tribal confederations on weaker ones. In the eighteenth century, before the Russians advanced into southern Altai, local tribes had to deliver fur tribute to the Zunghar "empire." After the Russian empire adopted the Altaians under her wing, she simultaneously incorporated not only the practice of tribute payments but also the tributary units defined by a Mongol word *duchins*. These "archaic" administrative entities survived until 1913. On the whole, until 1917 the entire *Kabinet* and state policy toward indigenous populations in Siberia was essentially subordinated to the goal of extracting the tribute.

Until the 1830s, the amount of the *iasak* was never exactly defined. The first attempt to standardize the payments was attempted in 1763 by Catherine the Great, who sent to southwestern Siberia a special commission headed by second major M. Shcherbachev, which eventually developed tribute regulations for all of Siberia. In 1764, the use of Russian tribute collectors and the taking of hostages to ensure payment were abolished. Instead, native leadership was charged with the task of collecting and delivering the *iasak*, which made indigenous chieftains part of the governmental bureaucracy. Most importantly, the government introduced the practice of the mutual responsibility of all clan members as a guarantee of regular delivery of the tribute.[42]

Per capita *iasak* payments for specific pelts and their monetary equivalents were finally fixed in 1834, and remained unchanged until 1917. The amount of the tribute did fluctuate, but it depended on the number of clan and tribal members who were periodically reregistered. In western Siberia, the *iasak* payments were quite lenient and comprised 15 percent of native income, while in eastern Siberia they reached 38 percent of native income.[43] Although throughout the eighteenth and the nineteenth centuries the portion of the *iasak* in the general *Kabinet* income was constantly declining,[44] authorities still found it profitable to maintain this tribute practice. At first the tribute was paid exclusively in furs. In the eighteenth century, when the fur resources became depleted, the *Kabinet* permitted indigenous Siberians to deliver the tribute either in furs or in cash at the natives' own choice. Such practice was confirmed in the beginning of the nineteenth century.[45] Still, throughout the eighteenth and at the first half of the nineteenth century, contrary to economic and social changes in native life, the *Kabinet* authorities made persistent attempts to force indigenous people to deliver the tribute in furs, because the sale of pelts brought more profit than the tribute delivered in rubles.

To understand the status of the Siberian natives, we should keep in mind that until the early twentieth century the government viewed all of them as direct or potential providers of fur tribute. For successful fulfillment of their tributary obligations, "zones" of their settlement were to be protected from intrusion by outsiders. Siberian settlers who disregarded the borders of regulated zones hindered imperial interests and therefore faced potential persecution and punishment.[46]

For example, in the Altai it was formally forbidden for non-tribute payers to move southward beyond the line of the "Kalmyk nomadic encampments."[47] Although Russian runaways and later settlers widely ignored this border, restrictions were occasionally used against intruders, especially if they were Old Believers. By the turn of the twentieth century, when a large number of Siberian nomads left their hunting occupations, the authorities still continued the policy of closing tributary areas to non-*iasak* people. In the 1880s and 1890s with the beginning of mass colonization in Siberia, it was informally stipulated that Russian settlers might sublease land from native communities. Non-tribute paying newcomers had to negotiate with the native administration to receive permission to settle on indigenous lands.[48] Even though settlers frequently ignored this stipulation and widely practiced land seizures, natives did sue intruders. Along with the chaotic settlement policy of the government, this did not make settlers feel secure on their lands. Indigenous self-government could restrain the spread of commercial life. As late as 1906, in the Ulala village, which grew as a trade center and commercial center of the mountain Altai, the local indigenous administration successfully stopped Russian merchants' and craftsmen's plans to transform Ulala from a native village into a town because such a change would threaten to release the area from the status of a tributary zone.[49] Preservation of "archaic" tributary practices certainly harmed the settlement process and the development of commerce, but, to the benefit of the natives, softened the blows of Slavic peasant colonization.

Although by the end of the nineteenth century many indigenous Siberians switched from hunting to settled life and agriculture, they still remained in the nomadic category, and the authorities continued to treat them as fur hunters. Under *Kabinet* pressure, for instance, some semi-settled indigenous groups were forced to return to a "primitive" existence in order to fulfill their tributary obligations. In addition, to guarantee both the quality and quantity of tribute, in the 1850s the *Kabinet* attempted to discontinue free trade between natives and Russian merchants. This unrealistic and totally unsuccessful measure only harmed the development of commercial life on the Siberian borderland. Despite a personal appeal of the governor-general of Eastern Siberia to Nicholas I "to abandon this custom of feudal times,"[50] the authorities continued to send agents who attempted to ward off merchants from native camps and "preserve" fur tribute for the *Kabinet*. It was not until 1910 that the Kabinet finally ordered natives to pay the tribute only in money.[51]

Although, later, the status of Siberian natives acquired the attributes of a separate social estate, at first, in 1724, those classified as "Siberian tribute-paying people" (*Sibirskie iasachnie liudy*) were formally subsumed in the larger category of state peasants. In addition, at the beginning of the 1700s, official documents also used the word *inozemsty* (people living in a different land) and *inovertsy* (people of a different belief). Yet, *iasachnie*, as indication of the major fiscal obligation of native subjects to the empire, remained the most widespread definition. It is notable that these different definitions point to natives' subject status, their residence beyond European Russia, and their belief, and do not say anything about their ethnic origin.

At the same time, from the very beginning, the nature of their dues to the imperial family set natives apart. The 1822 Statute of Alien (*Inorodtsy*) Administration compiled by Mikhail Speranskii confirmed the separate status of indigenous Siberians as tribute payers.[52] Incidentally, it was the first official document that used the word *inorodtsy* ("aliens") to define Siberian indigenous groups. Ten years later, such usage was formally codified as follows: "The name *inorodtsy* defines all tribes of non-Russian origin residing in Siberia."[53]

The Speranskii Statute for the first time attempted to categorize Siberian indigenous people in ethnic terms. It also separated them into three major groups on an evolutionary ladder leading to civilization: "wandering aliens," who were "permanent" nomads and considered the most primitive, "nomadic aliens," who moved around depending on a season, and "settled aliens." Speranskii and his colleagues assumed that at some point in an undefined future all Siberian natives would eventually merge into the settled category, adopt an agricultural lifestyle and be assimilated into the Russian peasantry. Although all three groups were to pay regular *iasak*, these three categories still differed in their subject duties. In addition to their tribute obligations, "settled aliens" carried the same responsibilities as the state peasants except the most hated and burdensome one, the military draft. "Nomadic aliens," the majority of indigenous Siberians, were responsible for a few local (*zemskie*) duties, such as maintenance of roads, postal stations, and carrying imperial cargoes. "Wandering aliens" (the minority in native Siberia) were excluded from all responsibilities except for the payment of *iasak*. All three groups maintained their internal clan and tribal self-government. The general approach was to introduce an indirect rule over indigenous communities and to reduce the meddling of Russian authorities with the administration of natives, which could prevent them from performing their major tributary functions. Even "settled aliens," whose administration was structured along the lines of the state peasantry, enjoyed considerable autonomy in their internal life.

The Speranskii legislation was a peculiar combination of the "modern" approach to natives and the "archaic" one. On the one hand, the statute mentioned Siberian aliens' rights in addition to a traditional emphasis on subject responsibilities. In the spirit of Enlightenment, it also placed natives on the evolutionary civilization ladder and permitted free trade between Russians and natives. On the other hand, the statute maintained all attributes of the "aliens" as a tributary population. Native clans with their mutual responsibility were defined as major tribute-paying groups. We also find in the statute the traditional "archaic" approach to the use of land, which was viewed as the state or *Kabinet* property (as in the case of the Altai). This practice was clearly an outdated stipulation, because by the 1820s in Siberia, despite a lack of private ownership of land, it was nonetheless informally leased and bought. Although natives were redefined from *iasachnie* (a subject category) into *inorodtsy* (an ethnic category), the statute of 1822 continued to view *inorodtsy* in an estate manner. For example, the statute indicated (paragraph 57) that "nomadic aliens" could move from *inorodtsy* to the ranks of state peasants, the burgher (*meshchane*) estate, and even to merchant guilds.[54]

It seems that the highly divergent assessments of the 1822 statute that we find in Russian scholarship[55] only proves the duality of this document – and it is this "dual" nature of the statute that might explain its unusual durability. Its contradictory nature corresponded to the contradictory imperial policy on the Siberian borderland. *Kabinet* attempts to "freeze" natives in their tributary units explains the fact that the phrasing of the later 1892 Statute of Alien Administration almost exactly repeated the text of the Speranskii legislation.[56] Not only did the empire drag it into the twentieth century, but even the general modernization drive in Russia that demolished traditional indigenous administrations in Siberia between

1910 and 1913 could not kill the statute, which maintained the indigenous population in the tributary category.[57]

Since historically their major obligation to the crown was delivery of *iasak* in furs, under both the 1822 and 1892 laws, *de facto* Siberian "aliens" carried only mild financial obligations compared to surrounding peasant communities. When V.I. Vagin, a biographer of Speranskii, wrote that "the *inorodtsy* were granted such broad self-government that no other estate of our country has enjoyed until recently,"[58] he was not totally wrong. Indeed, the amount of tribute paid by Russian peasants or even the "settled aliens" did not encourage indigenous people to move up the "civilization ladder." In 1824, in Tomsk province, the overall amount of all dues and taxes paid by the settled native was equal to 18 rubles, while the nomad delivered only 1.5 rubles.[59] By 1869, in Enisei and Irkutsk provinces, the tribute paid by the native was one third of the dues paid by the peasant. Even in eastern Siberia, where the amount of *iasak* paid by "aliens" was higher than in western section, V.S. Korsakov, governor-general of Eastern Siberia, complained in 1869 that the natives maintained a higher living standard than the Russian peasants; they did not carry the heavy burden of the military draft and paid half as much dues as did the peasants.[60]

Throughout the entire nineteenth century, the Teleuts in northern Altai feared mingling with the Russians. The "aliens" were afraid that such close relations, along with taking up agricultural pursuits, might result in their relegation to the status of peasants. Despite their obvious financial losses, some natives insisted on paying their tribute in furs,[61] which they considered an essential attribute of the *inorodtsy* status they hoped to maintain. There was also a fear of being reregistered from the nomadic category to the "settled aliens" category – a rank that drew natives closer to regular peasants. For example, one of the reasons the powerful Altai Orthodox mission failed to turn Altaian nomadic stock raisers into settled agriculturists was natives' fear of becoming peasants.

Considering the aforementioned, it is not surprising that the status of tribute payers, which the government had imposed on the "rock people," came to look alluring to neighboring Russian communities. At the turn of the nineteenth century, joining the tribute-paying "rock people" became an attractive alternative for "ascribed peasants" and lifetime mining workers who fled to the Altai Mountains. At least a few Old Believer parties that embarked on the search for the famous *Belovod'e*[62] sought to negotiate for themselves a status similar to the one received by the "rock people." One of the most documented cases – of the 1827 abortive escape of mining workers and "ascribed peasants" from a polishing plant in search of *Belovod'e* – shows that the runaways had planned to live in hiding and then to appeal for the status of "tribute *inorodtsy*"[63] For some of these parties, the "rock people" acted as inspirations or as guides not only because they were familiar with the area where "the government will not find you," but also because they knew "how to search for freedom." The villages of "rock people" with their "alien" status similarly attracted "stray" settlers who wished to join them.[64] Karl Ledebour, who visited the "rock" villages in 1826, wrote about the Bukhtarma and Uimon valleys as a favorite "hang-out" for about 800 people who wanted to entrench themselves in one of those settlements.[65] Frequently, the Russian "aliens" themselves joined the "scout" parties searching for better lands and drifted southward to the Chinese border.[66] It was hardly surprising that in 1827 P.K. Florov, head of the mountain administration of the *Kabinet* works, recommended that all residents of the "rock" village of Uimon be evicted as potential troublemakers and resettled beyond Lake Baikal, far from the Chinese border.[67]

Although this project never materialized and the "rock people" continued to reside in the southern Altai living as tributary-paying "aliens," 50 years later, as part of a general modernization drive, authorities eventually revoked their peculiar status. In 1878 all their specific privileges were waived, including the exception from the military draft, and "rock" settlements were reorganized into regular peasant districts (*volosts*). Although the Russian "aliens" fiercely protested, and even sent a special delegation to St Petersburg in 1882, their appeals were ignored.[68] Incidentally, in 1880 the government made a similar attempt, which they soon abandoned, to discontinue "alien" administration for indigenous communities in the Altai by replacing traditional hereditary leadership with elected leaders. The "aliens", however, were able to bypass these formalities by "electing" to the chieftain positions the same people who had held power before.

The "rock people" romanticized

Despite the long-time tributary status of the "rock people," or rather precisely because of this status, the writings of Siberian regionalists singled them out as spearheads of progress in the Altai. It is known that the educated nineteenth-century Russian public drew an ambivalent picture of peasant colonizers on the eastern borderland. Some observers portrayed them as agents of progress and Russianness, while the others gave them low scores, insisting that they too easily went native and essentially acted as regressive elements.[69] As active participants of these colonization debates, regionalist Siberian observers tended to share the former assessment. In their desire to upgrade the cultural and social status of Siberia in the eyes of European Russia, they portrayed Siberian peasant settlers as people of a better caliber than their counterparts west of the Ural Mountains.

For such leading regionalist authors as G. Potanin and N. Iadrintsev, Siberian colonizers were enterprising individuals and "free spirits," not burdened with the heritage of serfdom. Constantly scrutinizing Siberian colonization through the lens of Western experiences, regionalist writers and scholars portrayed Siberian settlers as carriers of modernity and essentially as a Russian equivalent of American pioneers.[70] It is notable that for the construction of such a romantic blueprint the "rock people" served better than any other Russian settlers. Downplaying the tributary status of these Russian "aliens," regionalists freely recast the administrative and financial leeway that the "rock people" enjoyed into a form of folk democratic rule – and an alternative to the existing social and political realities. The logic of this intellectual exercise was simple: if Siberian peasants were "free spirits," the "rock people" with their peculiar status were even more so.

Figure 5.1 "Rock people" (*Kamenshchiki*) meet visitors with a gun salute, Bakhturma valley, early nineteenth century. From Grigorii Spasskii, ed., *Noveishiia ucheniia i zhivopisniia puteshestviia po Sibiri*, v. 1 (St Petersburg, 1819), after 73.

The origin of the idealized portrait of the "rock people" as the best manifestation of Russian "free spirits" on the Siberian borderland can be traced to the writings of the early nineteenth-century Russian and Baltic German explorers (scientists and artists) such as Grigorii Spasskii, Karl Ledebour, Alexander von Bunge, Alexander Gelmersen, and Gerhard Meyer. These observers noted the unusual people planted amid the attractive landscape ("Siberian Switzerland"). Legends about unsupervised life in the "Rock" – beyond the suffocating control of imperial bureaucracy, the culture tinged with Old Belief ideology, and residence "close to nature" – were equally attractive to early Romantic travelers and later to Siberian regionalists.

Although he was not impressed with the messy and anarchic rule practiced by the "rock people," the geologist Spasskii (1809) praised their mores, which surpassed those of the "inhabitants of the Swiss Alps."[71] Baltic German zoologist Ledebour (1826) called them "bold seekers" and "adventurers" who penetrated "impassible wilderness" and who "because of their diligence" prospered and lived a well-to-do life in "elegant cabins."[72] Moreover, to Ledebour, the "rock people" acted as spearheads of a growing Russian imperial vitality that he believed would overcome the Chinese empire, "a sleeping relic animal":

"Residents of the Russian border villages create a favorable contrast to their clumsy southern neighbors. They are strong, well built, energetic and fast, and present a pleasant picture in this wilderness."[73] Gelmersen, who visited "rock people" eight years later, joined Ledebour in his assessment of Russian settlers' vitality: "Local residents are strong and healthy and have a pleasant appearance. They are rich and joyful."[74]

Later, these assessments were incorporated into the classic works of German geographers Alexander Humboldt (who personally visited the Altai in 1828) and Karl Ritter (who had a great impact on Siberian regionalism). In their popular and scholarly writings, Potanin, Iadrintsev, Belosliudov, and Grebenshchikov took this imagery for their regionalist purposes and continued to expand on the idea of the "rock people" as proud mountaineers: a physically strong race of people, bold and brave, whose women were analogous to Amazons.[75] Thus, Potanin used the "rock people" to create a generalized image of the early Siberian settler, who lived and acted in the "period of the Middle Ages for Siberia."[76] Continuing his "medieval" analogies, Potanin added, "I consider a sable hunter no less than a knight of minor rank. In his way of life we can see the same neglect of a family life and replacement of it for dangers."[77] These artificial European analogies obscured the fact that authorities categorized these "knights" as tribute-paying subjects of the empire, albeit belonging to the rank of so-called "settled aliens", who stood closer to the category of state peasants.

A member of the Potanin circle, musician and ethnographer Andrei Anokhin, compared the Russian Altai and its "rock" communities with the Cossack *Zaporozhie Sech* and even called the area "Siberian Sech."[78] On the other hand, for the same observers, the "rock people" served as symbols of the unleashing of the national forces of the Russian people in the colonization process.[79] The writer Belosliudov stressed that it was unwise to hinder the movement of those people who stretched imperial borders southward, thereby making the work of diplomats much easier.[80] Continuing to praise the colonizing potential of the Russian "aliens," Belosliudov exclaimed: "Do not restrain these, I do not know how to call them, half-bandits or half-adventurers, and in 50 or 60 years we will conquer all of Mongolia without wasting a pound of powder or sacrificing a single company of soldiers."[81]

Having visited the central and southern Altai in the summer of 1878, Iadrintsev described his impressions of the mountain Altai as an encounter with "paradise on earth." For him, its Russian residents were not only the backbone of colonization in the Altai, but even "the most pure race of the Great Russian people."[82] He also underlined that their vitality would infuse fresh blood in the veins of Siberian colonization as a whole. Stressing that the affiliation of these Russian "aliens" with Old Belief had educated them in a spirit of "high morality," Iadrintsev argued that the "rock" communities would be the best candidates to lead Russia's civilizing mission on the Siberian borderland. Moreover, he viewed the Altai as a laboratory where the "great colonization work of the Russian population" went on.[83] Interestingly, under the spell of these writings, some current Russian scholars still generalize about the uniquely heroic character of the "rock" residents.[84]

What these observers downplayed, did not see, or did not want to see is the fact that their peculiar "alien" status set the "rock people" apart from the rest of the Slavic settlers and made them superficially look "special" and "democratic." Thus, neither Potanin nor Iadrintsev, who characterized the "rock people" as pioneers and bearers of modernity, ever expanded on the origin of their "freedoms" or placed these "freedoms" in the context of the Russian political, administrative, and estate structures.

To be fair, at least one regionalist writer who closely observed their traditions and lifestyle did try to draw a somewhat different picture of the "rock people," stepping away from portraying them as the carriers of progress. Stressing that the life of these communities was as "frozen in time as stone," G. Grebenshchikov, a popular Siberian reporter who later emigrated to the United States, pictured them as a living slice of "Muscovite Russia." Still, Grebenshchikov did not expand on his own assertion, and, like Potanin and Iadrintsev, preferred to generalize about the "rock people" as communities "full of extraordinary power that makes them absolutely different from the downgraded and narrow-minded peasants of central Russia." It appears that as a writer, he was more interested in playing with the "rock" metaphor than with social and historical generalizations. To Grebenshchikov, the "rock people" looked and acted like people made of "rock": they were healthy, handsome, and beautiful. On top of this, they were skillful marksmen and riders who enjoyed a life of danger and bravery, and proudly looked straight in the faces of strangers without lowering their eyes.[85] Grebenshchikov's inconsistency reflects in large part the general ambivalence of educated Russians about peasants as model colonizers.

Conclusions

For such an ambiguous empire as Russia, which had to deal with her own cultural insecurities in relation to the West,[86] "archaic" paternalism in governing the Siberian frontier was still a valid approach in the nineteenth century. Moreover, the attitudes and component elements of the Muscovite ethic of empire survived to 1917 in regulating both the Siberian land and subject population.[87] Singling out specific ethnic groups either for prioritization, for oppression, or for treatment as sovereigns, as it was practiced on the Anglo-American frontier, was not the practice here. Although it appears that the conditions of Siberian natives were no worse than those of the Russian peasantry – in some areas (especially in western Siberia), they were even better – from an imperial viewpoint it hardly mattered. What mattered more was that all of them were the subjects of the Russian empire with their obligations and duties. The assertion – found in a great deal of writing about Siberia – that Russian settlers acted as agents of modernity and that Russian interests targeted Siberian natives for oppression owes its origin to the 1880s and 1890s, when Siberian regionalists created these ideas in an effort to boost their political agenda. Unfortunately, a few scholarly works still perpetuate some of this imagery today.[88]

It is obvious that estate-type tributary status, which the government assigned to Siberian indigenous tribes and which it also applied to the "rock people," was not a deliberately lenient treatment of Siberian natives by the Russian empire. Nonetheless, my suggestion is that this status was one of the elements of enduring "archaic" paternalism that the Russian empire extended by default to the Siberian borderland.[89] It is essential to note here that the annual fur and monetary *iasak* (tribute) delivered by all indigenous Siberians, whether they lived on state or *Kabinet* lands, was considered *Kabinet* property. Concerned about the security of the crown's income, authorities viewed the entire Siberian native population as the source of furs for the crown treasury right up until 1917. Treated as a group with fixed subject obligations, especially after 1822, the Siberian *inorodtsy* eventually acquired many of the attributes of a social estate.

It is also essential to note that in Siberia, the empire continued to practice the "archaic" approach not only to the *inorodsty* subject population, but also to the land worked by peasant settlers. Although, as part of the 1860s reform movement, the government eliminated such categories as ascribed peasants and ascribed miners, the attitude to Siberian land did not change. People could settle on it, cultivate it, even informally sell and mortgage it, but they never owned it as their own property, because it was state or, as in the case of the Altai, *Kabinet* domain.[90] In the second half of the nineteenth century, this paternalist approach became increasingly intertwined with elements of modern political and colonial practice, creating a symbiosis that preserved much of the old structures along with the new approaches and discourses. This symbiosis essentially replicated the contradictions of Russian modernization writ large.[91]

Still, let us return to the "rock people," whose case I use here to illuminate my major premise. The ease with which the empire at first placed the "rock people" into the existing estate-type category of tribute-paying "settled aliens," and then maintained them in this capacity without regard for their ethnic origin until the 1870s, serves as an example of the endurance of pre-modern imperial paternalism on the Siberian borderland. In the 1870s and 1880s, authorities initiated a package of modest modernization measures that, among other things, included the abolition of such "splinters of the past" as the tributary status of the "rock people." Nonetheless, the colonization process, at least in the Altai, shows that by the turn of the twentieth century clashes between the interests of the *Kabinet* and those of the tsarist state – that is, the crown's desire to maintain "alien" tributary areas and peoples for its own profit, versus the goals of advancing mass colonization for the greater economic development of all of Russia – created administrative and imperial chaos at the heart of the modernization process. At the turn of the twentieth century, then, the conflict between emerging Russian "modernity," on one hand, and the "ethic of empire" attitude, on the other hand, created a situation, at least as applied to the Altai, where because of the contradictory policies of the state (boosting peasant colonization and simultaneously preserving "archaic" *Kabinet* institutions) neither natives nor Russian settlers felt secure on their lands.

Notes

1 I am grateful to Nicholas Breyfogle, Willard Sunderland and Abby Schrader for their detailed comments, feedback, and criticism, which eventually helped me to sharpen the central thesis of this essay.
2 *Natsional'naia politika imperatorskoi Rossii: pozdnie pervobytnie i predklassovie obshchestva severa Evropeiskoi Rossii, Sibiri i Russkoi Ameriki,* ed. Yu.I. Semenov (Moscow, 1998), 141.
3 Some present-day historians of the American West associate the word "frontier" with the Eurocentric concept of Frederick Jackson Turner and prefer to use such neutral definition as the "borderland." Since in Russian historical scholarship the word "frontier" is not politically charged, in this essay I use both definitions interchangeably.
4 For a study of Russian religious dissenters as borderland colonizers, see Nicholas B. Breyfogle, *Heretics and Colonizers: Forging Russia's Empire in the South Caucasus* (Ithaca, 2005).
5 My view of a pre-industrial empire is informed by the works of Ernest Gellner, specifically by his *Nations and Nationalism* (Ithaca, 1983).
6 Jeremy Adelman and Aron Stephen, "From borderlands to borders: empires, nation-states, and the peoples in between in North American history," *American Historical Review* 104, no. 3 (1999): 830.
7 On the efforts of Petr Stolypin and Aleksandr Krivoshein to overcome these regulations and change the nature of colonization in Siberia after 1906, see Charles Steinwedel in this volume.
8 Edward H. Judge, "Peasant resettlement and social control in late imperial Russia," in *Modernization and Revolution: Dilemmas of Progress in Late Imperial Russia,* eds Edward H. Judge and James Y. Simms, Jr. (New York, 1992), 77, 80–1, 89; Willard Sunderland, "The 'colonization question': visions of colonization in late imperial Russia," *Jahrbücher für Geschichte Osteuropas* 48, no. 2 (2000): p.214.
9 Nicholas B. Breyfogle, "Heretics and colonizers: religious dissent and Russian colonization of Transcaucasia, 1830–1890" (Ph.D. diss., University of Pennsylvania, 1998), 11.
10 Incidentally, these methodologies affected me so much that eventually my major research, which is not related to the "rock people," shifted into the realm of ethnohistory and anthropology.
11 For examples of seminal works of so-called "new Western historians," see Richard White, *The Middle Ground: Indians, Empires, and Republics in the Great Lakes Region, 1650–1815* (New York, 1991); Daniel Usner, Jr., *Indians, Settlers, and Slaves in a Frontier Exchange Economy: The Lower Mississippi Valley before 1783* (Chapel Hill, 1992); and William Cronon, *Changes in the Land: Indians, Colonists, and the Ecology of New England* (New York, 1983).
12 One can find recent creative incorporation of these methodologies in Thomas M. Barrett, *On the Edge of Empire: The Terek Cossacks and the North Caucasus Frontier, 1700–1860* (Boulder, 1999) and Breyfogle, *Heretics and Colonizers.*
13 Patricia Nelson Limerick, *Legacy of Conquest: The Unbroken Past of the American West* (New York, 1987).
14 White, *Middle Ground.*
15 Colin G. Calloway, *New Worlds for All: Indians, Europeans, and the Remaking of Early America* (Baltimore, 1997); Andrei A. Znamenski, "'Vague sense of belonging to the Russian empire': the reindeer Chukchi's status in nineteenth-century northeastern Siberia," *Arctic Anthropology* 36, no. 1–2 (1999): 19–36.
16 Incidentally, in the eighteenth and nineteenth centuries, this attitude gave rise to the widespread practice of treaty-making on the North American frontier that connected Native American clans and communities and their Anglo-American counterparts (townships, states, and central governments) in a web of mutually negotiated agreements.
17 On this topic, see also Valerie Kivelson in this volume.

18 For more about the Spanish borderland in North America, see John Francis Banon, *The Spanish Borderland Frontier, 1513–1821* (Albuquerque, 1974); and David J. Weber, *Spanish Frontier in North America* (New Haven, 1992). Sampling recent methodological approaches to the study of colonial encounters, Ann Stoler and Frederick Cooper stress that such Western empires as England, the Netherlands, and France assessed their colonial policies through the prism of notions of citizenship, sovereignty, and participation. It is notable that these two authors save their reservations for Spain and Portugal, which, according to them, were ambivalent about these notions. Ann Laura Stoler and Frederick Cooper, "Between metropole and colony: rethinking a research agenda", in *Tensions of Empire: Colonial Cultures in a Bourgeois World*, eds idem (Berkeley, 1997), 3.

19 For a brief review of regionalists' vision of the Siberian frontier, see Sunderland, "The 'colonization question'," 219; for the assessment of the post-war Western scholarship of Russian frontier, see Breyfogle, "Heretics and colonizers," 6–7.

20 For more about this contest, see Fred W. Bergholz, *The Partition of the Steppe: The Struggle of the Russians, Manchus, and the Zunghar Mongols for Empire in Central Asia, 1619–1758* (New York, 1993).

21 About admission of the Altaian tribes into Russia, see G.P. Samaev, *Prisoedinenie Altaia k Rossii: istoricheskii obzor i dokumenty* (Gorno-Altaisk, 1996).

22 The 1822 Speranskii statute confirmed this peculiar status of these *dvoedantsy* (people of double affiliation). *Natsional'naia politika*, 142, 149.

23 N.D. Putintsev, *Statisticheskii ocherk Tomskoi gubernii* (Samara, 1892), 18–19.

24 I. Tyzhnov, "Obshchie zamechania ob organizatsii sosloviia gornozavodskikh liudei Kolyvano-voskresenskikh gornykh zavodov," *Altaiaksii sbornik* 6 (1907): 5

25 E.G. Blomkvist and N.P. Grin'kova, *Bukhtarminskie staroobriadtsy* (Leningrad, 1930), 7; L.I. Sherstova, *Etnopoliticheskaia istoriia tiurkov Iuzhnoi Sibiri v XVII–XIX vekakh* (Tomsk, 1999), 195; N. Zobnin, "Gornoe delo i khoziastvo Kabineta," *Altai, istoriko-statisticheskii sbornik po voprosam ekonomicheskago i grazhdanskago razvitiia Altaiskago gornago okruga*, ed. P.A. Golubev (Tomsk, 1890), 394.

26 Tyzhnov, "Obshchie zamechania," 22. Incidentally, the managers of the Kolyvan-Voskresensk works held military ranks equal to those established in artillery and the core of engineers. The works' administration also combined management tasks with judicial and police responsibilities.

27 Zobnin, "Gornoe delo," 395, 397, 414.

28 A.S. Zuev, *Sibir': vekhi istorii* (Novosibirsk, 1998), 219.

29 Ibid.

30 V. Otpetyi, *Altai, budushchaia Kaliforniia Rossii, i tsarstvovavshie na Altaie poriadki* (Leipzig, 1882), 63; Zobnin, "Gornoe delo," 408; V.A. Lipinskaia, *Starozhily i pereselentsy: Russkie na Altae v XVIII–nachale XX veka* (Moscow, 1996), 17.

31 Zobnin, "Gornoe delo," 413.

32 N.S. Modorov, *Rossiia i Gornyi Altai: politicheskie, sotsial'no-ekonomicheskie i kul'turnie otnosheniia, XVII–XIX vv.* (Gorno-Altaisk, 1996), 143.

33 For more about "flights" to and the life in the "Rock" in the second half of the eighteenth century, see T.S. Mamsik, *Pobegi kak sotsial'noe iavlenie: pripisnaia derevnia Zapadnoi Sibiri v 40–90-e gody XVIII v.* (Novosibirsk, 1978), 90–105.

34 Roy R. Robson, *Old Believers in Modern Russia* (DeKalb, 1995), 23.

35 Robert O. Crummey, "Interpreting the fate of the old belief communities," in *Seeking God: The Recovery of Religious Identity in Orthodox Russia, Ukraine, and Georgia*, ed. Stephen K. Batalden (DeKalb, 1993), 150.

36 G. Spasskii, *Noveishia uchenia i zhivopisnia puteshestvia po Sibiri* (St Petersburg, 1819), v. 1: 95–6.

37 According to a 1792 official census, there were 318 "rock people" of both genders (250 men and 68 women). These official statistics, however, do not reflect the real number of the "rock people," many of whom simply avoided registration. A.N. Belosliudov, "K istorii

Belovodia," *Zapiski Zapadno-Sibirskago Imperatorskago Russkago geograficheskago obshchestva* 38 (1916): 14. By 1809, according to official registers, their number increased to 627 persons. Spasskii, *Noveishia uchenia*, 84.

38 Putintsev, *Statisticheskii Ocherk Tomskoi Gubernii*, 19; Otpetyi, *Atlai, budushchaia Kaliforniia Rossii*, 69; K.V. Chistov, *Russkie narodnye sotsial'no-utopicheskie legendy XVII–XIX vv.* (Moscow, 1967), 275; *Puteshestvie po Altaiskim goram i Dzhungarskoi Kirgizskoi stepi: K.F. Ledebur, A.A. Bunge, K.A. Meier*, eds O.N. Vilkov, A.P. Okladnikov, trans. V.V. Zavalishin, Iu.P. Bubenkov (Novosibirsk, 1993), 132. Although the amount of tribute the "rock people" had to pay (2 rubles 30 kopeks per person) was almost twice as much as that of the genuine natives (1 ruble 50 kopeks per person), this was far less than the amount of duties paid by local Russians. Otpetyi, *Altai, budushchaia Kaliforniia Rossii*, 69–70. From 1769 the "rock people" had to provide a tribute in sable furs at the amount of 3 rubles and 50 kopeks per person. Furthermore, since 1824, as for all other "settled aliens," the dues of the "rock people" increased to 8 rubles. D.N. Belikov, *Tomskii raskol* (Tomsk, 1901), 151. Yet the major benefit cherished by the "rock people" as well as by genuine natives was the total exclusion from military draft.

39 Guliaev, "Altaiskie kamenshchiki," *Sankt-Peterburgskie viedomosti* 20 (1845): 119–20.

40 Otpetyi, *Altai, budushchaia Kaliforniia Rossii*, 69.

41 The geologist G. Spasskii, who visited "rock" villages 20 years after their incorporation into the empire and who closely interacted with their inhabitants, stressed that the areas occupied by the "rock people" were abundant in wild game and that "they hunt these animals as skillfully as neighboring nomadic people." He also added that "local sables are of a very high quality." Spasskii, *Noveishia uchenia*, 84.

42 Yuri Slezkine, *Arctic Mirrors: Russia and the Small People of the North* (Ithaca, 1994), 67; see the text of the instructions to Shcherbachev in *Natsional'naia politika*, 103–12.

43 Zuev, *Sibir': vekhi istorii*, 252.

44 In 1889 the tribute composed 12.3 percent of the *Kabinet* income; by 1917 the portion of the tribute dropped to 2.2 percent. RGIA, f. 468, op. 9, d. 947, l. 23.

45 RGIA, f. 468, op. 9, d. 913, l. 179.

46 Sherstova, *Etnopoliticheskaia istoriia*, 150.

47 The order stated that "beyond this border no peasant settlements hindering the Kalmyks shall be established without permission of those Kalmyks." N. Sinel'nikov, "Gornii Altai," *Voprosy kolonizatsii* 3 (1908): 274.

48 M. Abyshkin, "Iz Gornago Altaia," *Pravoslavnyi blagovestnik* 3, no. 20 (1905): 163–4.

49 *Ulala – Oirot-Tura – Gorno-Altaisk: stranitsy istorii*, comp. V.I. Edokov and A.V. Edokov (Gorno-Altaisk, 1997), 25–6.

50 RGIA, f. 468, op. 9, d. 911, ll. 303–4.

51 L.M. Dameshek, *Iasachnaia politika tsarizma v Sibiri v XIX–nachale XX veka* (Irkutsk, 1983), 132.

52 For more about the 1822 statute and detailed explanation of its articles, see Marc Raeff, *Siberia and the Reforms of 1822* (Seattle, 1956), 113–28; Slezkine, *Arctic Mirrors*, 83–8.

53 *Polnoe sobranie zakonov Rossiiskoi imperii*, 1833, v. 3–4, 358. For more on the evolution of the definition of *inorodtsy*, see John W. Slocum, "Who, and when, were the inorodtsy? The evolution of the category of 'aliens' in imperial Russia," *Russian Review* 57, no. 2 (1998): 173–91.

54 *Natsional'naia politika*, 146.

55 Some Russian researchers assert that the Speranskii statute was "modern" legislation driven by Enlightenment ideas, whereas others argue that it was a "conservative" document that sought to preserve old tribal systems for the purposes of tribute collecting. For more on this historiographical debate, see A.Iu. Konev, *Korennie narody Severo-zapadnoi Sibiri v administrativnoi sisteme Rossiiskoi imperii (XVIII–nachalo XX v. v.)* (Moscow, 1995), 23–4.

56 For the text of the law, see *Natsional'naia politika*, 229–66.
57 I.N. Smirnov, an observer who raised the banner of Russificaton at the end of the nineteenth century, stressed with disgust that "policy toward the *inorodsty* in the eighteenth and nineteenth centuries remained the same as it had been practiced by the first Russian princes: turning the *inorodsty* into tribute payers." I.N. Smirnov, "Obrusenie inorodtsev i zadachi obrusitel'noi politiki," *Istoricheskii viestnik* 47 (1892): 761. Incidentally, elements of the "archaic" attitude could be found in relations toward the rest of the Siberian population. For example, the reforms of the Russian peasantry (*volost* self-government) started in European Russia in the 1860s but did not reach Siberia until the turn of the 1880s.
58 V.I. Vagin, *Istoricheskie svedeniia o deiatel'nosti grafa M. M. Speranskago v Sibiri* (St Petersburg, 1872), v. 1, 335.
59 Sherstova, *Etnopoliticheskaia istoriia*, 240.
60 RGIA, f. 468, op. 9, d. 913, l. 137.
61 N.M. Iadrintsev, *Sibir' kak kolonia* (St Petersburg, 1882), 111.
62 *Belovod'e* was the utopian land of plenty, which preliterate peasant culture usually associated with a free and unsupervised agricultural paradise or simply with good fertile lands. For the Old Believers it also meant the land of free worship. *Biblioteka dlia Chteniia*, a popular nineteenth-century literary periodical, noted that *Belovod'e* meant "the land plentiful in all life necessities and convenient for settlement." Mamyshev, "Altai," *Biblioteka dlia Chteniia* 129 (1855): 37. There is a large literature on *Belovod'e*, especially in pre-1917 Russia. For the most recent assessment of such peasant dreams and stories, see David Moon, *Russian Peasants and Tsarist Legislation on the Eve of Reform: Interaction Between Peasants and Officialdom, 1825–1855* (London, 1992), 23–61.
63 TsKhAD, f. 2, op. 10, d. 4, l. 592.
64 Spasskii, *Noveishia uchenia*, 87.
65 *Puteshestvie po Altaiskim goram*, 119.
66 One of the last *Belovod'e* "flights" was initiated by the "rock people" in 1888. It might be assumed that one of the reasons for this "flight" was the abolishment of their "alien" status.
67 TsKhAD, f. 2, op. 10, d. 4, l. 597–8.
68 Belosliudov, "K istorii Belovodia," 15; and Chistov, *Russkie narodnye*, 276.
69 For an insightful analysis of these ambivalent assessments, see Sunderland, "The 'colonization question'." Compare also with Jeff Sahadeo in this volume.
70 Sunderland, "The 'colonization question'," 219.
71 Spasskii, *Noveishia uchenia*, 100.
72 *Puteshestvie po Altaiskim goram*, 121.
73 Ibid., 122.
74 G. Gelmersen, "Teletskoe ozero i Teleuty vostochnago Altaia," *Gornii zhurnal* 2 (1840), 244.
75 It was the legendary physical stamina of the "rock" women that drove Iadrintsev to exclaim that "the inner Altai can be compared with the kingdom of the Amazons." N. Iadrintsev, "Poezdka po Zapadnoi Sibiri v Gornii Altai," *Zapiski Zapadno-Sibirskago otdelenia Russkago Imperatorskago geograficheskago obshchestva* 2 (1880): 101; see also another of his works with similar assessments: idem, "Sibirskaia Shveitsariia," *Russkoe bogatstvo* 8 (1880): 66.
76 Potanin, "Polgoda na Altae," *Russkoe slovo* 9 (1859): 101.
77 Ibid.
78 A.V. Anokhin, "Burkhanizm v Zapadnom Altae," *Sibirskie ogni* 5 (1927): 162.
79 Mark Bassin reminds us that such expansionist enthusiasm was quite common for nineteenth-century Russian democratically oriented intellectuals. Mark Bassin, *Imperial Visions: Nationalist Imagination and Geographical Expansion in the Russian Far East, 1840–1865* (Cambridge, 1999), 13.

80 A. Belosliudov, "K istorii Belovodia," 25.

81 Ibid., 62.

82 Iadrintsev, "Poezdka po Zapadnoi Sibiri," 98.

83 Iadrintsev, *Sibir' kak kolonia*, 141; idem, "Sibirskaia Shveistaria.," 62. This idea of the Altai as the testing ground for the entire Siberian colonization process, with all its nationalist implications, was in a grotesque manner reflected in Leonid Bliummer's 1885 novel on the Altai. Bliummer noted that the Altai "emanates wild pristine charm and primitive pure beauty" and in future might replace the grandeur of the "Teutonic tribe" as the latter had replaced the Roman people. Leonid Bliummer, *Na Altae* (Novokuznetsk, 1993), 136–7. All this was actually a replay of the same "imperial visions" of the Russian educated public, which Bassin has discussed as applied to the Amur area in his *Imperial Visions*.

84 For an example of such views, see L.N. Mukaeva, "Nekotorie cherty sotsial'no-psikhologicheskogo i kulturologicheskogo tipa Russkogo naseleniia gornogo Altaia v dorevolutsionnoe vremia," *Problemy izucheniia kulturno-istoricheskogo nasledia Altaia*, ed. Elin (Gorno-Altaisk, 1994), 104.

85 G. Grebenshchikov, "Altaiskaia Rus'," in *Altaiskii Al'manakh*, ed. idem (St Petersburg, 1914), 13, 28, 37.

86 Nathaniel Knight, "Science, empire, and nationality: ethnography in the Russian Geographical Society, 1845–1855," in *Imperial Russia: New Histories for the Empire*, eds Jane Burbank and David L. Ransel (Bloomington, 1998), 132–3.

87 And, in some respects, I would like to add, well beyond 1917, which one can see in the existence of the "Stalinist *soslovnost'*" practice of ascribing class and nationality status categories. Although Terry Martin defines this practice as an "unintended neo-traditionalist outcome," which originated from "extreme Soviet statism," in my view, this points precisely to what he says it was not, the "persistence of traditional values." Terry Martin, "Modernization or neo-traditionalism? Ascribed nationality and Soviet primordialism," in *Russian Modernity: Politics, Knowledge, Practices*, eds David L. Hoffman and Yanni Kotsonis (London, 2000), 175.

88 James Forsyth, *A History of the Peoples of Siberia: Russia's North Asian Colony, 1581–1990* (Cambridge, 1992).

89 Another peculiar example of an estate category can be found in Russian America (Alaska) between 1790s and 1867. Driven by a desire to increase the meager Russian presence in this overseas possession, the government singled out Alaskan natives and mixed-bloods, who received elementary education and belonged to the Orthodox faith, into a special creole category (not to be confused, of course, with Creoles in the Americas). Defined by the government as a separate estate, it was never thought of as a racial or ethnic group. Creoles were endowed with particular hereditary privileges such as free elementary education, and exemption from taxation and military service. In exchange, these subjects of the empire were to perform obligatory 15-year service for Russian-American Company, the semi-governmental monopoly that controlled Alaska. Lydia T. Black, *Russians in Alaska, 1732–1867* (Fairbanks, 2004), 209–20.

90 It is notable that in the 1880s and 1890s, in southwestern Siberia, instead of using a common expression "to buy land," peasant settlers usually said "to buy a plowed field," or "to buy a forest plot." T.P. Prudnikova, "Vlianie idei uravnitel'nosti na obshchinnie poriadki poreformennoi sibirskoi derevni (60–90-e g. g. XIX v.)," in *Krestianskaia obshchina v Sibiri XVIII–nachala XX v.*, ed. L.M. Goriushkin (Novosibirsk, 1977), 202.

91 Reading Sunderland's detailed analysis of educated Russia's ambivalent visions of peasant settlers (Sunderland, "The 'colonization question'," 226–7), I could not resist the temptation to extend the words he uses for the description of peasants as ambiguous colonizers to the equally ambiguous borderland policies in the late nineteenth century. Very much as her peasant subjects, the "empire of peasants" acted as a "problematic representative of Russianness and 'civilization' on the frontier."

6 Resettling people, unsettling the empire

Migration and the challenge of governance, 1861–1917

Charles Steinwedel

In its lead story on 21 August 1910, *Russkie vedomosti* noted with surprise that Chairman of the Council of Ministers Petr Stolypin had "completely unexpectedly" departed for areas of resettlement in Siberia and the Steppe region. Since Stolypin's traveling companion, Aleksandr Krivoshein, the head of the Main Administration of Land Organization and Agriculture, had only just returned from Siberia, his sudden departure with Stolypin also came as a shock.[1] *Russkie vedomosti* suggested that the two had gone to address the imminent collapse of the state's colonization policy and hoped that they would give up on their goal of large-scale resettlement to Siberia. These desires were greatly disappointed. Stolypin and Krivoshein spent about one month in Siberia.[2] Upon their return, Stolypin wrote to Nicholas II that his "general impression [wa]s more than comforting ... Siberia grows fantastically (*skazochno*)." A "mixed stream of wealthy and poor, strong and weak, registered and unauthorized settlers – in general, a wonderful and powerful colonizing element" flowed from Russia to Siberia.[3]

The commitment of the two influential tsarist administrators to Siberian colonization tells much about both them and the role of migration in the empire's future. The movement of people to Siberia, most frequently resettlement (*pereselenie*) or colonization (*kolonizatsiia*), was a powerful force for social transformation in late imperial Russia.[4] In the last two decades of the tsarist regime, 5 million people migrated within the Russian empire.[5] The Resettlement Administration (*Pereselencheskoe Upravlenie*), subordinate to Krivoshein's ministry, had a vast jurisdiction. Stolypin and Krivoshein sought to use their great influence to attack the ideas that resettlement should be controlled and to de-emphasize the use of estate (*soslovie*) principles and nationality as criteria for building Russian influence in the empire's east – notions that had been central to state policy before 1905.[6] Instead, the two men sought to make resettlement easier, more universal, and based on the ownership of private property in land.

More broadly, Siberia provided an expansive field of action on which Stolypin and Krivoshein would attempt to realize their visions of what the empire should be. The two men's trip to Siberia provided an opportunity for a particularly clear statement of their understanding of the state's relationship to the population. Rather than the nineteenth-century model of the tutelary or police state, which assumed that the interests of the state were identical with those of the population and thus that the population's interests could be prescribed through state oversight, or *opeka*, Stolypin and Krivoshein articulated with clarity unprecedented for men of their authority that the interests of the population could not simply be identified with those of the state. The strongest state must instead base itself on the fullest expression of the people's "forces and capabilities."[7] Rather than regulating life through police power and external compulsion, the state should seek to inculcate social self-discipline and to bring about positive support from the population.[8] State officials like Stolypin and Krivoshein believed they could achieve this aim through the use of new techniques such as collecting information on and shaping popular attitudes, and developing private property.[9] The popular energy manifest in Siberian migration excited these two tsarist leaders and they were tantalized by the potential power of a state that could capture such energy. Yet migration also showed them the potential dangers to the tsarist state if it failed to do so.

Resettlement policy to 1905

A brief review of settlement policy establishes the context for the new governmental view of populations in the early twentieth century. Although migration policy is familiar in its outlines, scholarly treatments of it have tended to focus on how open or restrictive policies were and how they affected the peasantry and the agrarian question.[10] Without a doubt, these issues were central to discussions of settlement but do not exhaust the implications of migration policy.[11] Before 1905, migration policy stressed state control of resettlement, the need to reproduce estate hierarchies on the periphery, and the growing importance of nationality as a category for shaping the empire's population.

State officials in the nineteenth century considered control of movement essential for a number of reasons. For one, each subject's place in the social order – his or her estate status (*soslovie*) and religious confession (*veroispovedanie*) – had a concrete geographical location. Estate institutions were designed to fix lower social orders to particular places in order to extract taxes and military service from them.[12] Nobles belonged to particular noble assemblies. Local priests, mullahs, rabbis, or pastors kept birth records, the keys to civil status (property rights, inheritance, etc.). Second, the ability to choose one's place of residence itself constituted, in part, the hierarchy of privilege: nobles could choose their places of residence while members of lower orders could not. Third, officials believed that only through state regulation could officials match people and land in the most useful and rational manner, maximizing social welfare and state utility.[13]

The emancipation of the peasants in 1861 did not fundamentally alter the tsarist administration's determination to control movement. As emancipation ended serf bondage to landowners, the lower orders remained tightly tied to estate institutions, and emancipation legislation made no provisions for resettlement.[14] Authorities in St Petersburg feared that recognizing rights to movement would lead to large-scale, uncontrolled migrations that would disturb the social order and rural economy of central Russia. Decrees in 1871 and 1881 permitted settlement of certain peasants, mostly poor, to particular areas, but permission to migrate remained quite difficult to obtain.[15] Officials did not agree on all aspects of migration policy – some argued for more migration, some for less. But all officials agreed, and had long done so, that the government ought to direct all aspects of the migration process, from approval of those who were to migrate to the selection of places to which they would move.[16] All those discovered to have migrated without permission were subject to forcible return to their former homes.[17]

To be sure, the tsarist administration's ambitions for control of migration far exceeded its ability to do so. The small scale of official migration, from 9,000 families in 1887 to 7,600 in 1890, does not provide an accurate measure of migration in general. Most migration took place outside the state's knowledge and control. Such illegal migration accounted for as much as 60 to 85 percent of all migration in the late nineteenth century.[18] Different levels of the government had different interests, too. In contrast to central authorities, local governors and elites in comparatively sparsely settled border regions often welcomed migrants. The flow of rural laborers from central regions would increase the land's productivity and local elites' wealth. The region just west of Siberia, Bashkiria, for example, was an important destination for migrants in the 1860s and 1870s, before Siberian migration took off.[19] Orenburg Governor-General Nikolai Kryzhanovskii regularly appealed to St Petersburg to permit increased migration to the region,[20] while arguing that more ought to be done to integrate migrants into the political order.[21] The local administration's reach for new migrants considerably exceeded its grasp – its ability to situate them in the social order. Nonetheless, local officials' desires for new migrants and the state's lack of ability to control the actual flow of migrants did not alter central officials' views that the state ought to direct the movement of settlers for their own good and that of the state.

Official suspicion of migration decreased in the 1890s. With the construction of the Trans-Siberian Railway, more officials came to see the benefits of developing Siberia and perhaps reducing the relatively high ratio of people to land in parts of European Russia. The men most responsible for directing the Trans-Siberian Railway, Sergei Witte and Anatolii Kulomzin, believed that resettlement had a civilizing mission and would extend state control over Siberian territory.[22] The construction of the railway certainly made moving to Siberia much easier. According to official statistics, peasant migration to Siberia increased from roughly 260,000 between 1885 and 1893 to 1,115,000 between 1893 and 1902.[23] A Resettlement Administration was established within the Ministry of Internal Affairs to oversee the growing number of settlers.[24]

In the 1890s, Minister of Finance Witte's increasing openness to peasant resettlement often met opposition from the Ministry of Internal Affairs, which feared that excessive, uncontrolled migration threatened political stability and the economic interests of conservative landholders. Peasant uprisings in 1902 made clear to many hitherto reluctant officials the need to increase peasant migration as a way to relieve land hunger in European Russia, but differences of opinion still existed between Witte and his rival, Minister of Internal Affairs V.K. Plehve. Both favored resettlement and both certainly sought to advance state interests through it.

Plehve and his colleagues, however, saw a much greater role for the state in resettlement. The state should control from where migrants should be drawn, who should migrate, and where migrants should settle. Plehve and the head of the Resettlement Administration, Krivoshein, argued that settlement to Siberia had not corresponded to the government's interests. Settlement, to them, ought to move poorer peasants from overcrowded regions in central Russia to less densely settled regions. Migration should also increase the empire's presence in politically sensitive regions such as the Caucasus, Turkestan, and Far Eastern borderland areas. Instead, in the past decade, settlers had come from regions with plenty of land and from the Western borderlands, weakening the Russian position there.[25] To correct this situation, Plehve argued for the division of settlers into two categories, privileged and voluntary. Poor peasants who left overcrowded areas of European Russia and those leaving for areas perceived to need settlers would receive free transportation, state loans, military deferments, and tax exemptions. Those who did not meet these conditions would be considered voluntary. They would not be subject to compulsory relocation to their former homes, but would not receive the generous support of the state promised to settlers fulfilling state plans.

After the tsar dismissed Witte from his post in 1903, Plehve's emphasis on state control of migration became dominant. The Temporary Rules on resettlement, published on 6 June 1904, stipulated that the ministers of internal affairs, finance, agriculture, and, in some cases the minister of war should designate certain areas as overcrowded and others as desirable colonization targets. Privileged settlers bound for designated areas received substantial advantages over all others.[26] State interests dictated patterns of resettlement, not the goals of the tsar's subjects. Resettlement's purpose, as it had been before, was to direct particular people to particular places in a manner officials considered rational.[27]

Estate status

By its very nature, the migration of the tsar's subjects had powerful implications for the empire's system of estates. Migration complicated the maintenance of estate ties at both the point of departure and of arrival and the administration of peasants in general, which was one reason why some officials in the Ministry of Internal Affairs resisted it. For members of lower orders, severing connections with their communes or receiving permission to migrate could be difficult, since those remaining would have to assume a larger burden of taxes and other obligations. If peasants were not organized into communes and rural administrations promptly upon arrival, chaos could result.[28]

The difficulties of organizing rural life in comparatively more expansive and under-administered Siberia were even greater. Any attempt to extend the social system of central Russia to Siberia or Central Asia had to contend with the fact that the empire's most privileged estate, the nobility, was largely absent.

Throughout Russian history, the tsar's grants of land to noble servitors, sometimes as their personal property, or the nobles' purchase of land had been an important means of expanding Russian influence.[29] The government's ability to foster noble landownership ended at the Ural Mountains, however, though not because of an absence of effort. Beginning in the 1820s, the state on several occasions offered grants of land as private property to nobles or elite servitors. Such policies yielded meager results. An 1868 offer of land to retired officials and officers met with a bit more, but still modest, success.[30] Similar policies applied by Governor-General Kryzhanovskii in Ufa and Orenburg provinces in the 1870s largely discredited the entire system of land grants. Kryzhanovskii sought to improve the position of "educated landowners" in Bashkiria, and to draw new men "who would be recognized as useful."[31] On the advice of Kryzhanovskii, in June 1871 the central government enacted legislation that permitted retired officials and officers to purchase state land.[32] Rather than giving "excess" Bashkir lands to *pripushchenniki* (those allowed into Bashkir communes) with little land as law stipulated, provincial administrators gave land to noblemen, local officials, and privileged or non-privileged newcomers or sold it at extremely low prices.[33] Kryzhanovskii's efforts to strengthen the ranks of "educated landowners" initiated a land fever in Bashkiria and a "chaotic condition of landownership."[34] By 1880, the stripping of Bashkir lands for privileged servitors became a scandal that reached St Petersburg, eventually resulting in the removal of both Kryzhanovskii and Minister of Internal Affairs P.A. Valuev from office.[35] In the wake of the scandal, the state sought to exclude nobles and elite servitors from the resettlement process in Central Asia. In 1886 legislation permitted only "Russian subjects from the number of rural residents of Christian religious confessions" (*russkie poddannye iz chisla sel'skikh obyvatelei khristianskikh veroispovedanii*) to settle in Turkestan.[36]

The final effort to introduce large-scale noble landownership to Siberia took place in 1901. The tsar approved legislation allowing the sale outright or long-term rental with right of purchase of parcels as large as 3,000 *desiatin* "exclusively to persons of noble origins, who, according to their managerial reliability, are desirable in the government's perspective as landowners in Siberia."[37] A decade later, however, this initiative had largely failed. Land in Siberia remained almost exclusively in the government's possession.[38] The large, primarily noble landowners upon whom the state counted to serve in zemstvos and provide social and cultural leadership in European Russia were lacking in Siberia. Migration therefore created a society in Siberia unlike that of central regions despite the importance state officials gave to noble landownership.

Nationality

By the 1860s, categorizing subjects by estate status and religious confession proved inadequate to the state's engineering of settlement. In order to justify greater support for migration, for instance, Kryzhanovskii had argued that migration would bring greater "Russian" influence to the region in which non-Russian-speaking, Turkic, and animist peoples predominated.[39] Kryzhanovskii did not elaborate on this Russian/non-Russian divide. Non-Russians included primarily Bashkirs, but also other Muslim or recently pagan peoples. The "Russian element" he sought to draw to the region consisted of anyone from central or western Russia. The essence of the perceived boundary between the two groups was their relative backwardness or enlightenment. The "Russian element" would introduce more advanced agricultural practices, and would better provide labor for mines and factories in the Ural Mountains.[40] Other officials and writers associated different ethnic groups with different levels of agricultural development: Ukrainians were known as good farmers, Latvians excelled at milk production, and all were considered superior to the Bashkirs. Migration highlighted cultural and economic differences not accounted for by estate or religion. Latvian and Bashkir rural residents may have all belonged to similar estates, for example, but their perceived agricultural potential differed greatly. Similarly, Ukrainians and Russians might both be Orthodox, but differed substantially in their farming techniques. The management of migration required new ways to differentiate the tsar's subjects.

By the mid-1890s, resettlement administrators began extensive study of migrants to both Bashkiria and Siberia. Such study provided a vehicle for the working out of new ways of understanding the tsar's subjects. Understandably, officials primarily sought information regarding agricultural practices necessary to match settlers to the land. Inquiries regarding agricultural practices comprised most of the 59 questions asked of each migrant family. But the questionnaire included a question regarding nationality (*natsional'nost'*), too.[41] Resettlement administrators completed a similar, but shorter questionnaire on parties of settlers moving through Bashkiria's Ufa province in 1894 as well. This form categorized settlers by nationality, but omitted religious confession.[42] Nationality lacked systematic explication and publicity.[43] Nonetheless, categorization by nationality was novel at a time when the All-Empire Census of 1897 omitted the question. Military statisticians had begun to map the empire's population according to nationality, and colonial administrators in Central Asia had developed ethnic categorization of local populations, but the elaboration of nationality on the level of individuals or families was rarely undertaken by local administrators in European Russia.[44] By identifying the nationality of migrants, officials did more than attempt to engineer the Eastern borderlands to become more like European Russia. Since persons in European Russia were not typically categorized by nationality, the state was creating a nationally-identified population largely absent in the center.

The Temporary Rules of 1904 regarding migration centered on estate institutions and nationality. The rules authorized government loans to the communes in European Russia of peasants who intended to migrate. In this way, commune members could afford to compensate migrants for lands they left behind. Previously, the prospective migrant's obligations to the commune had substantially impeded legal migration. At the same time the Temporary Rules elevated the importance of nationality or Russianness. The law specified that only "persons of native Russian origins and of the Orthodox faith (*korennogo russkogo proiskhozhdeniia Pravoslavnogo ispovedaniia*)" or of approved "dissident sects" were permitted to resettle in Central Asia and the Caucasus.[45] What Kryzhanovskii and others earlier had described only generally as a "Russian element" received legal recognition. Before the rules fully took effect, however, events more urgent than migration intervened. The outbreak of the Russo-Japanese War in 1904 and the need to move soldiers and military supplies east brought a temporary halt to resettlement activity. Before the war ended, the empire was in revolution. When resettlement returned to the agenda, the political and social context had changed drastically.

Revolution and freedom of migration

The Revolution of 1905 and the near-collapse of the tsarist system that it brought about changed policy toward resettlement just as it did most other state endeavors. Sergei Witte, who had argued against Plehve for more freedom of movement before the latter's death in 1904, became Prime Minister. In March 1906, the tsar signed legislation that transformed the Temporary Rules of 1904. He granted all peasants the right to receive state benefits for migration, not just those whose resettlement fulfilled state objectives – those poorer peasants in certain provinces who were bound for officially approved, strategically important destinations – as had previously been the case.[46] The 1906 legislation provided the legal basis for migration in succeeding years and ended, for a time, the state's attempts to control migration through compulsion and through the forcible return of illegal migrants to their homes. State officials would not remain indifferent to resettlement, nor was free movement accepted by all. The state would continue to study migrants and the land that they settled, developing particular parcels of land for settlement. Funding for support of migration varied over time. Nonetheless, the law declared that resettlement administrators would no longer seek to control who migrated and to where. Administrators gave up their *opeka*, or tutelage of migrants. They no longer sought to achieve a specified balance of people and territory through the exercise of police authority. The legislation of 1906 provided the terms for migration to Siberia of a size unprecedented in Russian history.

Stolypin, Krivoshein, and the settlement of Siberia

The change in policy toward migration was in part simply a reaction to the revolution. As peasants burned manor houses, those who still saw the commune as a bastion of stability in the countryside soon supported migration as a means to ease land hunger and, if nothing else, place potentially trouble-making peasants far from central Russia. Yet a new approach to governance also motivated some officials to change their views. As the state regained control after 1905, the contours of a new political system became apparent. The October Manifesto offered the tsar's subjects basic freedoms and called for the creation of the State Duma. Some of these rights were codified in the Fundamental Laws of April 1906, which gave the empire a sort of constitution. Behind these reforms lay the notion that the regime could no longer rely upon the passive compliance of the population – its fulfillment of its obligations under the estate hierarchy. Rather, the revolution initiated a process of change in which influential officials viewed the population as active subjects whose attitude toward the government was crucial to the regime's survival. Minister of Internal Affairs Stolypin, appointed in April 1906, was one of the most prominent state officials who, in addition to suppressing opposition vigorously and often violently, sought also to cultivate support for the regime in new ways. One of Stolypin's contemporaries observed that Stolypin "realized ... that the stability of the state and internal order depended upon the attitude of the people toward the government."[47] Another argued that Stolypin was "a new phenomenon in our state life," because he sought "support not only in the strength of authority (*sila vlasti*) but in the opinion of the country."[48] The events of 1905 demonstrated to Stolypin that the very stability of the state depended upon the support of the people, although not necessarily of all the people and not only through popular sovereignty and elections.

In 1910, the implications of these views for resettlement policy emerged in full force when Stolypin and Krivoshein traveled to the Asian part of the empire – what they called Russia's only colony – to respond to setbacks in the migration process.[49] The immediate motivation for their trip was to investigate the declining flow of migrants to Siberia and what Stolypin and Krivoshein believed to be a reversion to excessive bureaucratic control. As the number of migrants soared in 1907, the Council of Ministers restored restrictions on migration. The head of the Resettlement Administration was allowed to halt the granting of settlement permits in cases where land was lacking or for whatever reason he deemed necessary. The Administration prohibited most scouting and began to allot parcels of land on the steppe to settlers from specific regions of European Russia. Migrants were selected by land-settlement commissions. These measures, in addition to a bad harvest in Siberia and two consecutive good harvests in European Russia, had slowed the volume of migration.[50]

Upon returning from Siberia, Stolypin's and Krivoshein's support for free resettlement was thorough and unconditional. They considered the decline in resettlement in large part the result of the inadequacies of what they called "organized" resettlement, and they intended their trip and the *Notes* (*zapiski*) it produced to challenge the idea of controlled settlement. In their opinion resettlement was still too regulated. A superficial "putting in order" (*uporiadochineniia*) and a "systematic character (*planomernost'*)" were too often demanded of settlement, when these were not appropriate to such a "complicated phenomenon of popular (*narodnoi*) life," they wrote. Resettlement and scouting for land should be as free as possible, with information on available lands widely disbursed and assistance given to people based on how difficult it was to set up in a particular area.[51]

Free settlement meant more than simply changes in policy on settlement. It required the introduction of "new economic principles" to Siberia. Stolypin and Krivoshein believed most of all in the need to establish Siberia's land as private property. Since nearly all land in Siberia belonged to the state or to Cossack units, buying and selling land legally could not take place with the exception of "Cossack officers' allotments." The sale of state land to peasants had been permitted in European Russia since 1906, and Stolypin argued that similar laws ought to be extended to Siberia. The sale of land would permit the distribution of land more efficiently to settlers. Stolypin and Krivoshein did not use the word "market" to describe the means of distributing land, but declared that private property in land would concentrate the population in "the natural means for the transfer of pieces of land into new hands by way of private financial transactions of rental and buying and selling." The most valuable pieces would command higher prices, while people with fewer resources would have an incentive to go to the less valuable, less accessible regions.[52] Second, Stolypin and Krivoshein believed that residents of Siberia should be allowed to consolidate their lands as private property in Siberia.[53] Finally, the establishment of private property, both of small scale and larger, more capital-intensive enterprises, would eventually attract educated men who would provide a basis for zemstvo institutions. Stolypin and Krivoshein called the lack of zemstvos the most major "deficiency" in Siberia's administration.

Figure 6.1 P.A. Stolypin and A.V. Krivoshein in Slavgorod, autumn 1910. From *Aziatskaia Rossiia*, v. 1 (St Petersburg, 1914), 488.

Stolypin and Krivoshein took essentially the same positions regarding European Russia. What made both men enthusiastic about Siberia was the fact that land sales and consolidations were *already* taking place. Even without legal sanction, land was in fact was being sold. In the region around Tomsk, slightly more scouts had purchased land for cash than had received land in allotments from the state. Without a legal basis, private teams of surveyors had begun the internal surveying of Siberian peasant communes as a prelude to separation and consolidation of the land as private property. Stolypin's and Krivoshein's reaction to such widespread circumvention of the law is striking. They seemed thoroughly undisturbed by these legal violations, considering them evidence that "life ... creates new forms of single proprietorship of land in accordance with the situation in fact, not considering the sluggishness in its legal justification."[54] They even considered the presence of large numbers of unregistered settlers in particular areas a sign of that area's good economic prospects. Officials could address problems caused by such concentrations of migrants by adjusting settlers' loans better to local conditions and by allowing private property. The market would then address these problems as much as the state would.[55]

The vigor with which Siberian settlers took to the reforms seemed to give the reforms added justification in the minds of Stolypin and Krivoshein. They used their commentary on Siberian migration to state their economic philosophy more broadly than they had when promoting reform in central Russia. There Stolypin's agrarian reforms were justified as necessary to prevent rebellions by undermining the commune and giving the autocracy a base in small proprietors. Peasant ownership of land would give peasants greater respect for the law that protected their property. It would reward peasant labor and promote more efficient, rational cultivation of the land, making small landowners the "nucleus on which rests the stability of the state."[56] Stolypin's "wager on the strong" meant an effort to reward the "energetic and enterprising" peasants with the ability to change their work and adopt "modern, rational methods of farming."[57] Stolypin and Krivoshein articulated in their report on Siberia a fundamentally different relationship between the state and the people from what they had proposed before. Unlike their cameralist predecessors, Stolypin and Krivoshein did not presuppose subjects whose economic interests could be identified with the state, and who would serve official designs for political stability. Rather, the strength and well-being of the state flowed from the population seeking to satisfy its own interests. Stolypin and Krivoshein considered the prosperity of individual migrants as essential to colonization:

> people, living people, ... go to Siberia, destroying the old life and building the new, each individually not in order, of course, to alleviate agrarian difficulties and to serve as a bulwark of the Russian state principle (*oplotom russkoi gosudarstvennosti*) in the borderlands. Their goal is to live more prosperously, to establish themselves better in Siberia than they lived in the native land.[58]

State intervention in support of resettlement had to keep this fact in mind. Stolypin and Krivoshein justified their attacks on the preservation of a state land fund since such lands amounted to "dead wealth" that should become private property. They considered this indicative of a new attitude toward state power:

> A certitude characteristic of all contemporary cultured countries grows strong in the public consciousness (*v obshchestvennom soznanii*): the primary wealth and power of a state [lies] not in the treasury and in state property, but in the wealthiest and strongest population.[59]

The reference to the "wealthiest and strongest" indicates not simply Stolypin's "wager on the strong" peasants, but the centrality of the population's strength as a whole. Finally, Stolypin and Krivoshein cited British liberal thinker John Stuart Mill in support of their conclusion that colonization benefited the old country as well as the new. To Mill, colonization was "the most profitable of all commercial matters."[60]

The conviction expressed by the two men in their *Notes* indicates a consideration of Western economic models considerably deeper than is often acknowledged.[61] They articulated a view of the collective interest as flowing from the actions of individuals pursuing their own self-interest rather than resulting from the decisions of state officials.[62] To say that Stolypin did not typically approve of individuals' disregard for state laws would be an understatement. Thus his acceptance and even endorsement of illegal acts to survey and convert Siberian land to private property demonstrates a surprising commitment to the popular will rather than to the observance of laws made in St Petersburg. The vast undergoverned spaces of Siberia presented them with a new vision of the empire's future once the politics of European Russia were at a distance.

The view of the economy as composed of individual subjects evident in Stolypin's and Krivoshein's *Notes* had important implications for their views of the importance of estate status and nationality. The view they articulated had much in common with the linkages, demonstrated above, between the decreased use of estate status to organize society, and the simultaneous increasingly common application of national criteria to the population observed before the 1905 Revolution. They argued that the 1901 legislation favoring noble landownership should be abandoned. They discussed the ethnic complexity of Siberian migration in a manner in keeping with developments in national categorization before 1905. Stolypin and Krivoshein expressed an interest in colonization as a means to spread Russian influence in a manner similar to Kryzhanovskii's 50 years earlier.[63] Stolypin and Krivoshein wrote that the influx of "vital Russian labor power" was the "chief motive force" in an otherwise "stagnant" milieu.[64] Previous residents of the region, including Siberian old residents and nomads, had to adapt themselves to the new conditions created by Russian migration.[65]

Stolypin's and Krivoshein's view of nationality, however, reflected the often underappreciated complexity of these concepts in late imperial Russia. The men operated with two definitions of nation in describing settlement of Siberia. One focused on Russian nationality as having particular cultural content – Russian ethnicity and the Orthodox faith. When reporting to Tsar Nicholas II, Stolypin emphasized the Russianness of settlers. He claimed the settler "element" was "properly monarchical, with a proper, pure, Russian worldview."[66] Stolypin and Krivoshein identified settlers as Russian and as fulfilling the Russian state interest by strengthening the empire's border with China. More often when describing Siberian resettlement, however, they stressed a sense of national/imperial identity based on geography, loyalty, and property rather than one based on Orthodoxy and Russian ethnicity.[67] What Stolypin and Krivoshein called the "gradual joining (*priobshcheniia*) of new spaces" in Siberia, "to Russian culture" was a phenomenon of "popular creative forces (*tvorcheskikh narodnikh sil*)" expressed by ethnically and religiously diverse settlers and forged in the experience of migration.[68] Stolypin and Krivoshein described the settlers to one area (the Kulundinskaia steppe) – where the "pulse of Russian life" now beat – as mostly "Ukrainians" and partly "German-Mennonites," whose purely Russian worldview could be questioned.[69] Stolypin and Krivoshein described the conditions of resettlement as favoring non-Russians and non-Orthodox. Settlers were forced to live "by bread alone," in constant battle with nature. Thrown together with other new settlers "without ties of common blood, without a common past," the settlers lived only for economic interests and without churches, markets, or cities. In difficult conditions, people of "stern temperaments, stubborn, and undemanding" such as "Latvians and religious sectarians" fared better than settlers from central Russia unaccustomed to the "wildness of new conditions."[70]

Stolypin and Krivoshein provided justification for the effort to track carefully the ethnicity of settlers, but not in order to move only ethnic Russians and Orthodox to Siberia. They stated that settlement would help the Russian empire fulfill its historic mission to protect territory occupied by "European tribes" from "Asiatic races" intent on spilling over onto it.[71] By contrast, Stolypin and Krivoshein wrote relatively little about Russian Orthodox religious and national concerns, perhaps 2 or 3 pages out of 130 in all. They had no fear that a lack of churches and schools would lead to the "moral running wild" of the settlers. The confrontation with nature made settlers serious. They achieved a sense of moral purpose and self-discipline in the absence of religious and educational institutions. Important differences thus existed between Stolypin's and Krivoshein's views and those of Nicholas II and others who identified the nation with the Orthodox tsar and Russian ethnicity.

By contrast, property was central to Stolypin's and Krivoshein's plans. The *Notes* of Stolypin and Krivoshein was widely disseminated and became the basis for the government's initiatives. As Minister of Land Organization and Agriculture, the ministry to which the Resettlement Administration reported, Krivoshein promoted his and Stolypin's agenda. Already in 1910, Krivoshein and Stolypin proposed that settlers be able to convert their land holdings into private property. When this effort failed, the Resettlement Administration increased the budget for demarcating settler allotments so that they would be used individually rather than made part of communal land tenure. Then Krivoshein sought to restore the policy of free migration. This was achieved in March 1911, when the Council of Ministers ordered the resumption of unrestricted resettlement to Siberia.[72] After Stolypin's death in September 1911, Krivoshein pushed for a law that would set aside tracts of land for private landowners to develop "larger and more cultured" agricultural enterprises than typical migrants. Unlike previous laws in Siberia and Bashkiria, this law did not target particular kinds of people, such as those of noble origins or educated state servitors. Instead, it was simply assumed that the development of large-scale private property would have "general cultural-political importance" by providing a flow of "fresh forces, educated and industrious activists" who would improve and diversify Siberian agriculture and were essential for the proper development of zemstvo and city government institutions.[73] By 1912, hereditary nobles who cultivated land could migrate with the permission of provincial governors, and non-cultivating nobles could do so with the permission of the Ministry of Agriculture. Finally, legislation introduced in 1913 would extend to all persons regardless of estate status the same privileges granted to rural residents.[74] With respect to migration, nobles would be like everyone else.

Only a few of the proposals of Stolypin and Krivoshein with respect to Siberia became law. This resulted in part from opposition to resettlement from the left, which saw it, at best, as an attempt to deflect attention from the problems of central Russia through activity in the East, and, at worst, as an effort to establish the types of reforms in Siberia – private property, the elimination of the commune – that it opposed in Central Russia. The political middle and right appear to have been generally sympathetic to resettlement, but without great interest. Propertied landholders from European Russia concerned with the development of their own regions dominated the Third and Fourth Dumas, and they lacked enthusiasm for the expenditure of funds for Siberian development.[75] Laws and policies on resettlement became entangled in the legislative impasse that developed even before Stolypin's death in 1911.

The most widely supported initiative of Stolypin and Krivoshein, however, suggests Siberian colonization's potential importance in the empire and how colonization shifted the terms of debate used in central Russia. On 21 June 1910, the tsar signed into law a measure that prohibited the hiring of Chinese labor at state enterprises in the Far East. In a rare display of unanimity, the State Duma had approved the measure as a way to improve Russia's security.[76] Since eliminating Chinese workers necessitated finding replacements, over the next five years, a government conference worked to increase the number of Russian workers in the Far East. After only 18 months, the officials responsible claimed success in attracting workers eastward, mostly through recruitment, the provision of transportation to and from the East, and advantageous settlement in the area. The precise nature and terms used to lure workers were not given, but according to the government, as much as 40 percent of Russian labor drawn to the region remained after the 1911 work season ended. What made the workers Russian was not specified, but the very idea of workers as "first pioneers in the matter of strengthening our [Russian] influence in the Far East" is notable.[77] Workers, generally considered a suspect element in the European Russian population became, in the Far

East, a bulwark of the Russian state ready to defend the "Motherland" in case of hostilities. Migration in this case was able to unite Duma deputies, the government, and at least some laborers in ways rarely observed with respect to other issues.

Conclusions

The tsarist state's approach to the migration of the empire's subjects changed markedly in the regime's last 50 years. Under Stolypin and Krivoshein, late nineteenth-century efforts to restrict migration and keep what did occur within a tight framework of administrative regulation gave way to the promotion of large-scale migration of people who moved of their own volition and received state support in order to do so. State officials gave up on efforts to reproduce European Russia's social hierarchy, dominated by the noble estate, in favor of a more inclusive and flexible society anchored in private landownership. The identification of settlers by nationality continued to be a feature of colonization policy before and after 1905, but the promotion of specifically Russian and Orthodox settlement no longer figured prominently in state plans. Members of non-Russian and non-Russian Orthodox groups could serve the empire's cause in Siberia, in some cases even better than Russians.

The changing approach to migration both reflected and motivated a new approach to the population among influential officials in late imperial Russia. Leading state officials such as Petr Stolypin and Aleksandr Krivoshein ceased to assume that the interests of the population were identical to those of the state and could be subsumed under them. Instead, such officials began to view the popular will as an essential grounding for state institutions. Stolypin's and Krivoshein's support for private property and for consolidation of communal land into personal property meant applying to Siberia essentially the same principles that they promoted in European Russia. Yet doing so did not mean making Siberia the same as European Russia. The lack of private property in Siberia made more stark the transformation involved in its introduction. The lack of large-scale landownership and the absence of the noble estate in Asian Russia meant that similar policies there produced a different social hierarchy. Stolypin and Krivoshein used migration policy to underscore the importance to the state of the tsar's subjects pursuing their own interests rather than taking direction from state officials. Regarding the consolidation of land as private property, Stolypin and Krivoshein were even willing to tolerate illegal activity to achieve their larger goal. The fact that these two influential state bureaucrats no longer believed officials knew best how to colonize Siberia marks the most important difference from nineteenth-century precedents.

Stolypin and Krivoshein's vision of Siberia's future obviously excited them, but also gave Stolypin pause. In a letter to Nicholas II upon his return in 1910, Stolypin sought to impress upon the tsar the need to undertake the reforms proposed in his and Krivoshein's *Notes*, and to do so in short order. If not, he wrote, a "vast crudely-democratic country would be created, unconsciously and formlessly, which would soon crush European Russia."[78] The state's lack of ability to police changes in Siberia made possible "spontaneous" changes in land-holding that seem to have impressed upon Stolypin and Krivoshein the limits of state power in directing the empire's economic life. The trip to the east suggested that Siberia provided a vast arena in which to work out their conceptions of reform, one distant from the radical opposition and conservative nobles who thwarted their initiatives in St Petersburg. It also showed how the colonization of Asian Russia unsettled considerations of social hierarchy and national identity that prevailed at court and in conservative society. Stolypin and Krivoshein embraced the possibilities for change. This embrace, however, seems to have been tempered by a disturbing thought: even if their proposals all became law, the crudely democratic Siberia might crush European Russia anyway.

Notes

1   *Russkie vedomosti*, no. 192 (21 August 1910): 1.
2   They inspected resettlement points throughout western Siberia and the northern Kirghiz (Kazakh) steppe, visiting four provinces and six *uezdy* in all. They primarily followed the route of the Trans-Siberian Railway, but traveled 500 miles on horseback away from rail lines and water routes in order to evaluate resettlement in a variety of geographic conditions. P.A. Stolypin and A.V. Krivoshein, *Poezdka v sibir' i povolzhe: zapiski P. A. Stolypina i A. V. Krivosheina* (St Petersburg, 1911), 3. For a thorough analysis of the *Notes* with different emphases, see Donald Treadgold, *The Great Siberian Migration* (Princeton, 1957), 153–83.
3   P.A. Stolypin, "Iz perepiski P.A. Stolypina s Nikolaem Romanovym," *Krasnyi arkhiv* 5, no. 30 (1928): 82.
4   I will use the expressions taken from my sources, "resettlement" and "colonization," interchangeably since my sources generally do. As Willard Sunderland has shown, in late imperial usage the concepts of resettlement and colonization were closely inter- twined, often interchangeable, and often paired. "Resettlement" sometimes meant a domestic process largely related to peasant movement, whereas "colonization" connoted greater "foreignness" and could be used to stress the imperial dimension of the process. After the 1860s, officials began to use "colonization" more than they had previ- ously. The relationship between the two terms remained unclear, however. Willard Sunderland, *Taming the Wild Field: Colonization and Empire on the Russian Steppe* (Ithaca, 2004), 88, 156, 158, 194.
5   S.I. Bruk and V.M. Kabuzan, "Migratsiia naseleniia v Rossii v XVIII–nachale XX veka (chislennost', struktura, geografiia)," *Istoriia SSSR* no. 4 (1984): 51–9, cited in Willard Sunderland, "The 'colonization question': visions of colonization in late imperial Russia," *Jahrbücher für Geschichte Osteuropas* 48, no. 2 (2000): 213.
6   On the pre-1905 period, see Andrei Znamenski in this volume.
7   V.F. Deriuzhinskii, *Politseiskoe pravo: posobie dlia studentov*, 3rd edn (St Petersburg, 1911), 9–10. I thank Peter Holquist for this citation.
8   State officials did not show particular concern for the protection of individual rights through the rule of law. Thus, I would argue that those who crafted migration policy assumed the creation of subjects in a manner like liberals in the West, but did not follow Western examples of the legal protection of individuals, beyond perhaps their interest in private property. The latter distinguishes them from state officials after 1917, I would argue. Laura Engelstein analyzes discussions of currents supporting and rejecting a shift from the *Polizeistaat* that functioned "in a crudely regulatory mode" to a *Rechtstaat* that sought to disperse efforts to inculcate "social discipline" in "Combined

underdevelopment: discipline and the law in imperial and Soviet Russia," *American Historical Review* 98, no. 2 (April 1993): 338–53.

9 On the political importance of property to Stolypin and Krivoshein, see Yanni Kotsonis, *Making Peasants Backward: Agricultural Cooperatives and the Agrarian Question in Russia, 1861–1914* (London, 1999), esp. chp. 3.

10 See for example, Treadgold, *The Great Siberian Migration.*

11 I will only touch on the connections between religious confession and migration to Siberia, a subject that merits its own study. Regarding sectarian colonization of Transcaucasia, see Nicholas Breyfogle, *Heretics and Colonizers: Forging Russia's Empire in the South Caucasus* (Ithaca, 2005).

12 Peasants were responsible to their communes and their rural administrations (*volost's*). Urban residents of lower orders were connected to particular urban administrations, such as *meshchanskie* or *remeslenie upravy*. Rural peasant or urban estate administrations had to give permission for trips more than 50 miles from their members' places of residence. See Charles Steinwedel, "Making social groups, one person at a time: the identification of individuals by estate, religious confession, and ethnicity in late imperial Russia," in *Documenting Individual Identity: The Development of State Practices Since the French Revolution*, eds Jane Caplan and John Torpey (Princeton, 2001); Mervyn Matthews, *The Passport Society: Controlling Movement in Russia and the USSR* (Boulder, 1993); and A.N. Beketov, "Pasport," in *Entsiklopedicheskii slovar'*, 82 vols (St Petersburg, 1891–1904), 44 (1897): 923

13 For a thorough account of motivations for state control of movement, see Sunderland, *Taming the Wild Field.*

14 The authors of the emancipation believed that to promote or even allow migration simultaneously with emancipation might destabilize a situation already fraught with tension. They suggested that limits on resettlement be removed nine years after emancipation. By 1870, however, new political actors were in power who did not see the need for such an action. Aleksandr A. Kaufman, *Pereselenie i kolonizatsiia* (St Petersburg, 1905), 18–19.

15 Any peasant who sought to migrate legally had to endure a very complicated process of permissions reaching as high as the Ministry of Internal Affairs in St Petersburg. D.P. Samorodov, *Russkoe krest'ianskoe pereselenie v Bashkiriiu v poreformennyi period 60–90-e gg. XIX* (Sterlitamak, 1996), 143. Subsequent to the publication in 1881 of rules on resettlement, the number of families officially permitted to migrate ranged from a low of fifteen in 1881 to as many as 13,109 in 1888 before falling slightly in the next three years. Kaufman, *Pereselenie*, 31. Permission to migrate did not mean simply that a family was supposed to leave their native village and head east or south, but was granted with the idea that each family would have state-owned land on which to settle. When in 1892 the existing stock of state lands surveyed for settlement was exhausted, official settlement came to a halt. Samorodov, *Russkoe krestian'skoe pereselenie*, 99.

16 Sunderland, *Taming the Wild Field*, esp. 114–15, 128, 130, 137–9, 153,178–80, 183; and Treadgold, *The Great Siberian Migration*, 77–8.

17 New legislation in 1889 increased the amount of state support for families which migrated, but those wishing to migrate still needed to furnish "reasons meriting attention" in order to do so and permission was contingent on the availability of free allotments of state land. Treadgold, *The Great Siberian Migration*, 79; and *Polnoe sobranie zakonov Rossiiskoi imperii* [hereafter *PSZRI*], series III, v. IX, no. 6,198 (13 July 1889), 535.

18 In some areas not specified for settlement, all migration was unofficial and illegal. The estimate comes from Kaufman, *Pereselenie*, 31.

19 Bashkir land was surveyed and by law the Bashkirs themselves were allotted 30 *desiatins* of land. Peasants who had assimilated into Bashkir districts, *pripushchenniki*, were allotted 15 *desiatins*. The remainder went into a land fund which could be sold to

migrants or local landowners. P. Shramchenko, "Zemel'nyi vopros v ufimskoi gubernii," *Russkii vestnik* 158 (March 1882): 449–532.

20 Kryzhanovskii had the strong support of much of the local elite in this endeavor. Many members of the local elite had been able to obtain Bashkir land, either legally or illegally, for next to nothing. Additional labor power would enable them to take full advantage of their windfall. N.V. Remezov, *Byl' v skazochnoi strane* (Ufa, 1986); and Shramchenko, "Zemel'nyi vopros."

21 Orenburg Governor-General Kryzhanovskii reported to his superiors in 1873 that migrants formed large groups who "lived outside the law, outside any police supervision," "without established authority," and thus failed to provide taxes and recruits. GAOO, f. 6, op. 8, d. 190, l. 105, cited in Khamza F. Usmanov, *Razvitie kapitalizma v sel'skom khoziaistve Bashkirii v poreformennyi period* (Moscow, 1981), 61. New settlements appeared without permission, and continued to be difficult to police. *Vsepoddanneishii raport Ufimskago gubernatora na 1884 god*, 11; *Vsepoddanneishii raport Ufimskago gubernatora na 1886 god*, 4. Some settlements, built as far as 40 miles from established churches, were considered especially subject to the influence of Old Believers and other religious dissidents. "Iz zapisok arkhiepiskopa Nikanora," *Russkii Arkhiv* 47, no. 5 (1909): 60.

22 Steven G. Marks, "Conquering the Great East: Kulomzin, peasant resettlement, and the creation of modern Siberia," in *Rediscovering Russia in Asia: Siberia and the Russian Far East*, eds Stephen Kotkin and David Wolff (Armonk, 1995), 28–9.

23 Edward H. Judge, "Peasant resettlement and social control in late imperial Russia," in *Modernization and Revolution: Dilemmas of Progress in Late Imperial Russia: Essays in Honor of Arthur P. Mendel*, eds Edward H. Judge and James Y. Simms, Jr. (New York, 1992), 77.

24 It produced a variety of pamphlets to increase prospective migrants' knowledge of what lay ahead of them and established medical and food supply points to support settlers en route. Government support for migrants in the form of loans and other privileges increased from 20,000 to 120,000 rubles from 1890 to 1896. Treadgold, *The Great Siberian Migration*, 125.

25 Judge, "Peasant resettlement," 75–93.

26 As Edward Judge has pointed out, the central thrust of the law was control. Ibid., 89. By contrast, Treadgold emphasizes the "freedom of migration" embodied in the law. Treadgold, *The Great Siberian Migration*, 129.

27 Sunderland, "The 'colonization question'," 218.

28 Orenburg Governor-General Kryzhanovskii frequently complained of difficulties administering migrants, and the problem continued to dog his successors into the twentieth century. In 1907, groups of "voluntary" settlers proved difficult for local authorities to register. "Samovol'noe pereselenie. Kor. Iz Orenburga," *Voprosy kolonizatsii*, no. 1 (1907): 301–3.

29 On this, see also Matthew Romaniello in this volume.

30 In the 1820s, Siberian officials were offered the right to allotments of land as private property. No noticeable response to the policy was received. In the 1840s, the circle of people offered 80 *desiatin* parcels of land expanded to include poor noblemen. Again, there were no takers. Generally, such grants were aimed at older nobles and servitors close to retirement who had little interest in remaining in Siberia at the end of their service careers. I. Vvedenskii, "Chastnoe zemlevladenie v Zapadnoi Sibiri," *Voprosy kolonizatsii*, no. 10 (1912): 37–8.

31 The overall intent of the sales was to enhance the position of educated landowners and a vaguely defined "Russian element" – migrants from central Russia with agricultural skills superior to the local Bashkirs – who would make the region more productive and able to support the newly reformed institutions and break up the "closed mass of the Muslim population." Shramchenko, "Zemel'nyi vopros," 476–7.

32 Those wanting to purchase land were to declare their intentions to the governor-general, who would forward them to the Minister of State Domains for final

approval. The average price per *desiatin*a was about 1 ruble, 80 kopecks, when the market price of land varied from 7 to 25 rubles per *desiatina*. Usmanov, *Razvitie kapitalizma*, 43.

33 In the period 1876–81 alone, 293 men purchased land in this manner, most of them noble servitors of high rank, including those in the local administration. Kryzhanovskii himself received 6,294 *desiatins*. Many subsequently resold their land at great profit, often to migrants from central Russia. Usmanov, *Razvitie kapitalizma*, 42.

34 Shramchenko, "Zemel'nyi vopros," 470.

35 The post of governor-general itself was eliminated. P.A. Zaionchkovskii, ed. and comp., *Dnevnik P.A. Valueva, ministra vnutrennikh del v dvukh tomakh*, v. 1, 1861–4 (Moscow, 1961), 50–1.

36 E. Iashnov, "Kolonizatsiia Turkestana za poslednie gody," *Voprosy kolonizatsii*, no. 18 (1915): 103.

37 *PSZRI*, series III, v. XXI, no. 20,338 (8 June 1901), 614–19.

38 Vvedenskii, "Chastnoe zemlevladenie," 37–8.

39 Ufa province's civilian governor Ushakov agreed with Kryzhanovskii that "only an influx of entire masses" of migrants from "internal provinces" would "convey to the Russian element" predominance among the local population. GAOO, f. 6, op. 6, l. 16, cited in Usmanov, *Razvitie kapitalizma*, 62. The need to introduce better farmers to the region remained a constant through at least the end of the century. *Vsepoddanneishii raport ego Imperatorskomu Velichestvu Ufimskogo Gubernatora Bogdanovicha 1899* (28 October 1900), 2.

40 *Vsepoddanneishii raport 1899*, 2; and Usmanov, *Razvitie kapitalizma*, 61–2.

41 *Tsifrovyi material dlia izucheniia pereselentsii v Sibir', izvlechennyi iz knig obshchei registratsii pereselentsev, prokhodivshikh v Sibir' i vovrashchavshikhsia iz Sibiri cherez Cheliabinsk v 1895 godu* (Moscow, 1898), I–XV. The questionnaire listed six nationalities – Great Russian, Little Russian, Mordvin, German, Pole, and Belorussian – and instructed that statisticians should write others in.

42 The categories of *natsional'nost'* given were *Russkii, Malo-Rossiiskii, Litovskii, Tatarskii, Latyshskii, Chuvashskii, Finskii, Mordvy, Evropeiskii, Tsyganskii,* and *prochii.* TsGIARB, f. I-11, Chancellery of the Governor, op. 1, d. 1272. ll. 17–17aob. On the local level, Ufa Governor Bogdanovich initiated a systematic investigation of the migrant population of the province in the mid-1890s.

43 At least before 1905, information on the nationality of migrants was not published along with other information about them.

44 For a discussion of military statistics and attempts to map the empire according to an ethnic grid, see Peter Holquist, "To count, to extract, and to exterminate: population statistics and population politics in late imperial and Soviet Russia," in *A State of Nations: Empire and Nation-Making in the Age of Lenin and Stalin*, eds Ronald Grigor Suny and Terry Martin (Oxford, 2001), 111–44. For a discussion of administration and ethnicity in Central Asia, see Daniel Brower, "Islam and ethnicity: Russian colonial policy in Turkestan," in *Russia's Orient: Imperial Borderlands and Peoples, 1700–1917*, eds Daniel Brower and Edward Lazzerini (Bloomington, 1997), 115–35.

45 *PSZRI*, series III, v. XXIV, no. 24,701 (6 June 1904): 603–7. On dissident sects in South Caucasia, see Breyfogle, *Heretics and Colonizers*.

46 Judge, "Peasant resettlement," 90.

47 Vladimir I. Gurko, *Features and Figures of the Past: Government and Opinion in the Reign of Nicholas II*, eds J.E. Wallace Sterling, Xenia Joukoff Eudin, and H.H. Fisher, and trans. Laura Matveev (New York, 1939, reissued Stanford, 1970), 462.

48 S. E. Kryzhanovskii, *Vospominaniia*: 215–16, cited in Francis Wcislo, *Reforming Rural Russia: State, Local Society, and National Politics, 1855–1914* (Princeton, 1990), 209.

49 Stolypin and Krivoshein, *Poezdka v sibir'*, 55, 117.

50 Treadgold, *The Great Siberian Migration*, 162, 193.

51 Stolypin and Krivoshein, *Poezdka v sibir'*, 17–18.

52 Ibid., 31–2.

53 Ibid., 58–9.

54 Some government surveyors had left state service to form private companies that conducted land surveys. Ibid., 30–1, 64–5.

55 Once again, Stolypin and Krivoshein did not use the word market, but their iteration of factors that would ease the problems of non-registered migrants – property, right of sale, and proper prices – suggests their reliance on market forces. Ibid., 71.

56 "K istorii agrarnoi reformy Stolypina," *Krasnyi arkhiv*, no. 17 (1926): 84, cited in Abraham Ascher, *P A. Stolypin: The Search for Stability in Late Imperial Russia* (Stanford, 2001), 156.

57 Ascher, *P A. Stolypin*, 158.

58 Stolypin and Krivoshein, *Poezdka v sibir'*, 17.

59 Ibid., 58–9.

60 Mill also wrote that "colonization ... is the best affair of business," and he advocated government intervention in colonization, though in terms of financial support for settlers. Ibid., 92.

61 Peter Waldron, *Between Two Revolutions: Stolypin and the Politics of Renewal in Russia* (DeKalb, 1998), 70.

62 According to Willard Sunderland, "'knowledgeable people' advising the Ministry of the Interior in the 1880s favored treating resettlement as a right and recognizing the peasant settler as a would-be rational actor," but those in power did not share such a view. Sunderland, *Taming the Wild Field*, 192.

63 Krivoshein, after all, had been one of Plehve's chief lieutenants in developing the policy of directing settlement from central Russia to strategically sensitive borderland regions to increase the Russian presence. See Gurko, *Features and Figures*, 192–4.

64 Elsewhere Stolypin and Krivoshein used a biological metaphor to describe settlement: "In the formerly lifeless desert the pulse of Russian life begins to beat." Stolypin and Krivoshein, *Poezdka v sibir'*, 83.

65 Ibid., 1.

66 Stolypin, "Iz perepiski P.A. Stolypina," 82.

67 Richard S. Wortman contrasts Stolypin's "state nationalism" with Nicholas's nationalism, which the tsar understood as his personal bond with his subjects. Richard Wortman, *Scenarios of Power: Myth and Ceremony in Russian Monarchy*, v. 2 (Princeton, 2000), 408–9.

68 Stolypin and Krivoshein, *Poezdka v sibir'*, 126.

69 Ibid., 82–4.

70 Ibid., 43.

71 People of nearly any nationality could participate in empire-building when the enemy against which Stolypin and Krivoshein defined Russia was racial, not national or religious in nature. Ibid., 125.

72 V. Voshchinin, "Kolonizatsionnoe delo pri A. V. Krivosheine," *Voprosy kolonizatsii*, no. 18 (1915): 8–9, 12–13; Treadgold, *The Great Siberian Migration*, 196. The only remaining restriction on settlers was that to receive government support they had to personally or through a scout inspect their allotment in advance in order to guarantee "consciousness" in settlement and reinforce their own choice in land.

73 "Proekt obrazovaniia v zaselennykh raionakh za Uralom krupnykh chastnovladel'cheskikh khoziaistv," *Voprosy kolonizatsii*, no. 9 (1911): 459.

74 Voshchinin, "Kolonizatsionnoe delo", 8–9; Treadgold, *The Great Siberian Migration*, 195, 200.

75 Treadgold, *The Great Siberian Migration*, 203.

76 "Postanovleniia Komiteta po zaseleniiu Dal'niago Vostoka o merakh privlecheniia russkikh rabochikh na Dal'nii Vostok," *Voprosy kolonizatsii*, no. 9 (1911): 446–8; "Mezhduvedomstvennoe soveshchanie po rabochemu voprosu na Dal'nem Vostoke," *Voprosy kolonizatsii*, no. 10 (1912): 308–13.

77 Ibid., 309.

78 Stolypin, "Iz perepiski P.A. Stolypina," 83.

7 Progress or peril

Migrants and locals in Russian Tashkent, 1906–14

Jeff Sahadeo[1]

Coming by the thousands, Russian settlers inundated the streets of Tashkent's "Russian section" in 1906. Unemployment, rural poverty, and repression in the central provinces drove these new arrivals to seek opportunities elsewhere. A recently completed rail line allowed settlers to escape harrowing treks across steppe and desert land that separated the tsarist province of Turkestan from European Russia. Administrators and other privileged Russians in Tashkent, despite their minority status in the city and region as well as their initial enthusiasm over the railway, greeted their new compatriots with scorn. Poor, dirty, and, in some cases, disease-ridden, recent migrants occupied all available housing in the Russian section, and squatted in old, dilapidated soldiers' barracks. They crowded the central city market, Voskresenskii bazaar, pleading with Russian or Central Asian passers-by for employment. Peasants refused official pleas to move to the surrounding countryside. Tsarist officials working with new settlers complained of "moral torment" from their shock at having to deal with so many members of Russia's lower classes.[2] By June, the city duma opened debate on enforcement of a ban on any movement to the capital city of Turkestan.[3]

Strains produced by this wave of migrants operated on several levels in the colonial city, illuminating and intensifying tensions along lines of class, race, and gender as well as local anxieties over the nature of tsarist colonialism. Leading imperial officials, professionals, intellectuals, and business leaders that formed overlapping elite strata in Russian Tashkent struggled to maintain their own image of the city as a symbol of European and Russian civilization (*tsivilizatsiia*) in the once renowned, but now decrepit, oases societies of Central Asia. Poor Russian migrants' lack of wealth and apparent disregard for "civilized" culture placed them at, if not below, the level of the colonized Central Asian population. New female settlers begged local merchants for food, violating the image of the pure and privileged Russian woman. Of greatest frustration to imperial officials in Turkestan was their narrowing control over the colonization process. St Petersburg, as it began to fund railway construction, sought to enforce its own vision of a populated and productive periphery that would overcome social and economic difficulties in central Russia. Economic growth and urban development that came with the railway failed to alleviate frustrations among Russian Tashkent's leaders that their city had lost its path towards progress (*progress'*); as migrants continued to pour into Russian Tashkent, moreover, some elites began to wonder whether progress was a goal worth pursuing after all.

Since the conquest and establishment of the tsarist province of Turkestan in the 1860s, tsarist officials maintained an ambivalent attitude towards large-scale colonization. K.P. fon Kaufman, the province's first governor-general, feared that waves of settlers from European Russia would provoke rebellion among an overwhelmingly Muslim Central Asian population deemed backward and fanatical. Kaufman proposed an evolutionary policy of "disinterest" towards Islam; he believed that local Muslims, upon witnessing Europe's achievements, would abandon their adherence to traditional ways.[4] Beginning in 1868, tsarist planners designed the wide, tree-lined boulevards and stately architecture of Tashkent's "Russian" (also referred to as its "new" or "European") section as a stark contrast to the crooked lanes and mud huts of what they referred to as the "Asian" (also called the "native" or "old") quarter. But who would inhabit this new urban space of power and privilege? The governor-general sought not only to dissuade Central Asians from taking up residence, but also to limit the number of lower-class Russians. Soldiers' barracks were relocated away from central Russian Tashkent after the city's police chief investigated complaints of strewn-about dirt, garbage, and feces.[5] Municipal authorities screened newcomers who sought to assume residence; poor Russians who arrived often remained in "temporary" mud huts they built for themselves on the edge of Russian Tashkent while awaiting official permission and designated housing in the city center.[6] As a symbol of an ostensibly superior civilization, Russian Tashkent's development was carefully managed by tsarist planners throughout the imperial period.

Local intellectuals in Russian Tashkent – primarily graduates of institutes of higher education serving in the tsarist bureaucracy – maintained a more aggressive attitude towards colonization. Formed in 1870, the Central Asian Scholarly Society sought to undertake a thorough survey of Turkestan's peoples and lands, in large measure to determine the region's suitability for settlement. Society members envisioned Russian colonization of steppe and oasis lands as the first stage in reinventing the Silk Road and enriching Russia through a railway link between Moscow and Beijing.[7] Yet these members shuddered when thinking about new settlers on their doorstep. A developing urban economy in the early 1880s based largely on the cotton trade attracted increased numbers of lower-class migrants to cross thousands of kilometers of steppe and desert to Tashkent, particularly as the economic situation in the center worsened.[8] Commentaries in the official newspaper *Turkestanskie vedomosti* condemned the slovenly dwellings and dead-end, garbage-filled streets of new suburban settlements that reminded many of Asian Tashkent. N.A. Maev, a member of the Central Asian Scholarly Society and editor of *Turkestanskie vedomosti*, complained that drunken "renegades" threatened to destroy "intelligent society," either through their lack of culture or their susceptibility to disease.[9] Maev lamented that the appearance of new settlers had destroyed one of the dreams of Russian intellectuals in Tashkent: to build a modern city without a "proletariat."[10]

At the same time, under Tsar Alexander III, the central government had begun to encourage migration to Asiatic Russia from central regions of the empire deemed overcrowded. St Petersburg and Tashkent reconciled respective goals and fears of migration in 1886, when the tsar signed an order allowing migration only to rural regions of Turkestan. Governor-General A.B. Vrevskii and N.I. Grodekov, military governor of the Syr-Dar'ia Oblast, which included Tashkent, sought out new rural lands for settlement, aggressively overruling district commandants who feared new settlements would spark local resistance.[11] Migration, however, proved an impossible process to control. Russian settlers continued to prefer Tashkent to the surrounding countryside, particularly after the most fertile lands of the district had been occupied. Thousands who fled famine in central Russia in 1891–2 remained in the city. *Turkestanskie vedomosti* pleaded with them to move to the countryside and assume Russians' "natural" role as peasant colonizers, thereby bringing pride to colonial society.[12] A devastating cholera epidemic in 1892 sharpened distrust of poor Russians, who were condemned by tsarist officials and intellectuals alike for failing to follow basic sanitary procedures. A new private newspaper, *Okraina*, in 1894 attacked a new "class" of "vulgar" people who sought to profit from their status as colonizers, all the while scorning any aspects of "civilized" behavior.[13] In 1897, Governor-General Vrevskii banned rural as well as urban colonization in Turkestan.[14]

Such a ban ran against evolving central policies towards the region. In the 1890s, after decades of failed lobbying efforts from governors-general from Kaufman to Vrevskii, St Petersburg decided to undertake railway construction in Turkestan. Minister of War A.N. Kuropatkin sold this plan to the tsar for military goals, as he sought to prevent any potential British or Chinese incursion into Russia's Asian lands. Even as Vrevskii formally ended colonization in Turkestan, Kuropatkin urged the use of Russian workers to build the direct rail line connecting European Russia to Tashkent, hoping that many would stay, as the region's "Russification [is taking on] an extreme political importance."[15] By that year, over 5,000 Russians were working on the rail lines, compared to fewer than 1,000 Central Asians, initially favored by Chief Engineer A.I. Ursati as they worked for lower wages.

Where Kuropatkin saw educated and skilled Russian workers as ideal settlers, Vrevskii and other tsarist officials saw a potentially seditious "fifth column." Many railway workers who arrived in Turkestan had been blackballed from their jobs for previous political activity. Socialist circles quickly formed in Russian Tashkent, and railway workers spearheaded the first strike against state administrators in the city in 1899.[16] Vrevskii's successor, Governor-General N.A. Ivanov, worried that these workers might make contacts with the Central Asian population, writing the minister of war in 1901 that subversive activities threatened to considerably shake the "native population's impression that the Russian people are inseparable, a strongly unified force, selflessly obeying the will of the MIGHTY TSAR (*sic*)."[17] Railways had nonetheless provided a significant boost to the region; an 1898 branch line linking Tashkent to the Caspian Sea had jumpstarted economic growth, as exports rose substantially.[18] Renewed vitality in the capital and the region led commentators to claim that after 40 years, Tashkent was fulfilling its potential of becoming "Asian Russia's St Petersburg."[19] Multiple strains in the decade following the 1906 completion of a direct line to Europe, however, led many privileged Russians to temper this enthusiasm with pessimism, seeing the railway more as a curse than a boon.

The 1906 migratory wave crashed upon a city torn by internal unrest. Railway workers had led opposition to the tsarist regime the previous fall as Tashkent joined the 1905 revolution. As across the empire, the tsar's promises of civil liberties and a democratically elected legislature (*duma*) as part of the October Manifesto split opposition forces. Russian liberal intellectuals in Tashkent – primarily mid-level state employees and professionals – shifted their anger from the regime and Cossack troops, who had killed two unarmed protestors during a November demonstration, towards subaltern groups in the city.[20] Leaders of the Tashkent branch of the Constitutional Democrat (*Kadet*) party saw the October Manifesto as a basis to advance progress in the empire. But democracy, one principal component of this progress, caused significant unease among this and other privileged groups. Kadet leaders urged new potential voters to consider "vanguard elements" like themselves, rather than railway worker activists.[21] One writer reminded readers of railway workers' effective blockade of the city during a November strike, and lamented that now all citizens of Tashkent were at the mercy of a small clique of radicals with "no sense of justice."[22]

Considering the possibility of "four-tailed" (equal, direct, universal, and secret) elections to a new state duma, these "vanguard elements" feared not only railway workers but also the majority Central Asian population. A lead article in the 24 November 1905 issue of *Sredneaziatskaia zhizn'*, entitled "Down with Progress," emphasized the danger of electoral reform to the Russian quest to modernize Central Asia.[23] Russians, who had provided European schooling, transport, and communication systems would be at the mercy of a people who lacked even the "beginnings of civilization" and saw "culture" as counter to their religious beliefs. Russians, as the "higher race," needed to complete their task of spreading enlightenment to the "dark" Muslim masses before the implementation of democratic government in Turkestan.[24]

Tsar Nicholas II's promulgation of the October Manifesto forced Tashkent Russians to wrestle with the paradox between civic freedoms and democratic government, on the one hand, and the fundamental inequalities that characterized imperial rule, on the other. Tsarist administrators quickly devised a solution to prevent the erosion of Russian superiority in Turkestan. "Natives," who composed over 90 percent of Turkestan's population, and "non-natives" would be divided into separate electoral franchises, each of which would send one representative to the duma. Such gerrymandering, which already applied to Tashkent's city duma where the minority "Christian" population received two-thirds of the seats, allowed the appearance of representative government while denying equal voting rights to Central Asians.

Leaders of Tashkent's Kadet party called a special meeting, open to all "progressive" political parties, to discuss this apparent violation of "four-tailed" voting rights for which they had fought so vigorously just months earlier. Kadet leader G. Reiser echoed the majority view supporting separate franchises, arguing that Muslims and Russians had "extreme" differences in culture.[25] Others justified separation on the grounds that it benefited the colonized; one delegate, Meier, argued that Russians, as "guests" in the region, needed to allow the native population representatives to address questions and problems that specifically affected them.[26] Such legitimations comforted attendees, despite one voice that called this new plan a "clear breach of the principles of equal voting."[27] Yet Reiser, Meier, and other Kadets rejected the views of N.G. Mallitskii, a prominent Orientalist scholar and current editor of *Turkestanskie vedomosti*, that the Muslim population, having no experience at popular elections and dominated by aristocrats and the bourgeoisie, should be deprived of representation completely. Mallitskii proved unique among the speakers in justifying unequal representation on the basis of common practice in European colonial states, using Algeria as an example.[28] Despite their willingness to accept separate franchises, fears persisted among Tashkent Russian liberals that unequal voting rights would establish Tashkent and Turkestan as "backward" areas within the empire. Such worries, however, did not threaten Russian support for the unequal voting rights, backed as well by Russian worker activists, who enjoyed their status a "labor aristocracy" in Central Asia.[29] The worker newspaper *Russkii Turkestan* argued that separate franchises would prevent "uncultured, conservative, and backward" Muslims from gaining power in a society destined to move towards socialism.[30]

Separate franchises also lessened the need for new Russian migrants, whose votes would not be needed in a seemingly more democratic Turkestan. However, adding to the rural unrest and sputtering central economy that had already pushed thousands of migrants to Turkestan in early 1906, Prime Minister P.A. Stolypin designed a plan to open Siberia, the Kazakh steppe, and Central Asia to millions of new settlers. As with earlier policies of exiling political opposition, Asian Russia operated as a "safety valve" for unrest, in this case among poor peasants who had risen against the regime in 1905. Millions of rubles flowed to a new Resettlement Agency. Stolypin promoted his policy as more than an attempt to ease rural poverty, arguing that new settlers, freed from stifling peasant traditions, could transform the future of farming in imperial Russia as well as assure the security of Asiatic possessions. Central Russian elites followed these plans with great interest, discussing them in the press and launching a new periodical dedicated to the issue, *Questions of Colonization (Voprosy kolonizatsii)*. The Asian frontier offered a way to revitalize the empire following the tumult of 1905.[31]

Central attention, combined with initial economic growth, led Tashkent Russian administrators and intellectuals briefly to shelve long-held reservations regarding mass migration. Since 1869, the city had been unable to shake the reputation given it by renowned author M.E. Saltykov-Shchedrin, whose "Tashkent gentlemen" symbolized a tsarist empire that sought conquest and profit over culture and the common good.[32] Frustration over this continued stereotype mounted among Tashkent Russian intellectuals following Alexander II's assassination in 1881. At a gathering in 1891 to mark the 135th anniversary of Moscow University, agronomist N.N. Kas'ianov denounced the reactionary policies of Tsar Alexander III. The spirit of the Great Reforms, which had informed the statutes and visions of a new, progressive Turkestan in the 1860s, had evaporated. The central government, not Tashkent, was a source of disorder and backwardness; the only reason for the continued resonance of Saltykov-Shchedrin's "Tashkent gentlemen" was St Petersburg's sending of corrupt and reactionary "freaks" to serve as administrators in Tashkent.[33] Now, however, high-ranking officials and central correspondents regularly visited Tashkent to publicize migration efforts and report on vanguard efforts on the frontier, culminating with Minister of Agriculture A.V. Krivoshein's high-profile visit in 1912. *Na rubezhe*, another new Tashkent private newspaper, reported in 1910 the "stunning success" of the initial wave of migrants, who were spearheading an independent farming class and a Christian, Russian society in Asia.[34] Some *Sredneaziatskaia zhizn'* writers noted that new migrants would prevent Central Asians from "colonizing" lands now made far more valuable as a result of the railway link with central Russia.[35] Tashkent Russians' enthusiasm for this movement, however, continued to envision settlers uniquely as rural inhabitants; indeed, an anticipated major benefit of Stolypin's plans was that settlers from central Russia would be less likely to remain in their city.

Officials in Tashkent directly involved with the settlement process realized the difficulty of finding quality farming lands for the tens of thousands of migrants anticipated to arrive annually. *Sredneaziatskaia zhizn'*, realizing that past migrants destined for new agricultural settlements in Turkestan had abandoned farming and returned to Tashkent, placed faith in a new generation of professionals, capable of using "academic" relations and "scientific" methods to develop lands suitable for colonization.[36] Newspapers reported regularly on meetings of the Turkestan Agricultural Society, whose members engaged in vigorous debates on the feasibility of tsarist plans for colonization. The society gained the privilege of meeting at the governor-general's mansion, an honor now shared with the Turkestan branch of the Imperial Russian Geographical Society, an organization chaired by the governor-general and composed of leading intellectuals, businessmen, military officers, administrators, state inspectors, and Church members, which also lent its efforts to locating land for colonization.[37] These vanguard Russian liberals hoped that civic culture would lead the state to success in its new venture.

Hopes placed on rational settlement plans, as well as the settlers themselves, quickly faded. Syr-Dar'ia district officials prioritized allotments for peasants from southern regions of the empire, believing experience working in warmer climates would smooth their transition to Turkestan.[38] Regardless of their origin, however, settlers favored growing food over more valuable export goods and proved unable to master the intricacies of irrigation in a subtropical climate. Their attempts to farm the land having failed, Russian peasants began as early as 1907 to return to Tashkent in search of work.[39] The 1912 Syr-Dar'ia Regional Statistical Committee's annual report stated that peasant migrants' behavior made them "less desirable" inhabitants of Russian Turkestan.[40]

As Governor-General Kaufman had feared a half-century earlier, substantial Russian migration destabilized the countryside. New settlers' seizure of land from Central Asian villagers, sometimes with the authorization of central resettlement officials, triggered resistance. By 1909, increasing rural violence led the Office of the Military Governor to foresee a general breakdown in order.[41] Another trend that concerned central and regional tsarist officials involved Russian colonists selling their lots to Central Asian farmers, who then irrigated the land and employed the Russians as sharecroppers.[42] Many of these peasants now produced export goods, particularly cotton, but not at all in the way imperial officials envisaged. Instead of peaceful, prosperous, independent farmers, migrants were attacking or submitting to the colonized population, threatening the fragile balance of colonial superiority and stability established over previous decades.

Central officials further upset this balance through their imperious behavior. Ignoring rising statistics of rural violence, the Main Administration of Land and Agriculture in St Petersburg sought to quicken the pace of colonization, and took control of the entire process on 19 December 1910. Rules governing settlement in Turkestan's official statute were loosened to allow any land "deemed in excess" of the local population's needs to be freed for settlement. For the first time, survey commissions expropriated lands claimed directly by Central Asian villagers or on well-established nomadic routes. Krivoshein announced during his tour of Turkestan massive irrigation projects that would allow the transplantation of 1,500,000 settlers.[43] Numbers of migrants continued to grow; in 1912, 18,821 arrived in the Syr-Dar'ia Oblast alone.[44]

News of ongoing difficulties in the countryside and the increasing numbers of migrants returning to, or remaining in, the provincial capital blunted Tashkent Russian enthusiasm for migration. *Na rubezhe* condemned "huge crowds" of peasants who, after noisily descending on offices of resettlement authorities in failed attempts to find arable land, took up begging, destroying the peace of privileged inhabitants of the Russian city.[45] According to *Turkestanskie vedomosti*

> [p]assenger trains are bringing to Tashkent the unemployed, coming from hungry provinces in the hope of finding any kind of work. Many under the category of "independent migrants" are staying at the way station [a temporary dormitory for migrants headed to rural Turkestan] and some are living under the open sky. This whole mass comes to Voskresenskii bazaar, where there are no jobs.[46]

After a brief interlude, disdain towards new, poor migrants returned as a central feature of Tashkent Russian society.

Even as the local press shied away from direct criticism of the central authorities, stressing instead settlers who had come without official permission, officials in Tashkent grew increasingly disenchanted with St Petersburg. Massive rural migration appeared to them as a tool to turn Turkestan not into a center of diverse new industries, as they had envisioned, but rather a supplier of raw goods, principally cotton. Senator K.K. Palen made his opinion clear during a 1908 tour of the province:

> [The growth of cotton] has already been extremely profitable for the nation, as in creating an internal cotton market, Russia will not be in dependence on various foreign trusts and arbitrary prices established by the London and American markets, but will be in position to regulate prices itself. Moreover, money now wasted for buying foreign cotton will no longer go abroad, but stay within the country.[47]

Central taxation and tariff policies, set to favor cotton growth, sparked the leader of the Moscow Exchange Committee, G.A. Krestovnikov, and the "Young Industrialist" P.P. Riabushinskii to form the Moscow Irrigation Company, with plans to irrigate hundreds of thousands of *desiatins* of land.[48]

Governor-General A.V. Samsonov surveyed these developments with concern. Exploiting the region as a producer of raw cotton hindered a diversified economy that would fulfill the design of an "Asian St Petersburg." Samsonov accordingly asked Russian industrialists, entrepreneurs, traders, and "representatives of Russian culture" to recognize Turkestan's potential as a center for secondary, productive industry.[49] R.R. Shreder and other Turkestan Agricultural Society members launched detailed criticisms of central policy following St Petersburg's takeover of the colonization process. One critique concerned environmental damage. All areas sufficiently irrigated to support cotton planting had been exhausted by 1910; further planting risked destroying the surrounding lands, as irrigating barren fields would draw water away from existing canals.[50] Farmers, driven by tax and tariff policies to grow cotton, were becoming "unwilling accomplices in their own destruction," according to a Turkestan Agricultural Society's 1911 report.[51] Branches of central Russian banks worsened the situation for Russian and Central Asian peasants alike, directing loans to large trading and industrial groups instead of small farmers, who, now tied to world markets, were left to collapse in bad times. District statisticians also expressed misgivings concerning the increased land allotted to cotton. The land dedicated to cotton production in the Syr-Dar'ia district increased sevenfold, from 11,019 to 76,276 *desiatins* from 1903 to 1913.[52] The Regional Statistical Committee stated in its 1912 report that "the district is no more than a vast market of raw materials, and at the same time, a place for the sale of goods from Russian factories."[53] A young Turkestan, at the mercy of central economic policy, had become no more than a "colony" (*koloniia*) of Russia.[54]

Employing "colony" in place of other terms in use for their region among Tashkent Russians, including "province" (*krai*), "outlying region" (*okraina*), or "homeland" (*rodina*), was significant in contemporary Russian discourse. As early as the 1880s, Siberian regionalists used the term as a pejorative to describe the results of central policies that shipped raw goods directly to the metropole, preventing the development of a balanced economy.[55] "*Koloniia*" came to symbolize the dependence of a region upon a center ignorant of its needs.[56] In the nineteenth century, criticisms of the center focused on its neglect of Turkestan rather than any dependent relationship. Now, central interest had given Tashkent Russians one of their most deeply held desires – a railroad – but with it came subjection to St Petersburg's economic policy. Criticism of the center also revolved around its political maneuverings. Private newspapers criticized Prime Minister Stolypin for stripping Turkestan, along with other border regions, of duma representation and excluding them from important central debates, particularly concerning migration.[57] Once condemned for its absence, St Petersburg now stood accused of excessive meddling in local affairs and its retrograde policies.

The Syr-Dar'ia Statistical Commission placed blame for Turkestan's status as a "colony" of Russia not only on the central government, but also the local rural population. Unlike the Turkestan Agricultural Society, which expressed sympathy for the plight of Central Asian peasants under increased pressure to grow export goods, district statisticians argued that, beaten down by "centuries of oppression," local farmers had yet to grasp the skills necessary to build a diversified economy through intensive agriculture.[58] Central Asians, like Russian migrants, became linked to perceived failures to fashion Tashkent and Turkestan as showcases of imperial progress. Discussions over relationships with the local population proliferated in the Tashkent Russian press, connected to anxieties surrounding increased migration and patterns of economic development. These debates among tsarist bureaucrats as well as privileged Russians illuminated complex and ambivalent attitudes towards Central Asians, lower-class Russians, the metropole, and progress itself.

Casting Central Asians as backward, district statisticians nonetheless admitted their importance for the development of a modern economy in Turkestan. The idea and importance of a still incomplete civilizing mission gained increased attention in the post-1905 years, with blame spread from an obstinate and ignorant local population to Russians themselves, who had failed to transfer tools for progress. Even while trumpeting Russian achievements brought to Turkestan, the author of "Down with Progress" maintained that civilization is known only "by hearsay (*naslyshke*) to most of the Russian population."[59] Each wave of new Russian settlers, ragged and ignorant, demonstrated the distance the nation still needed to traverse before it reached modernity. Other articles in *Turkestanskie vedomosti* and *Sredneaziatskaia zhizn'* chided Russian administrators and intellectuals for failing to learn local languages, which hindered their ability to spread civilization to the Muslims.[60] Russians at both ends of social spectrum had failed to act as effective promoters for the "civilizing mission" that underpinned their sense of legitimacy as imperial conquerors.

Worse, the colonial encounter was now appearing to demonstrate that Central Asians possessed certain qualities that distinguished them as more civilized than the Russian colonizers. As Russians overindulged in alcohol and showed no respect for law and order, Central Asians remained teetotalers and honored elders and leaders. As early as 1883, such contrasts had precipitated important policy decisions, particularly the use of Central Asians as beat police on the streets of Russian Tashkent. A Russian who lived in Asian Tashkent highlighted these

Figure 7.1 Russian Tashkent: the horseracing track, September 1910. Copyright ©
Anahita Gallery, Inc., Santa Fe, NM. By kind permission of Anahita
Gallery, Inc.

differences in a 1906 *Sredneaziatskaia zhizn'* article. As poor migrants begged on
the streets of the Russian city in the wake of 1905 protests, the author appreciated
that Central Asians knew how live in peace, as a community. Crime rates were low
in Asian Tashkent and his neighbors were calm, tolerant, and disciplined.[61] Other
authors claimed that a superior work ethic, as well as comfort operating in a large
urban environment and with complex regional trading networks, allowed Central
Asians to master the intricacies of a growing economy better than Russians, from
recent poor settlers to leading merchants. Central Asians' purchasing of land from
Russian peasants confirmed the perception of the former as adept at exploiting the
advantages of Russian imperial rule, which had integrated the region into European markets.[62]

Stereotypes of superior Central Asian skill in business leading to their
perceived domination of the local economy intensified after the construction of
railway links to the city. A 1903 *Turkestanskie vedomosti* article, entitled "A
Possible Future for Tashkent" discussed the "danger of [Russian] economic
enslavement to [the local population]."[63] "Barons" such as Arif Khoja and Isabek
Khakimbatov dominated the cotton economy; by concentrating rough-
processing plants near the sources of the best cotton in Fergana, they had indus-
trialized this area before Tashkent.[64] Representations of business as controlled
by non-Russians were ubiquitous in the post-1905 local press; cartoons in the
satirical journal *Turkestanskii Kara-Kurt* represented capitalists as Central

Asians, or as Jews, enslaving poor Russian settlers.[65] A.I. Dobrosmyslov, in his history of Tashkent published in 1912, warned that "soon, we Russians, due to our laziness and absence of entrepreneurship, will be in full dependence on the local Jews and Muslims."[66]

Criticizing through racializing capitalism reflected the doubts of many among Tashkent Russian elites as to the compatibility of capitalism – which brought polluting factories and the dirty, downtrodden "proletariat" – with a civilized culture. Russian businessmen operated alongside their Jewish, German, and Central Asian counterparts. Dobrosmyslov noted the powerful role of the Tverskii manufacturing company and Moscow Trading Industrial Association.[67] Yet Russian intellectuals, including leaders in the tsarist administration, sought to avoid identification with capital gain, believing that the chaos of the market fit poorly with the sense of order and peace to be embodied by the Russian city. In 1909, petitioners decried a city duma decision to award exclusive advertising rights to wealthy local businessman Seid Azim. Residents complained about placards that turned Russian Tashkent into one giant bazaar.[68] Advertisements for cigarettes and drinks blanketed landmarks of civilization, such as Kaufman square and the local schools, offending the "eyes and aesthetic sense of residents."[69]

Tashkent Russian elites' sense of incompatibility between "culturedness" (*kulturnost'*) and capitalism prompted a questioning of commonly regarded centerpieces of a modern society. The railway in particular had brought turmoil instead of benefits to Tashkent. The direct line from Orenburg delivered tens of thousands of unwelcome migrants. Improved linkages between European Russia and Turkestan had placed the latter in a dependent position, no longer self-sufficient in food as farmers now grew cotton instead of grain.[70] Prices for foodstuffs skyrocketed. Residents also wondered at the aesthetics and the efficiency of the dirty, slow-moving engines that pulled in and out of Tashkent station. Were these machines, asked one author, really an improvement over the caravans of camels that had supplied Tashkent so well for decades?[71] What were the benefits of this changing economy that Russian elites had for so long desired?

Capital development and commoditization, alongside migration, complicated another pillar of civilization frequently cited by Tashkent Russians: the respectful treatment and elevated status of women. Since the conquest, Russian authors contrasted Europeans' esteem of women with Central Asians, whose females were subject to polygamous marriages and hidden from public sight in separate living quarters, or behind veils.[72] In a 1910 article entitled "Respect Women!," Evgenii Fedorov extolled women's roles in ensuring the moral, spiritual, esthetic, and cultural supremacy of Russian society in Tashkent. As with the Greeks and Romans, "mothers and women propelled men to heroism and great feats."[73] Women's status and roles were infallible markers of a society's progress, according to Fedorov, who equated the harem with Central Asian backwardness. Fedorov ignored, however, another aspect of European civilization that demonstrated an uglier side of gender relations, and also deeply concerned Tashkent Russian leaders: prostitution. Since early migratory waves of the 1880s, tsarist officials and Russian intellectuals sought to control the numbers of poor Russian women acting as prostitutes. Multiple efforts to eliminate prostitution from the Russian city's suburbs failed, however.[74] A renewed initiative in 1909 sought to create a designated zone for prostitution on the Chimkent road, which abutted Asian Tashkent. Muslim elites opposed this move, citing issues of health and sanitation as well as a desire not to expose their population to the sex trade. A *Na rubezhe* piece, once more tying Central Asians to capital gain, condemned this move as hypocritical. What was really at stake was a potential loss of profits from brothels owned primarily by Central Asians, who feared that Muslim clients and prostitutes would be less likely to use or work at brothels so close to friends and neighbors. Central Asian elites' hunger for profit led them to promote "depravity."[75] Prostitution nonetheless continued to evoke great concern among tsarist officials because of the numbers of soldiers that frequented potentially "disease-ridden" prostitutes, as well as uncomfortable images of Central Asian men having relations with Russian women.[76]

Not only had Russians spread prostitution in Tashkent; their tastes for the exotic were directly responsible for the maintenance of one of the most repulsive elements of local culture: *bachas*, Muslim dancing boys who performed for male audiences in local teahouses. An article in *Sredneaziatskaia zhizn'* noted that even Islamic priests, characterized as the most fanatical and ignorant segments of the population, had agreed with tsarist authorities following the conquest to institute a ban on the practice to protect against pederasty.[77] Wealthy Russians, however, had begun hiring dancing boys to perform at local commercial exhibitions, and their presence was once again ubiquitous in Tashkent.[78] Were Russians leading Central Asians forward or backward in time?

Feminist writer A. Almatinskaia complained that Tashkent Russian claims of respect and equality for women did not correspond to reality. In 1910, thousands of Russians attended the funeral of renowned actress V.F. Komissarzhevskaia, who died unexpectedly during a performance in Tashkent. Extensive press commentary claimed the respect given her was a symbol of "women's equal rights" in Tashkent.[79] Almatinskaia, however, complained that Russian women still served as little more than "objects of luxury," obsessed with fashion and flirtations. Russian women lacked the education to contribute to society, unable to advance a civilizing mission that seemed to be failing so badly. She urged Russian women to educate themselves in order to make contact with mistreated Muslim females, setting both "on a new path."[80] Imperial officials, however, frowned on contact between Russian women and Central Asians. In the 1890s, women's increased presence in public life as clerks, doctors, and service personnel in Tashkent provoked great concern among tsarist leaders, who, in a similar fashion to European imperial regimes across the globe, sought to isolate "their" females from "polluting" contacts with the local population.[81] Anatole Marie Bariatinsky, wife of a local officer, wrote in her memoirs of the isolation faced by Russian women expected to await their husbands on long military tours and of her boredom of "sitting at my window – about the only thing to do in this dead-alive place."[82]

Lower-class women migrants threatened this distance through their daily contacts with the local population, particularly Central Asian merchants. One writer in *Turkestanskie vedomosti* decried such dealings, especially as traders enjoyed the power in this relationship, reducing poor women to beg them for discounts or shoplift to feed their families. Forcing Russians to stoop to this level should provoke "moral disquietude [as it] offends our national pride."[83] Rising food prices caused by increasing numbers of farmers growing cotton placed Russian women in an increasingly submissive position to the colonized population in the post-1905 years. Satirical journals in Russian Tashkent parodied these encounters, with clever, greedy merchants swindling poor, naïve, and helpless migrants.[84] Russian lower-class women began in this period to demand improvements to their material situation, joining others across the empire in a wave of strikes from 1911–13.[85] Sixty female workers of Tashkent's new tramway, hailed in the Russian press following disillusionment with the railway as the most recent symbol of urban progress, struck against the Belgian concessionaire "Louis Zalm," demanding to be paid a living wage.[86] The strike extracted higher wages and lower workloads, but also drew the attention of the tsarist secret police, the *Okhrana,* which henceforth kept a close watch on female labor actions as a flashpoint for future conflict.

Growing tension along gender lines undermined Evgenii Fedorov's hopes that Russian colonizers could establish at least one clear domain of superiority before the colonized population. One year before his article on women, Fedorov had written a larger piece that questioned the motivations, effectiveness, and outcomes of European imperialism in light of changes to Tashkent society in the early twentieth century. The author tied his views to contemporary criticisms of western imperialism, most notably J.A. Hobson's renowned 1902 work, *Imperialism: A Study.* Fedorov argued that desires for new markets, rather than the "civilizing mission," motivated imperial conquest. But this desire had unexpected consequences: colonized populations, particularly Muslims, rapidly adjusted to this new economic system. Fedorov went a step further than other Tashkent Russian authors in making this allusion, linking Central Asian economic success to an ability to progress culturally. Europeans, exclaimed the author, must renounce the view that Muslim societies were not capable of cultural development. "Take for example our Sarts [locals] … the energy and receptiveness with which they have developed their trade, allowing them to acquire European cultural accomplishments." Local dynamism contrasted to the greed and apathy of the colonizer, leading Fedorov to argue that Muslims are "leaving us only with sadness to note … that we, who sowed the first seeds of progress, may remain behind them."[87]

Fedorov reacted with ambivalence towards his own conclusions. On the one hand, Europe and Russia were succeeding in the "civilizing mission." On the other, boundaries that divided colonizer and colonized grew ever more difficult to define. His confusion echoed across the colonial world, as non-western populations adjusted to colonial economies and societies. Alice Conklin has argued that French "republican universalism" conditioned a belief in an inherently superior metropolitan French civilization, but also one that could lift subject populations worldwide to the same level as their conquerors. These tensions were never fully resolved.[88] Muslim progress in Tashkent at once indicated Russian success and failure in the age of empire.

Evolving representations of the cultured and prosperous Central Asian reflected not only Russian self-criticism but social and cultural changes within Asian Tashkent. Increased Russian migration as well as the railway offered new markets and opportunities. Central Asian artisans and laborers supplied clothing, utensils, tools, and foodstuffs for new urban and rural migrants.[89] Asian Tashkent began to attract its own migrants, growing from 107,705 in 1890 to 141,047 in 1908, according to official censuses.[90] The extent to which this increase reflects employment opportunities or heightened competition over village land is uncertain. Many newcomers worked as poorly paid day-laborers in cotton-cleaning or other factories, at times under Russian overseers.[91] Dobrosmyslov, however, portrayed a vital Asian city, citing European architectural features that sprouted in the wealthier parts of town.[92] N.G. Mallitskii compared Asian Tashkent to the textile center of Moscow, an interesting complement to the image of Russian Tashkent as an Asian St Petersburg.[93]

Central Asian notables – those who occupied positions of authority in local society, worked in the colonial state, or had accumulated economic wealth – vigorously, if not always successfully, sought to defend the interests of Asian Tashkent.[94] The city duma offered a prime public forum; although duma regulations allotted only one-third of the seats to "non-Christians," votes were taken based on those present at sessions. In 1907–8, the number of Muslim deputies regularly equaled or surpassed that of "Christians." Senator Palen, noted, however disingenuously, that continued petitions complaining of unequal representation in the duma were unjustified, given Muslims' ability to defend their interests through high attendance and vigorous debate. Palen claimed that Arif Khoja had shaped Muslim deputies into the most effective voting bloc in the body.[95] Muslim deputies succeeded in having the new tramway system operate in both Asian and Russian Tashkent, and frequently expressed discontent with actions of colonial officials.[96] They failed, however, to achieve their most sought-after goals of obtaining equal representation to the assembly and equal spending for the Russian and Asian cities.

To overcome their subject status, select Central Asian elites worked to adapt western ideas of culture and education. At the forefront of this effort were modernist Jadids, who formed part of a larger contemporary movement for Islamic renewal that had so impressed Evgenii Federov. Jadids united behind a belief in historical change and "progress" (*taraqqi*).[97] Critiques of their own society demonstrate Jadids' attraction to certain European ideas. Pederasty and the unequal treatment of women came under attack, as did the Islamic clergy, whose conservatism prevented local society from gaining the knowledge necessary to combat tsarist rule. Jadids focused much of their energy on "new-method" schools that taught history, geography, and mathematics alongside religion, and adapted European pedagogical methods.

Jadids nonetheless saved much of their criticism for the colonizer's culture, the least attractive features of which were identified with poor migrants. Along with some Russian liberals, they decried alcoholism, prostitution, gambling, and other unsavory trends they associated with the west. The Jadid newspaper *Sada-yi Turkestan* applauded traditional religious courts for their harsh treatments of Muslim drunkards who indulged their habit in the Russian city, hoping to escape sanction.[98] Jadids, along with other Central Asian elites, also directly expressed their distrust of lower-class Russians. Central Asian duma members approved of a Cossack presence on the streets of Tashkent even after their violent actions of October 1905. *Tujjor*, a newspaper published by Seid Karim, noted perpetual disorder on railway lines and deteriorating relations between Russian workers and Central Asians.[99] Jadids shared with many Tashkent Russians a distrust of their "own" peasant migrants, seen as uneducated, ignorant, and unskilled, and therefore incapable of grasping progress.[100] Progress was coming far too slowly for a society still under the colonizer's grip; only a handful of Jadid schools existed alongside more traditional Islamic forms of education, and conservative Muslim elites met new ideas with great hostility, considering the Jadids to be "impetuous youth."[101]

Jadids, however, felt more comfortable with one aspect of European progress than did their counterparts in Russian Tashkent. Economic development and capital accumulation appeared as useful tools to develop local society and overcome European domination. Unlike Russian liberals, Jadids themselves operated in the world of business – Munawwar Qari ran a bookstore, for example – and they derived their support from wealthy businessmen and traders.[102] Mahmud Behubdi forcefully expressed his desire that Muslims should pursue financial gain, stating "may God increase [their wealth]!"[103] Accumulation, however, was viewed as an absolute good only when it benefited the entire community. "Young businessmen" who whittled away their savings gambling or supported extravagant ritual feasts received sharp Jadid criticism.[104] Capitalism nonetheless appeared as a useful tool to subvert, rather than enforce, the inequities of colonial rule in Tashkent.

Poor migrants and a perceived loss of control, to the center as well as to Central Asians, came to symbolize the outcome of increased economic development for leading tsarist officials and commentators in the Tashkent Russian press in the post-1905 years. Even in their "natural role" as peasant colonizers, Russian settlers destabilized colonial society. Rural villages as well as city streets now teemed with new arrivals who were upsetting racial, social, and gender hierarchies. Russian Tashkent lost its perceived sense of order and progress that ostensibly differentiated it from the Asian city, as well as making it a symbol of the advance of "civilization" to the colonized world. The tsarist government, fighting for time after the revolutionary events of 1905, chose to export its problems and seek solutions on the periphery; in so doing, they ignored the needs and desires of local officials and elites. Political exiles, railway workers, and poor migrants all appeared not as welcome additions to a minority Russian community, even during the brief period when the possibility of a fully democratic Turkestan made demographic weight of critical importance; rather, they were seen as the latest in the line of "freaks" sent from St Petersburg to Tashkent. In the capital of the newest Russian province, born during the optimism of the Great Reforms, officials and elites envisioned their city as a vanguard for progress, not a trading post and depot for raw goods to be manufactured for the city. Post-1905 central policies seemed to be favoring the colonized population, which used well-established urban and merchant traditions to vault ahead of the Russian colonizer. As ever greater numbers of migrants arrived in Tashkent without any sense of "civilization," these colonizers began to ask who was colonizing and who was civilizing whom? Such a pessimistic discourse dominated the Tashkent Russian press even at a time when trade and growth was booming, when new restaurants and theatres appeared, and when the railway allowed leading cultural figures from central Russia to perform in the city for the first time. Jadids, themselves isolated from the Islamic clerics that formed the inner power circle in their own society, also lamented the future, not only because of their status as the colonized, but also because of the qualities of their own poor and peasant population, which, despite participating actively in a new burgeoning economy, still appeared as ignorant and backward. For them, as for the Russian liberals, Tashkent's growing lower classes no longer afforded them the opportunity to see the city as a refuge from the darker sides of the "progress" they so keenly espoused.

Notes

1 The Social Sciences and Humanities Research Council of Canada, the University of Illinois of Urbana-Champaign, and the University of Tennessee provided funding for the research for this chapter.
2 TsGARUz, f. I [Istoricheskaia chast']-16, op. 1, d. 29a, ll. 30, 180.
3 *Sredneaziatskaia zhizn'* [hereafter *SZ*], 9 April, 3 May, 7 and 13 June 1906.
4 On Kaufman and Turkestan, see Daniel Brower, *Turkestan and the Fate of the Russian Empire* (London, 2003), 26–56.
5 TsGARUz, f. I-36, op. 1, d. 525, ll. 20–1.
6 TsGARUz, f. I-1, op. 16, d. 224, l. 5.
7 TsGARUz, f. I-591, op. 1, d. 1, l. 2.
8 Jeff Sahadeo, *Russian Colonial Society in Tashkent, 1865–1923* (Bloomington, 2007), chps 1 and 4.
9 *Turkestanskie vedomosti* [hereafter *TV*], no. 49 (1884).
10 Ibid.
11 G.P. Fedorov, "Moia sluzhba v Turkestanskom krae (1870–1906 goda)," *Istoricheskii vestnik*, no. 10 (1913): 455.
12 *TV*, no. 20 (1893).
13 *Okraina*, 19 March 1894.
14 N. Gavrilov, *Pereselencheskoe delo v Turkestanskom krae (oblasti Syr-Dar'inskaia, Samarkandskaia, i Ferganskaia)* (St Petersburg, 1911), 4.
15 G.S. Kunavina, *Formirovanie zheleznodorozhnogo proletariata v Turkestane (1881–1914 gg)* (Tashkent, 1967), 57–8.
16 F. Azadaev, *Tashkent vo vtoroi polovine XIX veka: Ocherki sotsial'no-ekonomicheskoi i politicheskoi istorii* (Tashkent, 1959), 221.
17 TsGARUz, f. I-1 op. 31, d. 212, l. 1.
18 *Obzor Syr-Darinskoi oblast' za 1906 godu* (Tashkent, 1908), 168.
19 *TV*, 8 January 1908.
20 On the 1905 revolution in Tashkent, see A.V. Piaskovskii, *Revoliutsiia 1905–7 gg. v Turkestane* (Moscow, 1958).
21 *TV*, 6 January 1906
22 *SZ*, 25 November 1905.
23 *SZ*, 24 November 1905.
24 Ibid.

25 *SZ*, 6 January 1906.
26 Ibid.
27 Ibid.
28 *TV*, 6 January 1906.
29 K.K. Palen, *Otchet po revizii Turkestanskogo kraia, proizvedennoi po vysochaiemu poveleniiu Senatorom Gofmeisterom Grafom K.K. Palenom* (St Petersburg, 1910), 1: 378–9.
30 *Russkii Turkestan*, 9 January 1906.
31 On this, see Charles Steindwedel in this volume and Donald W. Treadgold, *The Great Siberian Migration: Government and Peasant in Resettlement from Emancipation to the First World War* (Princeton, 1957), 184–204.
32 M.E. Saltykov-Shchedrin, "Chto takoe 'Tashkentsy'?," *Otechestvennye zapiski*, no. 5 (October 1869): 187–207.
33 *TV*, no. 5 (1891).
34 *Na rubezhe*, 9 October 1910.
35 *SZ*, 11 January 1907.
36 *SZ*, 24 January 1907.
37 TsGARUz, f. I-69, op. 1, d. 1, l. 26.
38 A.I. Ginzburg, *Russkoe naselenie v Turkestane (konets XIX–nachalo XX veka)* (Moscow, 1992), 66.
39 *SZ*, 11 January 1907.
40 *Obzor Syr-Dar'inskoi oblasti za 1912 god* (Tashkent, 1914), 38.
41 Ginzburg, *Russkoe naselenie*, 51, 122; P.G. Galuzo, *Turkestan-koloniia. (Ocherk istorii Turkestana ot zavoevaniia russkimi do revoliutsii 1917 goda* (Moscow, 1929), 195–208.
42 *SZ*, 11 January 1907; Ginzburg, *Russkoe naselenie*, 87, 95.
43 Richard A. Pierce, *Russian Central Asia 1867–1917: A Study in Colonial Rule* (Berkeley, 1960), 136.
44 *Obzor Syr-Dar'inskoi oblasti za 1912 god*, 163.
45 *Na rubezhe*, nos. 95, 109 (1909).
46 *TV*, no. 250 (1911); on hostility to migrants, see also *Na rubezhe*, nos. 95, 109 (1909).
47 Palen, *Otchet po revizii*, 1: 378–9.
48 Muriel Joffe, "Autocracy, capitalism, and empire: the politics of irrigation," *Russian Review* 54, no. 3 (1995): 373.
49 Gavrilov, *Pereselencheskoe delo*, 99–100.
50 Galuzo, *Turkestan-koloniia*, 113.
51 I.M. Slutskii, "Khlokpovodstvo v Turkestane (doklad)," *Turkestanskoe sel'skoe khoziaistvo*, no. 4 (1911): 48.
52 A.P. Demidov, *Ekonomicheskii ocherk khlopkovodstva, khlopkotorgovli i khlopkovoi promyshlennosti Turkestana* (Moscow, 1922), 36.
53 *Obzor Syr-Dar'inskoi oblasti za 1912 god*, 125.
54 Ibid., 126.
55 The most renowned example of this was N.M. Iadrintsev's *Sibir kak koloniia: k iubileiu trekhsotletiia* (St Petersburg, 1882). See his arguments on 258–62, 295.
56 On the definition of *koloniia*, see *Entsiklopedicheskii slovar'*, 82 vols (St Petersburg, 1891–1904) [hereafter *ES*], 24: 518.
57 *Tashkentskii kur'er*, 13 February 1906.
58 *Obzor Syr-Dar'inskoi oblasti za 1912 god*, 125.
59 *SZ*, 24 November 1905.
60 See, for example, *SZ*, 26 February 1906; and *TV*, 12 January 1912.
61 *SZ*, 25 July 1906.
62 N.N. Karazin, *Russkaia Sredniaia Aziia, Zhivopisnaia Rossiia*, v. XX (1885), 150.
63 *TV*, no. 74 (1903).
64 In 1914, 159 cotton-processing plants were operating in Fergana, compared to 28 in the Syr-Dar'ia oblast. V. Suvorov, *Istoriko-ekonomicheskii ocherk razvitiia Turkestana* (Tashkent, 1962), 35–6.

65 *Turkestanskii Kara-Kurt*, no. 1–4 (1911): 6, 8.
66 A.I. Dobrosmyslov, *Tashkent v proshlom i nastoiashchem: Istoricheskii ocherk* (Tashkent, 1912), 374.
67 Ibid.
68 TsGARUz, f. I-36, op. 1, d. 4699, ll. 28–32.
69 *Na rubezhe*, 12 September 1909.
70 *Obzor Syr-Dar'inskoi oblasti za 1912 god*, 136; Marco Buttino, "Turkestan 1917: La révolution des russes," *Cahiers du monde russe et soviétique* 32, no. 1 (1991): 63.
71 *Turkestanskii sbornik*, 502: 221.
72 See, for example, *TV*, no. 83 (1903); no. 25 (1909); and *Turkestanskii kur'er*, 4 May 1913.
73 *Na rubezhe*, 24 January 1910.
74 Sahadeo, *Russian Colonial Society*, chp. 4.
75 *Na rubezhe*, 6 October 1909.
76 See, for example, *Na rubezhe*, 24 November 1910; and TsGARUz, f. 36, op. 1, d. 3492, l. 8.
77 *SZ*, 17 March 1906.
78 Ibid.
79 *TV*, no. 12 (1910).
80 *Turkestanskii kur'er*, 15 June 1914.
81 TsGARUz, f. I-1, op. 16, d. 843, ll. 1–2; f. I-36, op. 1, d. 4230, ll. 12–13, 123; and *TV*, 11 January 1904. On these uses of gender, see Anne McClintock, *Imperial Leather: Race, Gender, and Sexuality in the Colonial Contest* (New York, 1995), 352–74.
82 Anatole Maria Bariatinsky, *My Russian Life* (London, 1923), 175.
83 *TV*, no. 3 (1890).
84 *Turkestanskii skorpion*, no. 2 (1907).
85 On Russian women and strikes, see Rose Glickman, *Russian Factory Women: Workplace and Society, 1880–1914* (Berkeley, 1984).
86 TsGARUz, f. I-36, op. 1, d. 6100, l. 27.
87 *Na rubezhe*, 24 September 1909.
88 Alice J. Conklin, "Colonialism and human rights: a contradiction in terms?" *American Historical Review* 103, no. 2 (April 1998): 419–42.
89 See *Obzor Syr-Dar'inskoi oblasti za 1912 god*, 131; and *Istoriia Uzbekskoi SSR* (Tashkent, 1956), 2: 176–7.
90 Dobrosmyslov, *Tashkent*, 79–80.
91 Muslim workers earned an estimated 37 percent less than Russian workers in Tashkent. *Istoriia Uzbekskoi SSR*, 2: 202–3, 336–7.
92 Dobrosmyslov, *Tashkent*, 79.
93 N.G. Mallitskii, "Tashkentskie makhalle i mauze," in *V.V. Bartol'du Turkestanskie druz'ia ucheniki i pochiteteli* (Tashkent, 1927), 108–9.
94 On notability in Tashkent, see R.N. Nabiev, *Tashkentskoe vosstanie 1847 g. i ego sotsial'no-ekonomicheskie predposylki* (Tashkent, 1966).
95 Palen, *Otchet po revizii*, 3: 50–2.
96 *Sada-yi Turkestan*, 4 December 1914.
97 Adeeb Khalid, *The Politics of Muslim Cultural Reform* (Berkeley, 1997), 93.
98 *Sada-yi Turkestan*, 17 April 1914.
99 *Tujjor*, 21 November 1907.
100 Khalid, *Politics*, 221–2.
101 Ibid., 141–4.
102 *Sada-yi Turkestan*, 2 May 1914.
103 Behbudi, quoted in Khalid, *Politics*, 219.
104 *Sada-yi Turkestan*, 4 April and 17 May.

Part III

Population politics and the Soviet experiment

8 Acclimatization, the shifting science of settlement

Cassandra Cavanaugh

Medicine as a "tool of empire" aided European conquest of tropical regions by blunting the impact of infectious disease on soldiers and settlers.[1] Yet the persistently high rates of European morbidity and mortality in overseas colonies prompted intense debate as to whether the natives of a temperate climate could truly prosper in tropical lands, and vice versa. The fields of tropical medicine and tropical hygiene developed in the late nineteenth century to examine what were seen as environmental barriers to European settlement, to study both the particular pathogens of the colonies and to develop practical measures to promote acclimatization.[2] More broadly, "acclimatization studies" united scientists from many different disciplines – including geographers, medical scientists, anthropologists, agricultural specialists, zoologists, and biologists – in the pragmatic aim of settling, administering, and making profitable Europe's colonial outposts.[3] Environmental challenges to European settlement threatened to undermine unquestioned faith in European superiority, shored up in this period by faith in the possibilities of science.

By the early twentieth century, Russian scientists, mainly biologists and zoologists, were enmeshed in these debates, exploring the implications of their own empire's enormous environmental diversity. Although huge numbers of peasant families left European Russia for Siberia and the Kazakh steppe from the late nineteenth century onward, it was only in the 1920s that the problem of human acclimatization gained the attention of medical scientists and anthropologists in the Soviet Union. At that time, population movements into the southern reaches of Central Asia, or the Turkestan ASSR, were on the rise. Dubbed informally "*nasha tropika*" (our tropics), Central Asia since its conquest in the 1860s and 70s had become in the Russian public mind the equivalent to Europe's new overseas possessions, providing an opportunity to assert Russia's proper place among the "civilizing" powers of the West.[4] Civilization meant settlement, according to tsarist military officials who governed the province, in order to "inspire the natives to improve agriculture and industry through the Russian example."[5] But as "Europeans," Russian settlers would necessarily face the same environmental threats that rendered the English and French presence in the tropics of Africa and Asia so hazardous.

Views on the possibility of Russian acclimatization in the Central Asian "tropics" would radically shift in the first two decades of Soviet rule. During the 1920s, scientists in the Union's scientific centers and those in the region cast doubt on the possibility of Russian physiological adaptation in Central Asia. However, by 1935, Soviet medical and biological scientists, sometimes the very same ones, began to insist that full acclimatization was not only possible, but required only simple alterations in lifestyle and habits. Whether or not Russians had the ability to successfully colonize Central Asia reflected not only observers' views about the region, its climate, and its indigenous residents, but also their beliefs about the nature of the Russian people, and its biological, cultural, and political identity. The acclimatization question gave scientists the opportunity to underline the firm distinction they drew between indigenous "Asians," and immigrant "Europeans."

Russians as Europeans: early Soviet anti-acclimatization views

Early Soviet explorations of the acclimatization question relied heavily on the Western European literature on the subject. Leading Soviet specialists adopted the most radical anti-acclimatization stance as if to sharply underline Russians' European-ness. The first systematic statement came in 1923, when V.V. Bunak, the Soviet Union's most prominent physical anthropologist and head of the Moscow University Anthropology Laboratory, surveyed the European literature on acclimatization. He expressed deep pessimism about the possibility of humans from various races settling successfully in foreign climates.[6] Race and acclimatization were inextricably tied in European scientific and popular understandings. According to Bunak and others at the time, the somatic differences anthropologists catalogued in human groups classified as "races" corresponded to internal, physiological, and functional characteristics (the constitution) that also varied by race, and these characteristics determined vulnerability to various pathogens and climatic influences.[7] Contact with unfamiliar indigenous peoples, even within the same temperate climatic zone, would inevitably expose European settlers to new local illnesses or unfamiliar strains of other, more widespread diseases. The immigrant population might gradually build up immunity, but only "through a lengthy and severe process of natural selection."[8] As to settlement in the tropics, Bunak considered that "the impossibility for the European organism to adapt to the meteorological conditions of a hot climate is beyond doubt."[9] If Europeans did manage to survive in the tropics, it was only because they did not perform any physical work, living "as lords, served by an enormous quantity of slave labor," and even so had difficulty adapting. The "colored races," on the other hand, thrived in the tropics because, in Bunak's view, their requirements for sustenance and other necessities of life are so low. In order to adapt to the tropics, Bunak wrote, "the European must either abandon his European style of life, and lower himself to the living standards of the native [*opustit'sia do urovnia sushchestvovaniia tuzemtsa*]," or he will inevitably fall victim to tropical "wasting" or anemia.[10]

Those Europeans who did survive could not thrive, according to Bunak, since they were deprived of "the beneficial effect of the change of season on the life activity of the organism."[11] Even after gradual acclimatization, in tropical and subtropical regions, the bodily functions of the European would inevitably be depressed, leaving them less able to carry out life activities, weakened, and vulnerable to disease. In European women, fertility would wane, whereas men would experience "intensification of the sexual functions."[12] European settlers could only acclimatize in new regions beyond 10 degrees of latitude, according to French anthropologists working in Algiers, by moving gradually from one climatic zone to the next, and only if the new region did not differ too greatly from the home environment.[13] Racial makeup could confer a heightened propensity for adaptive physiological changes, but would not guarantee that the organism would function normally: those peoples from relatively hot climates, such as the Spanish, had greater chances of acclimatizing than those from more northerly lands, such as the English (although, for Bunak, the Spanish practice of intermarriage left the question of true acclimatization, which presumed the maintenance of the true type, unanswered).[14] Bunak believed that Europeans could more easily adapt to arid climates than to humid ones, and noted that the flow of Slavic settlers into the Central Asian steppe came mainly from the southern regions of Russia and Ukraine. He strongly doubted the success of a colony in Turkestan created by natives of Russia's northern regions.[15]

Representatives of fields such as medicine and biology adopted a slightly more optimistic view than Bunak, presuming that human biology was somewhat more malleable. The second major Soviet statement on acclimatization came from another Moscow specialist, a biologist, and, more importantly, a proponent of eugenics: Nikolai Konstantinovich Kol'tsov, director of the Institute for Experimental Biology and one of the founders of the Russian Eugenics Society. At the core of eugenics, of course, lay the belief that beneficial human traits could be advanced, and negative ones discouraged, so the eugenic approach to acclimatization necessarily meant a search for solutions.[16] Kol'tsov clearly recognized that the economic importance of migration issues in the early years of the USSR could yield opportunities to advance his research, and indeed, the Eugenics Society drew support from the People's Commissariat for Public Health (Narkomzdrav). Yet Kol'tsov was careful not to promise more than he thought his fledgling field could deliver, and did not minimize the acclimatization problem. "A European who finds himself in a tropical climate has a completely different susceptibility to disease than does the native," Kol'tsov wrote in 1928. "The important economic goal of settling tropical, subtropical, and polar regions demands that we discover whether or not the cause of these differences is the absence of acquired immunity or rather the effect of inborn constitutional traits of the European."[17] Like Bunak, Kol'tsov looked overwhelmingly to hereditary and biological factors to explain differential rates of all manner of disease observed among various "racial" groups, and he promoted the study of what he dubbed "racial pathology" in order to isolate each race's particular profile of resistance or susceptibility to disease. Yet, because disease susceptibility likely stemmed, according to Kol'tsov, from inherent racial factors, in the short term, until those factors were understood, little could be done to lessen European vulnerability in foreign environments.

Kol'tsov drew much of the supporting evidence for his theories from a tour of Central Asia in 1928, during which physicians in the region recounted their clinical observations that various diseases affected native and immigrant populations differently. While some struck indigenous Turkestanis with particular virulence (tuberculosis, syphilis), others seemed to bypass them entirely (including certain types of cancers). Tashkent physicians related the story of a scarlet fever epidemic in 1925–6, which seemed only to infect Russian and other European children. Citing German research, Kol'tsov hypothesized that the Uzbek children were hereditarily immune to the disease but carried its infectious agent. "In many southern, tropical, and sub-tropical countries, where epidemics of scarlet fever and diphtheria are hardly found among the local population," Kol'tsov wrote, "it has been shown that the infectious agents are carried by healthy children no less frequently, and are even more common than in northern countries, where diphtheria and scarlet fever carry away many victims."[18] The consequences of placing non-resistant Europeans in such a threatening disease environment were clear. Kol'tsov did hold out the hope, however, that the study of evolutionary processes, which he maintained were progressing more rapidly than ever before – "before our very eyes, and not over the course of endless centuries" – could eventually point to ways to reduce European vulnerability to disease.[19]

Both Bunak and Kol'tsov warned of the dangers posed by migration not only for Europeans in new environments, but also for the peoples they encountered there. Kol'tsov noted the lethal effect that exposure to contemporary European cultures and populations could have on indigenous groups, causing them to die out or "degenerate," a fact that also demanded investigation to clarify whether culture and *byt* [way of life], or these groups' particular physiologies lie at fault. According to Bunak, different racial immunity characteristics meant that in the encounter between settlers and indigenous peoples, one or both populations "would encounter serious threats to their survival." Only the process of biological competition between them would reveal the stronger group. As an example, Bunak cited the successful English colonization of North America, which he attributed to the fact they encountered there "a sparse, half-wild population, the primitive tribes of Indians, unable to resist them, and who quickly died out and freed the land." In India, settlement produced a much higher mortality rate for Europeans, because the English were met there by "stable racial types with whom the newcomers were unable to compete."[20]

Though written in the ostensibly neutral language of science, appraisals of European viability conveyed judgments about overall biological strength and worth, and expressed anxiety about the ability of Russians to accomplish the tasks of settling and ruling over what tsarist elites had deemed the empire's "colonies," but were now firmly fixed in the Soviet periphery. Though biologically vulnerable in the tropics, European dependence on a temperate climate provided for their cultural and intellectual superiority, which in itself helped underpin the idea of a civilizing mission. Together with their European counterparts, early Soviet scientists clearly considered the role of climate fundamental in shaping the various human races, and not only their physical traits but their psychological makeup as well. In this they echoed European colonial stereotypes of the lazy native, which attributed character to climatic influence.[21]

Acclimatization and the tasks of provincial science

What effect did these scientists have on state policy? The same year that Bunak published his anti-acclimatization views, the Party articulated its policy towards the non-Russian nationalities, substituting the promise of economic and cultural development for the local autonomy that had seemingly been proffered in 1917. "Overcoming the colonial legacy" of impeded development in those areas deemed "backward" vis à vis European Russia became the stated goal of that policy. In April 1923, the Twelfth Party Congress stated conclusively that the only solution of the national question lay in overcoming the non-Russian peoples' economic and cultural disadvantages. This strategy, known as *korenizatsiia* (indigenization, from *korennye narody*, or indigenous peoples) dominated Soviet policy towards the non-Russian nationalities throughout the 1920s and 1930s.[22]

Yet how could the indigenous peoples of such "backward" regions as Central Asia be raised to the level of development in Russia if their very biological makeup contributed to that backwardness? *Korenizatsiia* rejected any possibility of Russian migrants "lowering themselves to the living standards of the natives," as Bunak maintained, but rather insisted that the natives be brought up to European standards of development in their own territory. The tension between the political mandate of the Party and the research and practice agendas of physicians and public health officials in Soviet Central Asia grew into the 1930s.

Acclimatization was a familiar problem to the earliest physicians in Russian Turkestan, though they did not, for the most part, use the term. From the beginnings of the Russian conquest of Central Asia in the nineteenth century, migrants reported states of ill-health they suffered due to the unfamiliar environment. Whether from the intense summer heat, the elevation or dryness, or new, unfamiliar diseases, both Russian patients and physicians frequently attributed these sicknesses to Russians' special vulnerability to the Central Asian climate.[23] Settlers, soldiers, and administrators from the Russian metropole complained frequently of weakness, shortness of breath, and general malaise during the hot Central Asian summer.[24] These accounts, drawing on the European literature in the growing specialty of tropical medicine, often conflated the effects of local meteorological conditions and other disease-promoting factors, such as sanitation, water quality, or exposure to specific disease agents. Indigenous bodies and their pathogens constituted another threatening aspect of the new environment, and Russian medical writings warned that contact with indigenous peoples, while impossible to prevent, could spread sickness.[25] Through their acquaintance with the British and French colonial medical literature, Russian physicians knew that in some cases European powers attempted to limit their soldiers' contact with colonized peoples, fearing that Indians would pass contagion on to unacclimatized and vulnerable

Europeans. Most Russians judged such attempts impractical for tsarist Turkestan.[26]

Imperial-era Russian physicians, like their European counterparts, held differing opinions on the possibility of successful adaptation to what many labeled the "tropical" climate of Central Asia. Some believed the "foreign, unhealthy climate" to be "fatal" for Russians and Slavs; while others claimed that if locations of settlement were chosen to avoid the unhealthiest spots, and with the proper alterations in their daily regimen, Russians could fully adapt to the region's conditions.[27] Russians, as northerners and "Europeans" would always remain vulnerable to climatic stresses, which could only be mitigated to a greater or lesser degree, some physicians argued. Others insisted that Russians, unlike other Europeans, were uniquely adaptable to different climates, and that specific features inherent in the Russian physical and mental makeup would allow them to flourish in the region.[28]

With the consolidation of Soviet power came several institutional changes that shifted regional scientists toward a more consistently anti-acclimatization position. The Soviet state sponsored extensive efforts to scientifically map and catalogue the peoples, geographies, and natural resources in the non-Russian periphery during the 1920s, causing specialists in various fields to focus more closely on the problem of acclimatization.[29] A new institutional base for medical research (in Turkestan's Narkomzdrav), the Central Asian State University (TsAGU) medical school, a regional Bacteriological Institute, and a branch of the Moscow Tropical Institute all emerged in the early 1920s. The physicians governing these institutions conceptualized the region's health problems largely in terms of Central Asia's unique pathogens.[30] The study of epidemiology in Central Asia grew more systematic as well, thanks in part to the expansion of health care networks after 1925, allowing the region's new public health authorities to better quantify levels of disease in the population.[31] Stimulus to consider the acclimatization problem came from central authorities as well: the Academy of Science's Conference for the Study of Productive Forces (KIPS) urged scientists across the Union to assess the human populations of their regions, their strengths, and weaknesses, under the rubric of "Man as a Productive Force." The Central Bureau on Regional Research in the Uzbek SSR, charged with gathering this information for the Soviet Academy of Sciences, sponsored the first regional conference on Man as a Productive Force in 1925. Scientists presented findings on the national-cultural features of Central Asian peoples, the anthropological traits of various ethnic groups, as well as the topography of disease, rates of illness, specific features of local diseases [*mestnye bolezni*] and the means to treat them.[32]

Two directions in medical thought in the region produced findings that called into question the possibility of acclimatization: medical *kraevedenie* (study of the locality) and race-based research. Regional researchers' focus on "tropical" diseases emphasized the alien, threatening nature of the environment for Europeans, colored by the influence of western European colonial medical writing.[33] In 1925 the Central Asian Medical-Scientific Society sponsored a conference on the import of their members' research for the study of the region (*kraevedenie*), and thus promoted the idea of specific local pathogens. University medical clinics, student research circles, and independent physicians presented findings on the spread of these diseases and their treatment.[34] Many of the studies pointed to the special risks that these diseases posed to Russians and other immigrants who lacked immunity, although few indicated whether such immunity might be acquired.[35]

The study of local pathogens, then, suggested conclusions about the varied reactions to those pathogens shown by human groups – groups that were understood at the time to be representatives of different races. At the same time, physicians, anthropologists, and anatomists undertook anthropomorphic surveys of indigenous populations to define the physical types of the regions' various peoples, and in so doing, helped to reify the national distinctions being drawn among those peoples, and between the Russian and Slavic "Europeans" and indigenous "Asians." Physicians promoted their research on the grounds that the results would yield measures to improve health and fitness of these populations, in part by explaining the discrepancies in disease rates between indigenous and European groups. The idea that certain diseases did not strike indigenous Central Asians at all, or only rarely, had been gaining in strength since the world war and civil war. High death rates from malaria and other diseases among Russian settlers, prisoners of war, and refugees from the Volga implied to local doctors that indigenous Central Asians were innately immune to prevalent local illnesses.[36] At the First Congress of Turkestan Physicians, held in Tashkent in 1922, and at succeeding regional conferences, physicians claimed that they rarely observed a whole series of illnesses in native Turkestanis (cancer, scarlet fever), and that biological as well as cultural factors were responsible for this fact.[37] Assumptions of indigenous invulnerability, however, were accompanied by warnings that the indigenous peoples faced "degeneration" from the combined effects of tuberculosis and syphilis, to which their contact with Russians had exposed them.[38] Indigenous Central Asians' "weakened constitution" left them particularly susceptible to these illnesses, physicians claimed. These diseases also influenced the creation of new (negative) constitutional types, damaging the heredity of the indigenous people even further.[39]

Physicians and researchers in Soviet Central Asia shared Bunakov and Kol'tsov's skepticism about acclimatization, based on their assumptions about the specificity of local pathogens, and the role of race in governing responses to disease. The most prominent physician-anthropologist in the region, Dr Lev Vasilievich Oshanin, located the rationale for his own work on anthropology in its potential to contribute to the study of racial pathology, the concept promoted by Kol'tsov:

> Identifying the basic types, elements of which combine to create the complicated mosaic of the anthropological structure, is a necessary foundation to understanding the problem of racial and geographic pathology. Only when we explain the correspondence of defined complexes of anthropological characteristics to distinct geographical landscapes, and the correlation of these

complexes with constitutional types, serological characteristics and functional traits, can we begin to understand the problem of morbidity in a population, in connection with the environmental-geographic landscape and the heredity of the race.[40]

By 1928, despite the volume of research devoted to ameliorating the affects of the local climate and disease environment, the anti-acclimatizationist stance became more and more clearly pronounced among Soviet scientists in Central Asia. It was another scientist from the metropole who addressed the problem most directly, in an account clearly colored by the personal malaise he suffered in Central Asia. Professor Aleksandr Alekseev of Moscow University was among the specialists sent to staff the newly-created Central Asian State University medical school in 1920. He taught in the department of internal medicine there, specializing in gastro-intestinal disorders (which were for Russian physicians one of the clearest indicators of the region's harmful effects on non-natives). Alekseev argued that the effects of the environment could be blunted, but not overcome because of the unique links between racial physiology and native environment. "There are no cosmopolitan races that do equally well under all climatic conditions," he maintained.[41]

Nevertheless, correct hygiene would lessen (but not eliminate) the harm of the region's climate. Quoting the English malaria specialist Patrick Manson, he cautioned that "an acclimatized European is one who has learned careful and rational behaviors."[42] Chief among those rational behaviors for Alekseev was diet. Citing other European tropical hygiene specialists, he castigated the Russian insistence on maintaining their habitual diet of meat- and fat-filled *borsch* and *shchi* (beet and cabbage soup, respectively): "With this crude, fatty and low-quality diet, Europeans cannot be healthy in Turkestan."[43] Adopting the "French" cuisine based on vegetables such as artichokes and asparagus would help Russian settlers to adapt to the hot weather. However, such delicacies were not to be found in Tashkent, where, Alekseev lamented, even the potatoes were bad. He found the locally grown fruits and vegetables "crude" and "tasteless," claiming that the only palatable fruits there were causing gastro-intestinal distress, and so should be avoided.

Even more than the poor diet, Tashkent's bleak cultural landscape threatened to further dull the sensibilities of immigrant Europeans, and further inhibit their ability to acclimatize. "For a person with developed cultural taste, there is no more depressing sight than this large dusty gray town," he wrote. The low, architecturally undistinguished houses, dusty streets, lack of flowers, the impediments to physical culture since "the whole town lacks even one tennis court or swimming pool" all weighed heavily on Russians "of developed taste" (like himself), as did the reigning "philistinism" of local immigrant culture. More theater, cinema, and in general opportunities to fulfill what he termed the "requirements of the soul" would be necessary if Russians were to fully acclimatize in the region.[44] Alekseev suggested that, in principle, indigenous culture might yield insights into the most rational means for adapting to the local climate, and he urged scientists of acclimatization to "become acquainted with the Uzbek way of life and the requirements of the spirit." He insisted that the effects of climate cannot be studied in the abstract, and urged physicians to pay close attention to cultural and lifestyle factors, allowing that "even the undemanding Uzbeks have their own culture and way of life," and that they should be studied.[45]

However, even if Russians in Turkestan studied whatever might be gleaned from indigenous *byt*, and implemented all of the hygienic measures urged by European tropicologists, as Europeans they would still remain vulnerable to the climate's oppressive and even fatal effects. While Alekseev wrote that "it is possible to imagine that with a lifestyle that harmonizes with the climate in an ideal fashion, no climate would be inhospitable," from his description of the climate's effects, even such an ideal lifestyle, as remote as that possibility was, could not fully blunt the climate's harm to Russians.[46] The sun's rays, according to Alekseev, are extremely dangerous, even "sterilizing" (in the physiological, not hygienic sense) and threaten to strip the European of his productive capacity. "The too intense rays of the sun destroy the tissues of the white person just as x-rays broke down the tissues of many researchers before they were aware of the dangers."[47] He bemoaned Tashkent's still air, and cited an unnamed American climatologist to show that the absence or presence of breezes is a key for determining whether or not Europeans can tolerate a climate.[48] Altogether, what he called Turkestan's "tropical" climate had a deeply depressive effect on all the physiological functions of "the white person," according to Alekseev, lowering the metabolism, suppressing glandular secretions, and leading to psychological depression as well. His own misery fairly seeps through his description of the climate's effects: "Among sensitive people and those used to making themselves aware of their physical sensations there is often a kind of sun-phobia; they begin to hate this day-in, day-out burning sun, and begin to long for the overcast northern sky."[49]

Discussions of acclimatization, then, focused on the purportedly inherent biological differences among the "races" and provided a scientific justification for the generally low estimations of indigenous peoples and cultures that many Russians held. Biological differentiation ensured that differences in climate could not be overcome easily, or at all, and that the migration of Slavic peoples to Central Asia was inadvisable and to be kept to a minimum. Descriptions of climate connoted the negative qualities attributed to the Asian residents of the territory, echoing European ideas about the effects of hot climates on the psychology of indigenous peoples.[50] Alekseev's account of the sun's effects on Europeans calls on stereotypical images of the Asian character. The sun's rays are "insidious" (*kovarnye*), deceptive, and strike "quickly and without warning."[51] He compared the still air to a stagnant swamp, claiming that "eastern peoples" have a special love for flowing streams and gurgling waterfalls because of "the burdensome sensation of complete stillness, stagnation – in the absence of wind. Life is movement, and at is best is expressed through intensive, rhythmic movement. Any lasting stagnation or calm becomes unbearable." The stillness and the heat together cause indigenous residents to "avoid any mental or physical exertion whatsoever," rendering them as inert and unmoving as the air.[52]

Not only Russian scientists unhappily transplanted from the center, but those born and reared in Central Asia itself shared these assumptions of the harmful effects of the local climate on Europeans, as well as their determinative effects on the indigenous character. Professor Isaac Kassirskii, a native of the Russian colonial town of Novyi Margelan and a faculty member of the TsAGU medical school (after 1931, the Tashkent Medical Institute), became one of the region's most prolific specialists on the diseases particular to warm climates. His 1926–8 study of indigenous Uzbek subjects' metabolisms led him to attribute "the well-known phlegmatism and inertness of people populating the tropics and subtropics in general" to the long-term inherited effects of the hot climate. "It is not for nothing," he claimed at a 1928 medical conference in Tashkent, "that the 'languor of sweet southern indolence' (*istoma sladkoi iuzhnoi leni*) has become a saying. But we must not see in this any ill-will of the southern and eastern peoples, but rather seek a biological basis for this phenomenon."[53]

From anti-acclimatization to "socialist acclimatization"

Industrialization and collectivization during the first five-year plan set off waves of migration not seen in the USSR since the Civil War, accompanied in many areas by outright famine.[54] The mass movement of hunger-weakened peoples yielded predictable effects, sparking epidemics of typhus, diphtheria, and malaria across the USSR, and particularly in areas of new, haphazard industrial settlement, which often lacked any sanitary infrastructure. In Central Asia, the usual malarial sites in the Hungry Steppe and Tashkent province flared up again with the influx of new, non-immune bodies. Rapid, ill-planned expansion of irrigation networks, a component of plans to make the USSR self-sufficient in cotton, ensured the disease even more numerous victims than during the Civil War.[55]

Not surprisingly, this combination of high morbidity and the drive to meet the production targets of the Plan put increased pressure on medical researchers, particularly those involved in assessing labor productivity, to contribute to the achievement of state goals.[56] The Plan's emphasis on expansion of the Union's industrial base into new regions made acclimatization a priority issue. Reorganized and placed under the direct supervision of the Sovnarkom, in 1932, Leningrad's Institute of Experimental Medicine became the All-Union Institute of Experimental Medicine (VIEM), now charged with "the study of all aspects of the human organism."[57] Already in 1931, the Institute had begun to research the health of non-Russian minorities as well as labor hygiene; in 1934, the Institute created a formal research unit for acclimatization studies, or "man and climate," with a focus on the Arctic.[58] By 1931, the polar branch of Leningrad Institute for Labor Hygiene had also begun to study the acclimatization of residents of the town of Kirovsk in the far North.[59]

Migration to Central Asia, both spontaneous and planned, brought tens of thousands of new settlers from the Russian Republic (RSFSR) and Ukraine. Despite the urgings of Party officials to employ indigenous workers, economic managers in the region's new plants and construction sites preferred to recruit workers, even unskilled workers, from outside the territory.[60] The Party also sponsored large-scale migration of peasants from the RSFSR and Ukraine to areas to be newly planted with cotton, such as the Tajikistan lowlands.[61] Between 1927 and 1938, 650,000 people, mainly from the RSFSR, migrated to Uzbekistan, with the peak year 1934, when 113,900 came.[62] From 6.4 percent of the population in 1926, Russians grew to 15 percent of the Uzbek SSR's population in 1939. A rising number of studies on applied techniques for Russian acclimatization in Central Asia coincided with this period of migration. No longer could physicians be content to explore the theoretical aspects of migrants' responses to local conditions and pathogens. Military physicians studied soldiers' endurance in desert marches; labor hygienists measured the effects of summer heat on thirst and metabolism; physiotherapists studied the relative effects of solar radiation on immigrants and indigenous Central Asians.[63] And in 1934, the Uzbek SSR public health commissariat (Narkomzdrav) authorized the creation of the Uzbek Institute for Experimental Medicine (UzIEM), which, like its central counterpart, contained a special department devoted to the study of acclimatization, headed by the physician-anthropologist Professor Oshanin.

Research on acclimatization may have enjoyed renewed state support, but this support came linked with new constraints that limited discourse on the issue. The push for plan fulfillment made any suggestion of insurmountable environmental or inherent physiological barriers to maximum productivity politically unwise. Researchers began to reverse previous positions on the limits to physiological adaptation, and to conclude that while the climate may place particular stresses on European migrants, with the proper hygienic accommodations they could nonetheless recover their full productivity and well-being. The role of race in acclimatization became a more sensitive topic. In 1931–2, the fraught political atmosphere of the Cultural Revolution included an attack on alleged "great power chauvinism," and an initial intensification of the policy of *korenizatsiia*.[64] In the region's medical institutions, activists demanded the dismissal and punishment of those researchers who had warned about the possibility of indigenous degeneration brought on by contact with Europeans. At a conference of district health department heads in the spring of 1932, deputy Commissar for Public Health Nikolaev warned that "Uzbeks get sick the same as Europeans do. The Uzbek population is not degenerating, and will not degenerate!"[65] Scientists therefore searched for an approach to acclimatization that would take into account the race factor, but which avoided "biologizing" the question, and so did not risk political censure.

Acclimato-pessimism's days were numbered also because of its association with German racial hygiene theories after the breakdown of Soviet–German scientific cooperation with the rise of the Nazi party to power. Race itself became a politically suspect category in Soviet science, though not yet anathema. The first issue of the Uzbek Institute for Experimental Medicine's journal contained an article outlining the new parameters for discussion of race and acclimatization. Nikolai Kuznetsov and N.P. Sokolov, heads of the climato-physiology and biology departments of the Institute, began by denouncing existing definitions of human acclimatization for giving too much importance to the race factor. Bunak's approach to human acclimatization was harshly criticized as one that logically supported the theory of "higher" and "lower" races, and for his uncritical use of "bourgeois" science.[66] They argued that Bunak had mechanically applied the botanical and zoological view on acclimatization to humans, and that he reduced acclimatization to a biological process, founded on bourgeois racial theory, which, citing Stalin, they condemned as fascist. "Racial theory in the study of acclimatization is used by fascism in order to justify the existing shameless exploitation of colonized peoples."[67]

Reliance on European science, if that research cast doubt on the possibility of acclimatization, became grounds for political condemnation for racism. Kuznetsov and Sokolov discounted Bunak's denial that humans could adapt to extreme, unfamiliar climates as an unfounded tenet of bourgeois science; European scientists, they contended, concluded that full adaptation to the tropics was impossible because the colonist-exploiters they studied did not observe a "scientific, hygienic" lifestyle. Finally, they accused Bunak of bolstering theories that promoted stereotypes of indigenous inferiority, and therefore justifying the exploitation of colonized peoples. Professor Kassirskii, in his 1935 textbook, *Notes on the Hygiene of Warm Climates based on the Conditions of Central Asia*, also took pains to dispel what he termed the "bourgeois theories" of the warm or tropical climate's influence on both the indigenous people's character and the temperament of immigrant Europeans (without mentioning his own earlier views on "tropical indolence"). Colonial social relations and alienation from local life, not the climate, lay at the heart of Europeans' affliction with hypochondria, alcoholism or other psychological anomalies in the tropics, according to Kassirskii.

> It is obvious that all these bourgeois theories are groundless … in the conditions of Soviet Central Asia, where the mutual contact, respect, and the complete elimination of racial and national antagonism between peoples … does not permit the appearance of the so-called specific hypochondria of hot climates.[68]

But how to separate the "bourgeois" use of race concepts from the necessary physiological comparisons of different human groups? Kuznetsov and Sokolov admitted that natural selection, the historical evolution of human groups in different environments, and the study of the physical constitutions of those groups, were keys to unraveling the acclimatization problem. They hoped to salvage the Marxist credibility of race as a concept by citing Engels to the effect that labor, and not climate, helped differentiate the races of man. Furthermore, they denied the absolute biological distinctiveness of racial categories, arguing that "racial distinctions do not constitute an unbridgeable gulf between different human groups, and are not a barrier to their existence in various climatic zones."[69] They only partially rejected Kol'tsov's proposed "racial physiology" and "racial pathology," calling their existence "doubtful" and "exaggerated," and condemning their link to fascist racial theories.[70] Nevertheless, they upheld the need to study possible racially linked differences in physiological functioning in various climates.

These caveats do not seem to have seriously limited the exploration of race and acclimatization in the Institute's anthropology department for a few years.[71] Professor Oshanin continued to hold that "the study of the anthropological composition of Central Asia is ... a transitional step in the investigation of human acclimatization and the natural processes of adaptation of the Central Asian peoples to the conditions and peculiarities of their environment."[72] To plan the research agenda and consult with senior specialists working on "climate and man," Oshanin was sent in early 1935 by the Institute to VIEM in Moscow and to the Academy of Sciences Anthropological laboratory. He also spent time consulting foreign literature on the topic held in the Academy library. The works that he studied, in English and French, uniformly advanced radical anti-tropical acclimatization views, and in the case of the American climatologist Ellsworth Huntington, argued that the temperate climate of the north was uniquely suited to promoting human intellect and achievement.[73] It is not clear what precisely Oshanin concluded from his study of these works; however, his belief in the existence of racially defined physical constitutions that determined an individual's fitness for particular environmental conditions could have only been strengthened by them. Over the next two years, Oshanin directed research comparing the blood chemistry of indigenous and immigrant groups in the Pamirs, the "racial and constitutional types" of peoples of the Pamir mountain range and Pamir foothill region, and on comparative anatomy of indigenous and immigrant groups in Uzbekistan.[74]

The study of racial biology in the region finally came to a halt in 1937, when medical genetics fell into disfavor.[75] That year, UzIEM eliminated Oshanin's anthropology department; work on "climate and man" continued in the physiology department, but without any comparisons across indigenous and immigrant groups. The Institute as a whole was disbanded in 1940, its parasitology department transferred to the Uzbek Republican Bacteriological Institute (reorganized as the Institute for Microbiology, Epidemiology and Parasitology).[76]

While scientists continued to explore the racial basis for physiological adaptation, any suggestion of biological limits to acclimatization disappeared after 1934. Soviet scientists in Central Asia began to insist that not only could Europeans fully acclimatize in alien environments, but that neither racial factors nor socio-cultural ones would inhibit this process. Acceptable views of the climate itself changed, and assessments of the climate's effects shifted from harmful and dangerous to positive and healthful. From 1934 on, researchers took pains to emphasize that Central Asia was not in fact a tropical or sub-tropical climate, but rather an extreme continental one, within which there were numerous regional variations.[77] Professor Kassirskii rejected the view of the Central Asian climate as particularly harmful, and began to promote its health-giving qualities, if the proper hygienic accommodations were made.[78] "Each climate has its own plusses and minuses," he wrote, contrasting the warmth of Central Asia with the cold and damp of more northerly regions in Russia and in Europe, where diseases such as rickets and rheumatoid arthritis, rare in Central Asia, were common.[79] Russians should have no special troubles acclimatizing in Central Asia, according to Kassirskii, because of the lack of humidity in the air – a relative dryness that contrasted to the tropics, where the high moisture levels hindered the body's ability to regulate its temperature.[80] Kassirskii's view of the Central Asian climate and its effects could not contrast more directly with that of Alekseev's sun-phobe longing for cloudy northern skies:

> In spite of the dryness of the surrounding landscape, the abundance of sunshine, light, and the eternally cloudless blue sky are so attractive to those who come from the northern zones of the Union that many remain to live permanently in Central Asia, unable to "deacclimatize," or, as they put it, "part with the dear sun" (*rasstat'sia s solnyshkom*). It is not for nothing that in the public view, a person who even for a little while lived under the warm sun of Central Asia is unable to give it up, and must frequently return there. We know of thousands of such cases ... Therefore, this is an example of "psychological acclimatization."[81]

Rather than climate, Kassirskii claimed, it was the low sanitary standards and primitive element of local *byt* that created conditions for the spread of "cosmopolitan" (no longer tropical) diseases, or those that occurred across regions, and parasitic and other infections particular to hot climates. But Soviet power was well on its way to eliminating these conditions through sanitation and hygiene.[82]

The task of distinguishing "Soviet" approaches to acclimatization from "bourgeois" ones demanded a careful use of European scientific literature. Kuznetsov and Sokolov admitted that the scarcity of data on the region meant that scientists would need to refer to European studies, especially in order to investigate those areas of Central Asia that approached sub-tropical conditions, at least until Soviet scientists could produce their own research.[83] Kassirskii marshaled works of European scholars who considered acclimatization to be possible to support his arguments. He cites one Dr Arnold to the effect that full acclimatization requires that three conditions be met: natural population growth; the preservation of the main constitutional features; and of the ability to perform physical and intellectual labor. Arnold also proposed that Russians were among the ethnic groups particularly able to make the physiological adaptations necessary for acclimatization.[84] The changes in daily life instituted by Soviet power had made all of these conditions possible, Kassirskii argued, and so there could be no doubt that Russian and other European settlers were already acclimatizing in Central Asia. As the question of labor productivity was of primary concern for Soviet science, Kassirskii took special pains to counter theories that European acclimatization was possible in hot climates only if settlers abstained from manual labor, writing that "this colonizing approach is characteristic of many European authors' works on tropical pathology!"[85] If allowed to gradually become accustomed, immigrant workers rapidly acclimatized to the new conditions, according to Kassirskii, and were no less productive than either the acclimatized European or the indigenous population.

If some European findings on tropical acclimatization could be utilized, cautiously, then European hygienic prescriptions required even more vigilant scrutiny. Soviet acclimatization measures would necessarily focus on the socio-economic and cultural basis of everyday life. Previous Soviet approaches to acclimatization, according to Kuznetsov and Sokolov, over-influenced by European writings, failed to take into account the human capacity to alter the very climate in which he is adapting through labor. By reducing acclimatization to a question of biology, they discounted social and economic factors, through which man can foster adaptation, or technological measures, such as irrigation of the desert or housing construction and urban planning to regulate the microclimate, all of which the Soviet state was actively implementing.[86] Soviet acclimatization precluded the adoption of European styles of gear, such as the pith helmet, although Kassirskii acknowledged, ruefully, the superiority of its design and material as a defense against heat. But "political reasons" made pith helmets unacceptable, because of their association with English colonization of India.[87] On the other hand, socialist culture allowed more latitude than did "the narrow framework of prejudice that oppresses bourgeois society" for the development of styles of clothing more rationally suited to hot climates, he pointed out. By way of illustration, he described how, during his 1925 trip abroad, he suffered through a humid New York summer in a dark suit and tie required for his visits to medical institutions, and was refused service in a restaurant where he appeared without a jacket.[88]

In Soviet acclimatization, the European should not try to maintain his habitual way of life, but adopt those aspects of indigenous *byt* that proved to have a scientific basis.[89] Indigenous *byt* had many negative features, it was acknowledged, but thanks to its radical transformation under Soviet rule, some indigenous ways, developed over centuries, will certainly be scientifically proven to aid Europeans in adapting to local conditions.[90] Kassirskii described in detail the indigenous ways that could promote acclimatization. Both the native diet, with the preponderance of calories consumed late in the day and its emphasis on carbohydrates, and style of dress, with its loose-fitting tunics and insulated robes, should be emulated, though not without the proper "ideological" alterations. Because of their religious associations, turbans, for instance, though rational, should be excluded from use on ideological grounds.[91]

Conclusions

During the time at which they wrote, Soviet acclimatization specialists' prescriptions were seldom implemented systematically, if at all.[92] These writings reveal much more about Russians' visions of themselves as colonizers, first on par with, then more advanced than the Europeans to whom they compared themselves, than they do about actual conditions for new settlers in Central Asia.

A reductionist view of the sociology of science would attribute the drastic shifts in Soviet approaches to acclimatization during this period to direct political intervention in the shaping of scientific discourse, beginning in the period of Cultural Revolution, that followed a decade of more candid and scientifically legitimate investigation. It is clear, however, that both the racially based anti-acclimation view of the 1920s, and the later "acclimatization maximalism" were each rooted in their contemporary political and social contexts. Discourse about the role of race in acclimatization paralleled the trajectory of Soviet nationality policy, from one that, during the heyday of *korenizatsiia* in the 1920s, emphasized indigenous distinctiveness (though pronouncing it surmountable), to one that, by the mid-1930s, trumpeted the victory over indigenous backwardness and therefore denied any essential underlying differences. Indigenous *byt*, while primitive, could be said to contain some grains of rationality that might be emulated. In the pre-revolutionary and early Soviet period, scientists associated themselves with European colonial science, accepting research on Bombay or Tunis as fully applicable to Central Asian problems. Later, emphatic declarations of their social and ideological distance from European scientific assumptions allowed scientists to participate in the international conversation, but at the same time to declare the superiority of socialist acclimatization.

Notes

1 Daniel Headrick, *The Tools of Empire: Technology and European Imperialism in the Nineteenth Century* (London, 1981).
2 Michael Worboys, "The emergence of tropical medicine: a study in the establishment of a scientific speciality," in *Perspectives in the Emergence of Scientific Disciplines*, eds G. Lemaine et al. (Mouton, 1990), 75–93.
3 David Livingstone, "Human acclimatization: perspectives on a contested field of inquiry in science, medicine and geography," *History of Science* 25 (1987): 359.
4 In addition to Jeff Sahadeo in this volume, see also Seymour Becker, "Russia between East and West: the intelligentsia, Russian national identity and the Asian borderlands," *Central Asian Survey* 10, no. 4 (1991): 61; Daniel Brower, *Turkestan and the Fate of the Russian Empire* (London, 2003); and Jeff Sahadeo, *Russian Colonial Society in Tashkent, 1865–1923* (Bloomington, 2007).
5 L. Kostenko, *Srednaia Azia i vodvorenie v nei russkoi grazhdanstvennosti* (St Petersburg, 1871), 356.
6 V.V. Bunak, "Ob akklimatizatsii chelovecheskikh ras i sravnitel'nom znachenii opredeliaushchikh ee faktorov," *Russkii antropologicheskii zhurnal* [hereafter *RAZh*], no. 15 (1923): 45–59. N. Bogoiavlenskii, the author of the medical encyclopedia entry on acclimatization, also held that an individual's adaptive potential was a function of race. "Akklimatizatsii," *Bol'shaia meditsinskaia entsiklopediia*, v. 1 (Moscow, 1928).
7 See V.V. Bunak, "Neskol'ko dannykh k voprosu o tipichnykh konstitutsiakh cheloveka," *RAZh* 15, no. 2–3 (1923): 76–93; idem, "K antropologicheskoi kharakteristike tuberkuleznoi konstitutsii, v sviazi s voprosom o ee morfologicheskom znachenii," *RAZh* 15, no. 2–3 (1923): 60–75.
8 Bunak, "Ob akklimatizatsii," 57.
9 Ibid., 47.
10 Ibid.
11 Ibid., 46.
12 Ibid.
13 Ibid., 50.
14 Ibid., 47.
15 Ibid., 53.
16 The founder of eugenics, Francis Galton, defined it in 1905 as "the study of agencies under social control that may improve or impair the racial qualities of future generations

either physically or mentally." Quoted in Ivan Hannaford, *Race: The History of an Idea in the West* (Baltimore, 1996), 330.

17 N.K. Kol'tsov, "Zadachi i metody rasovoi patologii," *Russkii evgenicheskii zhurnal* 7, no. 2–3 (1929): 69.

18 Ibid., 83.

19 Ibid., 70. The rapidity with which biological mechanisms of adaptation could be developed by an organism, and their heritability, divided acclimatization scholars from the first, and reflected the basic split between Lamarckian and Darwinian biology. Some early plant biologists and zoologists in Russia supported the Lamarckian position that traits induced by climatic stresses were heritable, a view which ultimately contributed to the phenomenon of Lysenkoism. Douglas R. Weiner, "The roots of 'Michurinism': transformist biology and acclimatization as currents in the Russian life sciences," *Annals of Science* xlii (1985): 244–60.

20 Bunak, "Ob akklimatizatsii," 57.

21 Livingstone, "Human acclimatization," 372.

22 Gerhard Simon, *Nationalism and Policy toward the Nationalities in the Soviet Union. From Totalitarian Dictatorship to Post-Stalinist Society,* trans. Karen Forster and Oswald Forster (Boulder, 1991), 24; Terry Martin, *The Affirmative Action Empire: Nations and Nationalism in the Soviet Union, 1923–39* (Ithaca, 2001); and Francine Hirsch, *Empire of Nations: Ethnographic Knowledge and the Making of the Soviet Union* (Ithaca, 2005).

23 Reports of military physicians on the threat posed to soldiers by the climate can be found in RGVIA, f. 1402, op. II, d. 32, ll. 19–48, "Sanitarnyi uchenyi meditsinskii otchety po Kokandskomu uezdu Turkestanskogo Voenno-narodnogo upravleniia za 1883"; for one of the earliest accounts, see "Putevye zametki maiora Blankennagelia o Khive v 1793–4gg.," *Vestnik russkogo gegraficheskogo obshchestva,* no. 5 (1858): 90.

24 I.A. Kassirskii, "Klimatopatologiia Srednei Azii," *Klinicheskaia meditsina* [hereafter *KM*] XIII, no. 5 (May, 1935): 640; for a patient's view, see the memoirs of Varvara Dukhovskaia, wife of the governor-general, *Turkestanskiia Vospominaniia* (St Petersburg, 1913), 23.

25 For European debates on medically motivated segregation, see Philip D. Curtin, *Death by Migration: Europe's Encounter with the Tropical World in the Nineteenth Century* (Madison, 1989); Mark Harrison, *Climates and Constitutions: Health, Race, Environment and British Imperialism in India, 1600–1850* (Oxford, 1996), 209–14; Dane Kennedy, "The perils of the midday sun: climatic anxieties in the colonial tropics," in *Imperialism and the Natural World,* ed. J.M. MacKenzie (Manchester, 1990), 118–40.

26 A Dr Pevnitskii cited an article by Stephens and Christophers, "The native as the prime agent in the malarial infection of Europeans," in his study of malaria in the Termez and Merv garrisons. He concluded, however, that it is impossible to completely eliminate the fraternization between the garrison and the local peoples, and so other measures of fighting malarial infection would be necessary. "Pervyi opyt ratsionalnoi borby s bolotnoi likhoradkoi v Turkestane," *Russkii vrach* 1, no. 2 (1902): 585.

27 The miasmatic theory of contagion, gradually supplanted by germ theory in the 1880s and 1890s, gave rise to belief in the harmfulness of the region's environment. For this view, see A.M. Satinskii, *K voprosu o Tashkentskikh likhoradkakh* (Tashkent, 1878); "Poezdka A.I. Maksheeva v Turkestanskii krai letom 1867 goda," *Izvestiia Russkogo Geograficheskogo Obschestva* t. III (St Petersburg, 1868); and M.I. Kushelevskii, *Materialy dlia meditsinskoi geografii i sanitarnogo opisaniia Ferganskoi oblasti* (Novyi Margelan, 1890–1). Kushelevskii and others argued that studying the particular properties of specific locations could reveal areas less "miasmatic" and more conducive to settlement. After the establishment of germ theory, the risks posed by the climate and by local sanitary conditions replaced the threat of miasmas. See *Protokoly zasedanii Turkestanskogo meditsinskogo obshchestva* (Tashkent, 1899–1905), v. 1, no. 9.

28 On the difficulties of acclimatization, see *Turkestanskie vedomosti*, no. 48 (1888); on the Russian special ability to acclimatize, see I.L. Iavorskii, *Opyt meditsinskoi geografii i statistiki Turkestana* (St Petersburg, 1889), 473. Willard Sunderland has remarked on the nineteenth-century belief in the Russian capacity to assimilate other peoples, an assumption that was challenged, however, by the physical and cultural admixtures produced by contact with the peoples of the far north. "Russians into Iakuts? 'Going native' and problems of Russian national identity in the Siberian north, 1870s–1914," *Slavic Review* 55: 4 (Winter, 1996): 806–25.

29 For the use of ethnographic surveys during the 1920s, see Hirsch, *Empire of Nations.*

30 N.I. Khodukin, "Dostizheniia profilaktiki i izucheniia tropicheskikh zabolevanii za piatnadstat' let sovetskoi meditsiny v Sr. Azii," *Za sotsialisticheskoe zdravookhranenie Uzbekistana* [hereafter *ZSZUz*] no. 1–2 (1933): 104–10.

31 Cassandra Cavanaugh, "Biology and backwardness: medicine and power in Russian and Soviet Central Asia, 1868–1934" (Ph.D. diss., Columbia University, 2001), chp. 2.

32 Khronika, *Turkestanskii meditsinskii zhurnal* [hereafter *TMZh*], no. 11 (1925): 766–7.

33 The claim made by the Bukhara Tropical Institute, founded in 1924, to have better scholarly ties with foreign tropical institutes in London, Hamburg, and Calcutta than it did with Russian medical and biological research centers attests to the fact that the influence of Western European medical literature remained strong. Khronika, *TMZh*, no. 3 (1925): 195–6.

34 Dr V.A. Dobrokhotov, "Kraevedcheskaia deiatelnost' medfaka SAGU," *TMZh*, no. 12 (1925): 671–6.

35 One exception is the work by M.F. Mirochnik, "Immunitet i reaktsiia komplementa pri maliarii," *TMZh*, no. 1 (1925): 1–10. Mirochnik could not conclusively prove the existence of antibodies in malaria patients, but believed that immunity was likely to be inherited.

36 Ibid.

37 *Trudy pervogo nauchnogo s"ezda vrachei Turkestanskoi respubliki. Tashkent, 23–8 oktiabria 1922 g.* (Tashkent, 1923); "Godovoi otchet nauchnykh konferentsii vrachei st. gor. Tashkenta za 1926–7g.," *Meditsinskaia mysl' Uzbekistana* [hereafter *MMUz*], no. 4 (January, 1928): 72–4; "Protokoly zasedanii nauchnoi konferentsii pri kr. Uzbekskom bakteriologicheskom institute," *MMUz*, no. 5 (February, 1928): 88; *Trudy 3-ogo nauchnogo s"ezda vrachei srednei azii, 20–24 dekabria, 1928 g.* (Tashkent, 1930).

38 *Podvizhnye obsledovatelski-lechebnye otriady i ikh znachenie v organizatsii medpomoshchi selskomu naseleniiu v Srednei Azii (po dannym raboty otriadov v Turkestane v 1924 g.)* (Tashkent, 1925), 3.

39 V.K. Iasevich, "K voprosu o konstitutsionalnom i antropologicheskom tipe uzbechki Khorezma," *MMUz*, no. 5 (February, 1928): 34.

40 *Trudy 3-ogo*, 10–11.

41 A.G. Alekseev, "O vlianii zharkogo klimata v sviazi s kul'turno-bytovymi usloviami na zheludochno-kishechnye zabolevaniia v Turkestane," *KM* 6, no. 13 (July, 1928): 742.

42 Ibid., 750.

43 Ibid., 749.

44 Ibid., 751.

45 Ibid., 743.

46 Ibid., 744.

47 Ibid., 752.

48 Ibid., 745.

49 Ibid., 752.

50 Harish Naraindas has pointed out the anthropomorphic quality in European discussions of 'tropicality' with its lethargy, disease, and corruption. "Poisons, putrescence and the weather: a genealogy of the advent of tropical medicine," in *Médicines et Santé: Les sciences hors d'Occident au XX siècle*, ed. Anne-Marie Moulin (Paris, 1996), 31–57.

51 Alekseev, "O vlianii," 743, 748.

52 Ibid., 749.
53 I.A. Kassirskii, "K geograficheskoi patologii Srednei Azii. O gazoobmene u zdorovykh liudei v zharkoe vremia," in *Trudy 3-go*, 89.
54 For an overview of migration in this period, see Sheila Fitzpatrick, "The great departure: rural-urban migration in the Soviet Union, 1929–33," in *Social Dimensions of Soviet Industrialization*, eds William G. Rosenberg and Lewis H. Siegelbaum (Bloomington, 1993), 15–40.
55 A. Nikol'skii, "Perspektivy maliariinosti i bor'ba s neiu v Golodnoi i Dal'verzinskoi stepiakh v sviazi s vypolneniem kholpkovoi piatiletki," *Meditsnskaia mysl' Uzbekistana i Turkmenistana*, no. 9–10 (1930): 74–80.
56 "Obrashchenie ko vsem zdravotdelam, vsem uchrezhdeniam zdravoookhraneniia i ko vsem medrabotnikam Uzbekistana," *ZSZUz*, no. 9–10 (1933): 197–8; Lewis H. Sieglebaum, "Okhrana Truda: industrial hygiene, psychotechnics, and industrialization in the USSR", in *Health and Society in Revolutionary Russia*, eds Susan Gross Solomon and John F. Hutchinson (Bloomington, 1990), 234–40.
57 T.I. Grekova and K.A. Lange, "Tragicheskie stranitsy istorii instituta eksperimental'noi meditsiny (20–30-e gody)," in *Repressirovannaia nauka*, ed. M.G. Iaroshevskii (St Petersburg, 1994), II: 12–14.
58 Ibid., 14.
59 N.E. Kuznetsov and N.P. Sokolov, "K ucheniiu ob akklimatizatsii cheloveka," *Biulleten' Uzbekskogo Instituta eksperimental'noi meditsiny* 2(3) (1935): 4.
60 TsGANTMD, f. 10, op. 1, d. 1974, ll. 79–86. "Dokladnaia zapiska o natsional'nykh kadrakh v promyshlennosti srednei azii po materialam statsektora sredazgosplana" (1931).
61 "O pereselenii v Tadzhikistan (Postanovlenie Sredazbiuro TsK VKP(b) ot 16 ianvaria 1930)," *Partrabotnik*, no. 2 (1930): 16.
62 T.S. Mel'nikova, *Formirovanie promyshlennykh kadrov v Uzbekistane* (Tashkent, 1956), 80.
63 V.I. Magnitskii, "Medikosanitarnoe obespechenie voisk v usloviiakh pustyn' Srednei Azii," *ZSZUz*, no. 7 (1934): 54–9; S.R. Dikhtiar, "K postanovke issledovaniia pit'evogo rezhima v klimaticheskikh usloviiakh Srednei Azii," *ZSZUz*, no. 4 (1934): 109–11; G.A. Avanesov, "Vlianie solnechnykh luchei na teploregulaitsiiu u cheloveka v usloviiakh Srednei Azii," *ZSZUz* (August, 1932): 51–6; and B.A. Grekov, "Biodoza korennogo naseleniia," *ZSZUz*, no. 4 (1932): 61–5.
64 In the early 1930s, pressure for affirmative action hiring of minorities in industry and government dropped off, and emphasis on building indigenous (socialist) culture gradually gave way to the inculcation of Russian language and cultural markers, leading many scholars to conclude that the state abandoned *korenizatsiia*. See Martin, *Affirmative Action Empire*; and Simon, *Nationalism and Policy*.
65 "O zadachakh zdravookhraneniia," 52.
66 Kuznetsov and Sokolov, "K ucheniiu," 4.
67 Ibid., 8.
68 I.A. Kassirskii, *Ocherki gigieny zharkogo klimata v usloviiakh Srednei Azii* (Tashkent, 1935), 56.
69 Kuznetsov and Sokolov, "K ucheniiu," 4.
70 Ibid., 11.
71 In Moscow's Institute for Experimental Biology, however, while research on acclimatization (mainly in the Far North) continued, references to the racial identity of study subjects disappeared. By 1939, problems of high-altitude physiological adaptation of humans were still studied, but the Sukhumi branch of the institute conducted research on sub-tropical adaptation only on monkeys. See *Biulleten' eksperimental'noi biologii I meditsiny* I–VIII (1935–9); "Narodnyi komissariat zdravookhraneniia SSSR," *Otchet o nauchno-issledovatel'skoi deiatel'nosti vsesoiuznogo instituta eksperimental'noi meditsiny im. A.M. Gor'kogo za 1938–1939* (Moscow, 1940), 273–4.

72 TsGANTMD, f. 61, op. 1, d. 21, l. 6.
73 *Civilization and Climate* (New Haven, 1915). Other works consulted by Oshanin included E.V. Cowdry, ed., *Human Biology and Racial Welfare* (New York, 1930); William Z. Ripley, *The Races of Europe: A Sociological Study* (New York, 1910); Griffith Taylor, *Environment and Race: A Study of the Evolution, Migration, Settlement and Status of the Races of Man.* (London, 1927); Glenn T. Trewartha, "Recent thought on the problem of white acclimatization in the wet tropics," *Geographical Review* 16 (1926). On the anti-tropical acclimatization views of Huntington and the Anglo-American climatological school, see Livingstone, "Human acclimatization," 363. TsGANTMD, f. 61, op. 1, d. 22, ll. 54–5 ob. "Otchet o komandirovke prof. L.V. Oshanina v Moskvu I Lenigrad (srokom s 19/I 35 g. k 20 II 35 g.)."
74 TsGANTMD f. 61, op. 1, d. 21, ll. 1–15, "Rabochaia programma otdela sravnitel'noi antropologii i sravnetel'noi morfologii narodov srednei azii na 1934 god."; Ibid., ll. 16–20, "Dokladnaia zapiska, k planu rabot otdela sravnitel'noi antropologii i sravnitelnoi morfologii narodov Srednei Azii pri UzIEM."
75 Mark Adams, "Eugenics as social medicine in revolutionary Russia: prophets, patrons, and the dialectics of discipline-building," in Solomon and Hutchinson, eds, *Health and Society*, 222.
76 TsGANTMD, f. 61, op. 1, d. 35, ll. 1–2, "Rezoliutsiia Sovnarkoma UzSSR, 11 fevralia 1940g."
77 L.A. Molchanov, "Klimaticheskie usloviia Srednei Azii," *Sanitarnii sputnik vracha Srednei Azii* (Tashkent, 1935); and V.I. Magnitskii, "Mediko-sanitarnoe obespechenie voisk v usloviakh pustyn' Srednei Azii," *ZSZUz*, no. 1–2 (1934).
78 Kassirskii taught at TashMI until 1934 (from 1931 as a docent, and then professor and head of the Institute's tropical disease clinic). That year he left his research work in the region to become director of Moscow's Railway Hospital Institute, although he continued to publish articles on parasitic diseases. A. Lysenko, "Tropicheskie bolezni," *Bol'shaia meditsinskaia entsiklopediia,* izd. vtoroe, v. 32 (Moscow, 1963), 824–5; and R.I. Vorob'ev, *I.A. Kassirskii i ego vklad v meditsinu* (Moscow, 1988).
79 Kassirskii, *Ocherki*, 4.
80 I.A. Kassirskii, "Klimatopatologiia Srednei Azii," *KM* XIII, no. 5 (May, 1935): 640.
81 Kassirskii, *Ocherki*, 75.
82 I.A. Kassirskii, "Tropicheskie bolezni i osobnnosti techeniia nekotorykh kosmopolitnykh zabolevanii v Srednei Azii," *KM* XIII, no. 8 (August, 1935): 1125.
83 Kuznetsov and Sokolov, "K ucheniiu," 23.
84 Kasirskii, *Ocherki*, 72. Kassirskii cites Arnold only by name, and does not include his works in his bibliography.
85 Ibid., 75.
86 Kuznetsov and Sokolov, "K ucheniiu," 16.
87 Kassirskii, *Ocherki*, 95.
88 Ibid., 84.
89 Kuznetsov and Sokolov, "K ucheniiu," 9.
90 Ibid., 27.
91 Kassirskii, *Ocherki*, 96.
92 Kassirskii describes conditions at an irrigation construction site in the Hungry Steppe where, despite his counsel to the administering state agency, manual laborers received poor rations and had no special clothing to shield them from the sun; many were taken ill with gastrointestinal disorders and vitamin deficiencies. *Ocherki*, 155.

9 The aesthetic of Stalinist planning and the world of the special villages

Lynne Viola[1]

> Pulling out his notation sheets and his class-stratification register, the activist began to make marks on the paper; his pencil was two-colored, and sometimes he would use the dark blue, sometimes the red …
>
> Andrei Platonov, *The Foundation Pit*

In 1930 and 1931, the Soviet state forcibly exiled almost 2 million peasants in an operation euphemistically labeled "special resettlement." In early 1930, in practice, this operation was primarily auxiliary to wholesale collectivization, exhibiting in the main "confiscative-repressive" features[2] to remove and isolate state-defined enemies (the *kulak*), to expropriate kulak properties for use in the newly emerging collective farm system (as well as to prevent destruction of such properties), and to intimidate "wavering" peasants into joining collective farms. Later in 1930 and in the years to follow, the state would combine dekulakization with what had been in the 1920s still vague ideas about utilizing what were supposed to become self-sufficient penal populations in colonization, in agricultural expansion, and for the labor needs of the resource-rich but labor-sparse far north and east. The state created out of this amalgam what amounted to a parallel Gulag[3] of special resettlement villages, housing first dekulakized peasants and, later, additional contingents of social and ethnic "enemies."

The world of the special villages constituted a dark underside to what Stephen Kotkin calls Stalinist civilization, an example of "progressive modernity," whereby the Soviet state sought to create an enlightenment utopia based on socialist desiderata.[4] The road to utopia in the Soviet context traversed treacherous political, social, and cultural terrains, populated by individuals and groups perceived to be alien or in some way obstructive to the Soviet project. The construction of socialism under Stalin entailed the purification of Soviet society. The "desire to excise and expunge" enemy elements became an imagined prerequisite to reordering and mastering Soviet society on the way to the new civilization.[5]

The special settlements were vast laboratories of experimentation, replete with the most exquisitely detailed plans of control, regimentation, and order, designed to isolate noxious elements from healthy Soviet society, to keep them under constant observation and surveillance, and to re-educate through labor those who could be re-educated. On paper, the special villages exhibited all the traits of "scientific planning" from on high, ranging from centrally imposed schedules for everything from transport to village construction to reporting; to blueprints for homes, barns, and *bania*s; to plans and interestingly precise schedules for the "liquidation" of epidemic diseases.

Yet the awful reality of the special villages was anything but planned. Epidemic illnesses swept through the villages; exhaustion from hunger, neglect, and over-work took a continuing toll; brutal, corrupt, and drunken commandants exercised unlimited power; and tens of thousands of people died. The story of the special villages, like so many of the grand utopian projects of those times, marked a radical, if predictable, disjuncture between "scientific" planning and reality, a seemingly unbridgeable gulf between discourse and practice. In the case of the special villages, Moscow planners not only had to execute their plans with the bluntest of instruments – the Soviet Union's underdeveloped rural administration – but had to do so in the conditions of an emergency state (whether artificially designed or not) that grafted secrecy, excessive haste, and military procedure on to planning, all in a context of state terror. To make matters worse, the tempos of collectivization outpaced dekulakization and even the deportation operation, making "planning-*na- khodu*" (or along the way, as one official put it)[6] – however "scientific" it may have appeared on paper – an essential feature of this process. And the more the operation developed beyond the control of Moscow, the more Moscow responded with its endless plans, directives, orders, and threats, in an attempt to paper over reality, to assert control over provincial Oblomovs and Nagulnovs,[7] and to "ideologize" existing practice in order to bring it under the umbrella of Stalinist civilization.

In the 1980s, in response to Cold War interpretations that took at face value Soviet plans and totalizing visions,[8] Western revisionist historians called attention to these kinds of disjunctures between policy and actuality, exploring as causal factors center–periphery conflicts, inter- and intra-bureaucratic struggles, and the weaknesses of Soviet administration.[9] Although revisionists provided a clearer empirical picture of Soviet realities than had hitherto existed, and although many of their viewpoints have, in fact, been reinforced by the opening of Soviet archives in the 1990s, the story they present is still partial. The exclusive focus on the reality of the disjunctures may have obscured the plan – and, in the process, the centrality and very *idea* of planning in Soviet historical development under Stalin. In the 1980s, when most of the "blueprints" (writ small and large) of the totalizing state were largely locked up in closed archives, revisionist scholars assumed that the state ruled by ambiguous policy signals, mobilization, and repression. The opening of the archives in the 1990s, however, revealed an entire paper world of intricate plans, a world that existed and would continue to exist mainly on paper.

The all-mighty and omnipresent blueprints that characterized every detail of Soviet life were a reality unto themselves, although it is important to note that they did not therefore translate into a world controlled by a totalitarian state or a levia-than bureaucracy. Instead, they represented a *vision* of control and rational order projected on to the chaos of Russia by an urban state determined to transform and control a largely agrarian administration and peasant economy. In this sense, Soviet development under Stalin had much in common with what James Scott has dubbed "high modernism" – that is (in short), the state's desire for "the mastery of nature (including human nature), and, above all, the rational design of social order commensurate with the scientific understanding of natural laws."[10] Scott adds, "The carriers of high modernism tended to see rational order in remarkably visual aesthetic terms. For them, an efficient, rationally organized city, village, or farm was a city that *looked* regimented and orderly …."[11] High modernism, in combination with an authoritarian state and a weak or nonexistent civil society, could transform modern techniques in social engineering into societal disaster as was the case in Nazi Germany, communist China, and the Soviet Union, to mention a few of the worst cases from the twentieth century.[12] The disjunctures between planning and reality which we see in the Soviet case, therefore, should be viewed less as an aberration than an essential feature of twentieth-century social engineering, imposed from outside on subject populations, in a void of local knowledge, and within the context of an illiberal polity.[13] In a sense, this phenomenon was a signal feature of Stalinism and one, moreover, that continually rebounded in excesses, violence, and terror.

This essay is a case study in the rarefied world of Stalinist planning based on the early history of the special villages.[14] The special villages left a vast paper trail of vanquished intricacy, revealing visions of order, regimentation, discipline, control, and productivity that would remain largely ornamental in the brutal reality of their existence, but illustrative nonetheless of the aesthetic of Stalinist planning during the first five-year plan.

Part I: special settlement

> All fell silent, patiently enduring the night. Only the activist continued to write noisily, and achievements spread out ever more broadly before his politically aware mind, so that he already thought to himself: "[…] it's long since time to send off the whole population in whole train loads into socialism …"
>
> Andrei Platonov, *The Foundation Pit*

As early as 1925, G.L. Piatakov, then deputy chairman of VSNKh (*Vysshyi sovet narodnogo khoziaistva*, or Supreme Council of the National Economy), penned a secret report for his chairman F.E. Dzerzhinskii (who also continued to head the Soviet security police), outlining a plan for the use of penal labor in the extraction of mineral resources in a series of remote regions above the Arctic Circle, on Sakhalin Islands, in Nerchinsk, and in Kazakhstan. The report built upon an existing legislative framework, which included as standard penal practice compulsory labor for inmates in places of detention (from 1918) and the use of administrative exile (from 1922).[15] In 1928, People's Commissar of Justice, N.M. Ianson, reiterated these ideas in a recommendation to utilize penal labor in the northern timber industry to stimulate the all-important hard currency generating timber export industry. His recommendations seemed eminently practical given the instability of peasant seasonal labor in the north and general prison overcrowding in what had become a very costly institution to maintain. Moreover, Ianson's suggestions arose within the context of a fierce and ongoing institutional battle for control of the penal population being waged by the People's Commissariat of Internal Affairs for the Russian Republic (NKVD – Ianson's chief rival) and OGPU (*Ob"edinennoe gosudarstvennoe politicheskoe upravlenie*, or internal security police – Ianson's temporary ally). Ianson – and others – looked to the OGPU's penal system of labor camps as a solution to a variety of problems, ranging from penal overcrowding and reform to colonization and economic development.[16]

The first five-year plan pushed the issue of penal labor to the top of the agenda for Soviet planners. Genrikh Iagoda, de facto head of the OGPU, spearheaded these initiatives. In April 1929, the commissariats of justice and internal affairs and OGPU jointly submitted a report calling for the creation of a network of concentration camps that would be based on labor service rather than just isolation and that would be self-supporting. The authors of the report recommended that all prisoners serving sentences of three or more years should be transferred to such camps.[17] One month later, the Politburo issued a decree confirming the report's conclusions, and, in late June 1929, issued an extremely important decree calling for the expansion of the existing camp system, the creation of additional facilities, and the transfer of all prisoners serving more than three years to the OGPU for its work in colonization and the economic exploitation of a series of northern and eastern territories.[18] The OGPU had bested its institutional rivals, and took control of what was to be a rapidly expanding penal population and forced labor system.

In April 1930, Iagoda wrote a memorandum for his colleagues at OGPU, articulating his vision of the new penal system. Iagoda argued that the concentration camps in their current configuration were little more than holding pens for prisoners, whose labor was wasted. He called for the transformation of the camps into "colonization villages" of 200 to 300 households each. The prisoners would build the villages themselves, send for their families if they wished, and work as a permanent labor force in the forestry industry and elsewhere, while occupied "in their free time" in various agricultural pursuits that would allow them to support themselves and free up the government budget from supporting its unfree labor. Iagoda was ostensibly inspired by the need "to colonize the North in the fastest possible tempos."[19] Although the camps would never be displaced by such "colonization villages," Iagoda's proposal envisioned the emerging order of special villages that would house a continuing assortment of state-defined social and ethnic enemies through the remainder of the Stalin years.

In this context, collectivization and the mass repression that accompanied it presented vast possibilities for addressing a host of pressing economic and political problems. In late 1929, the regime launched a policy of rapid, forced collectivization of agriculture. On 27 December 1929, Stalin articulated the new policy toward the kulak as its "elimination as a class." Stalin's statement came at the end of a long debate over the "accursed question" of the kulak and the collective farm.

By this time, it was clear that the regime had closed the door to the collective farm on the kulak, but the kulak's exact fate was not so clear. At the Conference of Marxist Agronomists, where Stalin announced the new policy, Bolshevik leaders presented a series of opinions. Iuri Larin, who said "we don't take the position that all kulaks and their descendents (*potomstvo*) must be quickly shot," called for a "disarming" of the kulak through expropriation, resettlement, and re-education. Most other speakers objected vociferously to Larin's seemingly sufficiently radical position, arguing that the kulak was incorrigible and the "most evil enemy." V.P. Miliutin said it was impossible "to make a deal" with the kulak and quoted V.M. Molotov, who said, "Relate to the kulak as the most evil and unvanquished enemy." Like others, Miliutin said it was not a question of re-education but of class struggle, implying that the two were irreconcilable. And Stalin pronounced, "To advance on the kulak means to get down to business and strike the kulak, yes strike him, so that he will never be able to get back on his feet again."[20]

Collectivization and dekulakization brought their own imperatives, not always complementary to Iagoda's vision. Collectivization took place in the midst of, partly as a result of, a crisis atmosphere that militated against careful planning and a controlled campaign. As a consequence, dekulakization in the first half of 1930 exhibited more of a "confiscative-repressive" semblance than a well-ordered, utilitarian response to the needs of the day. The Stalinist war mentality, so clearly on display at the Conference of Marxist Agronomists, was given free rein. In the heat of the day, the main object became simply to strike a blow at the kulak from which he could not recover, to paraphrase Stalin. Meanwhile, in the field, the collectivization campaign progressed so rapidly that local cadres made their own decisions on the "kulak question" while awaiting instructions. They used dekulakization to intimidate other peasants into joining the collective farms – as a "stimulus," to use local parlance; they dekulakized to prevent peasants from selling or "squandering" their properties in the face of dekulakization or forced entry into the collectives; and they expropriated kulaks to take their properties and possessions for the newly emerging collective farm system (if not for themselves).

While Stalin may have been satisfied with this state of affairs – at the November Plenum of the Central Committee of the Communist Party, he did say that "not everything can be organized ahead of time"[21] – Iagoda had little patience for such "revolutionary spontaneity," raging against local initiative in dekulakization and reminding his subordinates that, "We lead *all* the [Soviet] Union" in the dekulakization operation.[22] Iagoda sought order and control in the extraction of his future army of forced laborers.[23]

Concrete policy directives on dekulakization were slow to materialize. Although the December 1929 Politburo commission on collectivization had endeavored (largely unsuccessfully) to introduce some order and clarity to the collective farm movement, it had not put forward its final proposals on the kulak question, probably as a result of a lack of consensus on the issue. The draft proposals, however, did set up certain parameters on the kulak question. The draft proposals established a differentiated approach to the kulak population (estimated at 5–6 million people), dividing it into three groups: a counter-revolutionary *aktiv*;

a larger stratum of less dangerous, but still economically powerful kulaks; and a final category of rank-and-file kulaks, who could be used as a work force in the collective farms. The emphasis was on isolation and punishment of the most dangerous kulaks through arrest and exile, and re-education through labor of the rest. The subcommission on the kulak formed their decisions on the basis of the assumption that "the power of the kulak has weakened."[24] None of this sat well either with Stalin, who derided re-education and stressed class struggle, or Iagoda, who claimed that the rural class struggle was worsening and called for decisive measures. As a result, the 5 January 1930 Politburo decree on collectivization paid scant attention to the kulak question.[25]

From early January 1930, Iagoda and the OGPU assumed a central (if not *the* central) role in planning the operation against the kulaks. Where the Politburo's December commission failed, the OGPU excelled, demonstrating in no uncertain terms its organizational and planning advantage over the party. And although the Politburo created another commission to deal with the kulak question, under Molotov's direction, this commission served largely as a rubber-stamping agency for OGPU's initiatives. Unfortunately, OGPU planning came in the midst of the ongoing campaign, therefore frequently arising as a reaction to seemingly irrepressible developments.[26]

The OGPU was the most important actor in the planning and implementation of dekulakization for first- and second-category kulaks, leaving the third category to local party organs.[27] The OGPU worked through its provincial (*krai/oblast'*) plenipotentiary representatives (*polnomochnye predstaviteli*, hereafter PP) in planning for the numerical size of the contingents of deportees, transport, temporary housing, and security measures. Operational procedures, arrests of first-category kulaks, and general oversight lay in OGPU hands. In early February (in some instances earlier), the OGPU carried out operations against first-category kulaks as a pre-emptive strike to remove village notables from the countryside. The OGPU arrested 140,724 kulaks between 1 January and 15 April 1930, and an additional 142,993 between 15 April, and 1 October 1930. Slightly over 30,000 first-category kulaks received death sentences in 1930 and 1931. The families of first-category kulaks were subject to deportation along with all second-category kulaks. In 1930 and 1931, the OGPU sent just under 2 million peasants into internal exile, primarily to the North, the Urals, Siberia, and Kazakhstan.[28]

Central responsibility for the coordination of settlement and administration of the special settlers once they had made their way into exile belonged to a special commission set up on 1 April 1930 under the all-union Council of People's Commissars (Sovnarkom or SNK) and presided over by V.V. Shmidt. The Shmidt commission was assisted – and paralleled – by an additional coordinating commission for the Russian Republic, a special Russian Republic Council of People's Commissars commission under People's Commissar of Internal Affairs V.N. Tolmachev which functioned from 9 March to 13 August 1930. By the time these two commissions were set up, the first contingents of special settlers were already in temporary housing, awaiting dispatch into the interior, or, in the case of adult males, on their way into the interior to build the special villages and/or begin their new work as special-settler laborers. Of the two commissions, the Tolmachev commission was the more active, and by the time it was dissolved in mid-August, the Shmidt commission appears to have faded into documentary oblivion, leaving special-settler affairs uncoordinated and largely decentralized for almost a year.

From August 1930, almost every commissariat and a variety of party and soviet agencies up and down the provincial hierarchy would have some role in special resettlement. The two primary roles belonged to the People's Commissariat of Agriculture for the Russian Republic (land and agricultural issues) and VSNKh (industrial employment issues).[29]

On the provincial level, the *krai/oblast'* soviet assumed general responsibility for special resettlement through 1930. A special *troika* (three-member commission) led by the provincial soviet chair with representation from the GPU and provincial land administration (*zemupravlenie*) coordinated work on resettlement, provisions, land, and labor. Responsibility for the organization of the settlers' agricultural work belonged to the provincial administration of migration, which worked through county- (*okrug*) level land agencies and colonization parties and was subordinated both to Main Migration Administration under the Russian Republic People's Commissariat of Agriculture and the provincial soviet. Responsibility for the employment of settlers and the construction of the special villages belonged to the industrial administrative organs making use of special-settler labor, which, in turn, worked through a variety of local agencies and answered to VSNKh and the provincial soviet.[30]

Throughout 1930 and the first part of 1931, administrative anarchy and poor coordination plagued special resettlement affairs, compounding what was intrinsically a disaster in the making. On 18 October 1930, a Russian Republic Council of People's Commissars decree entrusted E.G. Shirvindt with overall observation of special resettlement business, calling upon all Russian Republic-level agencies to keep him regularly informed. Within days, however, in a speech to the Communist fraction of the all-Russian Central Executive Commission (VTsIK), A.S. Kiselev inveighed against the absence of coordination and responsibility in special resettlement, warning that "someone must answer for this."[31]

The OGPU's nemesis, the Russian Republic People's Commissariat of Internal Affairs, through the Council of People's Commissars, had a larger role in the resettlement operation at this time, perhaps because the Politburo believed it could run the special resettlement operation through routine administrative channels, perhaps because the People's Commissariat of Internal Affairs had not yet given up the fight for control over the penal population. Whatever the case may be, special resettlement affairs were not routine business, and the experience of deportation and resettlement in 1930 would prove disastrous, claiming thousands of lives and leaving the entire operation in chaos. As a result, in mid-1931, the Politburo handed over *all* operations to the OGPU's GULAG, creating a Department of Special Villages (*otdel spetsposelenii*).[32]

Stalinist planning in this phase of operations was little more than an amorphous conglomeration of orders, directives, decrees, and special commissions, beset by a multitude of contradictions. Besieged by intra- and inter-institutional conflict and confusion, center–periphery tensions, and the confiscative-repressive aspects of collectivization and dekulakization that consumed the village, Iagoda's plans for self-supporting, well-ordered, and productive "colonization villages" were frustrated from every direction. The realities of dekulakization and expropriation meant that most settlers arrived penniless and without the OGPU's stipulated food supply, thus causing untold suffering, necessitating the mobilization of the food and supply bureaucracies, and making a mockery of the idea of self-supporting penal institutions. The pressing demands of production would lead local industry to exploit its special laborers mercilessly, thinking only of the short term and leaving little or no time for the settlers to build their special villages and farms. The wretched living conditions and the harsh reality of slave labor, a potentially fatal occupation, more than militated against re-education. Yet, in spite of such dire realities, the entire operation was blanketed with a dense cover of plans, directives, and orders, adorned with the most intricate detail.

The realities of the times meant that special resettlement would be anything but a "pure" experiment in planning. Pure experiments of this kind, however, are difficult to come by in life and most especially in the life of the crisis-ridden Soviet Union of the early 1930s. Crisis, in fact, was a necessary if sometimes self-defeating ingredient in Stalinist planning; without crisis it was impossible to mobilize the enormous inert agrarian bureaucracy on which the state rested. Moreover, crisis fueled the fires of ideological desire, compounding with urgency, not to mention enemies, Soviet transformative goals. Nonetheless, the OGPU and other Soviet planners saw their task as the creation of a rational and utilitarian order of repression. Plans would be grafted on to what had become a revolutionary war, one that would undermine planning at every step, but, at the same time, facilitate and indeed necessitate all such efforts.

Part II: plans

> "Disorganization!" the activist said wearily of this chilling wind of nature.
> Andrei Platonov, *The Foundation Pit*

There was a terrible clarity of vision in the planning of the special villages, but one that recalls Nikita Khrushchev's depiction of Stalin mapping World War II strategy on a globe. ("Yes, comrades, he used to take the globe and trace the front line on it.")[33] I do not mean this analogy as irony, but rather as a metaphor for understanding Stalinist planning as, at once, global and inexact. This remarkable, yet myopic, clarity of vision derived from the veritable cult of scientific planning that overlay Stalinist transformative policies, but that was scarcely reflected in the reality of the special villages. The latter resembled a dystopia refracted through a fun-house mirror of utopia.

Transport

Transport constituted the first major task of the special resettlement operation. The theoretical design of the transport operation was a planner's dream, replete with the most detailed specifications, rules of administration, and order.

The provincial OGPU PP was to be in general charge of all operations pertaining to the extraction of first- and second- kulak families from their villages; in turn, the PP would organize operational *troika*s at the county and district levels. These OGPU functionaries were to follow several sets of detailed instructions worked out in Moscow by the OGPU Secret-Operations Department and Transport Department. The instructions accompanied the OGPU's 2 February 1930 general directive (*prikaz* 44/21) on dekulakization.[34]

The first step on the special settlers' itinerary was to be the collection or concentration point (*sbor-* or *kontspunkt*), where peasants from one and sometimes more counties (*okrugs*) gathered to await further transportation, most often by railway. Accompanied by ad hoc convoys of regular police (*militsionnery*), Party and komsomol activists, collective farmers, and *batrak*s (landless agricultural laborers)[35] – as well as grieving friends and relatives – the families were permitted (on paper) to bring up to 30 *pud*s of property, including a two-month supply of food, basic household items, simple tools, and warm clothes.

Operational groups under the county department of the OGPU were to organize the concentration points; in cases when concentration points served more than one county, the provincial PP operational *troika* on dekulakization was to take charge. Military barracks and other buildings were to be used for temporary housing. Each concentration point was to be led by a commandant (appointed from OGPU personnel and subordinated to the county operational group or PP depending on the number of counties serviced) and two assistants. The commandant would be in charge of organizing the guard, food, medical, and sanitary services, and uninterrupted communications with the operational group. In case of any "incident," the commandant had full authority "to take all necessary measures." The commandant prepared dekulakized peasants for transport and transfer to the jurisdiction of the OGPU Transport Department and echelon commandant.

The OGPU Transport Department was to assume general leadership of all transport issues through a *troika* composed of representatives from its department, the People's Commissariat of Transport, and other transportation agencies. This central *troika* would be in charge of all personnel questions (railroad, "chekist," and armed convoy), finances, selection of feeding points en route, and the compilation of transport schedules. Road (*dorozhnye*) *troika*s, made up of the heads of various road agencies (including the Road Transport Department, or *Dorozhno-transportnyi otdel* of OGPU) were responsible for the formation of echelons, observation and leadership of loading and unloading of train cars, and for ensuring the fulfillment of the central *troika*'s schedule.

The Transport Department was to assign each echelon a number (per region, by the hundreds) and its own commandant. Echelon commandants were to be provided – at least three hours prior to transport – with lists (containing family and age structure) of special settlers. Echelon commandants heading for most regions were to separate out (by secret list) all able-bodied family members (in practice, mainly men) for earlier unloading. Each train car would have an "elder" (*starosta*) and assistant, both appointed from the settlers by the commandant. The commandant was also responsible for unloading ill settlers (if under six years of age, with the mother) and the dead. The guard, consisting of 13 riflemen (including a political instructor) with 60 ammunition cartridges per rifle, could open fire in the case of escape attempts or other "incidents." At stops, the elder and his assistant were allowed to disembark for food purchases (using the settlers' own money) and boiled water for their train car's occupants. Train-car doors could be slightly ajar when the train was in motion; at and near stops, the car doors were to be closed, and "tightly" (*naglukho*) closed in the vicinity of Moscow. The road *troikas* appointed two chiefs (one for loading and one for unloading) to take charge of the technical organization of echelons, embarkment, and disembarkment.

Each echelon was to consist of 44 train cars (supposedly *teplushki* or heated cars, but more often cattle cars), eight goods cars, and one fourth-class car for the command staff. Each car was to carry 40 people, with one stove, 28 plank beds, one chimney flue, two window frames, one lantern, and three buckets (two for boiled water and one for human waste). The command car was assigned two buckets, three army lanterns, and one signal lamp.[36]

Once the special settlers reached the first stop on their journey – generally a district (*raion*) center in the region of exile – they were to disembark at a reception point (*priemnyi punkt*), where – according to directive – the unloading chief was to ensure that the train was emptied in no more than three hours and the able-bodied were separated out from the non-able-bodied. In parties of 500 to 1,000, under convoy, the able-bodied were then to set out for the interior for work in the timber and other industries and to build the special villages. In the North, they traveled distances ranging from 20 to 40 kilometers per day, taking anywhere from eight to 25 days to reach their final destinations.[37] The non-able-bodied (the elderly, the ill, mothers and children) were to remain temporarily in the district centers, generally somewhere along the railroad routes, awaiting the summer, when river navigation and ground transportation would be more feasible. While they waited, they would live in a variety of make-shift housing, ranging from barracks and warehouses to monasteries and churches. Although detailed plans and discussions had gone into the construction of temporary barracks for these people, generally the short time between dekulakization and transport, not to mention the high costs, derailed such planning.[38]

It is perhaps superfluous to note that the plans did not flow like clockwork, that they materialized only on the very eve of the special settlers' departure, that the transport system was strained beyond its capacities, that people went hungry and became ill during the long and crowded journey, and that the center's only recourse was to rage against provincial officials who violated quotas in dekulakization and did not ensure that their dekulakized peasants were left a basic food supply. This disjuncture between plan and reality would continue, and became a basic feature of the special resettlement operation as the settlers moved into the interior and began the construction of their special villages.

Locating and building the special villages

While the special settlers were en route, provincial- (and lower-) level land and colonization agencies began the difficult process of finding suitable locations on which to build the special villages. Because it normally took at least four years to prepare land for migrants,[39] some agencies attempted first to make use of lands that had been prepared earlier for (regular) migration.[40] In most cases, though, the special settlers would arrive in the midst of virgin forest or marsh on totally unprepared lands. In Vologda (Northern Territory), the county land administration was fully aware that "correctives" would be needed later given the urgency of the assignment.[41] In Siberia, the provincial NKVD branch (*administrativnoe upravlenie*) complained that the areas for kulak resettlement had only been indicated on maps, with no actual survey work.[42] In Severo-Dvinsk (Northern Territory), the colonization party mapped out locations in the centers of forestry work and as far as possible from populated areas. The Northern provincial migration agency criticized Severo-Dvinsk for making decisions based only on "theoretical" thinking without any consideration of actual living conditions.[43] In many cases, entire special villages would be relocated or simply closed down in later years because of the complete unsuitability of the land; in some cases, special settlers would find themselves without a specific location at least for the first summer while the land agencies scrambled to find appropriate lands.[44]

The special villages were supposed to be located on lands that would support agricultural pursuits.[45] They were to be isolated, far from population centers and railways.[46] They were also not to be located near borders; in Siberia, the OGPU forbade any special villages within 150–200 kilometers of the border.[47] Each village was to house approximately 120 families (or about 600 people), and, as a rule, families were settled together with their fellow villagers from home.[48]

Industries using special-settler labor were responsible for the construction of the special villages. In the Northern Territory, each special village was to be home to 120 families and approximately 15 housing units of the "primitive standard log type."[49] Designed according to central plan and blueprint (which often arrived late, if at all), each home was to house eight families (estimated at five persons per family), one room per family, four square meters per person to a maximum of 20 square meters per family, with two kitchens, two stoves, two windows, and two entrance ways. The dimensions of each home were to be 24.5 × 9.40 × 3.5 meters with a total area of 991.08 meters. The homes were to be one-story log cabins, each to be situated not less than 30 meters from one another.[50] In Vologda, one bathhouse was to be constructed for every 15 homes (one per village). The bathhouse was to be 70 square meters long, divided into two parts, one for dressing and one for washing, one half for men and the other half for women. They were expected to service up to 200 people per 10-hour day.[51] In addition, construction plans included one barn and one warehouse for every eight families, as well as a separate building for the administration.[52] In the North, expenses for housing on a per family basis were estimated at 35 rubles 35 kopeks.[53]

The construction of the special villages entailed much more than simply building barracks and auxiliary buildings. The special villages had to be erected from scratch, on land tracts where colonization parties may or may not have conducted proper surveys and where the land may or may not have been suitable for agriculture. In addition to homes and auxiliary buildings, there would be (over time) plans for building schools, clinics, hospitals, post offices, and registry offices (ZAGS). The authorities also had to install telephone and telegraph lines and "import" security personnel, medical personnel, teachers, skilled carpenters, agronomists, and veterinarians. Apart from lumber, the industrial concerns employing special-settler labor had to bring in all building materials and tools from the outside, while supplying (with the agricultural agencies) manufactured goods, food, horses, cows, and agricultural inventory in the first couple of years. All of these tasks took place in remote, virgin territory. The villages were generally accessible only by boat, small cart, or on foot, and only for part of the year, given weather conditions. The authorities "mobilized" tens of thousands of carts and boats from the local population just to get the settlers to their villages, never mind the transport of food, supplies, and building materials. Road construction represented one of the most formidable tasks. In Vologda, the resettlement operation necessitated the repair or construction of 455 kilometers of roads; in Severo-Dvinsk, local authorities estimated that they would have to build up to 600 kilometers of roads. It is perhaps redundant to note that the special settlers themselves would do all of this.[54]

Set against the backdrop of the ongoing first five-year plan, it was unlikely that such exquisitely intricate plans would be even dimly reflected in reality. The myopic failure to make use of peasant know-how in the design of the villages, most especially in housing;[55] the irrational decision to transplant peasants onto lands vastly different from their native soil; the unmasterable details of construction; and the sheer enormity of the tasks involved doomed all plans from the inception, resulting in the formation of a world of special villages bogged down in the larger and more consuming realities of rural Russia. The Stalin regime attempted to compensate for these realities by administering the special villages from Moscow and imposing rules of internal order that were expected to transform the villages into model penal-colonization villages.

Rules of internal order in the special villages

On 24 August 1930, an OGPU *spravka* noted that work on the "Statutes for the Kulak Villages" had begun in March and was continuing. In the meantime, the *spravka* concluded, no one knew exactly how to organize the internal administration of the special villages.[56] That the regime had entered into operations without an exact notion of how the special villages would be run is further evident in an 11 January 1930 letter from Iagoda to his top deputies in which he asks whether it would be possible to organize the "kulak" villages without guards.[57] In light of the detailed, although not necessarily feasible plans on transport and the physical construction of the special villages, it is at first glance surprising that the OGPU had such an unclear vision of special-village administration. However, given the "*na khodu*" nature of those plans (not to mention the "confiscative-repressive" priorities of the entire operation in 1930) and the fact that NKVD RSFSR, not OGPU, had administrative jurisdiction over the special villages through 1930 and the first half of 1931, it is not surprising that rules and regulations were slow to materialize.[58] That statutes were drawn up at all is a reminder of the "special" (and indeed unprecedented) nature of this resettlement operation.

It was only in the fall of 1930 that VTsIK-SNK RSFSR issued a series of decrees on special village administration. Up until mid-1931, when the OGPU took over, the combined forces of the soviet apparatus and the NKVD had overall responsibility for resettlement issues once the dekulakized peasant families had reached their final destination. The coordination of all practical work was in the hands of the provincial soviet presidium, which then appointed a permanent conference (*soveshchanie*) under the chairmanship of the head of the provincial NKVD (police) branch (*administrativnoe upravlenie*) with representatives from OGPU, the land organs, and a series of labor, education, and health agencies to lead all work in the special villages. The provincial NKVD branch was responsible for organizing a *komendatura* (a kind of headquarters) in each special village, to be led by a commandant appointed by the provincial NKVD and confirmed by the district soviet executive committee and the OGPU. The commandant was subordinated directly to the provincial NKVD and corresponding district soviet executive committee and assisted by a staff of one to four (regular) police officials (one per each 50 families).[59]

Within the special villages, the settlers were forbidden to assemble without the permission of the commandant and, in general, had no right to self government of any kind. The commandant could appoint special commissions of five to 15 settlers to assist him with various agricultural, cultural, and public services (*blagoustroistvo*) issues. The committees would have their own set of centrally mandated statutes and were to be based primarily on the supposedly politically malleable youth of the village. For help on various "technical" questions, the commandant could also appoint an *ispolnitel'* (a kind of executor) from among the settlers of not less than one per every ten households.[60] Within a short time, a system of collective responsibility (*krugovaia poruka*) was also introduced to try to stem the massive flight of settlers from the special villages. All settlers had to sign a collective responsibility agreement, and one elder for every 10 households was responsible for monitoring the movement of settlers and reporting escapes and escape plans to the commandant.[61] In the North (and likely elsewhere), one settler was appointed in every home to take charge of hygiene issues and ensure the cleanliness of homes and the surrounding area as well as overseeing fire prevention.[62]

All able-bodied settlers were to work for various economic concerns, which, in turn, signed contracts for settler labor with the provincial authorities. Those who could not be thus employed remained in the village to open up and farm the land. Special settlers who worked outside the village were to receive the same salary and benefits as free workers, minus a 25 percent deduction for "administrative servicing." The administrative industrial organs (*khozorgany*) were responsible for guaranteeing their laborers housing, food, medical aid, and a series of other benefits.[63]

Special settlers could leave their villages only with the commandant's permission. Visitors to the special villages were allowed only with the permission of the district NKVD police office (*administrativnyi otdel*). For violations of the rules of

Figure 9.1 A utopian view of special settlement: propaganda drawing depicting the planned, but never real, goals of re-education through labor and regional economic development. From *Narym: ocherki i stat'i* (Novosibirsk, 1936), 184.

internal order, work violations, and petty crimes, the commandant could fine (up to 10 rubles) or arrest (up to 30 days) settlers. For more serious violations covered by the penal code, settlers could be sent to corrective labor colonies or camps.[64]

The commandants, who were supposed to be physically strong, preferably Red Army veterans and communists, were to receive a salary equivalent to or greater than that of the chief of the district NKVD police office (their boss), with periodic raises. Their police assistants were to receive a salary equivalent to divisional police inspectors, also with periodic raises.[65] The commandant's responsibilities included:

- observation of fulfillment of laws and decrees, holding accountable those settlers who were in violation of the same
- headcounts of the population and registration of all civil deeds and vital statistics
- preliminary investigations of crimes
- fulfillment of the economic tasks of the village
- organization of a fire brigade; care of roads and paths; observation of public services and the sanitary condition of the village
- organization of political-educational work, first of all among youth
- preparation of a budget for the village's economic and cultural needs and the costs of administration (to be confirmed by the district soviet executive committee).[66]

When the OGPU took over in mid-1931, most of this administrative structure remained in place, with certain refinements. In October 1931, the OGPU published what was to remain a *temporary* statute for the special villages through the 1930s.[67] Centrally, GULAG OGPU led all operations on the special villages through its Department of Special Villages (*otdel spetsposelenii*). Regions with large special-settler populations had their own Department of Special Villages under the PP OGPU. Depending on the size of a territory, there also may have been divisional (*uchastkovye*) and district *komendatury* as well as production *komendatury*, which worked on the sites where kulak labor was employed. At the base of the structure was the village commandant.[68]

Within the special villages, the commandant was to divide the population into sectors, each with an elder assisted by several helpers elected by villagers and confirmed by the commandant. These special-settler "officials" formed a group to aid the commandant and worked under the direction of one of the commandant's "free" assistants. In addition to their regular full-time employment, the elders' duties included the fulfillment of all of the commandant's orders; the provision of information on all escapes, incidents, and disorders; regular headcounts of the population; the observation of all rules of hygiene for the village and its homes; the transmission of all complaints and requests from settlers to the commandant; the announcement of the commandant's orders; and observation of rights (or lack thereof) of assembly. The elders could take no decisions independently of the commandant.[69]

All special settlers were required to be employed in "socially useful labor," as determined by the OGPU and paid and provisioned the same as free workers minus a (newly reduced) 15 percent deduction from their salaries to pay the costs of their administration. Exceptions occurred only with the sanction of a special medical commission that determined whether a villager should be exempted from work for health reasons. Special villagers could not leave the territory of the village or even relocate within it without the commandant's permission. The settlers were obliged to observe all rules unswervingly, carry out all orders of the commandant, as well as take care of all state and collective property in their use.[70]

The commandant drew up further rules of internal order, which were subject to confirmation by the Department of Special Villages under the PP OGPU and had to be posted so that all settlers could see them. He was responsible for the whereabouts of all settlers at all times. He was also responsible for ensuring that both the industrial administrative organs and the special settlers fulfilled all their respective obligations as specified in the contracts concluded by the OGPU with the corresponding industrial administrative organ. The commandant was responsible for reviewing all complaints and requests from settlers; if he could not resolve them, he was to redirect them to an institution or higher organ that could. The commandant answered for the political and social order of the special village, including all matters of hygiene and protection of state and collective property.[71]

For violations of order (quiet, hygiene, use of state property), work truancy, and drunkenness, the commandant could either fine (up to five rubles) or place under arrest (up to five days) the offending special settler. For "systematic" violations of this type, the divisional or district *komendatura* could apply fines (up to 10 rubles) and arrest (up to ten days). For more serious crimes, the commandant could transfer a settler to the jurisdiction of the People's Commissariat of Justice or the OGPU Collegium. Under no circumstances were settlers to be deprived of their ration as a means of punishment.[72]

The special settlers also had a series of defined rights. In theory, they were eligible for full rehabilitation of all civil rights five years from the time of exile if they observed the laws and worked honorably. (In practice, this was not to be the case.) They and their families were also to be paid (minus the 15 percent deduction) and provisioned the same as free workers, with the same rights to medical and social benefits. They were eligible to enroll in local schools and courses and if none were available, special networks of schools were to be built. They had the right to organize – with the commandant's permission – cultural-educational circles (*kruzhki*); the unlimited right to receive newspapers and literature published in the USSR, as well as correspondence, packages, and money gifts; the right to send children under 14 and non-able-bodied elderly home to relatives or friends; and, by 1931, the right to build their own individual homes and to obtain property and livestock.[73] Special settlers were also allowed by statute to marry free citizens, without the latter losing civil rights (or the former gaining them).[74] By 1932, special settlers could organize voluntary societies in the villages, provided that these societies had no potential for military training. Any kind of physical culture that could turn into preparation for military preparedness was forbidden, and settlers were not allowed to receive military literature of any kind.[75] In individual special villages, the commandant could add or subtract from the rights of settlers according to whim. In one case, for example, special settlers required a *propusk* (pass) to go to the baths.[76]

Needless to say, the world of the special settlers on paper reflected an order, regimen, discipline, and productivity that scarcely matched the experience of sometimes drunken, violent, corrupt commandants; deadly exploitative work bosses; settlers without rights or much real hope of ever leaving; and conditions of extreme and dire poverty, filth, and hunger. Visions of settlers opening up new territories, participating in "honorable" labor, and being re-educated became little more than a hollow facade for a system that most settlers viewed as no more than an unwarranted penal, if not death, sentence. Yet in spite of this reality, Moscow refused to let go of this facade of re-education and transformation, attempting to hold it up with a scaffolding of checks and controls, every bit as "scientific" as the plans.

Part III: controls

> There is not a drop of unregulated elemental force in our village anymore, and there is nowhere to hide either!
>
> Andrei Platonov, *The Foundation Pit*

Central plans were checked, recorded, and reviewed through an intricate web of controls that included both the "extraordinary" (special commissions, on-site inspections, judicial oversight, etc.) and the "ordinary" or "everyday" forms of seemingly routine reporting, scheduling, and classification. The "routine" appearance of such practices, however, was in fact a cloak to disguise the anything-but-routine nature of such controls, controls that ended most often in failure, scapegoating, and the application of "administrative measures," the Stalinist euphemism for repression.

A system of reporting developed alongside the special resettlement operation from the very beginning. The OGPU issued detailed instructions on the organization of registration and investigative (*uchetno-sledstvennye*) groups in the concentration points where dekulakized peasants gathered to await transport. An operative official of the OGPU not lower than a GPU county department plenipotentiary led the registration and investigative groups, which included OGPU and People's Commissariat of Justice officials and were subordinated to the concentration point commandant. The groups were to check settlers with an eye to anything of "special interest" to the organs of the OGPU, and select informers from the ranks of the settlers (one per 30 to 50 adults) for work in the concentration points, en route, and in the places of exile. Each settler family was to have two personal data cards (*lichnye kartochki*), one of which would be sent to the registration and investigative groups if there was a problem. Under ordinary circumstances, one card would go to the settler's native county and the other to the place of exile.[77]

The OGPU also issued a schedule for reporting at this early stage of the operation. In areas of exile, PPs were to provide precise statistical information on special settlers, "liquidated" counter-revolutionary groups and organizations, numbers of people arrested, and basic information on operations ("excesses," the political situation, disturbances, and so on) every five days by telegram to the Secret-Operations Department, the Counterintelligence Department, and other OGPU departments. The same PPs were to submit operational reports (*opersvodki*) by post every five days to the Secret-Operations Department, the Counterintelligence Department, and the OGPU Information Department on political conditions in the districts, the general course of operations, excesses, revolts, banditry, the work of the *troikas* (for first-category kulaks), and so on. Three separate standardized forms for statistical data were also included. The OGPU Transport Department was to report daily on the numbers of echelons, statistical data on their composition, the numbers of echelons en route, and the political atmosphere of the echelons.[78] The echelon commandant was required to send the OGPU Transport Department a standardized telegram, reporting the time of each echelon's departure. Echelon commandants were also expected to keep a special log on the trip.[79]

This "method" of required reports would continue throughout the early phases of the operation. In late April, OGPU ordered its PPs in the North, the Urals, and Siberia to report every five days on a detailed array of issues connected to the settlement of kulaks.[80] Up to July 1930, PPs sent *spetssvodki* (special reports) every five days to the center and, after that, every ten days.[81] Scheduled reports were required from every agency at every level of the provincial hierarchy for at least the first year. Even the land surveyors were bogged down in paperwork, reporting weekly on their progress.[82] And reports were going not only to the center; provincial agencies duplicated the center's reporting system, requiring their subordinates to provide similar types of information.[83]

Complementing this system of ascending, scheduled reports was a system of descending, scheduled orders for information and policy implementation. Throughout the operation, orders for information and policy implementation were inevitably accompanied by the incessant and generally impractical reminder to respond or act "in five days," "in three days," and so on. For instance, on 25 January 1930, the Politburo told the People's Commissariat of Transport and OGPU to work out a transport plan for the kulaks in five days.[84] On 11 January, Iagoda ordered his PPs to provide by 14 January data on the numbers of people arrested in the countryside for the last six months, the numbers of category-one kulaks, and a plan for sending category-one kulaks to the concentration camps.[85] Similar plans for the employment of settlers were to be provided "in ten days" according to an 18 March OGPU memo to PPs.[86] In May, the People's Commissariat of Trade was called on to provide food and other goods for the northern settlers in ten days, while the People's Commissariat of Transport was asked to obtain additional transport ships in the same number of days.[87] Even local health organs were thus mobilized; in June, the Vologda county soviet executive committee asked its health department to give directions on the "struggle with typhus" in two days.[88] These types of orders almost inevitably included threats and warnings that failure to fulfill this or that desiderata would entail reprimand, party expulsion, or worse.

This kind of scheduling assumed absurd proportions at times. Centrally, there was a complete (and hardly fulfilled) schedule for the entire operation – from land surveying and transport to the construction of barracks and roads, to food supply and the settlers' own agricultural work for the period from February through September 1930.[89] In the North, there were schedules for the construction of settler homes that included specific dates for the erection of walls, floors, ceilings, stoves, chimneys, and roofs.[90] In the Urals, there was even an "operational plan" for the struggle with epidemics, with exact dates for the liquidation of each type of disease.[91]

As time went on, in addition to somewhat less intensive reporting schedules, there was a series of specific investigative commissions, on-site inspections, and demands for a census of special settlers.[92] The great irony of all of this was that it was only from 1932 that a systematic accounting of settlers began, when Registry Offices (*ZAGS*) were formally established in the *komendatury*.[93] Before that time (and surely after), it was not unusual for officials to report, like a Tomsk county soviet executive committee official, that they did not know where "their kulaks" were or, like a Totemsk district party committee official in Vologda, "To this time, we do not know how many special settlers there are in the district."[94] Even the Andreev Commission, which presided over the special resettlement operation for the Politburo from March 1931 complained in August 1931 "of the absence at the present time of any exact data on the numbers of people" arriving in exile.[95]

Secrecy was an additional feature of this system of control. The entire special resettlement operation was veiled in secrecy, beginning with the fact that the settlers were to be strictly isolated from any populated areas.[96] The People's Commissariat of Agriculture and other agencies found themselves unable to receive or transmit basic information to subordinates because of OGPU secrecy rules. In early September 1930 (close to nine months into the operation), the Russian Republic People's Commissariat of Agriculture was forced to ask OGPU for permission to declassify certain types of technical information, receiving an affirmative response at the end of the month.[97] By November, the People's Commissariat of Agriculture Secret Department announced to its provincial land organs that OGPU had declassified the following information regarding the special resettlement operation: financial issues, the construction of homes, the provision of construction materials, food supply, land reform issues, and agricultural and veterinary questions. Still classified were the exact districts of resettlement, administrative statutes for the special villages, the commandant's rights and responsibilities, employment issues, and discussion of new contingents of special settlers.[98] The omnipresent secrecy of the system surely served in many cases to hamper the correct and timely provision of information from center to province and back.

Moshe Lewin has written eloquently of the controls that animated what he calls the "administrative monolith" of the USSR. In an essay from the early 1990s, he characterized the elaborate system of bureaucratic checks, controls, plenipotentiaries, envoys, and instructors as a manifestation of the "institutional paranoia" of a regime in fear of losing control and, one might add, a desperate effort to combat the inertia, indolence, and excess of provincial and local officialdom. Quoting Bazarov's February 1929 warning to *Gosplan* in his classic essay on "the disappearance of planning in the plan," Lewin wrote that "chaos [was] guaranteed in advance" in the absence of real knowledge and real possibilities. As a consequence, and in the absence of extra-state controls and initiatives, plan failures simply led to more plans and more controls as the system endeavored to repair itself in an all-too-frequently *na khodu* dynamic that inevitably led to bureaucratic parallelism, an absence of responsibility, scapegoating, and, ultimately, repression.[99] In the end, "administrative measures," that is, repression, became the usual recourse of the regime as repression became a simple and bluntly effective substitute for routine administration and control. The inevitable failure of the visions inherent in Stalinist planning led directly to the escalation of Stalinist repression.

Conclusions

> [I]s not truth merely a class enemy? After all it could now appear even in the form of a dream or imagination.
>
> Andrei Platonov, *The Foundation Pit*

Andrei Platonov captured the realities of the times in *The Foundation Pit*, a grim satirical depiction of "socialist construction" set amidst backwardness, ignorance, undigested Marxist theory, planning mania, military machismo, and supreme Bolshevik confidence. *The Foundation Pit* exposed the contradictions and, indeed, pathos of the desperate drive to socialist utopia undertaken during the first five-year plan, a drive to master and control society through "rational" visions of order, regimentation, discipline, and productivity that ended as a mere facade grafted on to a complex society and bureaucracy that resisted order and instead simply continued on in more "normal," messy human ways.

While Cold War scholars traditionally highlighted the totality in the visions of control, 1980s revisionist historians saw improvisation in the implementation. But in a sense, neither school was incorrect; they were simply incomplete. There was hyperplanning and there was chaotic enactment, but the two were more nearly reinforcing than contradictory, and, in any case, characteristic of the Soviet state's efforts to master its bureaucracy en route to socialism.[100]

In the end, Stalinist planning was more state aesthetic than totalitarian reality.[101] In fact, it shared much more in common with socialist realism than with "scientific" social engineering. Planning represented reality as it was imagined and intended, more often than not in a lofty and terrible isolation from actuality. It represented life as it *should* become, not as it was becoming. And like socialist realism, planning had an added dimension; it was both a denial of and a compensation for reality – in this case, the realities of an overcentralized and repressive state, an underdeveloped provincial bureaucracy, and an agrarian society resistant to state-imposed change. Unlike socialist realism, the aesthetic of planning was superimposed on to reality, translating in the case of the special villages, and the thousands of special settlers, into utopian quagmire and dystopian nightmare.

Notes

1   I would like to thank *Kritika* for permission to reprint this version of the article I published under the same title in *Kritika: Explorations in Russian and Eurasian History* 4, no. 1 (Winter 2003): 101–28.
2   V.P. Danilov and S.A. Krasil'nikov, eds, *Spetspereselentsy v Zapadnoi Sibiri*, 4 vols, (Novosibirsk, 1992–6), v. 1, 14.
3   *Glavnoe upravlenie ispravitel'no-trudovykh lagerei*, or Main Administration of Corrective Labor Camps.
4   Stephen Kotkin, *Magnetic Mountain: Stalinism as a Civilization* (Berkeley, 1995), 6–23. See also his highly engaging, "Modern times: the Soviet Union and the interwar conjuncture," *Kritika* 2, no. 1 (Winter 2001): 111–64, where he notes that the Soviet government sought to carry over its practices in modernity into the Gulag (p. 160).
5   Peter Holquist has demonstrated how the "desire to excise and expunge" such elements in society was a part of "mapping" social collectivities and populations in what he terms the "population politics" of the modern Russian state. See his article, "To count, to extract, to exterminate: population statistics and population politics in late imperial and Soviet Russia," in *A State of Nations: Empire and Nation-Making in the Soviet Union, 1917–53*, eds Terry Martin and Ronald Suny (New York, 2002). Also see David L. Hoffmann, *Cultivating the Masses: The Modern Social State in Russia, 1914–41* (Ithaca, forthcoming); and the important collection edited by Amir Weiner: *Landscaping the Human Garden: Twentieth-Century Population Management in a Comparative Framework* (Stanford, 2003).
6   GARF, f. 393, op. 43a, d. 1796, ll. 2–18.
7   Oblomov is from I.A. Goncharov's nineteenth-century novel of the same name, while the wildly excessive Nagulnov is the prototypical "dizzy" collectivizer from M.A. Sholokhov's *Virgin Soil Upturned*.
8   Needless to say, there were many exceptions, Merle Fainsod's *Smolensk under Soviet Rule* (Cambridge, MA, 1958) being the most notable.
9   E.g., J. Arch Getty, *The Origins of the Great Purge* (Cambridge, 1985); Lynne Viola, "The campaign to eliminate the kulak as a class, winter, 1929–30: a reevaluation of the legislation," *Slavic Review* 45, no. 3 (1986): 503–24; idem, "'L'ivresse du success': Les cadres Russes et le pouvoir soviétique durant les campagnes de collectivisation de l'agriculture," *Revue des études slaves* 64, no. 1 (1992): 75–101.
10   James C. Scott, *Seeing Like a State: How Certain Schemes to Improve the Human Condition Have Failed* (New Haven, 1998), 4. For a brilliant application of the notion of high modernism to the state's relations to the peasantry in the 1920s, see Tracy McDonald, "Face to face with the peasant: village and state in Riazan, 1921–30" (Ph.D. diss., University of Toronto, 2002).
11   Scott, *Seeing like a State*, 4.
12   Ibid., 5.
13   I thank Amir Weiner for making this point to me.
14   For an examination of the actual experience of the special settlers, as opposed to the abstract world of planning, see Lynne Viola, "'Tear the evil from the root': the children of the *Spetspereselentsy* of the North," *Studia Slavica Finlandensia*, tomus XVII, 34–72; and "The other archipelago: kulak deportations to the north in 1930," *Slavic Review* 60, no. 4 (2001): 730–55.

15 Galina Mikhailovna Ivanova, *Labor Camp Socialism: The Gulag in the Soviet Totalitarian System*, trans. Carol Flath (Armonk, 2000), 10, 18, 69–72; Peter H. Solomon, Jr., *Soviet Criminal Justice under Stalin* (Cambridge, 1996), 29. For the 1922 legislation on administrative exile, see *Sbornik zakonodatel'nykh i normativnykh aktov o repressiiakh i reabilitatsii zhertv politicheskikh repressii* (Moscow, 1993), 12.

16 S.A. Krasil'nikov, "Rozhdenie GULAGa: diskussii v verkhnikh eshelonakh vlasti: postanovleniia Politburo TsK VKP (b), 1929–1930," *Istoricheskii arkhiv*, no. 4 (1997): 142; E.A. Rees, "The people's commissariat of the timber industry," in *Decision-Making in the Stalinist Command Economy, 1932–7*, ed. idem (London, 1997), 126–31; Solomon, *Soviet Criminal Justice*, part I.

17 Krasil'nikov, "Rozhdenie GULAGa," 143–4.

18 Ibid., 144–6, 152–3. For the Politburo's June decree, see A.I. Kokurin and N.V. Petrov, eds, *GULAG, 1917–1960: Dokumenty* (Moscow, 2000), 62–3.

19 A.N. Dugin, *Neizvestnyi GULAG: Dokumenty i fakty* (Moscow, 1999), 7–8.

20 *Trudy pervoi vsesoiuznoi konferentsii agrarnikov-marksistov. 20–27 dekabria 1929* (Moscow, 1930), v. 1, 55, 74–5, 270, 445–6; v. 2, 157–8.

21 RGASPI, f. 17, op. 2, d. 441, vyp. 1, l. 70.

22 *Tragediia Sovetskoi derevni. Kollektivizatsiia i raskulachivanie. Dokumenty i materialy, 1927–1939*, 5 vols. (Moscow, 1999–2006), v. 2, 137–8.

23 As a consequence of which, the OGPU often appears as the main petitioner on behalf of the peasantry.

24 RGAE, f. 7486, op. 37, d. 40, ll. 58–53. [Ed. Note: the *listy* numbers in this and other endnotes below are indeed supposed to run in reverse order.]

25 See Lynne Viola, "The role of the OGPU in Dekulakization, mass deportations, and special resettlement in 1930," *Carl Beck Papers in Russian and East European Studies*, no. 1406 (2000): 8, 12.

26 See Viola, "The role of the OGPU," for detailed information on the two Politburo commissions and the role of the OGPU in dekulakization.

27 See *Tragediia Sovetskoi derevni*, v. 2, 163–7, for the 2 February 1930 OGPU *prikaz* (no. 44/21) on dekulakization.

28 See Viola, "The role of the OGPU," 21; idem, "A tale of two men: Bergavinov, Tolmachev and the Bergavinov Commission," *Europe-Asia Studies* 52, no. 8 (2000): 1451; and idem, *Peasant Rebels under Stalin: Collectivization and the Peasant Culture of Resistance* (New York, 1996), 245, note 67.

29 See Viola, "A tale of two men," 1451–2.

30 Ibid., 1452.

31 Ibid.

32 Ibid.

33 Nikita Khrushchev, "The crimes of the Stalin era," *The New Leader* (New York, 1962), 41. (I will not comment on the accuracy of Khrushchev's depiction.)

34 See *Tragediia Sovetskoi derevni*, v. 2, 163–7, for the 2 February 1930 OGPU *prikaz* (no. 44/21) on dekulakization. The central OGPU instructions on transport are in GARF, f. 9414, op. 1, d. 1944, ll. 42–64.

35 VOANPI, f. 1855, op. 1, d. 10, ll. 253–7 (*Instruktsiia po raskulachivaniiu i vyseleniiu kulatskikh semei II kategorii v Severnom krae*).

36 GARF, f. 9414, op. 1, d. 1944, ll. 42–64.

37 GAOPDFAO, f. 290, op. 1, d. 378, l. 11; f. 833, op. 1, d. 70, ll. 29–31, 33–4, 45.

38 GAOPDFAO, f. 290, op. 1, d. 378, ll. 11–12; on the discussion about barracks in the North, see Viola, "A tale of two men," 1460–1.

39 RGAE, f. 5675, op. 1, d. 23a, ll. 48–46, 50–49.

40 GAVO, f. 399, op. 1, d. 182, ll. 5–9.

41 Ibid.

42 GARF, f. 393, op. 43a, d. 1796, ll. 442–3.

43 GAVO, f. 399, op. 1, d. 219, ll. 163–4. (It was illogical to locate special villages in the midst of timber works because the center of gravity of such work was constantly changing as timber was "harvested.")
44 E.g., VOANPI, f. 5, op. 1, d. 277, ll. 23–4; GAAO, f. 621, op. 3, d. 204, ll. 1–21; d. 268, ll. 1–3; d. 269, l. 122.
45 GAVO, f. 399, op. 1, d. 182, ll. 5–9.
46 GARF, f. 1235, op. 141, d. 776, ll. 4–1.
47 TsAFSB, f. 2, op. 8, d. 267, l. 9. (In 1939, the state would order all *spets/trudposelenii* within five kilometers of the border or of railroads to be relocated. See GARF, f. 9479, op. 1, d. 65, l. 209; d. 57, l. 78; and Danilov and Krasil'nikov, eds, *Spetspereselentsy*, v. 4, 8, 290–1, n. 4.)
48 *Istoricheskii arkhiv*, no. 3 (1994): 128. (In the North, the average size of "free" villages was 22 households. See GARF, f. 393, op. 43a, d. 1796, ll. 2–18.)
49 GAOPDFAO, f. 290, op. 1, d. 379, ll. 2–4.
50 GAVO, f. 395, op. 1, d. 39, l. 22; f. 399, op. 1, d. 219, ll. 3–9; GARF, f. 393, op. 43a, d. 1796, ll. 2–18.
51 VOANPI, f. 1855, op. 1, d. 86, ll. 32–3.
52 GAVO, f. 399, op. 1, d. 219, ll. 3–9; GARF, f. 393, op. 43a, d. 1796, ll. 2–18.
53 GARF, f. 393, op. 43a, d. 1796, ll. 2–18.
54 See Viola, "The other archipelago."
55 E.g., the largest contingent of special settlers in the North – Ukrainian peasants – were expected to work with wooden logs in the construction of their homes, despite the fact that they had always built their homes with clay and straw back in Ukraine.
56 GARF, f. 9414, op. 1, d. 1943, ll. 74–5.
57 *Tragediia Sovetskoi derevni*, v. 2, 103–4.
58 Some key regions had statutes (generally "temporary") drawn up as early as April 1930, suggesting initially a decentralized approach. See GARF, f. 393, op. 43a, d. 1797, ll. 81–6 (Siberia); and f. 1235, op. 141, d. 786, ll. 19–16 (Urals). In the North, temporary statutes were produced only in July 1930. See GAAO, f. 621, op. 3, d. 49, ll. 180–5. These provincial statutes may have formed the basis for later VTsIK-SNK rules.
59 GARF, f. 1235, op. 141, d. 776, ll. 4–1, 13–12, 11–10.
60 Ibid.; and GARF, f. 1235, op. 1, d. 786, ll. 19–16; f. 9414, op. 1, d. 1944, l. 100.
61 GARF, f. 9414, op. 1, d. 1944, l. 168; *Tragediia Sovetskoi derevni*, v. 2, 526–9. For statistics on flight, see Viola, "The role of the OGPU," 31.
62 GARF, f. 393, op. 43a, d. 1797, ll. 92–3.
63 GARF, f. 1235, op. 141, d. 776, ll. 4–1.
64 Ibid.
65 VOANPI, f. 5, op. 1, d. 276, l. 16; GARF, f. 1235, op. 141, d. 776, ll. 4–1. (In the North as of July 1930, 76.6 percent of commandants were communists. GAOPDFAO, f. 290, op. 1, d. 388, ll. 77–8.)
66 GARF, f. 1235, op. 141, d. 776, ll. 11–10.
67 On the eve of the war, in 1939, Beria was working on plans to reform the special or labor villages as they were then called. The plans never came into affect and a new regulation for the villages only came into being in 1944. See Danilov and Krasil'nikov, eds, *Spetspereselentsy*, v. 4, 7–8, 34–5, 42–7.
68 Danilov and Krasil'nikov, eds, *Spetspereselentsy*, v. 2, 68–9.
69 Ibid., 75–6.
70 Ibid., 69–70.
71 Ibid., 71–2.
72 Ibid., 73–4.
73 Ibid., 70–1.
74 GARF, f. 9479, op. 1, d. 5, l. 43.
75 GARF, f. 9479, op. 1, d. 11, l. 39.
76 Danilov and Krasil'nikov, eds, *Spetspereselentsy*, v. 2, 152–8.

77 Viola, "The role of the OGPU," 18–9; GARF, f. 9414, op. 1, d. 1944, ll. 31–3.
78 GARF, f. 9414, op. 1, d. 1944, ll. 37–8.
79 Ibid., ll. 51–60.
80 Ibid., l. 93.
81 *Tragediia Sovetskoi derevni*, v. 2, 602–3.
82 GAVO, f. 399, op. 1, d. 182, ll. 20, 356, 391.
83 On reporting within the Communist Party in the North, see GAOPDFAO, f. 290, op. 1, d. 384, l. 15.
84 RGAE, f. 7486, op. 37, d. 78, ll. 55–3.
85 *Tragediia Sovetskoi derevni*, v. 2, 103–4.
86 GARF, f. 9414, op. 1, d. 1944, l. 97.
87 GAOPDFAO, f. 290, op. 1, d. 386, ll. 147–9.
88 GAVO, f. 395, op. 1, d. 40, ll. 160–70.
89 GARF, f. 393, op. 43a, d. 1796, l. 285; also see RGAE, f. 5675, op. 1, d. 23a, l. 21.
90 GAVO, f. 395, op. 1, d. 39, l. 17.
91 V.V. Alekseev et al., eds, *Raskulachennye spetspereselentsy na Urale (1930–6 gg.). Sbornik dokumentov* (Ekaterinburg, 1993), 80–3.
92 GARF, f. 9479, op. 1, d. 5, ll. 25–6; d. 19, l. 10; RGASPI, f. 17, op. 162, d. 10, ll. 132–3.
93 S.A. Krasil'nikov, *Na izlomakh sotsial'noi struktury: marginaly v poslerevoliutsionnom Rossiiskom obshchestve* (Novosibirsk, 1998), 65–6.
94 Danilov and Krasil'nikov, eds, *Spetspereselentsy*, v. 1, 182; VOANPI, f. 1855, op. 1, d. 86, ll. 43–6.
95 RGASPI, f. 17, op. 120, d. 52, l. 186.
96 GARF, f. 393, op. 43a, d. 1796, ll. 184–90. (In practice, special villages were sometimes quite close to "free" peasant villages.)
97 GARF, f. 393, op. 43a, d. 1798, ll. 154–153.
98 GAAO, f. 621, op. 3, d. 19, l. 58; RGAE, f. 5675, op. 1, d. 23a, l. 233.
99 Moshe Lewin, *Russia. USSR. Russia. The Drive and Drift of a Superstate* (New York, 1995), 84, 88–9, 96, 120, 193.
100 See Scott, *Seeing Like a State*, for a discussion of how state transformational visions fall short of their aims.
101 In this context, it is worth quoting Boris Groys: "When the entire economic, social, and everyday life of the nation was totally subordinated to a single planning authority commissioned to regulate, harmonize, and create a single whole out of even the most minute details, this authority – the Communist party leadership – was transformed into a kind of artist whose material was the entire world and whose goal was to 'overcome the resistance' of this material and make it pliant, malleable, capable of assuming any desired form." From *The Total Art of Stalinism: Avant-Garde, Aesthetic Dictatorship, and Beyond*, trans. Charles Rougle (Princeton, 1992), 3.

10 "Those who hurry to the Far East"

Readers, dreamers, and volunteers

Elena Shulman[1]

I am from the Union's heart – from the flowering capital
I bring to the Far East my greetings
Let my song run across the eastern sky
Carried by the storm of spring, our victory song

I am just like all of them, those tens of fervent
Young women of our great Motherland
We will work diligently with a happy tune –
We are full of health, energy and strength!

And there are not a few who hurry to the Far East
Pedagogues, poets, actors, doctors:
We want the country to blossom everywhere
So that it bubbles with joy, like a mountain brook.[2]

Khetagurovka, 1937

The Soviet Far East, located on the Pacific coast of northern Asia, appeared with ever increasing frequency in Soviet print and cinema during the late 1930s. This late addition to the Russian empire, having only become a Russian territory in 1860, was also a latecomer to the Soviet Union, delayed by a prolonged Civil War and a Japanese occupation well into the early 1920s.[3] Although the region had been a source of special concern for some time, Far Eastern development and security skyrocketed in importance in 1936 and 1937 because of increased international tensions. The Far East's distance from the center, its low population density, and, in the 1930s, the swelling numbers of Japanese forces in Manchuria intensified insecurities within the Politburo and saturated public discussion of the region with an aura of jingoism. Japanese activity in Manchuria did not consist solely of an expansion in their military presence but also encompassed resettlement programs for impoverished Japanese and Korean farmers along its northern frontiers.[4] Soviet authorities responded with their own military build-up and a renewed emphasis on establishing permanent settlers as the first line of defense.[5]

During the closing months of 1936, the region's poor performance in attracting and retaining voluntary settlers compelled the Communist Party to redesign and revive settlement programs that had withered in the chaos of collectivization.

Although the Far East contained a significant number of "special" (forced) settlers and labor-camp inmates, these population groups were hardly a reliable source of manpower to repel invading forces. Accordingly, newspapers aimed at Communists and young people became conduits for a variety of programs that mobilized politically vetted volunteers for permanent settlement. As part of this emphasis on the area, press accounts and official pronouncements sought to articulate and disseminate among a wide audience a sense that the far-flung Soviet Far East was part of a coherent and irrevocably linked national entity. The main thrust of this coverage aimed at explaining the strategic importance of the region, the need to exploit its natural resources and the urgency of fortifying it against certain enemy encroachment.

This chapter discusses the representations of the Far East in official propaganda and popular beliefs, and especially the gender connotations therein. Hundreds of thousands of people volunteered for migration in response to such publicity. Why? What were the cultural and emotive dynamics motivating Soviet voluntary migrants – and young women in particular – to embark for a precarious life thousands of miles from home? Using documents produced for and by those who participated in this migration process – including official publicity materials and letters and memoirs of settlers – I illustrate how the gendered aspects of official discourses on nation building, Soviet civilization building, and frontier life structured men's and women's self-image and expectations. In addition, letters written in response to mobilization campaigns lend themselves to an examination of reader reception and a better understanding of how men and women digested official messages and deployed them in their displays of patriotism.

The Far Eastern landscape – pristine, primordial, and simultaneously vulnerable to enemy predations – functioned as a congenial space for performing patriotic fantasies. Soviet citizens moving to the Far East came with notions of the region they picked up from official propaganda and from popular beliefs about Siberia and its natural world.[6] Between 1937 and 1939, the Soviet Far East came to play a dominant role as a stage for dramatizing threats to national integrity, and the Far Eastern theater steadily spawned heroic prototypes.[7] Journalists, Party officials, and propagandists took great pains to identify their audiences and to tailor their message accordingly. Press coverage and police actions intimated that the right kind of settler for the border zone was to be Slavic, young, patriotic, and politically reliable.[8] This new crop of heralded patriots struggled against the chaotic natural world and directly participated in securing Soviet territorial claims. Such heroes either contributed to border defenses or fortified the nation's might by their very presence in a forbidding environment where they endowed former culturally and ideologically marginal spaces with elements of the Soviet modernizing project.

Resettlement publicity appealed directly to young women, especially in 1937 and 1938. The Far East suffered from a long-standing shortage of women, which contributed to a dismal record of new settler retention and slow regional development. Because of increasing interest in the region from the center and a resolve to address some of its obvious inadequacies, a campaign to attract young single women to the region began in February of 1937.[9] On the pages of the 5 February

1937 issue of *Komsomol'skaia pravda* (newspaper of the League of Young Communists), a young wife of a Far Eastern officer, Valentina Khetagurova, appealed to women to join her in this "marvelous land."[10] Several months after the publication of her appeal, the Communist Party established in the Far Eastern city of Khabarovsk the *Khetagurovite Committee for the Resettlement of Young People in the Far East*. Officials and journalists called those who migrated in response to Valentina Khetagurova's appeal "Khetagurovites" in her honor. Khetagurovites became the most widely publicized and recognized participants of the Far Eastern resettlement programs. Initially, the campaign appealed expressly to young women. However, men and married couples also applied for migration through the Khetagurovite program. Close to 300,000 individuals volunteered. In 1937, over 11,000 young women arrived to settle in the region. Eventually, over 20,000 women and approximately 5,000 men had migrated as Khetagurovites by the time the campaign ended at the close of 1939.[11] Such a lively response points not only to the popularity of frontier myths among the Soviet public but also underscores women's aspirations to participate in state-sponsored projects. I argue that the dream of frontier exploits effectively struck a chord among young women because it was one of the few spaces where womanly virtues seemed to be a decisive force both in history and in revolutionary struggles against nature and savagery.

When *Columbus* came to Komsomol'sk

All public appeals emphasized that migrants should come out of a sense of patriotic duty in order to assist in the exploitation of natural resource for the good of the nation. Although the state maintained and periodically adjusted material incentives to facilitate permanent settlement, migrants who came only in search of better pay were potentially less desirable and possibly politically suspect. Promotional literature avoided discussions of material incentives (*l'goty*) in part because they were reminiscent of pre-revolutionary resettlement campaigns that were squarely based on a promise of self-enrichment for enterprising peasants and merchants. On a more practical level, financial inducements in the 1930s did not adequately compensate migrants for the abysmal living conditions that they inevitably found on the frontier. The lack of goods, a catastrophic housing shortage, and the high cost of living in the Far East offset most gains in salaries and benefits. Moreover, material rewards for resettlement were offered to a limited number of highly skilled workers and professionals and few were headed to the extreme northern regions of the Far East, where special incentives were in effect in any case. Those who came to the region strictly in search of better pay quickly discovered the inadequacies of such incentives and typically left at the first opportunity.

A predetermined schema for explicating the need for resettlement and for writing about the Far East was always at work in promotional literature. When necessary, these concepts were reshuffled to fit their audiences, but never significantly altered between 1936 and 1939. The 11 November 1936 issue of *Pravda*, which was dedicated to the Far East, vividly illustrates this montage of patriotic culture and frontier mythologies.

The leading editorial piece in the 11 November issue took great pains to differentiate the Bolsheviks' rights of possession and exploitation from the claims of their Asian neighbors and capitalist predecessors. Although themes of a civilizing mission existed in occasional articles about the relatively small number of native people that lived in the area, literature promoting resettlement rarely noted their existence. Most often, the Far East was presented as an empty land where nature beckoned for a ruler. The empty land served as the dramatic canvas where Bolsheviks triumphed in a clash of civilizations. "Before the Bolshevik Revolution, capitalists – both native and foreign – were only hunters here. They took only what was strewn around."[12] According to this logic, capitalists and all others represented a lower level of human evolution who, as hunters and gatherers, forfeited their right of possession by their lack of industriousness. Moreover, "capitalists lacked the will and technology" to exploit natural resources. The Bolsheviks on the other hand had "a deeper feeling for the region" and dispelled its undeserved reputation as a "place of death" perpetuated by their fainthearted predecessors. *Pravda*'s editors concluded that: "The Bolsheviks, armed with technology and culture were the first real discoverers of the Far East and thus its rightful masters (*khoziaeva*)."[13]

The Japanese, their activities in Manchuria, and their predatory nature were recurrent themes in publicity soliciting migration to the Soviet-Manchurian border. Far Eastern commanders reported to *Pravda*'s readers that the Japanese were well on their way to establishing a Manchurian infrastructure with the intention of using it as "a platform for war against the Soviet Union."[14] Indeed, part of the appeal of the Far East in the newspaper coverage was that it was a geographic space that fostered a direct and visceral sense of competition with Japanese rivals. Those who stood on the banks of the Amur River, in the city of Blagoveshchensk, could observe Japanese troops and fortifications with the naked eye across the water. Thus an ordinary person was potentially engaged in "measuring up the power in development and culture of the capitalist world with the socialist world, and to be one of the builders in the Far East is to be a leading soldier of a new society on one of the most important sectors of the front."[15]

Soviet citizens could observe the predatory essence of Japanese militarism and the natural world on the "other" side. National boundaries supposedly coincided with stark differences in fauna and flora. Yellow tinged the landscape. "The Manchurian side has thick low bushes, egg-yellow flowers cover its steep cliffs; tiny fields reach to the river bank. Here is the settlement of Japanese reservists – dusty, cheerless, with gray metal roofs."[16] Readers could have easily picked up repeated references to "yellow" as a subtle echo of "Yellow Peril" anxieties so common in pre-revolutionary discourses in reference to the region's Asian neighbors, but no longer fit to print in their most brazen form in Soviet era publications.

Much of the campaign to attract settlement and to describe the Far Eastern region was presented using the metaphors of Russian folktales. Magic keys, enchanted forests, fantastic natural treasure troves, and mighty *bogatyry* (mythical Russian warrior-knights) populated the gallery of mottoes about the Far East under Bolshevik rule. Although late to join the Soviet Union, the Far East "would make up for this tardiness with *bogatyr*-like growth." Bolsheviks were the real masters of the area because they brought with them "Socialism, the enchanted key to the region's treasures."[17] Having brought this magic key to the wilderness, the new masters were the first to really unlock its "innumerable riches." Once "the spell of backwardness" was dispersed by its Bolshevik-*khoziaeva* "the *taiga* receded ... Just like in a fairy tale, roads and railroads now run across bottomless marshes and places where a human foot had never set."[18]

Throughout this period, films set in the Far East reiterated the themes outlined in the newspaper coverage. The Arctic and the Far East served as "key heroic spaces"[19] in the increasingly common adventure-frontier films of the Stalin era. In the cinematic representation of the Far East, "the task of the hero was to tame nature – to render the uninhabitable habitable."[20] Intrepid male partisans and keen-eyed border guards joined forces with burly working men to tame the wilderness on the silver screen. These images of powerful *bogatyry*, whether in the guise of border guards or unflinching Arctic explorers, were representations of the Far East that left no room for archetypes of female heroism. If one took the *bogatyr* theme to its logical conclusion, women could have no place in magical spaces because in Russian fairy tales they never accompanied men on their quests. Rather, the maiden sat wistfully in a tower awaiting liberation by her knight. However, the practical necessity of populating the region by the late 1930s dictated the promotion of Valentina Khetagurova to carve out, at least, a niche for women in frontier myths and to capture the imagination of women.[21]

In publicity aimed at young men and women, the frontiers were billed as extraordinary spaces for personal growth and character formation, with "conditions especially conducive for the education of strong, hard characters, and for fortifying the will."[22] The natural bounty of the region demanded special reverence and required special dedication from people who eschewed avarice and the "long ruble." Only those truly loyal to their Motherland and to their professions were capable of understanding the region and of becoming its masters. Personal growth was paired with conquests over the natural world that was at once fascinating and threatening. "Those who come here are the sort interested in the struggle for socialism in new, unique conditions, those who want to open up their own personal horizons and those who are bewitched by ocean storms."[23] Reiterating the same themes as other articles, Valentina Khetagurova stressed that because this region was untouched, those who wished to see the immediate fruits of their labors for the collective good could be readily satisfied. "It is gladdening to think and know that this recently wild and barren frontier is being transformed into one of the marvelous corners of our wonderful country by the strength of our own hands."[24]

Many of the cinematic and press representations of frontier life also tried to mirror frontiersmen from other historical contexts. Soviet exploration myths were often consciously patterned on interpretations of American experiences. The "discovery" of America and Western adventure stories *à la* Jack London were familiar to and extremely popular with Russian readers and resurfaced in narratives about Soviet settlement life.[25] Europeans and Americans had come to imagine the exploration of the far north as a particularly masculine undertaking because of "the physical duress involved in the conquest of the Arctic and because exploring was regarded as the conquest of virgin territory."[26] In a similar vein, Soviet citizens were genuinely captivated with northern exploits in the 1930s. And just as the themes of masculine endurance versus the ravages of a hostile natural world dominated western tropes about the Arctic, so it was among ordinary Soviets, who idolized Soviet Arctic male daredevils and aviators.[27] The urge to recreate these motifs in the Far East was obvious to the first contingent of young people who came to build what would become Komsomol'sk-na-Amure in 1932. They sailed to their destination on the ship *Columbus*, a detail that was not forgotten by the makers of the popular 1938 film *Komsomol'sk*.[28] At the same time, women's representations alongside men on the frontier did not alter the terms used to describe the mission of Soviet power in the Far East or the gender of its possessors. Although women and their valuable contribution were central elements in the plot of the film, its theme song "March of the Komsomol" turned to the Far East's natural elements and decreed that it was time to "Submit! Your master (*khoziaen*) has come!"[29] The reiteration of the word *khoziaen* gave a particularly masculine flavor to the imagery of frontier settlement, since it not only meant master of the house, or boss, but also husband and man.

Despite some of these obvious similarities there were important differences shaping collective imaginations about Soviet frontier life. Siberia and Far Eastern regions had reputations as simultaneously zones of freedom from the intrusion of the state, dangerous zones populated by criminals, and places of punishment. Until the 1930s, the darker themes competed with the motifs that promised liberation and renewal. However, all public discussion of the region as a place of punishment disappeared at the same time as the NKVD erected its empire of camps. By the mid-1930s, the harsh natural worlds of the Far East and Siberia were unambiguously presented as testing grounds to prove one's resolve and masculine endurance rather than as places of suffering or untrammeled freedom from the state.

The content of gender ideology in Soviet exploration and settlement narratives also departs from important components of Western experiences. First, the place of women differed because the accumulation of wealth and property, inducements for mass participation in expansion and settlement in other territories, were not supposed to be central elements in this Soviet patriotic migratory process. In films and literature such as Vera Ketlinskaia's 1938 novel *Muzhestvo*, Soviet women embarked for distant lands to demonstrate their resolve, strength, and commitment to the nation rather than as companions to pioneering men or to improve their material circumstances. Second, Russian and Soviet ideals of womanhood exalted women willing to sacrifice personal interests for the collective. Highly dramatic acts of self-abnegation were especially respected. Valentina Khetagurova garnered the national spotlight after she volunteered to abandon cosmopolitan Leningrad to live in a remote forest where she faced scurvy and predatory wildlife. Her public appeal to encourage young women's migration was replete with stories of her subsequent life on the frontier, where she selflessly labored in a struggle against low morale and an unforgiving natural world to provide sustenance for garrisoned troops. These components of Soviet gender ideology propelled young women's enthusiasm for this venture and shaped their sense of accomplishment and social worth.

Khetagurova's life story, which made up the bulk of her letter, was not one commonly found in official narratives about women's lives. Khetagurova was not a woman who had been oppressed or illiterate.[30] Although the piece was actually produced by the editorial staff of *Komsomol'skaia pravda*, Khetagurova's letter told the story of adaptation from the perspective of a woman. She was presented as a woman who acted on her own to take advantage of a chance to travel to an exotic land. Her adventure story also alluded to the peripheral status of women in revolutionary and heretofore frontier mythologies by positioning them as envious observers. Khetagurova noted that "Soviet young women are ruled by a great envy, envy for everything heroic."[31] When she first volunteered to go, unsympathetic men in authority tried to keep her from going to one of the most remote outposts of the Far East because it was "no place" for a young woman. Almost unable to fulfill her fantasy of living in the *taiga* because she was a woman, now Khetagurova pronounced that women were finally welcome into the geographic space of the Far East and by extension into the grandiose epic of Soviet accomplishments.

The immediacy of the threat from the Japanese created an arena in the Far East where women could participate in public acts of sacrifice in defense of the Motherland.[32] The appeal to women made in promotional literature such as Khetagurova's letter held out the possibility of entry into heroic realms.

Figure 10.1 "Meeting the women patriots," by Dm. Nagishkina. From *Tikhookeanskii komsomolets*, 8 March 1939.

Khetagurova made the claim that her work in the *taiga* was more difficult and perhaps more meaningful than the work of women in other regions.[33] On the frontier, women's labor outside the realms of production appeared as anything but the irrelevant daily drudgery of housekeeping. Their activities, whether at home or as voluntary workers in communal institutions, were touted as the most visible expression of women as "a second army" standing in the path of invaders. Valentina Khetagurova reasoned that,

> Lads of course can cut down trees, build roads. But only women's hands can make the region really lived in. Life runs somehow superficially, in a suitcase mood, if caring hands, the cheerful laughter of young women, and the eyes of a caretaker are missing.[34]

A chance to publicly display belonging and good citizenship by selflessly employing their "women's hands" proved to be an effective draw for female volunteers.

Women like Khetagurova ultimately found that there was a price to pay for claiming recognition in nation-building projects based on a specific feminine contribution. Soviet women were not the first to confront this dilemma. A wide body of literature on women's participation in expansionist projects in other historical contexts illustrates how gendered ideology punctuated and structured these undertakings.[35] For instance, suffragists construed Canadian women's participation in settlement as a potential avenue toward political equality. They "saw women's settlement work as the basis of their claim to a voice in the future of the West."[36] However, women's bid for public authority based on their role in a "pioneering partnership" also "had the effect of reinforcing dominant gender conventions," because they stressed the specificity of their feminine contributions in a masculine project.[37] Similarly, women's claims to their rightful place alongside men in Soviet civilization building projects stressed the specificity of feminine contributions and thus reinforced gender boundaries.

Although thousands of migrants traveled to the Far East in this period, the sight of single young women embarking for the frontier received the most coverage and appeared most curious. Once volunteers surfaced in response to Khetagurova's appeal, Soviet journalists did not hesitate to tout their example as yet another sign of socialist triumph. Part of the publicity campaign surrounding the migration assured volunteers that their efforts marked the beginning of a new civilization and that history would marvel at their sacrifices. A column on the front page of *Komsomol'skaia pravda* in April 1937 aimed at publicizing the success of the Khetagurovite call-up also attempted to distinguish this migratory process from those in capitalist countries. In particular, the author underscored the special significance of spatial movement for young women. While migration in capitalist countries was a product of "unemployment, hunger, and cold," Soviet migrants to the Far East were propelled by "boundless sacred love for their mighty socialist Motherland."[38] Examples of whole families, who had good jobs in good conditions but were moving to the Far East, "where difficulties and depravations awaited them," served as proof that only the most "noble" motivations explained such decisions.

The resolve of women to "move to the borderland with Manchuria" was placed into explicit contrast in comparisons with the fate of Japanese women. This theme was allowed to take on sensational overtones by the use of a letter from a Japanese farmer supposedly published in the Japanese newspaper *Sekai Undo Tsusin* (*sic*) and cited by *Komsomol'skaia pravda*. In the excerpt presented to Soviet readers, Japanese farmer Kisaragi was offering to sell his 16-year-old daughter Khanae. He explained,

> Life is so difficult that it is impossible to continue in this way ... She cried a great deal but has now agreed. She does not need luxuries. If necessary, send her to Formosa or to Manchuria. Save our home![39]

The fate of the Japanese farmer's daughter, forced by hunger "into a public house in Manchuria," afforded the polar opposite for the voluntarism of Soviet young women streaming to the other side of the border. Just in case the lesson was not clear enough, the column ended with yet another exemplary letter from young women wishing to go to the Far East and an invocation to readers.

> Contrast this with the wholly limitless grief and profound drama in the letter of the Japanese farmer we introduced to you. It is hard to find a more striking contrast for a graphic illustration of the state of affairs in the two worlds. The fate of a 16-year-old Japanese girl – this is the fate of all children of laborers in the capitalist world. The noble urge of young women patriots traveling to the Far East on the call-up of Khetagurova – these are the dreams and thoughts of the glorious and fortunate daughters of the socialist Motherland.[40]

The voluntary spatial mobility of Khetagurovites appeared in contrast with the lives of women in Japan and in a temporal contrast with the supposed immobility of Russian women in the pre-revolutionary period. In a column several weeks later, a correspondent quoted from a young woman thrilled to be traveling where she was "needed. Me, a small, inconspicuous person, I am going to do a great deed. They wait for me! Just think of how great that is!"[41] With a long urban pedigree, the young woman repudiated the notion that the world revolved around Moscow.

> I want to see other cities, rivers, forests, and mountains. I want to look into all the corners of my Motherland. My mother lived all of her life in Moscow; my granny was born and died in a house within the gates of Moscow, not having seen more than one city. Life after all is just too short to sit for years on end in one spot on a huge geographic map.[42]

"I just read the newspaper"

Letters from volunteers and their later memoirs reveal some of the ways volunteers digested the themes described above. What they selected to note or remember about their decision to migrate provides a glimpse into the public imagination about the Far East and the role women expected to play in Soviet frontier life. Although these sources do not offer unmediated access to the migrants' motivations and experiences, they are valuable indicators of the durability of formative perceptions. Certain themes that appeared in the 1930s reappeared almost unaltered in the women's memoirs 40 years later. Memoirs also indicate something about the personalities more likely to find life in the Far East attractive. These sources embody commonly held aspirations among this female cohort to position themselves in the most public forums possible, where they could display their standing as pivotal agents in empire building. Although the campaign was initially aimed at women, men disregarded this component and applied to become Khetagurovites. Their failure to notice that the program was meant for women provides an opportunity to compare responses from men and women to a distinct promotional campaign with overt gender connotations.

Letters from resettlement applicants in the 1930s contained information on age, education, work history, and sometimes statements of preference for future work and duties on the frontier. Single women, women with children, single men, and men writing on behalf of their families sent inquiries. A large proportion of correspondents came from towns (of all sizes) in the Ukraine, Belorussia and central Russia. Statistics on those who eventually arrived as Khetagurovites in 1937 and 1938 support the impression that although most applicants were under the age of 40, there was no rigid uniformity among them in terms of region of origin, profession, and Party or Komsomol membership.[43] Nevertheless, significant patterns emerged. About one-third of both men and women were currently or had once been propagandists and organizers either in their workplace or in their military regiments. Some of the women, in their thirties, had experience in Party and Soviet sectors for work among women and worked as orphanage administrators. A significant proportion of male respondents had a background in journalism or had been factory newspaper correspondents (*rabkors*) or village correspondents (*sel'kors*). There is no indication in the archival record of whether these letter writers were eventually selected for migration or their subsequent fate.

Letter writers did not apply on a soon-forgotten whim. There are many instances when applicants indicated that they had applied before and were rejected or never received a reply. Yet they continued to inquire and reapply by post and by telegram at considerable personal expense. Typical of this persistence were three female employees of the Southern Ural railroad. Because they "burned with desire to work in the Far East stirred by the appeal of Valentina Khetagurova,"[44] they refused to accept numerous rejections from the Khetagurovite Committee. The Khabarovsk archive retained their telegram that reiterated their suitability and rights to participate. Another married couple was so eager to be invited they enclosed an extra sheet of blank paper and an envelope in their correspondence with the Khabarovsk Regional Party Committee to expedite their invitation.[45]

Readers of promotional materials about the Far East fathomed the texts as categorical invitations to participate in revolutionary acts. Impatience to be heroic and exaggerated emotions were typical sentiments in letters volunteers sent to authorities. After reading *Muzhestvo*, a novel set in Komsomol'sk-na-Amure, being built by resilient male and female Komsomol members, Vera Ketlinskaia's readers, like Vera Nikitkina, wrote asking for advice on how to become a Khetagurovite.[46] The tone and urgency of the letter underscored the emotional allure of migrating to a place where Nikitkina could feel useful.

> I have wanted to go to the Far East for a long time in response to the call of Valentina Khetagurova. But I thought that I would not be useful there, but now after reading this book [*Muzhestvo*] I think that even I could be of use … I ask you to write to me and tell me if I can go there and how to get there, and please do not deny this to me. I want to get to Komsomol'sk so much.[47]

Many of those who responded did so because of a desire to emulate the supposed revolutionary resilience of young people who took part in the projects of the five-year plan and to feel useful in similar collective undertakings. Memoirs indicate that much of their identity evolved in direct opposition to the lifestyles and value systems of less politically engaged and non-Komsomol young women. Whether by the way they dressed or by their activities in organizations, female Komsomol activists who answered Khetagurova's call-up wanted to maintain a close and visible bond with a distinct social group of like-minded young people. M. Koliasnikova, as a teenager, read about the creation of a new life somewhere "far away." She impatiently waited for her turn to imitate Ostrovsky's literary hero Pavel Korchagin in *How the Steel Was Tempered* (1932–4).[48]

Women tended to be more laconic in their letters of application and seemed reticent to give more than only the vaguest of explanations for their enthusiasm. Typically, women like Tatiana Sharaia, from Chernigov oblast' in Ukraine, explained only that she "already had a long-term desire to resettle for permanent residence and work in the Far East."[49] Twenty-two-year-old Igalkina from Smolensk oblast' volunteered because "all the time I notice in newspapers interesting things about our beloved Motherland. Especially interesting to me is life in the Far East."[50] Women were also more candid than men about mundane personal reasons to relocate. Thirty-seven-year-old Seleznova volunteered for "work of any kind" in the Far East. She explained that "here I have nothing to hold me. I have no family." Press accounts compelled her to "give over all of one's strength and energy for the Far East."[51] Khatukhina sent two different letters to the Khetagurovite Committee. In one letter she stressed that she wanted to move to the Far East to extricate herself from some unspecified family circumstance and to follow her acquaintances who recently moved to Komsomol'sk-na-Amure.[52] Molchanova desired to live in Komsomol'sk and "this desire was especially strong" because she had a "good comrade serving in Komsomol'sk in the Red Army." She listed her attributes as a member of her Komsomol cell, assistant to the First Secretary, and an avid sportswoman.[53] "I have a great desire to enter nursing courses, over there I can probably do so," wrote Glevskaia.[54] Four young women in the Komsomol living in Smolensk were impatient to be officially invited. This group of friends, "wanted to live in the Far East and to receive a specialization." One of them expressed a desire to study for a professional degree and to "strengthen the power of the Soviet Union."[55]

Women proved to be parsimonious generators of ritual incantations that were the staple of patriotic culture. Not a single woman invoked Stalin as an inspiration or benefactor. The letter of Glevskaia's represents explanations most commonly found among women who wrote that they "wanted to work in the Far East honestly and bravely and to defend my Motherland, beloved country."[56] The evidence could suggest that applicants were aware that expressions of gratitude or gesticulations to Stalin were practices that had their time and place but that as ostensibly selfless expressions of volunteerism their letters did not require such conventions. It also appears that women were not as engaged as men in producing ritualistic incantations that became the staple of political culture in this period. One explanation for this may have been women's discomfort in participating in excessive public speech. Many of the female volunteers were from small towns and rural areas of the Soviet Union. It is plausible that their social context did not foster a place for women's voices and therefore women were not accustomed to this style. The implications of their brevity were also important in the ideological arena of Stalinist culture. Exactitude in expressions of correct sentiments and finesse in the display of Party loyalty carried a great deal of weight in securing authority. If many otherwise activist and upwardly mobile women were less inclined or less able to participate in these discourses they would suffer in contests for power or simply never engage in the mêlée.

There was one theme that regularly appeared in women's otherwise brief explanations for their desire to resettle. They were sure they were needed and their presence was a requirement for permanent conquest of a disputed territory.[57] This sense was so powerful that it pervaded women's statements in the 1930s, and figured prominently in memoirs written 40 years later. Efrosina Mishalova, in her memoir, vividly recalled the adulation with which the audience of Khetagurovites greeted the Far Eastern Commander, General V.K. Bliukher, and the emotions his speech stirred. She recalled that Bliukher told the audience to:

> Remember dear young women that although at this time you are wearing civilian dress, you are actually soldiers in the Red Army, defenders of the Far Eastern borders. Remember this always and everywhere … You are now residents of the Far East and we are all now on the border with Japan. Japan is a very sneaky and insidious enemy … Always be prepared to join the ranks of the defenders of our sacred Far Eastern borders.[58]

The audience jumped into raucous applause. "Everyone was in such a mood that one wanted to grab a rifle at that moment and go to fight the samurai. If a samurai was to have fallen into our hands at that moment he would not have walked out alive."[59] This was precisely the kind of rhetoric that many of the women found most exhilarating and easily integrated into their visions of their future in the Far East. V. Glevskaia from Nikolaevsk, Ukraine wrote a typically enthusiastic and jingoistic letter to the Khetagurovite Committee in September of 1939:

> I just read the newspaper about the Far Eastern region and I've read it now so many times, I have a desire and such a grand desire, that was born a long time ago, to go to the Far Eastern region … I am 24 years old, but now I only want to go the Far East, all my desires and aspirations (*sic*). I have a five-year-old son, I say to him, "Son, let's go to the Far East," and he replies, "Yes, to butcher (*rubit'*) the fascists!"[60]

In other studies of letters from this period, Soviet women figure prominently as victimized supplicants who emphasize their weakness, ill health, poverty, or motherhood to implore action on the part of the powerful.[61] None of these letter-writing strategies were evident in letters from female volunteers to the Far East. On the contrary, women presented themselves as adaptable, energetic, and specifically defined themselves as patriotic. Motherhood appeared to applicants as a possible disadvantage, with the potential of sabotaging their dreams of moving to the Far East. A divorced single mother, living with her own mother, worried that her family circumstances could undermine her application so she felt it necessary to reassure Party authorities that: "My family does not interfere with my work."[62]

Both men and women who wrote as volunteers presented themselves as potential equals in a common struggle to defend the borders or to build socialism. Chashchina from Cheliabinsk wrote to the Khabarovsk Party Committee because she "wanted to work in the Far East. If it is at all possible to join you."[63] Three male workers from a railroad factory in the city of Magnitogorsk wrote asking to resettle because they wanted to work on a new construction site, "where they need labor." They told the First Secretary that his speech at the Eighteenth Party Congress "moved their hearts." Now they impatiently sought to

> work in the Far East, together with you and with all the working class and peasantry of the Far Eastern Region, to strengthen its might. [We desire] with you to struggle to build new construction, to struggle for the full dawn of our flowering, unbeatable Motherland. And if the Japanese fascists try to stick their beastly paws into our loved unbeatable Motherland, then we are always ready at the first call of our government, at any minute, at any second to stand at the defense of our border.[64]

There are numerous examples of this loquacious style in the letters of men. Karpov-Karaev was the most extreme, if not the most adept, of those who enthusiastically consumed and then reworded texts to display his own standing as a conscious citizen. He claimed to have participated in the revolutionary days and the Civil War, and in 1937 wrote that the call of the Communist Party, government, and Khetagurova:

> forced every honest citizen of the Soviet Union to think about being battle-ready every day and in any sector of work … The Far Eastern *taiga* is now being remade into a marvelous region by the will of our wonderful fatherland (*otechestva*), our valiant Party of Bolsheviks in the thickest of forests where until recently roamed ferocious beasts, bears, and tigers, at this moment grows the construction of cities, villages, the building of railroads, and roads, the building of fortresses of socialism near to the Pacific Ocean.[65]

Thirty-two-year-old K. Dodoko explained that when he and his wife read about the region in the newspapers "we decided to go and live in your region and work for the good of our Motherland. If we are needed then we will stand at any minute for the defense of our Motherland and the Far Eastern border."[66] Dodoko was in charge of a department in a *sovkhoz* and his wife was a village teacher in the Vannov district of Krasnodar region. His use of a collective "we" is noteworthy because it was so unusual for men to write in the plural on behalf of themselves and their families when volunteering the whole family for relocation.

Female and male teachers were the most engaged in elaborating their interests and seemed to be the most enthusiastic consumers of Soviet-frontier mythologies. Teacher Pavel Martynov from the Gor'kovskaia oblast' was keen to teach in a Far Eastern school but had little luck getting hired by writing to the regional education department. After reading several articles in the newspapers on the Far East, he wrote to the region's First Secretary. Thirty-three years old, with a wife and two children, Martynov taught geography and natural history to fifth, sixth, and seventh graders. His wife was a preschool teacher who also wanted to work in the Far East. Martynov stressed that he was "committed with my whole soul to my grand obligation – the education of children. I want to give my still young strengths to the education of children of the Far East, the future defenders of our mighty fatherland, the future builders of socialism." This geography teacher was also the only one to demonstrate a cognizance that the region was not an empty wilderness or filled with wild savages, but was populated by a variety of indigenous people who sent their children to school. Martynov was particularly interested in teaching in a national minority school and although he had no special knowledge about these cultures, he was ready to learn any language necessary for the job.[67]

Thirty-three-year-old bookkeeper Nikolai Emel'ianov was the only man among the letter writers to mention mundane motivations for resettlement. He wanted to leave the only area he had ever known because, "I have only one aim for leaving the Donbass, and this is to change climatic conditions and at least slightly fulfill my duty to help our country in the matters of development of the Khabarovsk region."[68] His search for a better climate in the Far East was profoundly misguided because the Khabarovsk region is better known for its climatic extremes. His misperception of what was in store highlights the extent to which the region figured as a veritable Garden of Eden in the imagination of the nation's most dutiful sons.

Women were most adept at visualizing themselves as defenders of the Soviet border. T. Zhurikhina from Ivanov greeted her letter's recipient in a chatty tone. "Dear comrades, border-guards of the Far East. I come to you with a true desire." She explained that she wanted to work with them "in unison, in the defense of the Motherland from an enemy attack."[69] Thirty-one-year-old Lotikova "burned with desire to put in my own share of work into the task of strengthening our Far Eastern borders."[70] Eighteen-year-old Maria Glupikhina called herself "a loyal *patriotka*" who wanted to be included in the ranks of those who desire to work in the Far East.[71] Schoolteachers were the most proficient at this form, as demonstrated in a collective letter from four teachers from the Smolensk region. Their letter stressed their eagerness to educate youth on a distant periphery as part of the Far Eastern patriotic family. They wanted to "contribute our selfless labor together with the best people to strengthen the power of our Motherland, strengthen our borders against our enemies."[72]

Women's peripheral status in the prevalent mythologies of revolutionary bravado explains the appearance of "envy" as a motivating force among women. They may have picked up on this theme when Khetagurova mentioned it, but since they discarded so much else it clearly spoke to their own attitudes. Igalkina was "pleased and envious that other young women were going to the region."[73] She initially thought it was not possible for her to join them because she was in the retail industry, which seemed to lack relevance to historic missions. Claiming to be writing on behalf of other young women in her workplace, she promised that they would respond with great happiness if invited and pledged to become Far Eastern Stakhanovites. She also "promised not only to work but if necessary to go along with our fathers and brothers to the border and defeat the enemy on their territory." Thirty-one-year-old E. Iuzhina also wrote out of a sense of "envy for the younger women who I see leaving for the Far East" in response to Khetagurova. She explained, "I am not an engineer, nor a doctor, I am a Party worker and I have an immense desire to work in the Far East."[74]

"The whole country knew!"

If a superstar such as Valentina Khetagurova emerged out of the periphery, there was also the potential for other young women to gain their own acclaim and status out of their very public sacrifices for the good of the nation.[75] One of the inescapable benefits of becoming a Khetagurovite was the publicity lavished on participants. Becoming a Khetagurovite meant repeated appearances in photographs and articles in hometown newspapers, as well as in their new place of residence. Khetagurovites starred in a documentary film, *Khetagurovki*. They were eulogized in Matvei Blanter's 1939 operetta *On the Shores of the Amur*, which Khetagurovites saw performed in Khabarovsk.[76] There were other productions based on the Khetagurovites. The film *Girl with a Personality* (*Devushka s kharakterom*, 1939) was a musical comedy which revolved around the arrival of an officer's wife from the Far East with a mission to find female volunteers for migration. There were numerous poems, such as *Khetagurovka* cited at the opening of this chapter. All of these undoubtedly provided extraordinary outlets for self-affirmation and public acclaim.[77]

Those who migrated had already garnered a certain degree of limelight at their place of origin as either exemplary workers in production or as prominent activists. Many Khetagurovites genuinely enjoyed public speaking and ritual displays of their own authority. For instance, one woman loved being an "agitator." She enjoyed visits to workers' homes for talks and relished the times when, "whole families listened to me."[78] The opportunities for such prominence were thoroughly welded to public rituals affirming national loyalties. Most of all she delighted in appearing on a tribune, "I was so small but so proud that I am giving orders to such a large mass of people to raise the flag."[79] In Khabarovsk she became the secretary of her Komsomol factory organization, something she "had dreamed about" from her first days in the Komsomol.

Part of this longing for the limelight is obvious in the pleasure the memoirists experienced during the fanfare surrounding their departures and arrivals in the region. Memoirists lavished a great deal of attention on these experiences. Koliasnikova not only felt elated at the public festivities when she left her hometown, but was also taken by surprise and at the same time pleased by her reception in Khabarovsk, where "we were greeted with great warmth. An orchestra played once more, there were fine speeches. We were very uncomfortable because we had not done anything yet and we were being greeted as heroes."[80] Bazarova was also proud of the exciting send off and reception. "The whole country knew! A song was even written for us, 'Goodbye Young Women'."[81] Before Kapitalina Kostina left her Gor'kii factory for the Far East she was given a grandiose send off by her factory and drama circle comrades. In Khabarovsk her group was "greeted even better than they were sent off. The orchestra played, there were masses of people there and we smiled and cried from joy."[82] All of the greetings and special festivities along the way made women like Nadezhda Iur'eva feel that they were "traveling as people who are needed in the Far East."[83]

In hindsight, elderly memoirists offered a wider and somewhat more candid range of explanations for their own and their fellow migrants' eastward trek to the shores of the Pacific. Memoirists explained that many they knew simply wanted to see exotic locations. Others were attracted by the prospect of a far-flung adventure as a step toward autonomy from parental control. Some considered resettlement a test of their personal resolve precisely because few acquaintances and relatives believed that the young women could abide the difficult conditions of the Far East. All of these sentiments were mixed with a determination to participate in important national projects. According to Druzhevich the primary driving force for women like her was precisely not "a search for intense personal emotions", rather it was a test and exploration of "one's moral strength" and a chance to "live a life of purposefulness with passion in the name of the Motherland."[84] Sacrifices in the name of the Motherland were also opportunities for women to live autonomous lives. When asked to explain why they had answered the Khetagurovite call-up 40 years later, some pointed to the supposed natural propensity of young people to "dream about great feats and about extraordinary voyages."[85] Alekseeva remembered being told that young women should "Be ready for an autonomous life. We badly wanted to try out our strengths, to prove that we were not afraid of anything even though people tried to scare us."[86]

Young women thought of themselves not only as the agents of Soviet modernity but as the agents of civic mindedness. Women viewed "patriotism" as a work in progress. They assumed that patriotism and commitment to national goals were not unmediated natural emotions that stemmed from being a citizen. Rather, they regarded patriotic sentiments as products of living in a society where an individual's quality of life was a matter for concern for the larger collective. It therefore fell to them to exhibit concern about the living conditions of fellow-workers and instill patriotism among others in return. For instance, one young woman explained that she helped to make life better in barracks in order to "bring everything to life that will win patriotism."[87] What they sought were conditions where they could immediately impact the quality of life to demonstrate their own sense of cultured living and persuade others to remain committed to national goals. Poligonova explained that:

> We were called here by Valia Khetagurova not just to work in industry or help in public work. Valia Khetagurova called us to strengthen, to instill culture in the Far East, so that our people will not run from the Far East, so that they stay here as permanent residents.[88]

In 1938, as well as in the 1970s, Khetagurovites stressed that friends and relatives had warned them about the Far East. Even the publicity aimed at the women did not hide the fact that difficult living conditions and deprivations were in store.[89] Prior to coming to the Far East, young women knew what they had read in novels such as *In the East*.[90] Others picked up information about the region from books with telling titles such as *Japan's Secret Agent*; *Border under Lock*; *The Enemy Will Not Cross the Border*; and *My Reconnaissance Work*.[91] Alekseeva and her friends "imagined the Far East as a distant planet."[92] Dire warnings only added an extra layer of mystique to the venture and buttressed their stubbornness. Asikritova was told by acquaintances that:

> You'll perish there at the edge of the world. And there are savages living there who walk around naked, and there are shamans beating on their tambourines, and beasts. And misfortune awaits young women at every step [where they are] surrounded by nothing but convicts.[93]

Twenty-year-old Bazarova explained that she and her friends used to read everything they could about Komsomol'sk-na-Amure but only knew that:

> There somewhere at the edge of the world a new city has been born made by the hands of the Komsomol. We had scanty information about the region. We

mostly heard rumors about all kinds of difficulties: scurvy, harsh climate, life in tents and dugouts. Some just tried to scare us. "Where are you going? Lads are not able to stand it." But this only made our desire stronger and we could not be stopped.[94]

A common refrain both in the comments made in the 1930s and in the memoirs was a sense of disappointment experienced by women who thought they were headed for life in the most primitive conditions and untouched wilderness. Many of those who went had wildly distorted expectations, and the normalcy they found was a disappointment.[95] "We were expecting to see in Komsomol'sk not only the wild *taiga* with beasts, but also half-savage people, with whom we would be forced to struggle."[96] Valianskaia from Kiev "used to dream about the Far East. The *taiga*, the hills and the beauty of it all appeared in front of us."[97] She and her friends

especially wanted to end up in the *taiga*, in the real *taiga*. When we arrived we became disillusioned. Instead of the *taiga*, we saw three or four trees. But we had dreamed of seeing a real *taiga*, where snakes and animals are roaming.[98]

Bazarova remarked that the women who came to Komsomol'sk "were bothered by pangs of conscience since it was like we had come to something ready. We were greeted with a five-year-old city and not a remote *taiga*."[99] Plaskina, who went to Komsomol'sk at the age of 17, remembered that when she and her group arrived in Komsomol'sk

we saw finished houses and we became very disillusioned because we did not see the tents the way we had fantasized. We imagined tents and the *taiga* and impassible paths. Later we understood that we would get our share of good and bad.[100]

Activists blamed behavioral problems, poor work performance, and unreasonable demands among some on the fact that they "did not meet savages but ordinary people and a city under construction."[101]

The common experience of disappointment suggests that women sought public feats and encounters with savages and primitive conditions where they could graphically display their own civility. Khetagurovites hoped to find a sparsely developed land to function as a conspicuous platform for displaying the indispensability of women's work inside and outside of the domestic sphere. The more savage the locals or the more uncouth the workers, the more visible their own status as patriots and the more secure they felt themselves to be as agents of the nation.

The problem was not only that some were disappointed at finding familiar conditions where their contributions would possibly go unnoticed. The migrants also had to contend with skepticism among Far Easterners about their real motivations and widespread doubts about the ability of women in general to comprehend patriotism. Having stressed the specificity of their feminine contributions, the

Khetagurovite campaign reinforced a sense that women's essential differences might also render them ill-equipped to act out of purely patriotic sentiments.

If there were doubts about their motivations, there were further doubts about the ultimate worth of their apparent sacrifices. Popular attitudes about the meaning of exploration and migration deprived the young women of the full recognition they expected. The female-led campaign and the image of young women embarking for a land known for its overabundance of men complicated the meaning of migration and put many women in a defensive posture. Female participants could never overcome their anomalous place in frontier mythologies. Their intentions remained suspect, and observers assumed that women could only be motivated by a search for husbands or wealth, rather than patriotism. This attitude was so pervasive that some of the women were compelled to address the issue directly. Druzhevich rejected the idea that young women came in search of husbands or personal gain.

> We answered precisely because it was more difficult there. We were not offered any material incentives. There was a one-time travel subsidy. All of us were workers, after all. At the time, of course, marriage was not an end in itself for us.[102]

Memoirists and Khetagurovites obviously felt the sting of mockery that surrounded their decision to travel to the region. When Opryshko prepared to leave for the Far East with two of her factory co-workers,

> People laughed at us because [they said] we were going only to get married because there are many lads there. Or for a long ruble. But those who sympathized with us and knew what awaited us along the way told us that we would meet with great difficulties. We would have to be hungry and bare.[103]

Having succeeded as a train driver, a field traditionally dominated by men, Druzhevich remained cognizant of the treatment women received when they transgressed into male spheres. In this context she acknowledged that "certain narrow-minded people often with malicious smiles and crafty airs judged and measured us only as women who came to the Far East to get married."[104] Forty years later she continued to encounter people who demeaned "the most pure, exalted, and beautiful." The sting of such mockery was so tangible that it elicited a lengthy rejoinder.

> I will say it briefly: in our youth, and today, there was never and is not now a shortage of young men. However, to find a friend, to build with him a beautiful life like singing a song, is not always possible. If you are going to look for this specifically, then you won't find this in the Far East, and you can't write away for it "across the border." There are probably people today who crave to "earn" and to return home in their own *Volga* [a car] ... These are apparently the types who yearn to "get married" and "advantageously" no less. These sorts were always around with or without the call-up![105]

Only partially able to realize their hopes of sustained and genuine acclaim for their sacrifices, Khetagurovites continued to draw prestige by stressing how tightly their life paths intertwined with the development of Soviet society.

Despite the contentious meaning of their sacrifice, those who settled in the region garnered real satisfaction from the development of their new hometown. Egorova, who settled in Komsomol'sk-na-Amure, continued to identify herself and her group of friends as former Khetagurovites who were respected members of their community and authentic pioneers. Several dozen former Khetagurovites were still prominent public figures in the 1980s. They had formed not only lifelong friendships but also a strong civic pride in the urban landscape they inhabited. Egorova explained that:

> The "gals" meet often and now we call ourselves pioneer pensioners but we participate in the public life of our city and do not get sad. Our city has become unrecognizable, flowering and we all love it because our share has been put into its construction.[106]

Mariia Komarova, who originally hailed from Ukraine, concluded her memoir with this reflection on her decision to migrate. "I am very pleased that I ended up in the Far East. This is my second Motherland. I might even say that I love Russia more than Ukraine."[107] A visceral sense of having participated in turning a wilderness into a city made it possible for women like Komarova to identify their interests with a grander nation-building project transcending former allegiances.

Khetagurova's invitation to create a new society on a blank slate of wilderness was a genuinely popular sentiment that served the interests of the Communist Party in the immediate pre-war years. The search for recognition and a space where they felt needed suggests a profound sense of social isolation experienced by young women in a society that promised equality but denigrated traits and labor associated with femininity. The Far East continued to retain a strong association with rugged masculinity, notwithstanding efforts to interject women into the mythical landscapes in official culture. Despite or perhaps because of the Far East's aura of danger and challenge, young women were determined to play a role in the construction of a new Motherland and the defense of the nation.

Letters of application to resettle and memoirs of Khetagurovites reveal that young female volunteers shared a fascination with life in the most remote locations. They were convinced that demonstrable sacrifices for the national good would also bestow upon them the kind of social worth they craved. An empty space, the wild *taiga* was supposed to be the perfect context where all legacies of the past and the drudgery of the present day dissolved and an absolute new kind of social world took shape.

Notes

1 Research for this chapter was supported in part by a grant from the International Research & Exchanges Board (IREX), with funds provided by the National Endowment for the Humanities, the United States Department of State, which administers the Title VII Program, and the IREX Scholar Support Fund. None of these organizations is responsible for the views expressed. The author wishes to thank Nina I. Dubinina.
2 Anna Boriss, "Khetagurovka," *Na rubezhe. Zhurnal khudozhestvennoi literatury i publitsistiki* (May–June 1937): 22.
3 For a comprehensive discussion of the Russian and Soviet Far East see John Stephan, *The Russian Far East* (Stanford, 1994).
4 For further on the Japanese in Manchuria see Louise Young, *Japan's Total Empire: Manchuria and the Culture of Wartime Imperialism* (Berkeley, 1998); Yashihisa Tak Matsusaka, *The Making of Japanese Manchuria, 1904–32* (Cambridge, 2001); Prasenjit Duara, *Sovereignty and Authenticity: Manchukuo and the East Asian Modern* (Lanham, MD, 2003).
5 V.B. Zhiromskaia, *Demograficheskaia istoriia Rossii v 1930-e gody. Vzgliad v neizvestnoe* (Moscow, 2001), 68. A variety of voluntary resettlement campaigns had been in effect for the Far East since the mid-1920s and the population of the area grew by 195 percent between 1926 and 1937. Soviet planners deemed this pace inadequate for rapid industrialization and regional self-sufficiency. No new settlers arrived in 1935 and 1936 under the auspices of voluntary resettlement programs.
6 For further on this, see James R. Gibson, "Paradoxical perceptions of Siberia: patrician and plebeian images up to the mid-1800s," in *Between Heaven and Hell. The Myth of Siberia in Russian Culture*, eds Galya Diment and Yuri Slezkine (New York, 1993), 67–93.
7 For more on this see Emma Widdis, *Visions of a New Land: Soviet Film from the Revolution to the Second World War* (New Haven, 2003).
8 The area contained approximately 300,000 prisoners and special settlers in 1939. Zhiromskaia, *Demograficheskaia istoriia*, 72–3.
9 For more on the causes of this gender imbalance, see my article, "Soviet maidens for the socialist fortress: the Khetagurovite campaign to settle the Soviet Far East, 1937–9," *Russian Review* 62 (July 2003): 387–410.
10 Valentina Khetagurova-Zarubina, "Priezzhaite k nam na Dal'nii Vostok," *Komsomol'skaia pravda* [hereafter *KP*], 5 February 1937.
11 The final tally is from RGASPI M, f. 1, op. 23, d. 1351, l. 69, "Postanovlenie TsK VLKSM 'O rabote khetagurovskoi komissii'," 13 October 1939. [Communist Youth League records under the auspices of RGASPI are abbreviated as RGASPI M.]
12 "Forpost sotsializma na Vostoke," *Pravda*, 11 November 1936.
13 Ibid.
14 L. Aronshtam, "Osobaia Krasnoznamennaia," *Pravda,* 11 November 1936.
15 D. Zaslavskii, "Na Tikhom Okeane," *Pravda,* 11 November 1936.
16 B. Lapin and Z. Khatsrevin, "Vverkh po Amuru. Putevye zametki," *Pravda,* 25 June 1939.
17 "Forpost sotsializma."
18 Ibid.
19 Emma Widdis, "Borders: the aesthetic of conquest in Soviet cinema of the 1930s," *Journal of European Studies* 30, no. 4 (December 2000): 405.
20 Ibid.
21 A striking shortage of women in Komsomol'sk-na-Amure and the region first received attention in the coverage of the city's five-year anniversary in January 1937. V. Malev, Iu. Zhukov, L. Los', et. al. "Komsomol'sk segodnia. O unom gorode, psevdoromantiki i nasushchnykh potrebnostiakh 'Taezhnoi stolitsy'," *KP*, 14 January 1937.
22 D. Zaslavskii, "Na Tikhom Okeane," *Pravda,* 11 November 1936.

23 Ibid.
24 Khetagurova-Zarubina, "Priezzhaite."
25 For further on reading habits and the popularity of Jack London see Evgeny Dobrenko, *The Making of the State Reader: Social and Aesthetic Contexts of the Reception of Soviet Literature*, trans. Jesse Savage (Stanford, 1997).
26 Linda Bergmann, "Women against a background of white: the representation of self and nature in women's Arctic narratives," *American Studies* 34, no. 2 (Fall, 1993): 53.
27 See John McCannon, "Positive heroes at the pole: celebrity status, socialist-realist ideals and the Soviet myth of the Arctic, 1932–39," *Russian Review* 56 (July 1997): 346–65.
28 A.V. Kiparenko, "Na stroitel'stve goroda iunosti," in *Uchastnitsy velikogo zasedaniia*, eds A.V. Artyukhina et. al. (Moscow, 1962), 145–56.
29 The film's main protagonist Natasha was loosely based on Valentina Khetagurova. "Fil'm 'Komsomol'sk' gotov," *Tikhookeanskaia zvezda*, 4 April 1938. The role of women in the plot received attention in other publications. N. Likhobabin, "Kino 'Komsomol'sk'," *Tikhookeanskaia zvezda*, 15 June 1938.
30 Choi Chatterjee argues that the evolution of an ostensibly backward woman into the New Soviet Woman and heroine was at the center of Stalinist claims to modernity and was a consistent trope in public texts by and about women. See Choi Chatterjee, *Celebrating Women: Gender, Festival Culture, and Bolshevik Ideology, 1910–39* (Pittsburgh, 2002).
31 Khetagurova-Zarubina, "Priezzhaite."
32 Historian Karen Petrone found that confrontations with the Japanese in the Far East offered both tsarist and Soviet era publicists conducive platforms for elaborating upon "military-heroic masculinity." See Karen Petrone, "Masculinity and heroism in imperial and Soviet military-patriotic cultures," in *Russian Masculinities in History and Culture*, eds Barbara Evans Clements, Rebecca Friedman, and Dan Healey (New York, 2002), 172–93.
33 This sentiment was later repeated by those who came as Khetagurovites. Valentina Khetagurova, *Vsesoiuznoe soveshchanie zhen komandnogo i nachal'stvuiushchego sostava RKKA* (Moscow, 1937), 174.
34 Valentina Khetagurova, "Zdravstvui, iunost' 30-kh!" *Rabotnitsa*, 8 (1967). Quoted in Nina Dubinina, *Ty pozovi Dal'nii Vostok!* (Khabarovsk, 1987), 73.
35 For examples see Louis Montrose, "The work of gender in the discourse of discovery," *Representations* 33 (Winter, 1991): 1–41; Anne McClintock, Aamir Mufti, and Ella Shohat, eds, *Dangerous Liaisons: Gender, Nation and Postcolonial Perspectives* (Minneapolis, 1997).
36 Catherine Cavanaugh, "'No place for a woman': engendering western Canadian settlement," *Western Historical Quarterly* 28 (Winter, 1997): 509.
37 Ibid., 506.
38 "Molodye patriotki svoei rodiny," *KP*, 11 April 1937.
39 Ibid.
40 Ibid.
41 Elena Kononeko, "Schastlivogo puti, podrugi!" *KP*, 28 April 1937.
42 Ibid.
43 Documents related to the Khetagurovites are located in GAKhK, which now includes documents from the former Partiinyi arkhiv Khabarovskogo kraikoma VKP(b)-KPSS (PAKhK). Holdings from the former Party archive are designated as GAKhK P. GAKhK P, f. 2, op. 6, d. 358, l. 1, "Dokladnaia: O sostoianii dvizheniia molodezhi khetagurovskogo prizyva na DVK na 20/III/1938."
44 GAKhK P, f. 35, op. 1, d. 185, l. 160. Letter of Fedorova, Gladkova, and Ryzhnikova. They addressed their letter to the First Secretary "personally."
45 Ibid., l. 296. Letter from Dodoka and Svistula.

46 Letters to Ketlinskaia are in RGALI, f. 2816, op. 1, dd. 362–4. For a discussion of women writers, the portrayal of women, and V. Ketlinskaia in the 1930s, see Rosalind Marsh, "Women writers of the 1930s: conformity or subversion?" in *Women in the Stalin Era*, ed. Melanie Ilic (New York, 2001), 173–91.
47 RGALI, f. 2816, op. 1, d. 363, ll. 73–73ob. Letter from Vera Nikitkina, Vol'nogorskii *sel'kolkhoz*.
48 GAKhK P, f. 442, op. 2, d. 283, l. 86. Letter from Koliasnikova.
49 GAKhK P, f. 35, op. 1, d. 339, l. 272. Letter of T. Sharaia.
50 GAKhK P, f. 35, op. 1, d. 174, ll. 159–60ob. Letter from Igalkina.
51 GAKhK P, f. 2, op. 2, d. 146, l. 126. "Zaiavleniia i spravki chlenov VKP iziavivshii zhelanie rabotat' na DV i perepiska." Letter of Seleznova.
52 GAKhK P, f. 35, op. 1, d. 250, l. 38. Letter of Khatukhina, 17 May 1939. In another letter written just one month earlier she claimed that although she had personal reasons for migrating, these were superseded by her desire "to work in a new construction site." GAKhK P, f. 35, op. 1, d. 185, ll. 68–68ob. Letter of Khatukhina, 2 April 1939.
53 GAKhK P, f. 35, op. 1, d. 185, l. 299. Letter of Molchanova.
54 GAKhK P, f. 35, op. 1, d. 339, l. 270. "Zaiavlenie lichnogo kharaktera." Letter of Glevskaia.
55 GAKhK P, f. 35, op. 1, d. 359, ll. 95–7. Pegov personally forwarded their letter to the Khetagurovite Committee chair with the note, "Comrade Lapshin, I ask you to answer the young women with haste and help them move here to work." 3 May 1939. Letter of Ivantseva, Ivanova, Egorenkova, and Lukovnikova.
56 GAKhK P, f. 35, op. 1, d. 339, l. 270. "Zaiavlenie lichnogo kharaktera." Letter of Glevskaia.
57 Women's emphasis on taking up arms and readiness to participate in violence is a common theme in this period. See Anna Krylova, "Stalinist identity from the viewpoint of gender: rearing a generation of professionally violent women-fighters in 1930s Stalinist Russia," *Gender & History* 16, no. 3 (November 2004): 626–53.
58 GAKhK P, f. 442, op. 2, d. 284, ll. 114ob–15. Memoir of Efrosina L. Mishalova, "Vospominaia o moei miloi zadornoi trudnoi i schastlivoi komsomol'skoi iunosti," 18 February 1976.
59 Ibid., 114ob.
60 GAKhK P, f. 35, op. 1, d. 339, l. 270. Letter from Valentina Glevskaia.
61 For more on such strategies see Golfo Alexopoulos, *Stalin's Outcasts: Aliens, Citizens and the Soviet State, 1926–1936* (Ithaca, 2003).
62 GAKhK P, f. 35, op. 1, d. 185, ll. 87, 88. Correspondence of the Department of Cadres. Letter of Iuzhina from Orel, in the position of Third Secretary of a Communist Party district committee.
63 GAKhK P, f. 35, op. 1, d. 336, l. 43. Letter of Chashchina.
64 GAKhK P, f. 35, op. 1, d. 185, l. 366. Letter of Zemnukhov, Semenychev, and Chushkin.
65 GAKhK P, f. 2, op. 2, d. 146, l. 142. Letter of Karpov and family, 14 June 1937.
66 GAKhK P, f. 35, op. 1, d. 185, l. 296. Letter from Dodoka and Svistula.
67 GAKhK P, f. 35, op. 1, d. 185, l. 351. Letter of Martynov.
68 GAKhK P, f. 35, op. 1, d. 185, ll. 125–6. Letter of Emel'ianov.
69 GAKhK P, f. 35, op. 1, d. 185, l. 192. Letter from Zhurikhina.
70 GAKhK P, f. 2, op. 8, d. 146, l. 116. Letter of Lotikova.
71 GAKhK P, f. 2, op. 6, d. 341, l. 139. Letter of Glupikhina.
72 GAKhK P, f. 35, op. 1, d. 358, l. 87. Letter of schoolteachers: Nikol'skaia, Gavrilova, Fedorova, Novikova.
73 GAKhK P, f. 35, op. 1, d. 174, ll. 159–60ob. Letter from Igalkina.
74 GAKhK P, f. 35, op. 1, d. 185, ll. 87, 88. Correspondence of the Department of Cadres. Letter of Iuzhina.
75 Koliasnikova explained that she and others wanted to "join into something grandiose demanding all of your strength and wanting nothing in return like heroes from

Ostrovskii's book, *How the Steel was Tempered*, and Sholokhov. We wanted to be a little bit like our heroes." Memoir of M.N. Koliasnikova (Koturanova). GAKhK P, f. 442, op. 2, d. 283, ll. 85–85ob.

76 Mishalova loved seeing the operetta *Na Beregu Amura* in Khabarovsk in the late 1930s. Memoir of Mishalova, l. 119ob. *Na Beregu Amura* first appeared in 1939, composed by Matvei Blanter, also famous for the song *Katiusha.*

77 There were obvious references to Khetagurova in the 1938 film *Komsomol'sk.* A theatrical work, the 1938 play *Tania* by Aleksandr Arbuzov, told the story of a woman's personal growth through selfless labor and migration to the Far East along with Khetagurovites. Well received by audiences, *Tania* is still considered one of the finest plays of the Soviet period and was staged once more to critical acclaim in 2003.

78 GAKhK P, f. 442, op. 2, d. 282, l. 9. Memoir of Kapitalina Kostina.

79 Ibid., l. 10.

80 Memoir of Koliasnikova, l. 87.

81 "Goodbye young women," 1938, music by I. Dunaevskii and text by L. Levin. Memoir of P. Bazarova, GAKhK P, f. 442, op. 2, d. 283, l. 98. Similar focus on the fanfare of their send off is found in the memoir of A. Alekseeva, GAKhK P, f. 442, op. 2, d. 283, l. 15.

82 Memoir of Kostina, l. 6.

83 GAKhK P, f. 442, op. 2, d. 283, l. 44. Memoir of Nadezhda Iur'eva.

84 GAKhK P, f. 442, op. 2, d. 284, ll. 31–50. Memoir of Iu. Druzhevich, also quoted in Dubinina, *Ty pozovi*, 159.

85 GAKhK P, f. 442, op. 2, d. 298, l. 2. Memoir of Nina A. Asikritova, "Sorok odin god na Dal'nem Vostoke," October 1978.

86 Memoir of Alekseeva, l. 14.

87 GAKhK P, f. 618, op. 1, d. 325, l. 100. "Stenogramma kraevogo soveshchaniia khetagurovok – Shukhman," 16 September 1938. Similar pride in restructuring the behavior of men in crude settlements is prominent in the memoir of Anna Plaskina GAKhK P, f. 442, op. 2, d. 283, l. 52.

88 GAKhK P, f. 618, op. 1, d. 325, l. 316. "Stenogramma kraevogo soveshchaniia khetagurovok – Poligonova," 17 September 1938. A similar understanding of the need for women appeared in the memoirs. For example, see the Memoir of Koliasnikova, l. 86.

89 This message was a prominent theme in the recollections of participants as well as in comments made in the 1930s. Memoir of P. Egorova, April 1974. GAKhK P, f. 442, op. 2, d. 283, l. 9. 2.

90 GAKhK P, f. 618, op. 1, d. 325, l. 88. "Stenogramma kraevogo soveshchaniia khetagurovok – Beliakova," 16 September 1938. *Na Vostoke* by P. Pavlenko was a 1936 novel set in the Far East with a young female heroine, Olga, who struggles against a variety of hurdles including the natural world to aid border guards and security officials.

91 Memoir of Mishalova, l. 86.

92 Memoir of Alekseeva, l. 14.

93 Memoir of Asikritova, l. 3.

94 Memoir of Bazarova, l. 97.

95 On popular perceptions of northern regions and fascination with exploration see John McCannon, *Red Arctic: Polar Exploration and the Myth of the North in the Soviet Union, 1932–1939* (Oxford, 1998). The Far East also sparked a flurry of popular and scientific interest in the mid-nineteenth century. See Mark Bassin, *Imperial Visions: Nationalist Imagination and Geographical Expansion in the Russian Far East, 1840–1865* (Cambridge, 1999).

96 GAKhK P, f. 618, op. 1, d. 325, l. 17. "Stenogramma kraevogo soveshchaniia khetagurovok – Iliukhina," 15 September 1938. Khetagurovite Ilukhina worked in Komsomol'sk-na-Amure's factory no. 126.

97 GAKhK P, f. 618, op. 1, d. 325, l. 62. "Stenogramma kraevogo soveshchaniia khetagurovok – Valianskaia," 15 September 1938.

98 Ibid., l. 64.
99 Memoir of Bazarova, l. 95.
100 Memoir of Plaskina, ll. 53–4.
101 "Stenogramma – Iliukina," l. 18.
102 Memoir of Druzhevich quoted in Dubinina, *Ty Pozovi*, 159.
103 GAKhK P, f. 618, op. 1, d. 325, l. 295. "Stenogramma – Opryshko," 17 September 1938.
104 Memoir of Druzhevich quoted in Dubinina, *Ty Pozovi*, 158.
105 Ibid., 158–9.
106 GAKhK P, f. 442, op. 2, d. 283, l. 91. Memoir of Polina Egorova.
107 GAKhK P, f. 442, op. 2, d. 282, l. 145ob. Memoir of Mariia Komarova.

11 The "planet of one hundred languages"

Ethnic relations and Soviet identity in the Virgin Lands

Michaela Pohl

The Virgin Lands opening (its "mass phase" took place 1954–6) was the last large-scale Soviet-era migration project that contributed to the centrifugal movement of people from the centers to the borderlands of the Soviet empire. Nikita Khrushchev's project was initiated and implemented with the needs of Moscow and the Soviet nation in mind, rather than those of people in Central Asia, but despite that, it brought a lasting transformation of society and nature to Kazakhstan. The Virgin Lands were not "abandoned," and the project was not merely a chapter in the history of Soviet power struggles or an episode of voluntaristic agricultural policy, as some Western textbooks and the works of Sovietologists suggest.[1] Kazakh demographers have estimated that between one and two million Slavic settlers came to Kazakhstan as a result of the Virgin Lands opening, and throughout the 1990s, Kazakh and Western scholars and observers agreed that this was a "heavy price" to pay for the "mixed successes" of the Virgin Lands episode.[2] More positive assessments are rare nowadays. The former celebrations of internationalism, of the "great friendship of peoples," and of the Virgin Lands as a special "planet of 100 languages" have gone out of fashion. A new Kazakh history textbook for university students states more prosaically that one of the main results of the Virgin Lands was the "formation of a broad zone of socio-cultural and ethnic contacts, which invigorated the internationalization of public life," but the text provides little substantiation and no examples of culture in this Virgin Lands zone, pointing only to negative long-term effects on Kazakh culture as a whole.[3]

This chapter seeks to reappraise the notion of the *tselina* (Virgin Lands) as a multiethnic "planet," examining evidence from documents and personal narratives on three broad topics: inter-ethnic contact, religious and cultural life, and notions of Virgin Lands identity. The history of the Virgin Lands project has been written from Moscow's point of view, from that of Kazakh national history, and in the spirit of the Cold War. Only Russians and Kazakhs have appeared in the Virgin Lands discourse, while many other local people (Germans, Chechens, Ingush, and other Slavs, to name but a few) whose lives were changed have remained invisible.[4] As my discussion shows, it is not particularly revealing to reduce the Virgin Lands to an episode of demographic aggression, seeing the project's significance primarily in wreaking the "crushing final disintegration of traditional Kazakh culture."[5] Viewed from the Virgin Lands – at the peripheries of *both* Russia and

Kazakhstan – and despite economic and ecological setbacks, the Virgin Lands project, or rather what it was transformed into, turned out to be one of Khrushchev's most successful and lasting *social* reforms. It was a process that initiated the destalinization and rehabilitation of a region that had served as a dumping ground for punished nations and for labor camps. It took place rather differently from how we – or Khrushchev – had imagined. It was far more turbulent and even violent, and it involved many different groups of people besides Russians and Kazakhs. The processes of migration and construction evoked contradictory responses ranging from fervent support to bitter resistance. Ultimately, however, the Virgin Lands opening gave hundreds of thousands of the most varied people opportunities to build new lives and to reinvent themselves. Notions of moving to an "empty" space led to conflicts, but they also served to rehabilitate the region and to make way for a new identity for both settlers *and* local people.

This essay is based on archival and oral history research in what is now the Astana region of Kazakhstan, which served as the administrative and cultural center of the Virgin Lands. (To confuse matters, the region's principal town was called Akmolinsk from 1832–1960, then Tselinograd 1960–92, Akmola 1992–8, and Astana since 1998, and the name of the region has generally followed suit. Throughout, I use the historically correct designation.) When the campaign started, in 1954, its hinterland was a sparsely settled steppe territory of slightly more than 150,000 km^2 (about the size of South Korea). Akmolinsk was founded as a fort in 1832, in the course of extending Russian administration to the Kazakh Middle Horde. The Akmolinsk region was one of the main destinations of Slavic peasant settlement after emancipation, and a center of reformist efforts to transform agriculture in the 1890s. Most Russian and Ukrainian peasant settlements were clustered along the rivers, separately from Kazakh auls, but already by 1920, the Kazakh population of this region was reduced to 37 percent of the total.[6] In the Stalin era, the Akmolinsk region became a site for agricultural labor camps and a place of exile for the nations deported by Stalin. The two largest groups of exiles in Akmolinsk were Germans and Caucasians, primarily Chechens and Ingush. By 1946, 136,625 "special settlers" (*spetsposelentsy*) lived in the Akmolinsk region, the total population of the region being about 508,000.[7] Counting "kulaks" and prisoners, "special" populations in Akmolinsk made up about one-third of the total population. It is important to know for what follows, that after the initial shock wore off, the "special settlers" adapted to the local conditions very differently, depending on the national group and on their place of origin. A great variety of sources show that Chechen and Ingush resisted accommodation, while the Germans were obedient and worked as hard as they could to survive. Akmolinsk party bosses perceived Chechens and Ingush as working "significantly worse than the Germans," and they arrested far more Caucasians than Germans for crimes and misdemeanors.[8]

The political atmosphere in Akmolinsk was intensely oppressive from the beginning of collectivization until well into the 1950s. Kazakh communists about to be promoted were investigated to make sure their father or uncle had not been a *bai* or a member of the Kazakh intelligentsia purged in 1937, and they were closely

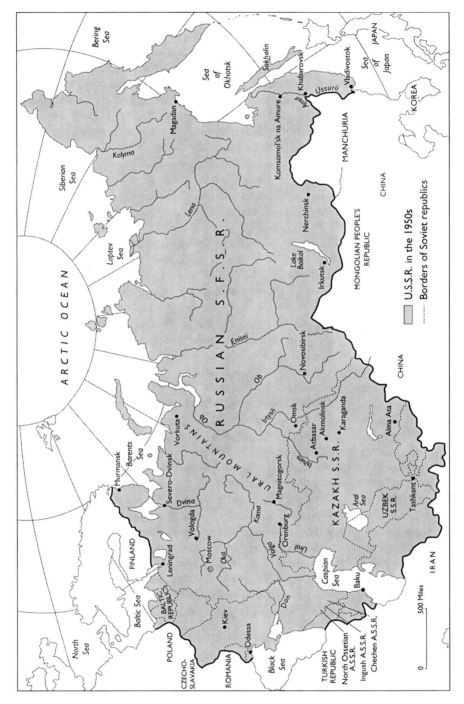

Map 5 The USSR, c 1950

observed for signs of "nationalist" sentiments and corruption.[9] If some of the local Stolypin peasants, resettled "kulaks," and even the German "special settlers" had built up relatively prosperous villages, the economic situation of the region as a whole was bleak and most work was done by hand and with draft animals. Many Kazakh villages had little contact with the outside world, and in the poorest districts, like Kurgaldzhino, children suffered from preventable diseases and few were sent to school. The Akmolinsk party chief, Nikolai Zhurin, along with the other party bosses from northern Kazakhstan, was one of the most enthusiastic supporters of the Virgin Lands project from its inception, hoping to seize a major opportunity for investment. Upon Khrushchev's request, he submitted a proposal for an increase in cultivated lands for the Akmolinsk region alone that was in excess of what the republican leaders considered possible for the entire republic.[10]

In opening the new lands, Khrushchev had the intention of reducing the burden on the Soviet Union's collective farmers. Most of his Virgin Lands memorandum to the Presidium of the Central Committee on 22 January 1954 (later published under the title "Means of Resolving the Grain Problem") is devoted to demonstrating how little grain the state had been able to procure in the years since 1950 and what a dismal effect the ever greater pressure had upon the collective farms and upon the morale of the *kolkhozniki* (collective farm workers). Opening so-called virgin and fallow lands in Siberia and Kazakhstan (the initial proposal called for 13–15 million hectares) would allow the state to reduce its demands on the central regions and would make it possible to buy more grain instead of extracting it.[11] Khrushchev was less alert to the needs of Kazakhstan and of the people who would work in the new lands.

His formula for opening the new lands can be summed up as "technology plus people." It was to be accomplished by pouring *all* new tractors and agricultural machines produced in 1954 into the new regions and by recruiting a permanent workforce (100,000 volunteers) by means of a large-scale publicity campaign. The settlers were recruited and sent at emergency speed by the Komsomol, the Party's youth organization. From the end of February 1954 to 20 April 1954, the total was reported as 146,710.[12] The recruiting commissions tried to fill the total required of them, and sent anybody who would sign up, including many 15–16-year-old teenagers (youth of draft age), who would have to leave again the next year. Over 20,000 volunteers arrived in Kazakhstan before any farm directors had been appointed. A significant number of people released under the amnesties of 1953–4 were sent to the Virgin Lands with Komsomol *putevki* (vouchers) during the first year, but it is difficult to say how many exactly. People from all over Kazakhstan complained about amnestied criminals who committed thefts and engaged in rude confrontations with locals. At a Party plenum in Akmolinsk in 1954, Party bosses said that one-third of the "volunteers" had a "dark past."[13] The Komsomol leaders attempted to avoid this in later years. It appears that the mass recruitment of formerly amnestied prisoners was not repeated, but the speed of recruitment in the second year was even greater than in 1954: 111,914 by 15 April; 162,099 by 1 June 1955.[14] In 1954 and 1955, the communist youth organization mobilized a total workforce of 330,375 people.[15] This was far more than initially projected. The oversupply of workers was supposed to combat the effects of out-migration, which ensued as soon as Virgin Lands workers arrived in their regions, but it also helped intensify the outflow when overcrowding and competition for jobs increased too much.

Suspicious of the mobilization results, some Western writers have placed the word "volunteers" in quotation marks when speaking of the Virgin Lands, or they have argued that "semi-compulsory methods" were used,[16] but the truth is that the project received a tremendously positive public response in 1954 and 1955. The verifiable (through unpublished documents and interviews) manifestations of this outpouring of enthusiasm and patriotism make clear that the project had a tremendous appeal for tens of thousands of young *kolkhozniki* stuck in bleak post-war villages. The work-days (*trudodni*) accumulated in *kolkhozy* amounted to nothing more than "little sticks" (*palochki*), while in the state farms of Kazakhstan one could earn money wages, and in addition receive an internal passport. In my interviews in the Akmolinsk region in 1994 and 1996,[17] almost all former Virgin Lands settlers sought to impress on me how desperate they were to leave behind the bitter poverty of the post-war years. One of the most vivid expressions of this came from Industrian Semenov, a Virgin Lands veteran who later became a local writer:

> We were a generation of fatherless children. The main thing that moved us, you see, is that we were people who experienced the most violent war, the terrible, destructive war ... and so from this destroyed country, we were the first who tried to escape the nightmare.[18]

The Virgin Lands held out prospects to nearly everyone. Students and some of the urban youth hoped they would "travel" and "live under the open sky,"[19] while demobilizing soldiers were more realistic in their expectations: "We are not afraid of difficulties. We are prepared to meet them. We have seen many hardships."[20] Many girls and young women wanted to get married in Kazakhstan,[21] while others had heard that Kazakhstan was a "rich country," that it was "great" there, that the wages were good.[22]

The Virgin Lands settlers inundated the region. The population of the Akmolinsk region grew by 133,761 during the first three years of the campaign, but this does not reflect the fluidity of people, as altogether at least 300,000 people came to the region, most to leave again after a few months or years.[23] Of the first waves of settlers in 1954–6, only a few hundred people stayed in the region. The bulk of settlers who remained came some years later, especially during the years 1960–5 (when Tselinograd was booming) and after (when an infrastructure and services had been built up).

The main reason for out-migration was that the years of the "mass opening" (1954–6) were terribly difficult and many of the volunteers suffered severe deprivations upon arrival. Local authorities were completely unprepared for the influx of people and materiel. Vast trainloads of tractors, tents, and supplies were sent, but remained piled up at train stations for months and even years because it was

НА НОВЫЕ ЗЕМЛИ
ЕДЕМТЕ С НАМИ!

Figure 11.1 "Come with us to the Virgin Lands!" (poster, V. Seleznev, Moscow, 1954).
From *Rossiia: Istoriia strany v plakatakh* (Moscow, 1993), no page number
indicated.

extremely difficult to transport the supplies to the sites of the new state farms. For the first two years, the food situation in the Akmolinsk region was frequently described as "extremely abnormal" and as "alarming," including cases in which tractor brigades starved for several days, and workers collapsed from hunger while they were working. Almost all the farms went through a succession of bosses. Common complaints were that the directors were constantly drinking, that they were rude towards the settlers, and that they committed many acts of random and bureaucratic abuse. The bosses had a heavy hand. Quite a few of them got into drunken episodes that were more "colorful" than those of the youth.[24]

Despite these rough beginnings the project transformed the region and the north of Kazakhstan. Between 1954 and 1956, Akmolinskaia oblast' received 3.29 billion rubles in investments, the settlers built about 10,000 of their own houses, and they built 77 brand-new state farms and settlements.[25] These Virgin Lands settlements represented the state of the art in rural construction, completely different from the older European villages and the Kazakh *auly* that existed in the region. The area of the state farms was large. The streets were wide, designed with space for trees and benches. One unique feature of the Virgin Lands farms was that work and public areas were designed to be separate. Garages, electric stations, storage facilities, grain silos, and cattle sheds were clustered at one end of the settlement, separate from living areas. Storage sheds, stables, and gardens attached to individual houses were accessible through back alleys, to preserve the neat appearance of the main streets. The centers of the settlements featured spaces for parks and squares. All of the settlements received electricity and telephone services by the mid-1950s. Living in such a settlement and becoming a paid worker was very attractive to *kolkhozniki* from the depressed villages of the western regions of the Soviet Union, and many of them stuck it out from the first, turbulent years – returning to Belarus and Ukraine only in the mid-1970s, when they were pensioned. A disproportionate number of my most enthusiastic Virgin Lands informants of all nationalities grew up in orphanages, and in the years after 1956 large cohorts of released prisoners from the camps quietly made the *tselina* their home. Workers and youth from the large cities, however, found little at first to make up for deprivations, and they came and left in droves. State and Party essentially viewed and treated these settlers as an endlessly renewable source. What started as a plan to permanently resettle 100,000 people turned into a *yearly* mobilization of that many workers.

When the Virgin Lands settlers started pouring into Akmolinsk, local people received few or no explanations of what was happening, and the settlers came expecting "empty" steppe lands. The entire presentation of the Virgin Lands in propaganda and in media prepared them to expect a Kazakhstan that was empty of culture or people, except for a few "native herders." They were astonished and dismayed to find thousands of people whom they had been taught to think of as "traitors" already living there, scattered in all the villages and small district towns. Antonina Azeeva, a construction worker in a state farm founded in 1955, had a very vivid recollection when I asked her why she came and what her expectations were.

Do you think I had any idea what Kazakhstan was like back then? [Laughs.] I thought it was this rich country, just as everyone else thought! We thought we knew, but we didn't know anything! And then, when we got here – [Louder.] Oh!! Oh!! If you could have seen what it was like! We went out of our minds!! Out of our minds! ... The train station was terrifying! [Loudly.] And the people there, all black! Chechens, and Ingush! And what kind of people they were, they all went with some kind of knife under their belt. ... Oh, how we cried! Oh! Where did we end up? Why did they tell us it was so great here (*sil'no khorosho*)? On the radio it said how in Kazakhstan, how it couldn't be better than that! Well, afterwards, after we opened the new lands, we really did have a great life. Only nature here remained strange, but we had all the goods we needed.[26]

It was easy to blame the deported people for problems, or to see them as "enemies" and "parasites." As soon as the new settlers began to arrive in Kazakhstan, dozens of incidents of unrest, violent confrontations, beatings, mass fights, and riots were reported by the militia and the special settler police force in each of the Virgin Lands regions.[27] To give some examples, one series of attacks and fights, which were typical for these first Virgin Lands months, happened at KazTsIK *sovkhoz*, a place where many of the new workers were amnestied prisoners and where the local population consisted of resettled Ingush and Poles. The Virgin Lands workers were left without direct supervision and without work for several months. Many confrontations took place during extended drinking bouts. A mass fight in March 1954 caused one death from knife wounds, that of a settler. The larger cases in this farm were reported to the Party only months after they occurred, and they were not fully investigated until almost one year after the events, in 1955. The report drawn up at that time showed that during 1954 smaller incidents (brawls, knife fights, rapes) involving between two and five people had been nearly daily occurrences at KazTsIK and that they had not been recorded by anyone.[28]

Several mass riots between Virgin Landers and resettled Chechens and Ingush took place in mechanization schools (which provided courses for tractor drivers) at the end of 1954, after the harvest, each involving hundreds of participants. These large confrontations were also preceded by a whole series of smaller violent incidents, including brawls at movie showings and other attacks and beatings. In the village of Elizavetinka, for example, the hostile atmosphere exploded on Soviet election day in December 1954, as the voting and holiday festivities brought crowds of all national groups out into the streets. The immediate cause of the fighting appears to have been an attempt by Virgin Landers to drive the Caucasian special settlers from the local club, which on that day served simultaneously as a polling station and dance hall. A scuffle at the club erupted into general fighting that spread all over the village, involving at least 120 persons directly, as active participants in the fighting. The Ingush fled to their houses, pursued by mechanization students, who armed themselves with sticks and rocks, and began to invade Ingush homes, dragging out inhabitants and beating them. The fighting went on

from noon until evening. Virgin Landers chased away and intimidated local officials, until they were driven back to their school by Ingush men armed with rocks
and axes, and finally dispersed into smaller groups by the school director and
teachers.[29]

Police and party records show that at least 135 separate violent crowd incidents
took place in the Akmolinsk region between 1954 and 1957.[30] In police reports and
write-ups made soon after such incidents occurred, several patterns emerge very
clearly. The police placed the blame for instigating the majority of the occurrences
squarely on the Virgin Landers. In almost all district towns and villages the
arriving Virgin Lands settlers created a hostile atmosphere and many of the
"special settlers" were soon afraid to go to rural stores and lunchrooms and to
public events like dances and movie showings. In addition, I found that while
deprivations and poor conditions clearly increased the level of stress and competition for resources, the number and the intensity of confrontations increased when
people *had* money, especially to buy vodka; that is, when the settlers first arrived,
after the harvest, and during major holidays. The great majority of direct participants in the fights were young single men, and small-scale confrontations turned
into riots or larger fights only where workers were concentrated in larger numbers.
Such incidents tended to occur in district towns, or in Akmolinsk, where workers
attended tractor courses, were crowded into construction trust dormitories, or
congregated at dances, in parks or clubs.[31]

The deported people not only adapted to their exile differently, they also reacted
differently to the violence. While Germans and Kazakhs generally tried to avoid
confrontations, many of the Caucasian men fought back, and this caused even
greater violence. A newspaper editor from Alma-Ata, sent to carry out "political-
explanatory" work among the Chechen and Ingush in the Akmolinsk region in late
1956, wrote that despite the efforts of the Akmolinsk Party organization to fight
"unhealthy phenomena,"

> [I]n Akmolinsk and in the districts of the *oblast'* murders of Chechen and
> Ingush frequently take place, committed by bandits and hooligan elements.
> This has created somewhat strained relations between the Chechen and a
> certain part of the rest of the population of Akmolinsk and rural districts. Just
> before we arrived several Ingush were killed, others beaten half to death, and
> wounded. In the evening, the latter are afraid to go out on the streets of
> Akmolinsk and of the Virgin Lands settlements alone.[32]

Local police officers were very concerned about these incidents at first. But after
about a year they stopped recording smaller incidents and concentrated on
breaking up large groups of "hooligans." The regional party organizations passed a
few resolutions "On Group Fights," which exhorted local officials to "carry out
explanatory work" among the affected populations, but except for firing farm
directors and Party secretaries *after* major fights had occurred, they took no
systematic action.[33] Judging by the declassified records of the special settler
police, which are available up to 1959, the fights decreased sharply in number after

1957, when the Chechens and some of the Ingush were allowed to return home to the Caucasus (more on this follows below).

Many of the oral testimonies that I collected in Akmola contradicted the documentary evidence, primarily because it was difficult to get people to talk openly about these disturbances. The most common responses to direct questions about ethnic relations and fights were to deny that fights had ever taken place, or to minimize their extent by blaming the violence on the amnestied criminals of the first years, on "youth excesses," or on so-called "outsiders" (*sluchainye liudi*). On the other hand, some interviewees brought up the violence spontaneously, as in this example from a conversation with a 60-year-old Kazakh woman, a dairy worker in a Virgin Lands farm for over 30 years.

M.P.: Tell me about how your life changed here, when they opened the Virgin Lands.
N.N.: Oh!! When the *tselina* opened, it was hard! People from Moscow came here. Muscovites came and put a trailer there. There was no house; there was a Kazakh *aul*, and a barracks, nothing else. The Kazakhs were all afraid. "Oh! People from Moscow came, they are killing people!" They all hid in their houses! When the Muscovites came with their trailer, everyone hid. They were afraid, Russians [as well], Kazakhs, very much. And then we got used to each other and people became like family. They started to work together, we [indicates herself and a German woman] were like real sisters. Right. Then they started to build housing. The first house they built was ours, where I live now; I've lived in that house for 30, for 40 years now.[34]

None of the interviewees who did consent to talk and reflect upon these matters brought up "ethnic hatred" to explain the violence. Instead they brought up the Soviet "collective." In a group discussion with Ingush and Chechen men, participants argued that the new arrivals "did not recognize" or "acknowledge" Kazakhs or Ingush as part of this collective.[35] Leonid Kartauzov, a much-decorated Virgin Lands veteran and former Supreme Soviet deputy, described some of the violent fights, and argued that they took place because the Caucasians were "fiery" and "considered themselves the bosses" in the Virgin Lands towns. The violence lasted, he said, until people "found a common language." He went on to explain:

L.M.: The thing is, you know, taken by itself; the *tselina* was one of the best measures to improve our internationalist education. Because they came here from all republics. People came here of all nationalities and faiths, so that's why they called Kazakhstan the "republic of 100 languages." In our state farm alone, somehow they counted it, were 125 nationalities.
M.P.: Just in that one place [unconvinced].
L.M.: Just there. … And you know, the common goal, the knowledge that our work was absolutely necessary, that's what brought us closer. Nobody could survive on their own in those conditions. Only the collective.

M.P.:   It seems to me, well, I read these protocols of the MVD about the fights, and I want to ask you this. The police said the fights started because those people [the Caucasians] were accused of being traitors to the motherland. Why were things so hard with *them*, and with others they were –

L.M.:   That's right, right – no, here's what I want to tell you, I'm not talking about the nationalities who lived here before we came.

M.P.:   But only the people arriving?

L.M.:   Right, you see what I mean? Only those who came. Slowly, bit by bit, those others who lived here started to come into our collective. But those who came, they represented some kind of general collective. You understand? And only thanks to that, we could really make an effort with this *tselina*, in a short time, and pretty successfully.[36]

The first part of Kartauzov's testimony could have been taken straight from the Soviet Virgin Lands literature, with its accolades to internationalism, and its emphasis on the creation of a "multinational family of Virgin Landers." It was a typical convention to point out a specific brigade or state farm, and to show how many nationalities were peacefully working side by side in it. The level of friend-ship was "measured" by the successes of such multinational work collectives in ploughing up the land, bringing in the harvest, or winning competitions.[37] What Kartauzov said about the local people slowly becoming part of the "general" Soviet collective, however, was unique, and reflects his personal and specific expe-rience of local culture as initially separate and different.

The most important impulse for bringing the "special settlers" back into the orbit of the Soviet collective was provided by a series of reforms of the exile system, which began two years before Khrushchev's "Secret Speech" and coin-cided with the influx of Virgin Landers.[38] In the summer of 1954, the government passed a decree which reduced the number of exiles by one-third all at once. All children under age 16 were released from their "special" status. Along with these measures to reduce their numbers came new regulations that eased the restrictions that the deportees lived under. It was made easier to travel and to change one's resi-dence within the republic of exile. The most immediate result of these new provi-sions was that Ingush and Chechens began to leave the Virgin Lands areas and to move to the south of Kazakhstan. By February 1955 about 19,000 persons had left the northern regions. The most important motivation was the harsh climate and unfamiliar nature of northern Kazakhstan, but a brigade from Moscow, sent to study the dislocation of special settlers and the violent clashes, found that the violence also played a role.[39]

A decree in December 1955 lifted the "special regulations" from the Germans. This reform was linked to the visit of German Chancellor Adenauer in Moscow in September 1955. The Germans received no compensation for their confiscated properties and did not receive the right to return to their former republics. Their removal from the special regime caused great unrest and resentment among the remaining special settlers, who could not understand how they were "any worse" than the Germans.[40] In the summer of 1956, all remaining exiles, including

Chechens and Ingush, were taken off the special settler rolls, but, like the Germans, they were still not allowed to go home. They were released without apology or rehabilitation, and they were forced to sign a document saying that they waived all rights to their former property, and that they were aware that returning to their former home was forbidden. Five thousand persons in the Akmolinsk region refused to sign this waiver.[41] Finally, in December 1956, apparently responding to spontaneous out-migration and growing unrest in the exile regions, the Central Committee passed a resolution that prepared for the repatriation of the Caucasians. The return migration was poorly organized and dragged on for months, as train stations and railroad towns were swamped with streams of people, and local authorities attempted to ease the pressure by announcing temporary stops on out-migration. The bulk of Chechen families left by 1958, but many Ingush ended up staying in the north of Kazakhstan, because their home region was split between the Chechen-Ingush ASSR and North Ossetia.

As these piecemeal and hesitant attempts at reform were carried out, and in the midst of the Virgin Lands influx, the special settlers revived their cultures and found a new confidence. One of the sources of this new confidence was grassroots political activity. Between 1955 and 1957, Germans and Caucasians who wanted to return home engaged in letter writing campaigns, trips to district and regional party offices, and even public demonstrations to achieve their goal.[42] A second source for restoring some measure of cultural autonomy was religious belief. Secret reports show that the religious culture of the exile population grew very strongly in those years. By 1959, the Akmolinsk region was home to more than 40 different religious groups (represented in most of the villages of the region), including Muslims (including Sufis), Orthodox Christians, Baptists, Mennonites, Polish and German Catholics, and many smaller sects.[43] While most of the religious groups acted in secrecy, others, according to a 1955 regional KGB report, openly proselytized, sought to draw village youth into prayer groups and choirs, distributed icons and candles, and carried out baptisms and weddings. For example, one of the most visible Sufi brotherhoods was based in Atbasar, a railroad town in the north of the region, led by Sheikh Bagautdin Deni Arsanov. In the mid-1950s the Sheikh moved to Alma-Ata, but the movement continued to flourish and the "*Arsanovtsy*" maintained connections in dozens of villages in the Akmolinsk region, and traveled throughout Kazakhstan.

Most remarkably, as I discuss elsewhere in greater detail, the Chechen Sufis founded an entirely new movement in Akmolinsk, the Vis Hadj *tarikat*, or sect of "White Hats" (*beloshaposhniki*). The "White Hats," named after the caps followers wear, are widely credited with inspiring the largest expansion of Sufism in exile, and after the 1950s the sect spread from Kazakhstan to Chechnya.[44] Throughout the late 1950s, Muslim and Christian preachers traveled around the villages of the region, organized Bible and Koran studies, advised believers in spiritual and practical questions, and collected money to support themselves and to build prayer houses. The major groups and those not suspected of carrying out "anti-soviet activities" were allowed to register, and German Lutherans were allowed to open a church in Akmolinsk in 1956.[45]

Clearly, the Virgin Lands were a very different place than many imagined (and imagine to this day). The most recent arrivals brought to this mixture their own vibrant and rough frontier culture, in which vodka and simple entertainments like dances, singing, and going to film showings featured most prominently. It was hardly "monolithic" (as Kazakhs now allege) and in the first few years it did not make a great impact, nor did it hinder the growth of all these different expressions of culture and identity.

"Special" and Virgin Lands settlers remember the 1950s quite differently. When I asked about entertainments or festivities, many former special settlers waved the question off, exclaiming there had never been any "good times," while Virgin Landers lit up with enthusiasm, remembered songs and *chastushki* (folk verses) from their home regions, and nostalgically described dances and holidays. The most important and satisfying holidays were the days immediately after the harvest (which in the 1960s turned into a "Day of the Agriculture Worker," a holiday that people said was specific to the Virgin Lands), the October Revolution Day (7 November), and New Year's Eve. A marked separateness also emerged when I asked people about specific practices. For instance, I asked couples who had married in the 1950s about their weddings. Several German women exclaimed bitterly that they "had no wedding," while others remembered primarily their poverty and absence of a dowry, and a very modest, quiet celebration: "My mother came, and her father, and we had a bottle of vodka, too. And that was it, we were married!"[46] Virgin Landers who married other Virgin Landers also spoke of their poverty at the time, but fondly recalled "brigade weddings" and the sense of community they engendered:

> The whole brigade had a party! How many people in the brigade, let's see, 20, or 30, and our neighbors. We were in this little tiny room, sat down, people everywhere! We never used to look who's friends with whom! We didn't make any distinctions, like, you're up there, you're a boss, you know, we were all the same. ... It was great, we celebrated for three days. No one paid attention, you know, director, worker, tractor driver, or whatever, we were all together.[47]

Virgin Landers who courted and married local women – whether Kazakhs, deportees, or from other groups living in the region – initially encountered resistance from the local special-settler police,[48] and frequently on the part of relatives on both sides of the future family. In one dramatic case recorded by the local police, the male relatives of an Ingush woman chased and threatened a young couple until the police interfered and helped them leave the republic.[49]

Officials measured the "friendship of peoples" by showing that the number of "mixed" marriages, or vows across national and ethnic lines, increased. The number of such weddings increased by about one-third in the Akmolinsk region (from 20.5 percent of all weddings in 1950 to 38.8 percent in 1960). [50] While this number shows little in itself, because it includes marriages of Slavs to each other, the narrative testimonies that I collected show that Virgin Landers who married locals indeed tended to have a better understanding of their neighbors' difficult lives, being able to recall more than the simple fact that they were present. Industrian Semenov, cited above, who married one of the Polish exile women, was deeply affected by the sharp contrasts between the newest settlers and the special settlers. The Virgin Landers, as patriots and Soviet citizens, felt the whole country to be theirs, and they felt free to go anywhere. At the same time in Akmolinsk existed "second-class" people who were not even allowed to go to the next village without permission.[51] Semenov wrote about an incident in which one of the special settlers was beaten and no one dared to defend him, because of his special status.

> That was my first collision with one of the innermost secrets of the Stalinist regime. I was amazed, just like the other *tselinniki* ... who worked in the MTS Virgin Lands brigades, made up of local people. To tell the truth, we knew about the repressed, the special settlers, we had heard about them, but we thought nothing of it. Used to working in multinational collectives every-where, we saw nothing special in the fact that local brigades and villages, besides Kazakhs and Russians, contained Poles, Germans, Chechens, Ingush, Kabardians, Balkardians, Koreans, and other people. But coming into contact with their "status," in practice, gave us this stunning piece of information: these were unfree people, almost prisoners. After that morning my comrades in the brigade warmed up to me and told me much about their lives. It's true; however, they did so gently, almost as if speaking to a sick person, and only partially ... [knowing that] otherwise I would experience difficulties.[52]

Others worked side by side, in the celebrated multinational work collectives, knowing very little about each other. Galina Tarasiuk, a land surveyor who came to Akmolinsk in 1954, admired the German farms of the region as "strong and well managed." She worked with German agronomists and collective farm chairmen for years, respected them as excellent workers and competent bosses, and learned much from them, but as she explained:

> We did not notice that they were under a special regime. I didn't even know that there was a *spetskomendatura*, that is something that they told us later. In general they behaved as if they were free, and I wouldn't say that there was any oppression.[53]

Hard work and the sharing of dangers, disappointments, and successes gradu-ally engendered mutual respect. In interviews, people of all nationalities insisted that they did learn to respect each other, even if their relationship had a stormy beginning. That respect was somewhat different from the official "friendship of nations." For instance, it was a commonplace of the Virgin Lands propaganda that local "herders" came to the aid of frozen or lost *tselinniki*, and that they met the settlers "gladly" or "warmly, like brothers." As discredited as that language may seem after 1991, *locally* the notion that the *tselina* was a place that fostered a special kind of mutual aid, and friendship remains a key component of Virgin Lands lore and of regional self-identification to this day. While most aspects of

Kazakh culture clearly remained invisible to my Russian informants, there was one important exception – the concept of hospitality. My interviewees frequently and spontaneously expressed their appreciation of the Kazakh traits of kindness and compassion for people, and they recounted instances in which Kazakhs helped newly arrived people when nobody else would. By a widely shared consensus, high Kazakh standards of hospitality were an important value and something to aspire to regardless of nationality. For instance, many of my non-Kazakh informants told stories of entertaining and receiving guests that are (at least on the surface) surprisingly similar to testimonies collected in Kazakh families about the prestige and satisfaction derived from successful feasts and celebrations.[54]

Many people of the older generation in Kazakhstan, as in the testimony by Kartauzov, cited above, see no contradiction between the tradition of remembering the Virgin Lands as an example of ethnic harmony and the evidence of the violence that took place. The "others," those who left, especially Chechens and Ingush, never became part of the Virgin Lands collective, and thus simply were not part of the story. Another interesting illustration of how this local consensus grew is provided by the way in which Virgin Landers *who stayed* (most of them former *kolkhozniki*), local Kazakhs, special settlers, and local officials alike came to view new waves of urban youth, especially Muscovites, who rotated in and out each year, as "outsiders." The students from the capital were supposed to set an example, but workers in Kazakhstan, regardless of their status, could hardly believe the strange "tastes" and "styles" that existed in Moscow, and they indiscriminately lumped together "*stiliagi*" ("mods" or stylish youth) with "hooligans" and "criminals."[55] "They think nothing of wearing trousers wide to the knees and sweaters that are just as long. They dance 'in style' (*tantsuiut stilem*). They sing songs that don't exist in the repertoire of Russian songs, nor as popular Soviet songs."[56] Local officials and workers alike perceived the youth from Moscow as troublemakers and slackers, who would flock to the district committees begging to be released from work for "medical" and "family" reasons just when the harvest began.[57]

Most importantly, high wages and the growth of prosperity engendered a local sense of community. In Akmolinsk, 1956 was the first year during which conditions for Virgin Lands workers became better than catastrophic. It was the first harvest season in which their efforts led to a great success.[58] The state procured over 180 million *poods* of grain from Akmolinsk,[59] and the workers were able to earn high wages and many of them were decorated and received gifts and bonuses. The best workers had the chance to win prizes, for instance motorcycles. These rewards and satisfactions were shared by many in the region, regardless of what "category" of people they belonged to. The records of the regional soviet show this very clearly. In 1954 a few dozen people were distinguished by becoming participants in the agriculture pavilion at VDNKh in Moscow. In 1955 the *oblispolkom* issued several pages-worth of lists of outstanding workers (*spiski peredovnikov*). In 1956 the lists of people decorated for Virgin Lands work suddenly grew to more than 1000 pages. Each year these lists included substantial numbers of people of all nationalities, and many local collective farmers (not just state farm workers).[60]

The food shortages of the first years disappeared conclusively from the picture by 1956. One major problem that was not solved even by the end of the 1950s was housing construction. New cohorts of settlers responded to the catastrophically slow pace of housing construction by leaving. By January 1958 out-migration of "cadres" had reached nearly 100 percent in both farms and construction units, that is the entire professional workforce (mechanizers, drivers, supervisors, and so on) brought in from other republics now turned over once each year – even as countless collective farmers, former prisoners, and others in need of a fresh start continued to stream to Kazakhstan on their own.[61] In 1960 Khrushchev decided to carry out an administrative reorganization to get this problem under control, based on the same thinking that led him to institute *sovnarkhozy* in 1957. The new unit was the so-called Virgin Lands Region or *Tselinnyi krai*, consisting of the five northern Virgin Lands regions of Kazakhstan.[62] The most important functional result of the *krai* was the creation of a new *krai* party organization (*Kraikom KPSS*) directly subordinate to Moscow rather than Alma-Ata. Akmolinsk oblast' was dissolved as a separate administrative entity. Although Akmolinsk became the capital of the new Virgin Lands region (and was renamed Tselinograd in 1960, at the suggestion of Khrushchev), the entire regional leadership was replaced in December 1959. The local Party bosses were criticized for neglecting the needs of the settlers, for their inability to lead rural cadres, and, in an unusual admission, for neglecting the former special settlers in the Party's political work. They, especially the Germans, were better at farming the Virgin Lands than the workers brought in from other regions.[63]

Although the *krai* would be dissolved again after Khrushchev's ouster from power, the Akmolinsk region and especially Tselinograd were decisively transformed during the *krai* years. It was a period of renewed investment, and of the streaming in of new volunteers from Russia, this time many students and members of the intelligentsia. The opening of television and radio stations and of new *krai* newspapers attracted a fresh generation, many of them enthusiastic young representatives of the national "thaw culture," who changed the cultural atmosphere of the Virgin Lands profoundly. Along with the name change came a popular awareness that the identity of the region had been transformed. For instance, it is during the *krai* years that monuments to the Virgin Landers of 1954–6 first appeared locally.[64]

Tselinograd "became cultured" and grew into the largest center of higher education in the north of Kazakhstan, as several major educational institutes were founded in the city. These institutes and the new *krai* administrations provided work for many people released from the labor camps and for the special settler intelligentsia. While the majority of Chechens and Ingush went home, the German special settlers had no autonomous region or republic to return to. As the Medvedev brothers have argued, they had to stay because they were needed as the basic permanent workforce in the *tselina*, while the Caucasians ended up being "more trouble than they were worth" and thus were allowed to go home.[65] The Germans found their niche in the Virgin Lands. Staying in Kazakhstan was not to their disadvantage, at least economically. After their political rehabilitation in

1964,[66] they ended up being granted a small degree of linguistic and cultural autonomy. Tselinograd Germans built up prosperous communities during the 1960s and 1970s and they were highly valued and respected as organizers and administrators. By the 1980s they even had considerable influence in local party organizations, and the first post-independence chief of the Akmola region was of German descent, Andrei Braun. Tselinograd became a German cultural center with a lively religious life, several official churches, and a German newspaper.[67] Many of my German interview partners remembered the Virgin Lands as the time "when things got better," when they got "easier," and they mentioned that many Germans were decorated for their participation in agricultural work. This is also reflected in published memoirs, in fieldwork and archival research conducted by local researchers.[68]

Most importantly, the *krai* years were a period of growing prosperity and of unceasing construction for the entire region. New housing appeared in the villages, and in Tselinograd new housing districts (*mikroraiony*) were built, as well as bridges and roads, a direct high-voltage energy supply from Karaganda, a new airport, a number of recreation complexes (Virgin Lands Palace, Pioneers' Palace), and other monumental public buildings, such as the House of Soviets. Conditions for Virgin Lands workers did not change immediately, but people who saw Akmolinsk grow into Tselinograd and who spent their whole lives in the region unanimously placed great emphasis on the economic transformation of the region and the city. A common thing for people to say (whether asked about it or not) was "there was nothing here before" and that the settlers built "everything" or that "everything was built during the *tselina*." Similar phrases were used by villagers, townspeople, workers, and members of the intelligentsia, both in formal interviews and in casual conversations. What "nothing" meant, as I came to understand, was not literal emptiness or the absence of people, but rather "there was nothing here for people to live on." It referred to the poverty that existed before the Virgin Lands opening, and also was a way of drawing attention to the great amount of work that people accomplished during the Virgin Lands years. Everyone who lived in Akmolinsk before 1954 agreed that life became more prosperous for all national groups. The daughter of a Stolypin settler from Ukraine, married to a Moldovan special settler, told me that a "second life" began with the Virgin Lands. Her reference to "the bridge" points to the *krai* years as the decisive ones.

> The youth were followed by special trains with products, with things, with beds. And together with them, our life began to turn around, it became different. After the *tselina*, they began to ship materials. Especially when the bridge was built, a second life began. ... After the *tselina* they began to supply us with goods, food products, completely different than before.[69]

Settlers who came in the 1960s were thrilled to find stores full of "deficit" goods:

Life was much easier here [in Tselinograd]. It was easier to get an apartment and to get consumer goods than in Ukraine. In the stores here they had goods from East Germany, Poland, Czechoslovakia, they had shoes.[70]

Here they had shops, full of everything. They had good streets. Where we came from everything had been destroyed by war.[71]

In rural regions, the economic situation changed for everyone, not only workers on the Virgin Lands state farms. Kan De Khan, a Korean collective farm chairman who had an extraordinary career and who contributed much to the regional economy during the 1950s ands 1960s, expressed what many other people in Kazakhstan told me as well, in an article published during the fortieth Virgin Lands anniversary.[72]

Our collective farm could hardly be called a Virgin Lands enterprise. It was organized in 1933, but before the opening of the Virgin Lands it was weak and it produced little for the state. The Virgin Lands opening not only improved the economy, but it significantly raised the standard of living and the culture of the village ... Before this, the youth tried to leave the village by any means, legally or illegally. With a seven-year education, back then considered very solid, working in a collective farm was considered a disgrace ... And of course, how could you keep people in the village, if the school, the hospital, the majority of houses were in a catastrophic state! After all, they were built from mud. So the Virgin Lands did not only consist of plowing the land. It was necessary to rebuild everything from scratch – the school, hospital, kinder-garten, club, the sports complex, stores, houses ... and economic buildings. With great difficulties, pushing us to the limit of our strength and possibilities, all these basic objects were built. They serve the economy to this day, and *zemlianki* (mud huts) have disappeared from the village altogether.[73]

People grew animated when talking about the 1960s in Akmolinsk. They clearly preferred this part of the story to talking about the initial, turbulent years. I collected numerous oral testimonies that showed how strongly people of all nationalities identified with these changes, but one of the most interesting testimo-nies was published in an article entitled "Virgin Lands Nostalgia," in 1994:

It seemed to us that we are living a new life, that the *tselina* represented a new planet, where people were nicer, better. According to Khrushchev's promise we had 20 years to go before communism – but here, in Tselinograd, it had already started.[74]

This was the local perspective, but was the Virgin Lands opening a success from Moscow's point of view, as well? The question of the profitability of the entire venture was one of Khrushchev's main preoccupations. At the December Plenum of the Central Committee in 1958 he reported that the Virgin Lands had paid for itself after four years, despite the predictions of its opponents that it would not be worth the investments. Between 1954 and 1958, 30.7 billion rubles had been invested in the Virgin Lands, according to the Central Statistics Office and the Ministry of Finances. During the same time period, the state had procured 48.8 billion rubles' worth of grain, thus receiving a "net income" (*chistyi dokhod*) of 18.2 billion rubles, 9.3 billion from the Russian Virgin Lands regions, and 8.9 billion from Kazakhstan.[75] Khrushchev singled out Dnepropetrovskii state farm in the Akmolinsk region as a particularly good example of the investments that had been made at the level of the state farms. The organization of the farm had cost the state 28.4 million rubles, in return it received 86.4 million rubles' worth of grain in procurements and purchases.[76] Martin McCauley, the author of the first mono-graph on the Virgin Lands, tracked these official calculations of net income in the Virgin Lands and concluded that the Virgin Lands indeed performed "creditably" until 1960, as net income kept "roughly in step" with investment. According to McCauley, the additional investments undertaken during the krai years "adversely affected the overall performance" of the project, and they had the effect of lowering the overall profit achieved after a peak in 1960.[77] This is an important conclusion. The Virgin Lands opening did not solve all of the problems of Soviet agriculture, and it was never designed to do so. Instead, precisely those invest-ments that Sovietologists chalked up as a waste transformed the lives of millions of people *in the Virgin Lands regions*, far from Moscow, from Alma-Ata, and from debates in scientific journals. Khrushchev's successors abolished the *krai*, but continued to invest in the Virgin Lands, and they continued to receive grain from the region.

During Kazakhstan's belated "glasnost" years in the 1990s, public debates of the *tselina* focused exclusively on Kazakhs and Russians. For the first time, Kazakh scholars showed that the percentage of Kazakhs in the republic was greatly reduced as a result of the Virgin Lands, and that Kazakh culture suffered: alto-gether over 700 Kazakh elementary schools were closed, and Russian ones were opened instead. Kazakh villages were neglected in favor of the Virgin Lands settle-ments, and by the 1980s, many stood empty because families moved in search of opportunities for work and education.[78] However, it is not entirely clear which of these processes were directly caused by the Virgin Lands opening, and which were the result of large-scale processes occurring in the entire Soviet Union. The more immediate impact on the deported populations of those regions has remained completely invisible. Why did the culture of the special settlers experience a modest revival in the Virgin Lands regions, even though they were on the receiving end of most of the violence of the first years, while that of the Kazakhs was suppos-edly "crushed"? Even among the special settlers there are unexplained differences: why did Chechens and Ingush preserve their languages, while subsequent German generations grew up believing it was "illegal" to speak German – even as they received preferential treatment in the job market, such as it was in the *tselina*? The culture that existed before the Virgin Lands started did not change very quickly. It became less visible, compared to the constant reiteration of the new Virgin Lands identity. In later years Akmolinsk was constantly presented as "primitive" before the Virgin Lands and as empty of culture, except for "backward" religious practices. In the Party, Muslim religious beliefs and customs like bride price were dismissed as "feudal remnants," perhaps more vigorously because of the influx of outsiders. However, Kazakh entertainment activities continued, including large public events like horse races and horse games, sponsored by the local soviet (the *ispolkom*). Many people observed religious holidays, holding feasts and slaughtering animals, and major Islamic holidays drew up to 3,000 believers to the central mosque in Akmolinsk. [79] Many, if not most, older Kazakhs *in the Virgin Lands* emphatically reject the notion that the Virgin Lands brought them harm. While members of recent generations might accuse them of being misinformed or even brainwashed, they insist on simple insights, such as: "We are all sleeping on beds now, whereas before, we slept on the floor."[80]

Public narratives of the Soviet past in Kazakhstan, or rather of the many different pasts that were characteristic of the multiethnic borderlands, contain many unresolved contradictions. The Virgin Lands past has remained the story contrived during the Soviet era, interpreted either positively or negatively, and tied to simple notions of either progress or loss. The *contradictory* (not just negative) effects on Kazakh culture and the dramatic and previously unknown evidence of clashes with others should not obstruct our view of the more durable processes through which ethnic relations improved, primarily the growth of prosperity. Soviet culture in the Virgin Lands was not unsuccessful, because it left spaces (perhaps unique to Kazakhstan or to the periphery of the Soviet Union) in which distinct cultures and groups and individuals could quietly create their own version of the Virgin Lands or of Kazakhstan. The Virgin Lands, as a newly created borderland, a new *pays* within the Soviet *patrie*, made a unique, regional contribution to Soviet identity. Tselinograd is now Astana, Kazakhstan's booming capital city. Even as the region has seen a great influx of Kazakhs from the south, the Virgin Lands work ethic, high educational level, and multiethnic social potential are at the very center of Kazakh identity in the twenty-first century. The regional ethnic harmony, while weakened, did not evaporate and serves as one of the foundations of the new Kazakhstan.

Notes

1 See, for instance, Martin Gilbert, *Atlas of Russian History* (New York, 1985), 136; Sidney Ploss, *Conflict and Decision-Making in Soviet Russia: A Case Study of Agricultural Policy, 1953–63* (Princeton, 1965); Richard M. Mills, "The formation of the Virgin Lands policy," *Slavic Review* 29, no. 1 (1970): 58–69; and Martin McCauley, *Khrushchev and the Development of Soviet Agriculture: The Virgin Land Programme 1953–64* (New York, 1976).

2 See, for instance, David M. Crowe, Zhanylzhan Dzhunusova, and Stephen O. Sabol, guest eds, *Focus on Kazakstan: History, Ethnicity, and Society*, Special Topic Issue, *Nationalities Papers* 26, no. 3 (September 1998): 405–6, 428.

3 N.E. Masanov et. al., eds, *Istoriia Kazakstana: Narody i kul'tury* (Almaty, 2001), 341.

4 Throughout this essay, when I refer to "locals" as a group, I am referring to Kazakhs, deportees, earlier settlers, and the many others who had lived for a while in the region before the arrival of the Virgin Lands settlers.

5 Ingvar Svanberg, "The Kazak nation," in *Contemporary Kazaks: Cultural and Social Perspectives*, ed. idem (New York, 1999), 3.

6 Zhanusak Kasymbaev, *Istoriia goroda Akmoly* (Almaty, 1995), 9–10; A.F. Dubitskii, *Proidemsia po ulitsam Tselinograda* (Tselinograd, 1990), 6–12; Nadezhda Strel'tsova, "S chego Akmola nachalas'," *Info-Tses* (Akmola), 12 April 1996, 6; R.N. Nurgaliev, ed. *Akmola entsiklopediia* (Almaty, 1995), 38.

7 Nurtai Agubaev, "'Zdes' nashi korni, ili o tom, kak Akmolinskaia oblast' stala mnogonatsional'noi," *Info-Tses*, 11 February 1994, 7.

8 See Michaela Pohl, "'It cannot be that our graves will be here': the survival of Chechen and Ingush deportees in Kazakhstan, 1944–57," *Journal of Genocide Research* 4, no. 3 (September 2002): 401–30.

9 OPDAO, f. 1, op. 1, d. 1915, l. 43, Zhurin to Ponomarenko, 13 April 1954, no. 435/s; also see ibid., d. 1857, l. 30.

10 RGANI, f. 5, op. 24, d. 519, ll. 3–31 and ll. 161–225, esp. l. 176, 16 November 1953, "O merakh dal'neishego razvitiia sel'skogo khoziaistva Akmolinskoi oblasti," from Tasbaev, Zhurin to Mikoian, Khrushchev; Nikita S. Khrushchev, *Khrushchev Remembers: The Last Testament*, trans. and ed. Strobe Talbott (Boston, 1974), 120–2; and Nikolai Zhurin, *Trudnye i schastlivye gody: Zapiski partiinogo rabotnika* (Moscow, 1982), 172.

11 RGANI, f. 5, op. 45, d. 1, ll. 1–14, 22 January 1954, Khrushchev to TsK KPSS, "V presidium TsK KPSS"; and see "Puti resheniia zernovoi problemy: Zapiska v Presidium TsK KPSS," in N.S. Khrushchev, *Stroitel'stvo kommunizma v SSSR i razvitie sel'skogo khoziaistva* (Moscow, 1962), v. 1, 85–100.

12 TsKhDMO, f. 1, op. 9, d. 296, ll. 135–6, 126–7, 166, 207, 210.

13 OPDAO, f. 1, op. 1, d. 1852, l. 202, 17–19 November 1954, "Protokol zasedaniia 4-ogo Plenuma Akmolinskogo Obkoma KPK."

14 TsKhDMO, f. 1, op. 9, d. 323, ll. 152, 185, 237, Saprykin to TsK VLKSM, TsK KPSS.

15 TsKhDMO, "Spravochnye materialy," d. 232, "Statisticheskaia spravka," l. 217; and see RGANI, f. 2, op. 1, d. 360, l. 5, "Stenograficheskii otchet Plenuma TsK KPSS" (where this figure was rounded up to "350,000").

16 See for instance Gilbert, *Atlas*, 136; Edward Crankshaw, *Khrushchev: A Career* (New York, 1966), 201.

17 I conducted about 50 full-length interviews (life histories) with former settlers and local people in the Akmola region in Kazakhstan between 1994 and 1996, during dissertation fieldwork. About a dozen of the interviews used for this article were with Russian informants; the rest include interviews with Kazakh, Ukrainian, Moldovan, Belorussian, German, Polish, Ingush, and Chechen respondents. My questions varied depending on nationality and background, but I followed a similar set of questions for both men and women. The interviews in 1996 were carried out with a Human Subjects Clearance for my project from Indiana University, and the interviewees cited by name signed a Human Subjects Clearance, agreeing to an "authorial" [*avtorskii*] interview, while all others cited agreed in writing or verbally (on tape) to be cited anonymously in my publications.

18 Interview with I.N. Semenov, Akmola, Kazakhstan, July 1994, Tape No. 94-01.

19 Fieldnotes Summer 1996, Tape No. 96-09.

20 OPDAO, f. 1, op. 1, d. 1983, ll. 19–21, and see ll. 28, 47, 58, 71–4, 81, 86.

21 See also my chapter "Women and girls in the Virgin Lands," in *Women in the Khrushchev Era*, eds Melanie Ilic, Susan E. Reid and Lynne Atwood (Basingstoke, Hampshire, 2004).

22 Fieldnotes July 1994, August 1996, Tapes 94–01, 96–41, 96–51, and others.

23 OPDAO, f. 1, op. 1, d. 1941, "Administrativno-khoziaistvennye kharakteristiki Akmolinskoi oblasti," (1954); d. 2169 (1955); d. 2554 (1957); d. 2714 (1958); d. 2856 (1959).

24 Michaela Pohl, "The Virgin Lands between memory and forgetting: people and transformation in the Soviet Union, 1954–1960" (Ph.D. diss., Indiana University, 1999), 278–304.

25 OPDAO, f. 1, op. 1, d. 2297, ll. 22–6, 11 April 1956, "O khode stroitel'stva sovkhozov i MTS v oblasti"; and ibid., dd. 1941, 2554.
26 Interview with Antonina Nikolaevna Azeeva, 19 August 1996, Manshuk, Tape No. 96–45.
27 OPDAO, f. 1, op. 1, d. 2049, ll. 74–5, Nikitchenko to Zhurin; ibid., d. 2049, ll. 83–106, 25 July 1954, Serikpaev to Zhurin, "O prestupnosti sredi komsomol'tsev i molodezhi pribyvshikh na osvoenie tselinnykh i zalezhnykh zemel', po sostoianiiu na 1.7. 1954 g."
28 GARF, f. 9479, op. 1, d. 903, ll. 50–1, 20 January 1955, Seitmukhambetov, "O faktakh ugolovnykh proiavlenii mezhdu pribyvshimi kontingentami na osvoenie tselinnykh zemel' i spetsposelentsami."
29 GARF, f. 9479, op. 1, d. 903, ll. 45–8, "O gruppovoi drake v g. Atbasare, Akmolinskoi oblasti."; OPDAO, f. 1, op. 1, d. 2077, l. 23, 19 January 1955, "O faktakh gruppovykh drak v s. Elizavetinka, Akmolinskogo raiona i gorode Atbasare"; and ibid., d. 2079, ll. 4–9, "O faktakh gruppovykh drak v Akmolinskom i Atbasarskom uchilishchakh mekhanizatsii sel'skogo khoziaistva."
30 GARF, f. 9479, dd. 903 and 847; and OPDAO, f. 1, op. 1, dd. 1929–31, 2049–50, 2137–9, 2336, 2348, 2470–1, 2542, 2652, 2655, 2630, 2779, and 2852. For a more detailed discussion, see Pohl, "Virgin Lands," 345–52.
31 Ibid., 321–68.
32 APRK, f. 708, op. 30, d. 625, ll. 3–4, January 1957, Abazatov, "Dokladnaia v TsK KPK."
33 See, for instance, GARF, f. 9479, op. 1, d. 903, ll. 45–8, "O gruppovoi drake;" OPDAO, f. 1, op. 1, d. 2077, l. 23, 19 January 1955, "O faktakh gruppovykh drak;" ibid., d. 2079, ll. 4–9, "O faktakh gruppovykh drak;" and ibid., d. 2138, ll. 122–8, 1 July 1955, Serikpaev to Zhurin, Butin, "O bol'shom roste narusheniia obshchestvennogo poriadka v gorode Akmolinsk."
34 Anonymous interview, Manshuk, Akmola region, July 1996, Tape No. 96–52.
35 Anonymous group interview, Akmola region, 12 September 1996, Tape No. 96–39.
36 Interview with Leonid Mikhailovich Kartauzov, 14 June 1996, Akmola, Tapes No. 96–07 and 96–08.
37 See, for instance, the chapters "Planeta sta iazykov," and "V sovmestnom trude krepnet mnogonatsional'naia sem'ia tselinnikov," in S. Shvachko, *Tselina preobrazhennaia, tselina preobrazhaiushchaia* (Tselinograd, 1968), 40–76; and Ie.N. Auelbekov, "Internatsional'naia druzhba – zalog uspekha," in Kh.S. Abdrashitov and Vladislav Vladimirov, *Shchedrost' tseliny* (Alma-Ata, 1974), 135–47; V. Kasatkin, *Osvoenie tseliny – zrimoe voploshchenie Leninskoi druzhby i vzaimopomoshchi narodov SSSR* (Alma-Ata, 1974).
38 For a detailed discussion of the special settler reforms, see Viktor Zemskov, "Massovoe osvobozhdenie spetsposelentsev i ssyl'nykh (1954–60 gg.)," *Sotsiologicheskie issledovaniia*, no. 1 (1991): 5–26. For the impact of the reforms on the Caucasians in Akmola, see Pohl, "It cannot be."
39 GARF, f. 9479, op. 1, d. 903, ll. 11–15, 16 February 1955, Karamyshev to Kruglov.
40 OPDAO, f. 1, op. 1, d. 2336, ll. 1–4, 2 February 1956, Akhmetov to Zhurin, "Spetszapiska ob osvobozhdenii iz pod administrativnogo nadzora organov MVD nekotoroi kategorii spetsposelentsev i nastroeniiakh spetskontingentov po oblasti."
41 Ibid., ll. 128–31, 25 June 1956, "Dokladnaia zapiska o nastroeniiakh i povedenii spetsposelentsev."
42 Pohl, "It cannot be," 423–4.
43 OPDAO, f. 1, op. 1, d. 2852, ll. 50–64, 22 April 1959, "Spravka o nalichii i deiatel'nosti razlichnykh religioznykh grupp na territori Akmolinskoi oblasti"; ibid., d. 2790, ll. 8–16, 2 June 1959, "Protokol 7-ogo Plenuma Akmolinskogo OK KPK" (speech by A. Andreeva about religion); B. Bobrovskii, "Sovremennyi baptism i ego moral," *Akmolinskaia pravda*, 8 December 1954.
44 See Pohl, "It cannot be."

45 OPDAO, f. 1, op. 1, d. 2139, ll. 46–59, 19 September 1955, "Spetssoobshchenie."
46 Anonymous interview, July 1996, Tape No. 96–51.
47 Anonymous interview, July 1996, Tape No. 96–41.
48 Interview with Industrian Semenov, July 1994, Tape No. 94–01.
49 GARF, f. 9479, op. 1, d. 903, ll. 43–4, 1 January 1955, Seitmukhambetov, "Spravka."
50 Shvachko, *Tselina*, 116.
51 Industrian Semenov, "Tainstvennyi znakomets: GULAG" (Typescript, 1995), 10.
52 Industrian Semenov, "Spetsposelentsy: kto oni?," *Gorodskie novosti* (Akmola), 13 May 1994, 3; and "Tainstvennyi znakomets," 9.
53 Interview with Galina Dmitrievna Tarasiuk, 1996, Akmola, Tapes No. 96-11 and 96-12.
54 See Cynthia Ann Werner, "The dynamics of feasting and gift exchange in rural Kazakhstan," in *Contemporary Kazaks: Cultural and Social Perspectives*, ed. Ingvar Svanberg (New York, 1999), 47–72.
55 Fieldnotes Summer 1996.
56 TsKhDMO, f. 1, op. 9, d. 566, l. 67, 17 August 1960, letter from brigade No. 3, Priishimskii state farm.
57 TsKhDMO, f. 1, op. 9, d. 566, ll. 65–6, October 1960, Selivant'ev/*Komsomol'skaia pravda*, TsK VLKSM.
58 See the published documents on grain procurement from the Akmola region, "Telegramma Esil'skogo RK KPK … po sdache khleba gosudarstvu," 21 September 1956, and "Iz pravitel'stvennoi telegrammy Akmolinskogo OK KPK … po sdache khleba gosudarstvu," 24 September 1956, in V.K. Savosko, ed., *Narodnoe dvizhenie za osvoenie tselinnykh zemel' v Kazakhstane* (Moscow, 1959), 510–14.
59 Ibid., 552–3; and I.M. Volkov, ed., *Velikii podvig partii i naroda. Massovoe osvoenie tselinnykh i zalezhnykh zemel': Sbornik dokumentov i materialov* (Moscow, 1979), 274–5.
60 GAAkO, f. 268, op. 8, d. 52, 1954, "Uchastniki Vse-soiuznoi sel'sko-khoziaistvennoi vystavki"; ibid., d. 58, 1955, "Spiski peredovikov"; ibid., dd. 68–70, "Spiski trudiashchikhsia v gorode Akmolinske, predstavlennykh k nagrazhdeniiu medaliami 'Za osvoenie tselinnykh zemel' za 1956 g."
61 OPDAO, f. 1, op. 1, d. 2673, 13 February 1958, "O sostoianii raboty s rukovodiashchimi kadrami, spetsialistami i o ser'eznykh nedostatkakh v trudovom i kul'turno-bytovom ustroistve mekhanizatorov sovkhozov."
62 The regions united in the *krai* were Akmola, Kustanai, Kokchetav, Pavlodar, and North Kazakhstan.
63 OPDAO, f. 1, op. 1, d. 2857, ll. 37–8, December 1959, "Doklad o realizatsii postanovlenii TsK KPSS i TsK KPK 'O rukovodtsve Akmolinskogo OK KPK sel'skimi p/o'"; and APRK, f. 708, op. 33, d. 171, l. 326, 17 December 1960, "Ob obrazovanii Tselinnogo kraia v Kazakhskoi SSR."
64 "Iz soobshcheniia gazety *Sel'skaia zhizn'* ob ustanovlenii v sovkhoze 'Dvurechnyi' Akmolinskoi oblasti pamiatnika trudovoi slavy tselinnikam," 8 December 1960, in Volkov, *Velikii podvig*, 410–11.
65 Roy A. Medvedev and Zhores A. Medvedev, *Khrushchev: The Years in Power*, trans. Andrew R. Durkin (New York, 1978), 122.
66 On 29 August 1964 the Presidium of the Supreme Soviet issued an announcement that accusations of active collaboration with the Nazis had been unfounded. Gerhard Simon, *Nationalism and Policy Toward the Nationalities in the Soviet Union. From Totalitarian Dictatorship to Post-Stalinist Society*, trans. Karen Forster and Oswald Forster (Boulder, 1991), 245.
67 Berta Bachmann, *Memories of Kazakhstan: A Report on the Life Experiences of a German Woman in Russia* (Lincoln, 1983); Joseph Schnurr, ed., *Die Kirchen und das religiöse Leben der Russlanddeutschen* (Stuttgart, 1972), 265–8.
68 AOM, Razdel: Deportatsiia, NVF No. KP 14127–9, "Istoria sel. Kamenka i Kamyshenka Astrakhanskogo raiona," and NVF No. KP 14347, "Vospominaniia: Bich,

A.A." See also Maria Terenik, "Einer aus dem Karlag: Im Neuland," in *Die bitteren Äpfel von 1941*, ed. Wandelin Mangold (Alma-Ata, 1991), 122–4; Aleksandr Frizen, "Uchastie sovetskikh nemtsev v razvitii sel'skogo khoziastva Kazakhstana" (Candidate Dissertation, Alma-Ata, 1991).

69 Anonymous interview, 1996, Tape No. 96–53.
70 Anonymous interview, Fieldnotes 4 July 1996.
71 Anonymous interview, Fieldnotes 22 June 1996.
72 From 1944 to 1975 Kan De Khan was the chairman of the "18 let Kazakhstana" collective farm, and he became a Hero of Socialist Labor in 1957. See Nurgaliev, ed., *Akmola entsiklopediia*, 335.
73 Kan De Khan, "Moe otnoshenie k proshlomu," *Vesti*, 18 February 1994.
74 Efim Chirkov, "Tselinnaia nostal'giia," *Info-Tses*, 25 February 1994, 2.
75 RGANI, f. 2, op. 1, d. 360, l. 5, 15 December 1958, "Stenograficheskii otchet Plenuma TsK KPSS."
76 Ibid. See also speeches of T.I. Sokolov, the secretary of the "Bureau on northern oblasts" that was founded in 1960: for instance, "Iz doklada sekretaria Tsk KPK predsedatelia Biuro Tsk KPK po Severnym oblastiam T.I. Sokolova na pervom respublikanskom slete molodykh tselinnikov v Kazakhstane," OPDAO, f. 3227, op. 1, d. 1, l. 13.
77 McCauley, *The Virgin Land Programme*, 147.
78 Zh. Kuanyshev, "Tenevye storony geroicheskoi epopei," *Zaria* (Alma-Ata), no. 5 (1991), and no. 7 (1991); A. Kopishev,"Zabytye auly," *Zaria*, no. 7 (1991); "O sud'be iazyka zemli kazakhskoi," *Kazakhstanskaia pravda*, 29 November 1990.
79 OPDAO, f. 1, op. 1, d. 1870, ll. 18–21, 11 August 1954, "O realizatsii postanovlenii TsK KPSS ot 7.7.1954 'O krupnikh nedostatkakh v nauchno-ateisticheskoi propagande i merakh ee uluchsheniia.'"
80 Anonymous interview, Fieldnotes 7 July 1994; see also Kimash Syzdykov, "Zemlia nastoiashchego bratstva," *Stolychnyi prospekt*, 7 March 1996, 3.

Part IV

Conclusions

12 Colonizing Eurasia

Alfred J. Rieber

A commentator reflecting on Russian colonization is immediately struck by a pair of paradoxes. For centuries, all Russia has seemed to be on the move. Yet throughout modern history greater restrictions have been imposed on population movement in Russia than most other European states. Few governments have been so determined to keep people in one place and yet so active in displacing them. It may be argued that the paradoxes notwithstanding, Russian colonization was not a unique phenomenon. The migration of the east Slavic tribes to the river basins of west Eurasia in the fifth and sixth centuries was part of the Volkerwanderung. The Germanic peoples continued to move eastward both as conquerors cum crusaders in the Baltic lands and as peaceful colonists throughout much of East Central Europe including Russia itself in the eighteenth century. In another of the great continental expansions, the Ottoman Turks attempted to settle Anatolian peasants in the Balkans through their policy of *sürgün*, or forced resettlement. Throughout parts of Western Europe during the medieval period a process of internal colonization also took place. And this is only to speak of the continental dimension. Overseas colonization shared some characteristics with the continental, but the differences were significant enough to make comparative judgments difficult and risky. The most important of these – and the distinction here is particularly important in comparison with and contrast to the Russian case – was the transformation over time of the overseas colonists into different peoples with different cultural values, political institutions, and social structures. What is striking about the Russian case is that despite the existence of strong regional characteristics and the construction of a multicultural empire, the Russian colonists and their descendants remained overwhelmingly Russian in speech, customs, and religious beliefs, including schismatic and sectarian variations on the Orthodox theme.

What distinguishes Russian colonization from all others is first its persistence over time, proceeding from the earliest Slavic migrations to the last decade of the twentieth century.[1] This was not, to be sure, an uninterrupted or uniform movement. But, as the chapter by Val Kivelson argues, the imperial policies of Muscovy in dealing with Siberian tribes, which imposed boundaries and identities upon ill-defined and amorphous indigenous populations, had its parallel in early Soviet practice and for similar purposes: to assert and testify to the organizing power and legitimate authority of the center over the periphery. Moreover, Elena Shulman and Michaela Pohl demonstrate another suggestive continuity when they point out how it was still possible in the late 1930s and again in the late 1950s to generate considerable enthusiasm among the population for voluntary resettlement in remote areas of the country. Second, Russian colonization at least from the sixteenth to the twentieth century gave rise to strongly ambivalent feelings among the ruling elites and many intellectuals, who were concerned in general about the effects of the process and in particular upon the character of the colonists and the loyalty of the colonized. And this brings us back to the paradoxes.

The leading Russian historians of colonization, S.M. Solov'ev, V.O. Kliuchevskii, S.F. Platonov, and M.K. Liubavskii, and such post-communist historians as Boris Mironov, located the roots of the double paradox in the contradictory needs of the state and its service people, on the one hand, and the clash between their interests and those of the mass of the Russian population, on the other. To state the problem in the broadest terms: during the medieval period the Moscow state perceived the advantages of settling service men and peasants on its vulnerable frontiers in every direction: in competition with Novgorod for the northern territories, with Kazan to the east, in defense against the Crimean Tatars to the south and the Lithuanian princes to the west. Yet at the same time, it opposed the flight to the frontiers of peasants and renegade petty service men who found unbearable the fiscal, labor, and service obligations of the state and landowners. From the earliest experiments in colonization, the state displayed flexibility in confronting the problems of settling Russians on the newly acquired lands. As Matthew Romaniello makes clear, the Muscovite government adopted its traditional policy of granting *pomest'e* in order to attract and keep military servitors on the frontiers of the newly conquered Kazan khanate. But this opened up the possibility of negotiation between the pomeshchiki and the central government over such issues as inheritance and land use with consequences for the social and economic character of the region. In retrospect, the experience on the Middle Volga established a precedent for the future of Russia's colonization. Different regions would require different solutions at different times.[2]

How different the solutions could be is demonstrated by Brian Boeck. His provocative essay argues that the major concern of the Muscovite government on its southern frontier was not to colonize but to contain the nomads and to prevent the hemorrhage of the Russian population through flight outside its control. He pounds another nail in the myth of Russia's penchant for unlimited expansion by pointing out that throughout the seventeenth century the government preferred to establish contractual arrangements with clients rather than promote colonization. In some ways his analysis echoes Liubavskii's view that the geography of the open steppe combined with the fierce attacks of the Crimean Tatars and other nomads were a deterrent to colonization rather than a spur to expansion. The failure of the first two settlement schemes under Peter illustrates the difficulties and underscores the wisdom of the Muscovite elites.

If the main object of state policy on the southern frontier was to stem the flight of peasants, Moscow recognized that settlement beyond the limits of its authority constituted more than a loss of revenue and manpower. The free colonizers represented an alternative way of life, a return to an earlier cultural pattern of hunting and gathering supplemented by raiding and pillaging. On the southern steppe the legendary abundance of fish, game, honey, and wild berries provided a richer and more balanced diet than the grain-dependent peasantry of the center enjoyed. The collecting of food and booty was a more adventurous, less labor-intensive activity than tilling the soil, and fit the masculine ideal of the warrior-provider. The Siberian frontier offered a different appeal for hunters in search of the "El Dorado" of furs that carried them all the way to the Pacific Ocean. Here was another example, according to Val Kivelson's perceptive article, when the interests of the state conflicted with the lusts and ambitions of the colonizers. Moscow sought to regulate in an orderly fashion both the fur tribute and the jurid-ical relations between the Russians and the indigenous peoples. The aim was to provide the state with a stable and reliable source of income and labor force. But the adventurer-colonizers could not always or even often be restrained. Their brutal treatment of the indigenous peoples undermined the assurances of the more benevolent but remote center. Moscow sought to mediate between them. In the process tsarist officials displayed an unexpected if not always even-handed recog-nition of local rights. Kivelson's most provocative finding is that this attitude mirrored the government's policies toward property relationships in the center where claims "were always layered and overlapping."

Tales and rumors of the free life were distilled into mythologies of the frontier that appealed to the discontented, the mistreated, the seekers, and the adventurers. From the government's point of view there were certain negative qualities of these mythologies that caused the greatest concern. They gave rise to utopian expecta-tions, even to apocalyptic visions, and to the fearful dichotomy between *voliia* (freedom) and *vlast'* (authority/power).

There were several reasons why no single overriding myth of the frontier, comparable to the Turner thesis in American history, prevailed in Russian history. First of all, there were as many different kinds of frontiers as there were different kinds of settlers. From a functional perspective, for example, there were the mili-tary, extractive, and settlement frontiers.[3] Second, the absence of an equivalent of the Turner myth in Russian historiography and popular culture (and the reason why it is often borrowed unsuccessfully as a substitute), also reflects the profound ambivalence of the elites within the government toward the frontiers and fron-tiersmen. As the preceding chapters illustrate, a number of contradictory themes, creating more paradoxes, run through the cultural imaginings of Russians about the colonizing process. Did the frontier settlements represent forms of utopia or dystopia? Were the settlers advancing state interests or challenging them? Was the aim of the colonizers a civilizing mission and cultural integration or the extension of toleration and cultural pluralism? Were the results of colonization a blending (*sliianie*) or a clash of cultures? Each one of these themes is worth a full-length study, but considerations of space require a more selective approach.

The remainder of this essay will focus on two interconnected themes that stood at the center of the paradoxes that characterized Russian colonization: the tension between utopian visions and dystopian results, and the ambiguity of the civilizing mission. What is meant by utopian in this essay is a project or set of aspirations envisaging an ideal society on the periphery that is either a perfection of, or in some respects an alternative to, the dominant socio-economic and, on occasion, hegemonic form of society and state in the metropolitan center.[4] The utopian aspirations from below, that is growing out of the popular culture, were more likely to take the form of an escape from and even a challenge to dominant values and institutions. Utopian projects from above aimed rather at perfecting the existing structures of state and society by settling colonists either by force or by concessions in sparsely inhabited regions outside the metropolitan area in order to maximize the conditions for experimentation.

In the pre-modern period and down into the nineteenth century utopian visions from below originated among secular malcontents and religious dissidents who fled or were expelled from the center and resettled on the periphery of empire. On the secular side the most obvious examples of an ideal community were the early Cossack brotherhoods, with their radical notions of egalitarian social structures and freely elected atamans. The religious utopias were of two types. The social reconstruction of the spiritual communities of Old Believers were backward-looking utopias seeking to reconstruct the world they lost in the great schism of the seventeenth century. The forward-looking religious utopias were represented by the sectarians who sought the new Jerusalem.[5] Both constituted movements from the center to the periphery, in part under state pressure so that their migration took on more the aspect of deportation. In the seventeenth and early eighteenth century the colonizing settlements of the Old Belief occupied what might be called the old frontier zones, on the edge of the pre-imperial Muscovite state; in the north, the Volga-Kama region, the southwest border with Poland, and later with the Habsburg Monarchy. The sectarians in the eighteenth and nineteenth century spread into the new frontier zones, especially Caucasia and Siberia all the way to the Amur Basin.[6]

Still, the utopian ideals must be placed in a larger context. The majority of peasant migrants, as far as it is possible to judge in the fact of unreliable statistics and official testimony, were motivated by more practical considerations, that is simply by the search for a better life. Utopias were the ideology of colonization. They attracted only pre-established, inner-directed groups who already shared a commitment to a better life within a formal structure of values. But it must also be recognized that the utopian ideals were related to more diffuse peasant notions of what a better life entailed. Among the Orthodox peasantry there was a rich mélange of myths, legends, rumors, and misunderstandings of government legislation that engendered visionary, even apocalyptic visions of Belovod'e.[7] In many cases it is difficult to draw a sharp distinction between these vague and elusive manifestations of popular culture and the more ideologically well-defined utopias. As several essays in this collection demonstrate, similar patterns of behavior among peasant colonists provided subsequent interpreters among the intelligentsia with sufficient material – they needed little encouragement – with which to embroider or invent utopian myths about them.

Figure C.1 Migrants, with their makeshift tents, at a resettlement meeting point near the Bogotol train station, Tomsk province, late nineteenth century. From *Velikii put':* *vidy Sibiri i velikoi sibirskoi zheleznoi dorogi*, vyp. 1 (Krasnoiarsk, 1899), 66.

From above, that is the state chanceries, colonization, when it was regarded in a positive light, was perceived as a means for defending or expanding territorial control and integrating the periphery into the body politic. In this period the major debates within the government came over questions of how best to adjudicate relations between Russian colonists and the indigenous population. For the most part tsarist officials both at the center and on the periphery were preoccupied with practical problems and proposed pragmatic solutions.[8] When they appeared, however, utopian visions were frequently related to ideas of a civilizing mission. That is to say that social experimentation and the image of the Russian kulturträger constituted the government's ideology of colonization. In the view of some state officials, regions not well endowed by nature or dominated by nomadic or semi-nomadic societies could be transformed by the application of new technologies and scientifically based ideas into productive and progressive lands fit for extensive colonization as proof of the moral and material superiority of Russia over the conquered peoples, demonstrating its equal status with the most advanced European societies.

The earliest plans to use colonization in order to create model communities in the spirit of Enlightenment projects were launched under Catherine II by importing foreigners in order to instruct by example Russian peasants in the uses of modern agricultural techniques and the virtues of social self-discipline. The impulse weakened under Alexander I and turned into a dystopian disaster in the military colonies. But the establishment of the universities and technical schools under Alexander I and Nicholas I and the diffusion of their graduates within government agencies created a new basis for state intervention in the process of organizing and transforming the imperial periphery as a means of enhancing Russia's power and prestige. By the late nineteenth century, colonization more and more took on the form of rational planning. The utopian impulse was taken up by Soviet authorities as social experimentation in a variety of forms, albeit with very mixed results. In brief, the modernizing form of utopia took shape as the ruling elite began to perceive the colonizing process as a means to overcome some of the persistent problems of domestic as well as foreign policy, that is overcoming economic backwardness, plugging the porous frontiers, and taming the wilderness as an emblem of European civilization.[9]

Among the religious colonists with utopian aspirations, the Old Believers occupied a special place. In his essay Andrei Znamenski brings into focus one of these groups known as the "rock people," who settled in the remote valleys of the Altai. Although they, like other Old Believers, were forced to the periphery of empire either by state legislation or simply in search of better lands, their decision to accept the status of *inorodtsy*, that is of native peoples, in order to escape the heavier burdens of being enrolled in the peasantry endeared them to romanticizing regionalists. What had been a rational calculation on the part of the "rock people" was transformed by intellectuals into a "back to nature" movement that could be used as an anti-modernizing utopia.

A different kind of religious utopianism developed in the southern Ukraine. In an essay not published in this collection but presented at the conference, Sergei Zhuk analyzed how the German, mainly Mennonite colonizers introduced into the area by the tsarist government as model agriculturalists interacted with dissident Russian religious colonists.[10] Together they stimulated a popular evangelical awakening that was linked by virtue of their shared "Protestant work ethic" to the highly productive and efficient communities. The result in his words was the creation in southern Ukraine of "a unique social and cultural laboratory." In terms of its social organization and economic enterprise, it stood at the opposite end of a civilizational spectrum from the "rock people," yet it shared with them a deviant religious vision of the ideal life.

In Russia as elsewhere most of the utopian aspirations from below to create the alternative and ideal society faded under the pressure of state intervention, the rigors of nature, and the hostility of the surrounding indigenous peoples. The Cossack brotherhoods split over the issue of ownership of private property and enrollment in state service, two of the most effective divisive tactics exploited by the state. The religious communities succumbed to internal dissention and the predatory opposition of neighbors who had no interest in emulating their social discipline and envied their economic success. Under these conditions it is surprising that even a few Old Believer communities survived in remote areas like the North Caucasus until the collapse of the Soviet Union. Moreover, the spark of utopian fantasies was not extinguished in the Soviet Union but rather rekindled by the state in such radically different forms as the model labor camp and the Virgin Lands movement.

With the development of scientific education and the formation of scientific societies in Russia, the utopian models of colonization acquired strong secularizing elements. But there were undeniable visionary elements that surfaced from time to time in ways that acquired a specifically Russian dimension. For example, many of the rational-scientific utopias were permeated by one form or another of geographic exceptionalism, a tradition going back to the classic interpreters of Russian colonization, S.M. Solov'ev and V.O. Kliuchevskii. As David Moon demonstrates, there were scientists who regarded certain sparsely settled areas that appeared poorly endowed by nature as in reality well suited for certain kinds of cultivation and colonization. Konstantin Veselovskii was one of the optimists who believed that it was possible to grow grain on the steppes, "when the forces of the mind will be partly victorious over the unfavorable influence of nature." He defined these forces as the application of "*promyshlennogo dukha*," a term Moon translates as "the spirit of diligence." But one could just as well translate it in its more literal sense of "the industrial spirit." This would introduce a meaning closely resembling that of the St Simonians, whose influence was considerable in mid-century among Russian engineers and officials connected to such enterprises as railroad building. The fact that Veselovskii was also an advocate of model farms set up in the steppes by the Ministry of State Domains in order to train agricultural specialists adds weight to the thesis that he can be ranked among those who perceived science not only as a means to transform an uncooperative nature, but also, in a way that would prefigure some of the more extreme Soviet experiments, from a counter-intuitive perspective. In the case of Veselovskii, the dubious argument proceeded from the assumption that the cultivation of wheat required far less rainfall than other crops and could sustain a much larger population on the steppes than nomadic animal husbandry. Other specialists interpreted the industrial spirit in terms of irrigation. This more practical harnessing of science to the production of food and cotton and turning deserts into lands of plenty was taken up by officials and entrepreneurs for different reasons. The former linked their projects to the political goal of consolidating Russia's control over Central Asia; the entrepreneurs sought profits. But both efforts were couched in terms of a civilizing mission.[11]

It was left to P.A. Stolypin and A.V. Krivoshein to undertake the most ambitious and deliberate attempt, in the words of Charles Steinwedel, "to remake the center in a new environment." One of the major contributions of his chapter is to demonstrate how they expanded the ideas underlying the agrarian reforms of the post-1906 period in Siberia as a corollary to Witte and Kulomzin's support for migration as part of Russia's civilizing mission. The difference lay in the determination of Stolypin and Krivoshein to reject the idea of oversight (*opeka*) and of matching the colonists to the needs of the state. Although they vacillated on whether or how much to limit migration, they ended up on the side of greater freedom of movement combined with socio-economic experiments in management and sale of state lands. They perceived an interaction among three linked concepts. First, there was the attempt to use colonization of the periphery as a means of creating a different society from the center in order to serve as a model of what could be achieved at the center. Second, they believed that massive resettlement would help Russia fulfill its historic mission to protect the imperial territory from the Asiatic races. Third, they stressed the difference between the older concepts of resettlement and a newer, more transformative idea of colonization: the all-round cultural development, the civilizing mission, of a weakly settled space. But there was already a shadow on their utopian horizon. A note of caution was sounded by the reformers, who wondered out loud about the potential danger of the promised land developing so fast and formlessly that it might crush European Russia.

Elsewhere in Central Asia, as the chapter by Jeff Sahadeo so clearly shows, the civilizing mission had already begun to fray at the edges, and the idea of building European cities as emblematic of progressive humanity produced tension rather than the resolution of deep social problems. After 1905, the colonization of Turkestan was shot through with ambiguous results. The elitist and racial assumptions of the civilizing mission were undercut by the influx of lower-class Russian settlers made possible by the new railroads, the duma elections allowing natives as well as Russians to vote, and the efforts of the Jadid movement to fuse European values and the Islamic moral code in order to outstrip the colonists. The local Russian population was caught in the rip tide of uncertainty and fear of marginalization.[12] Confidence and hubris gave way to the question: "who was colonizing and who was civilizing whom?"

The rulers and elites of imperial Russia from Peter I forward frequently looked to the periphery of empire as a field for social and political experimentation. The tradition lasted from the building of St Petersburg at the outer western edge to the government's drive to colonize the Far Eastern edge on the eve of World War I. Colonization was part of this process, but only a part. The idea that it was somehow easier to construct a progressive, indeed an ideal society or an urban framework, outside the old center of Russian life underlay projects as far removed as Catherine's colonization of the south with Europeans, through the constitutional projects of Alexander I in the Grand Duchy of Finland and the Kingdom of Poland, to Stolypin's plans to civilize and secure the eastern extremities of empire. At the same time, Stolypin anticipated that the preparation of fresh lands might provide better guarantees for his wager on the strong than the struggle to transform the hide-bound customs of the commune in central Russia.

In tsarist Russia, a tangled web of secular and religious motives linked utopian projects to various versions of a civilizing mission. The latter included spreading Christianity, more specifically Orthodoxy, replacing nomadic patterns of life with agricultural settlements, introducing western technology, and creating rationally planned urban spaces. From Peter's eagles to Stolypin and Krivoshein there was a breed of reformers who sought to reach beyond the incremental palliative toward a radical reconstruction of society. They shared more than we have given them credit for with the mental world of the intelligentsia in their search to find the ideal balance between European and Russian values and institutions. That their efforts ended in war and revolution should not diminish the pathos and heroism of their struggles.

The chapters on the Soviet period share, it seems to me, an understanding of how the Bolsheviks sought to close the gap between the utopian visions of the peasantry, intelligentsia, and officialdom of the old regime. To achieve their ends they combined the application of force and unprecedented violence with mass propaganda based in part on a pseudo-science of society. Coercion and ignorance turned utopian planning into dystopian nightmares, but as several of the chapters illustrate, the propaganda, at least in the post-Stalinist period, matched aspirations for a better life among elements of the population.

From an unusual perspective Cassandra Cavanaugh demonstrates how shifts in the paradigm of acclimatization among Soviet scientists reflected and reproduced the major policy shifts of the government toward colonization. As such, it is a neat case study of the contextual approach to science. For our purposes, it serves to demonstrate how science at the service of the civilizing mission could end up reaching diametrically opposite conclusions about the possibilities of Europeans – i.e. Russians – acclimatizing to the environments of sub-tropical regions of the Union. The ambiguity of the civilizing project resolves itself in a double irony. In the 1920s, racial biology, medicine, and environmental studies in the Soviet Union emulated Western European, i.e. the "civilized" world, in providing a scientific basis for establishing the superiority of the peoples of the temperate climatic zones. But they also implicitly discouraged colonization as unsuitable and dangerous for European types. This dovetailed nicely with the government's policy of *korenizatsiia*: the non-Russians had to be the instrument of their own civilizing under benevolent Soviet *opeka*. But industrialization accompanied by massive dislocation of populations required a new look at the difficulties of acclimatization that refuted the determinist implications of Western biology and environmental studies and substituted a voluntarist perspective that emphasized technological and medical intervention to overcome natural obstacles to colonization and economic development. The civilizing mission would be taken up by different hands.

Lynne Viola offers a dramatic portrayal of those different hands at work in the 1930s. The result was a radical disjuncture between utopian projects like those aimed at creating self-sufficient penal populations and harsh reality. What she calls "an entire paper world of intricate plans" remained on paper largely because they were produced in a void of local knowledge and an illiberal context, that is the mass deportation in 1930–1 of two million peasants to the far north. Bureaucratic in-fighting contributed to the chaotic results. In an imaginative metaphor she compares Stalinist planning for penal settlements with the socialist realist aesthetic, similar in its aspiration to represent a process of becoming an idealized socialist future, but radically different in its engagement with real human beings instead of painted images.

Elena Shulman's chapter is valuable as a study of the Stalinist discourse of colonization, with its blending of several persistent themes: images of the promised land, a civilizing mission, and concerns over state security in the borderlands. *Pravda*'s myth-making about the Far East as an empty land which capitalists lacked the will to develop was embellished by metaphors drawn from Russian folk tales, evocations of the civilizing mission in its refurbished Soviet form, and appeals to patriotism in defense against the Japanese (read Yellow Peril) threat to security. Women were singled out as a special target of the rhetorical onslaught, and some success in attracting them is attributed to the Khetagurovite campaign which accepted 20,000 out of 300,000 applicants in 1937–9. Once again the state entrusted the NKVD to organize the resettlement, under the aegis of a newly created Resettlement Department. The parallels with the projects of Stolypin and Krivoshein are self-evident. Even Shulman's conclusion that despite the best efforts of the party and police apparat, the frontier remained "a tenacious male space" reproduces an important but neglected theme of the tsarist experiments in colonizing the Far East.

The last effort to revitalize an old and well-worn utopian myth in the Virgin Lands program was, according to Michaela Pohl, one of the most successful social reforms in the post-Stalinist period, but also one that evinced a high level of turbulence and even violence. Once again the dystopian aspect of state-sponsored projects disappointed hopes and diminished the achievement of what began as a noble experiment. Her research documents the great enthusiasm for the project among the thousands of youth who volunteered, revising the prevailing view in Western literature that emphasized coercive measures. But the outcome was mixed. On the one hand, she demonstrates that as in the past, whether the 1930s or 1890s, the preparation and reception of the colonists was deplorably inadequate. In the first years, the familiar picture of food shortages, collapse of local transport, and poor housing was responsible for widespread disillusion measured in a high percentage of returnees. On the other hand, those who stayed constructed 10,000 homes of their own and founded new state farms and enterprises. Reinforced by a second, less well-known wave in the 1960s that brought students and intelligentsia who raised the cultural standards and recorded renewed enthusiasm for the material improvements. To be sure, the Virgin Lands program was a far cry from the agrarian utopia advertised. There were tensions with the older generation of the local Kazakh population and communities of deportees from the war. But Pohl stresses both the material and cultural successes that made substantial progress toward the establishment of a genuinely multicultural region. In her final assessment the author defines the experiment as "a new *pays* within the Soviet *patrie* [that] made a unique regional contribution to Soviet identity." It would be difficult to document a more optimistic approximation of a utopian outcome for any other region of the Soviet Union. All the more poignant then was the sequel that unfolded in the post-Soviet era.

The preceding essays raise a persistent question about colonization in Russia that requires further research and thinking. Why were certain colonizing efforts more successful than others in overcoming the natural obstacles and the resistance of indigenous peoples? In his magisterial work, M.K. Liubavskii argued against the main thesis of Solov'ev and Kliuchevskii that geography in the form of the great Eurasian plain and river system was highly favorable to colonization. He demonstrated how swamps, thick forests, and desiccated steppe were formidable obstacles to settlement. This led Liubavskii to the conclusion, supported by the foregoing essays, that colonization did not take place through the movement of large masses of people, but in a dispersed manner. Physical features, not politics set the boundaries of regions.[13] But the preceding essays also contribute to a more complex picture of colonization by enlarging the role of culture and agency in the process.

The essays bring out nicely the ambiguity of state officials, intellectuals, and the colonists themselves toward the civilizing mission. Because of the contiguous territorial character of Russian as opposed to overseas colonization, the interaction of cultures on the frontier affected the whole of society. It was more difficult to distance the metropolitan center from the colonial areas. This is why the terms settlement and colonization gradually became blurred in Russian official language.[14] The essays also capture the importance of leadership and social cohesion in promoting the adaptation of the colonists to their new environment. In the early period, boyars and monastic establishments often provided lands and even loans to peasants to resettle. The state played its role in constructing defense works. Another element of leadership came from the service nobles who petitioned the government for land grants in fertile areas and resettled peasants. Others, their numbers still unknown, deserted state service, and, either in small groups or together with some of their peasants, struck out into the "wild field", where they often joined the Cossack communities.

In the modern period the settlements that survived intact over the long-run were constituted by those who were already organized into coherent and self-contained communities like the Mennonites, the Old Believers, and the sectarians, or the Ukrainian Cossacks, who, after the dissolution of the Sech, became the main colonizers in the North Caucasus. Otherwise the work was done by the big estate owners, who received enormous tracts of land in Ukraine from Catherine and Paul, and who followed the example of their boyar predecessors in the north by organizing the resettlement of lands and even resorting to the recruitment of runaways from Poland and the central Russian provinces. A rough tripartite formula for a colonization with the best chances to survive and even flourish would be (1) the availability of ploughland that could be cultivated without large-scale capital investment or a high level of agricultural technology; (2) pre-existing social or religious cohesion of the colonists, or else experienced leadership in organizing and managing large-scale agricultural properties; (3) state support and protection.

Even a superficial comparison between the last major effort of the tsarist government to colonize Siberia and the several Soviet experiments discussed above illuminates their different approaches to the same persistent problems. In contrast to the efforts of the Committee on the Siberian Railroads, the NKVD and other Soviet agencies were woefully unprepared for the enormous tasks of resettlement that they undertook. At the same time, large-scale population movements from below took the form of migration to the cities and not settlement of the countryside. Time and again, the essays by Viola, Shulman, and Pohl demonstrate the gap between, on the one hand, the hyper degree of planning and the heavy reliance on coercion or propaganda accompanying the colonization projects, and, on the other hand, the failure of the central planners to allocate adequate resources, coordinate their plans with local authorities, or select suitable terrain for the colonists.[15]

The chapters in this volume stop short of the disintegration of the Soviet Union, but two thoughtful commentaries on the phenomenon of what has been called the "unpeopling of the periphery" shed light on the colonization process by examining its historical reversal in the 1990s.[16] The reverse migration of Russians and Ukrainians began in the 1970s as the result of four intersecting demographic processes. There was first of all a growing labor shortage in the Slavic republics for skilled workers and professional people. Second, Russians and Ukrainians in the Caucasian and Central Asian republics found themselves forced into an increasingly competitive labor market with the indigenous people, who were beginning to reap the benefits of higher education and a renewed state policy of *korennizatsiia*. Third, well-established groups like the Old Believers in the North Caucasus abandoned their centuries-old communities for fear of being engulfed in communal warfare among the indigenous peoples, even though the violence was not directed at them. Fourth, migrants moving from east to west sought relief from the harsh climate and alternatives to the underdeveloped cultural infrastructure of Siberia and the Soviet Far East. They were the new seekers for a better life, unencumbered by utopian visions, which had died a natural death by this time, or by a civilizing mission which had appeared to many Russians and Ukrainians to have succeeded only too well. The return to the center reached its peak in 1994 and thereafter declined in part because of the Chechen War, which exposed newly returning young Russians to the military draft, and in part because the economic benefits of leaving compared to those of staying had begun to level out.[17]

Most recently, depeopling has accelerated again. The Russian government has announced plans to resettle from 200,000 to 600,000 people from the remote parts of the Siberian north, although the Russian coordinator for the World Bank that is subsidizing the undertaking preferred the euphemism "migration assistance scheme" in order, presumably, to avoid invidious comparisons with dystopian Soviet resettlement plans.[18] Finally, during the 1990s, many Russians in Kazakhstan have abandoned what was the last great utopian project in Russian and Soviet history. The future development of the frontiers by new colonists will be driven by mostly different motive forces. There will be no search for constructing ideal communities or undertaking a civilizing mission, though concerns about security will still play a role in the calculations of the central government. It will be the profit motive embedded in the discovery and exploitation of natural resources that will take their place, perhaps more realistic, but perhaps no less ambiguous in its effect upon the new colonists and the primordial natural environment.

If the major motive forces for state-sponsored colonization were internal stability and external security, then what are the social and strategic implications of the great retreat of Russians from the outer borderlands – that is the former national republics – and from the eastern periphery of the Russian Federation itself? It is probably still too early to come to a firm judgment. It would also be a mistake to exaggerate the importance of in-migration as a factor contributing to domestic instability or posing a security risk on the frontiers. However, perceptions persist among the Russian population that external migrants are responsible for rising crime rates. Government officials and academic specialists express concern over the serious potential threat to Russian control over the Far Eastern and Eastern Siberian regions posed by Chinese immigrants.[19]

The chapters in this volume reinforce the views of the classic Russian historians on the centrality of colonization in Russian history, even as they reinterpret the process itself. At the same time they raise by implication the conclusion that "unpeopling" the periphery may have as profound an effect on the future of Russia as peopling it had in the past.

Notes

1 The great interpreter of Russian colonization, M.K. Liubavskii, argued that the process of colonization was virtually completed before Russia became an empire, noting that the addition of the Baltic region, Poland, Finland, Bessarabia, the Caucasus, and Central Asia had their own populations and by virtue of their natural geography did not attract Russian settlement. *Obzor istorii russkoi kolonizatsii s drevneishikh vremen i do XX veka* (Moscow, 1996), 539. (This seminal work had been completed in the early 1930s but remained unpublished for over 60 years.) He may have overstated the case, but, even granting the point, one of the main reasons for studying Russian colonization after Peter I is precisely because of the cultural interaction between the colonizers and the indigenous peoples.

2 For basic changes in tsarist policies from indirect to direct rule of the native populations of the southern borderlands in the eighteenth century see Michael Khodarkovsky, "Colonial frontiers in eighteenth century Russia: form the North Caucasus to Central Asia," in *Extending the Borders of Russian History*, ed. Marsha Siefert (Budapest, 2003), esp. 134–9. For a different kind of change in the South Caucasus to "colonization by contract," see Nicholas B. Breyfogle, "Colonization by contract: Russian settlers, South Caucasian elites and the dynamics of nineteenth century tsarist imperialism," in ibid., 143–66; and in the Eastern Caucasus from toleration of sectarian colonists to insistence on persons "of Russian origin and the Orthodox faith" who would be allowed to settle on the pasturelands of the native peoples, Firouzeh Mostashari, "Russian colonization of Caucasian Azerbaizhan, 1830–1905," in ibid., 167–81.

3 Andreas Kappeler, "Iuzhnyi i vostochnyi frontir Rossii v XVI–XVIII vekakh," *Ab Imperio*, no. 1 (2003): 47–64.

4 The leading Russian specialist on peasant utopias identifies three types of legends: the "golden age," the "far lands," and the "redeemer". K.V. Chistov, *Russkaia narodnaia utopiia* (St Petersburg, 2003), 38. I have focused on the "far lands," that is "Belovod'e" meaning pure or free lands beyond the seas, in metaphorical terms. Ibid., 311–12, 316.

5 Chistov calls such groups as the *beguny* and *stranniki* "peasant anarchist religio-social organizations." Ibid., 280.

6 For an examination of the role of sectarians in the colonization of Transcaucasia, see Nicholas B. Breyfogle, *Heretics and Colonizers: Forging Russia's Empire in the South Caucasus* (Ithaca, 2005).There is no general history of the Old Believers as colonizers but insights into their role may be gleaned from Paul Werth, *At the Margins of Orthodoxy: Mission, Governance, and Confessional Politics in Russia's Volga-Kama Region, 1827–1905* (Ithaca, 2002); and Roy R. Robson, *Old Believers in Modern Russia* (DeKalb, 1995), 21–3, 34–5, 64–6, 120; Firouzeh Mostashari, "The politics of colonization: sectarians and Russian orthodox peasants in 19th century Azerbaizhan," *Journal of Central Asian History*, no. 1 (1996): 16–29; and L.E. Gorizontov, "Raskol'nichii klin. Pol'skii vopros i staroobriadtsy v imperskoi strategii," *Slavianskii al'manakh*, 1997 (Moscow, 1998), 140–67.

7 For a cogent summary with supporting literature see Willard Sunderland, "Peasant pioneering: Russian peasant settlers describe colonization and the eastern frontier. 1880s–1910," *Journal of Social History* 24, no. 3 (summer 2001): 900–1. For the sectarian search for the new Jerusalem in the South Caucasus, see Breyfogle, *Heretics and Colonizers*, chp. two.

8 Tsarist confessional politics aimed at supporting the stable mainstream religious elites even at the cost of repressing the deviant Russian colonists on the frontiers in order to bolster the security of the state, another example of its paradoxical behavior. Firouzeh Mostashari, "Colonial dilemmas: Russian policies in the Muslim caucasus," in *Of Religion and Empire: Missions, Conversion and Tolerance in Tsarist Russia*, eds Robert P. Geraci and Michael Khodarkovsky (Ithaca, 2001), 229–49; and Robert Crews, "Empire and the confessional state: Islam and religious politics in nineteenth century Russia," *American Historical Review* 108, no. 1 (February 2003): 50–83.

9 For the relationship of these same persistent factors to foreign policy see Alfred J. Rieber, "Persistent factors in Russian foreign policy," in *Imperial Russian Foreign Policy*, ed. Hugh Ragsdale (Cambridge, 1993), 315–59. See especially the essays by Viola, Shulman, and Pohl in the present volume.

10 Sergei Zhuk, "The Ukrainian periphery of the European reformation: sociology of colonization, displaced peasants and religious awakening on the southern frontier of the Russian Empire (1780s–1878)," unpublished paper; and idem, *Russia's Lost Reformation: Peasants, Millennialism, and Radical Sects in Southern Russia and Ukraine, 1830–1917* (Washington, DC, 2004).

11 Muriel Joffe, "Autocracy, capitalism and empire: the politics of irrigation," *Russian Review*, 54 (July 1995): 365–88.

12 In a parallel case where "nativization" raised questions about who was civilized and who was primitive, see Willard Sunderland, "Russians into Iakuts? 'Going native' and problems of Russian national identity in the Siberian North, 1870s–1914," *Slavic Review* 55, no. 4 (Winter 1996): 806–25.

13 Liubavskii, *Obzor istorii*, especially the introduction by the editors A.Ia. Degtiarev, Iu. F. Ivanov and D.V. Karev, "Akademik M.K. Liubavskii i ego nasledie," 41–2.

14 Willard Sunderland, "The 'colonization question': visions of colonization in late imperial Russia," *Jahrbücher für Geschichte Osteuropas* 48, no. 2 (2000): 212–13.

15 The measure of the differences can be extrapolated from François-Xavier Coquin, *La Sibérie: peuplement et immigration paysanne au XIXe siècle* (Paris, 1969), esp. part five. Notwithstanding the relatively favorable balance on the side of the tsarist bureaucrats, particularly those on the Committee of the Siberian Railroads, the problems of surveying and land distribution, capitalization, inadequate markets for agricultural surplus and the conflicts with the *starozhiltsy* underline the enormity of the task they set for themselves. For general comments on "the disappearance of planning in the plan" see Moshe Lewin, *Russia. USSR. Russia* (New York, 1995), chp. 5.

16 In addition to the citations below, see Charles King and Neil J. Melvin, eds, *Nations Abroad: Diaspora Politics and International Relations in the Former Soviet Union* (Boulder, 1998); idem, "Diaspora politics: ethnic linkages, foreign policy, and security

in Eurasia," *International Security* 24, no. 3 (2000): 108–38; and Natalia Kosmarskaia, "Khotiat li russkie v Rossiiu? (Sdvigi v migratsionnoi situatsii i polozhenii russkoiazychnogo naseleniia Kirgizii)," in *V dvizhenii dobrovolnom i vynuzhdennom. Postsovetskie migratsii v Evrazii,* eds A. Viatkin, N. Kosmarskaia, and S. Panarin (Moscow, 1999), 180–8.

17 Dzheremi R. Azrael (Jeremy Azrael), Vladimir Mukhomel, and Emil Pain, eds, *Migratsii v postsovetskom prostranstve: politicheskaia stabil'nost i mezhdunarodnoe sotrudnichestvo* (Moscow, 1997), esp. E. Pain and A Susarov, "Politicheskii kontekst migratsii v post-SSSR," 49–65.

18 *Guardian*, 30 May 2003.

19 Galina Vitkovskaia and Sergei Panarin, *Migratsiia i bezopasnost' v Rossii* (Moscow, 2000).

Glossary

desiatina, desiatiny (pl.)	measurement equal to 1.09 hectares (2.7 acres)
iasak	tribute
inorodtsy	people of different race
inovertsy	people of different faith
inozemtsy	people of different lands
murzas	native leaders, "princelings"
oblast'	province, region
obrok	quitrent
pud	pood, measurement of weight, one *pud* = approximately 36 pounds)
soslovie	social estate
uezd	district
ukaz	edict, decree
ulus	settlement or nomadic camp of certain nationalities in Siberia
versta	unit of distance, 1 *versta* = 1.06 km

Index

Page numbers in *italics* refer to illustrations.

Abruzov, Aleksandr 236n77
Academy of Sciences, (Imperial/Soviet) 88, 99, 174
acclimatization theory 13–14, 169–84, 273; oppositional views in 170–3; socialist acclimatization and 178–83; tasks of provincial science and 173–8
Adelman, Jeremy 107
Adenauer, Konrad 248
adventure stories, American 217–18
agricultural production 9, 271; climate and 89–94, 97, 99; collectivization of 189, 192–3, 213; droughts and 85, 91–2, 95–8; meteorology and 94; modernization of 88, 93, 97, 137; population's value for 25, 133; in Siberia 133, 271; soil depletion/erosion and 68–9, 92–3, 96–7; soil science and 94–5; in the steppes 14, 41, 55, 81–99; in Turkestan 153–4, 156; Virgin Lands movement and 241. *See also pomest'e* land grants
Akmola/Akmolinsk 239, 241–2, 244, 246–55, 257. *See also* Tselinograd
Alamatinskaia, A. 159
Alaskan natives 127n88
Alekseev, Aleksandr 176–7, 182
Alekseeva (Khetagurovite) 229
Alenin, Ivan Alekseevich 70
Alexander I, tsar 270, 272
Alexander II, tsar 152
Alexander III, tsar 150, 153
Alferov family 70
All-Russian Central Executive Commission (VTsIK) 201
All-Union Institute of Experimental Medicine (VIEM) 178
Altai region 9, 12–13, 109, 270. *See also* "rock people"
Americas (North, South) 8, 107–8, 172. *See also* New World
Andreev Commission 207

syn Andreianov, Men'shov 68
Annenkov, M.N. 90, 97
Anokhin, Andrei 120
Anuchin, D.N. 97
Arctic exploration 218
Arnold, Dr. (acclimatization scientist) 182
Arsanov, Bagautdin Deni 249
Asanov family 64, 70
Asikritova (Khetagurovite) 229
Assemblies of the Land 44–45
Astana 239
Astrakhan province 81, 83
Atbasar 249
Atkeev, Iambulat 65
Atlasov, Vladimir 31–2, 34
Azeeva, Antonina 244–5
Azim, Seid 158
Azov 44, 53–55

bachas (Muslim dancing boys) 159
Bacteriological Institute 174
Bariatinsky, Anatole Marie 159
Bashkiria region 130, 132–3
Bassin, Mark 88
Bazarova, P. 228, 229–30
begging 12, 148, 160
Begishev family 65, 70
Behubdi, Mahmud 162
Belgorod line 45, 47–9, 52, 55
Belorussians 15
Belosliudov, A. 120
Belovod'e 117, 268
Beznosikov (Lieutenant-Colonel) 90
biological competition. *See* evolutionary theory
Bitiug settlements 55
Blanter, Matvei 227
Bliukher, V.K. 224
Bliummer, Leonid 127n83
Boeck, Brian 9, 14, 26, 83, 266
Bogdanov syn Dubrovskii, Aleksei 70
Bogoiavlenskii, N. 184n6
Bogoroditsii Convent 64

Bogtachevskii family 70–1
borders, territorial 7–8, 36; Belgorod line 45, 47–9, 52, 55; Don River as 53; Izium line 49; North American 107–8; Russian-Chinese 109, 139; security of 8–9, 13, 41–56, 61–7, 72–4, 139–40, 213, 266, 274; southeast Russian steppes as 81, 83, 87–8
Boris Godunov, tsar 27–8
Bratsk people 30, 35
Braun, Andrei 254
Bukhara Tropical Institute 186n33
Bukhtarmintsy. *See* "rock people"
Bunak, V.V. 170–2, 179–80
Bunge, Alexander von 119
Buturlin, Andrei 35

Calloway, Colin 108
Canadian women 220
Catherine II, the Great 2, 10, 56, 84, 112, 114, 270, 272
Cavanaugh, Cassandra 13–14, 273
Central Asian Medical-Scientific Society 174–5
Central Asian Scholarly Society 149
Central Asian State University (TsAGU) medical school 174
Central Bureau on Regional Research (Uzbek SSR) 174
Charles V, king of Spain 21
Chashchina (Khetagurovite) 225
Chechens 239, 245–9, 252–3, 256
Cherniaev, Valerian 96
Cherniaev, Vasilii 92, 96
China 9, 109, 139, 277
Chuvash 63
"civilizing missions" 10, 271–4; acclimatization theory and 169, 172, 273; ambiguity and 160, 162–3, 275; Khetagurovite movement as 216, 274; "rock people" and 120; in southeastern steppes 86–7; Turkestan and 156; as utopian visions 269
climate 89–94, 97, 99. *See also* acclimatization theory
collectivization 189, 192–3, 213
colonization history: distinguishing characteristics of 7–8, 265–6; historiography of 2–3, 5–6, 107–8, 266–7; reverse migrations and 15, 276; themes of 7–14
Committee on the Siberian Railroads 276
Conference for the Study of Productive Forces (KIPS) 174
Conference of Marxist Agronomists 193
Conklin, Alice 160
Constitutional Democrat *(Kadet)* party 151–52
conversions, religious 63, 74
convict settlement 8, 214. *See also* special villages
Cossacks 8, 275; agricultural production and

85, 90; as autonomous security forces 43–4, 48–50, 52–5; indigenous peoples and 11, 35; land ownership and 135; population statistics for 84; utopian visions and 268, 270
cotton industry 149, 155, 157, 178
Council of Ministers 135, 140
Council of People's Commissars (Russian Republic) 194–5
Council of People's Commissars (SNK) 178, 194–5, 201
creoles 127n88
Crimean Khanate 41–2
criminals and outlaws 10, 12, 42
cross-cultural interactions 8, 10, 13–14, 107–8; "civilizing missions" and 10, 86–7, 120, 156, 160, 162–3, 169, 172, 216, 272–4; violence in 11, 27, 30–32, 154, 245–7
Cultural Revolution (1931–2) 179

Darwin, Charles 86
Davies, Brian 45, 47
Davies, Norman 44, 48
decolonization. *See* reverse migrations
deforestation. *See* forests and deforestation
Demidov, Akinfii 109, 111
Derevii, Fedor Prokof'ev 72
disease and disease control 14, 42, 54, 150, 169–84, 190, 206–7
Dmitrev syn Ermolaev, Lev 69
Dnepropetrovskii state farm 256
Dobrosmyslov, A.I. 158, 161
Dodoko, K. 226
Dokuchaev, Vasilii 93, 94–5, 97–9
Don Cossacks. *See* Cossacks
dowries 12, 70, 71–2
droughts 85, 91–2, 95–8
Druzhevich, Iu. 228, 231
Dukhobors 8
Dutch settlement 8
Dzerzhinskii, F.E. 191

Eastern Cape (southern Africa) 8
ecological zones. *See* natural environment
economic development policies 9–10; population's value to 9, 25, 62–3, 113, 129, 174; taxation and 13, 23, 26–8, 106–7, 111–18. *See also specific industries*
education 87–8, 93, 97, 161
Egorova, Polina 232
Elizavetinka 245
Emel'ianov, Nikolai 226
empty lands 2, 8, 14, 26, 216, 239, 244
Enandarov, Iangil'd 64
Engels, Friedrich 180
England. *See* Great Britain
Enisei province 117
Enmametev family 65

environment. *See* natural environment
Epancha 27–8
Erlov, Matvei 69
Ermolov, A.S. 96–7, 99
erosion. *See* soil depletion and erosion
Esipov, Ivan and Kalin 68
ethnic difference 13–14, 113, 115–16; as
    identity determinant 132–3, 138–9
ethnographic surveys 13, 29–30, 33–4, 149,
    174–5
eugenics 171
European colonizing concepts 21–2, 25,
    34–6, 108, 169
evolutionary theory 86, 170, 172, 180

Far East, Russian/Soviet 9–14, 86, 140,
    213–14, 230, 274, 277. *See also*
    Khetagurovite movement
Federal Migration Service 15
Fedor Ivanovich, tsar 27
Fedorov, Evgenii 158, 160
Fedorovshii, Elbno 68
Filimonov, Kondratei 69
Filipenko, A.E. 96–97
films, adventure-frontier 217–18, 227–8
Florov, P.K. 118
folktale metaphors 216–17, 274
forestry industry. *See* timber industry
forests and deforestation 89–94, 99
Foundation Pit, The (Platonov) 189, 191,
    196, 205, 208
France 8, 21, 53, 108, 160, 169
Free Economic Society 95–6, 99
free people 45, 47
French Revolution 53
frontier myths 215, 217–19, 226, 231, 267
fugitives. *See* unauthorized migration
Fundamental Laws (1906) 134
fur tribute. *See iasak* (fur tribute) people

Gavrilov syn Ostrovskii, Boris 72
Gelmersen, Alexander 119, 120
gender 11–12. *See also* men; women
Geographical Society. *See* Imperial Russian
    Geographical Society
Germans 11, 13, 84–5, 139, 270; deported
    239, 246, 248–9, 251, 253–4, 256
Girl with a Personality (film) 227–8
Glevskaia, V. 224, 225
Glupikhina, Maria 227
Gmelin, Samuel Georg 88
Godunov, Boris 27–8
Godunov Map *29,* 29–30
Golitsyn, V.V. 52, 58n37
Gorchakov, Petr 27
Great Britain 8, 21–2, 25, 108, 169, 171–2
Grebenshchikov, Mikhail 31–2, 120–1
Grigorev syn Azter'ev, Dmitrev 64
Grodekov, N.I. 150

Groys, Boris 212n101

Hellie, Richard 44
Hobson, J.A. 160
Holland 8, 21
Hosking, Geoffrey 49
hostage taking 11, 31, 33
Humboldt, Alexander 120
Hungry Steppe 178, 188n92
Huntington, Ellsworth 181

Iachont'ev syn Karazulov, Timofei 69
Iadrintsev, N. 118, 120–1, 164n55
Iagoda, Genrikh 192–4, 196, 200, 206
Iakovlev syn Solovtsov, Bogdan 70
Iakuts 30–2
Ianchurin, Bakrach 64
Ianson, N.M. 191–2
iasak (fur tribute) people 27–8, 106–7,
    112–18, 267
Iaushev family 76n32
identity 8; determinants of 88, 129, 132–3,
    139; invented 47; "Russianness" and
    132–3, 138–9; Soviet 9, 251–3, 256–7;
    "stepmother" nature and 87, 95–6
Igalkina (Khetagurovite) 223, 227
Ikonnikov, I.S. 96–7
Imperial General Staff 86, 89
Imperial Russian Geographical Society 86,
    94, 99, 153
In the East (Pavlenko) 229
India 172, 183
Indians (New World) 21–2, 34–6, 172
indigenization *(korenizatsiia)* 173, 179, 184, 273
indigenous peoples: disease and 14, 42, 54,
    150, 169–84, 190, 207; *korenizatsiia*
    (indigenization) and 173, 179, 184, 273;
    lawsuits by 32–33; as military servitors
    61–7; oaths of loyalty/submission and 35;
    Russian superiority to 14, 90, 151, 172;
    social estate definitions of 115–16; violence
    against 11, 27, 30–2, 154, 245–7; women,
    treatment of, of 11. *See also* cross-cultural
    interactions *and specific groups and
    regions*
industrial production 9, 133, 158, 178
Ingush 239, 245–9, 252–3, 256
inheritance rights 70–1, 266
Institute for Experimental Biology (Moscow)
    187n71
Institute for Experimental Medicine (UzIEM,
    Uzbek SSR) 179, 181
Institute for Labor Hygiene (Leningrad) 178
Institute for Microbiology, Epidemiology and
    Parasitology (Uzbek SSR) 181
Institute of Experimental Medicine
    (Leningrad) 178
Internal Affairs, Ministry/Commissariat of
    130–1, 192

Irkutsk 10, 30, 117
irrigation systems 90, 93, 97, 155, 271
Isennaleevskii 67
Iugor princelings 30
Iur'ev Pol'skoi Province 24
Iur'eva, Nadezhda 228
Iuzhina, E. 227
Ivan IV, the Terrible, tsar 26, 30, 61, 63–4
Ivanov, D.L. 92–3
Ivanov, N.A. 150
Ivanov syn Stupishii, Prokofei 66
Izium line 49

Jadids 161–3, 272
Japan 9, 213, 216, 221, 274
Jews 158
Justice, Commissariat of 192

Kadet (Constitutional Democrat) party 151–2
Kahn, Kan De 255
Kalmyks 73, 109, 113
Kamchadaly people 31
Kan De Kahn 255
Karim, Seid 162
Karpov-Karaev (Khetagurovite) 225–6
Kartauzov, Leonid 247–8, 252
Kas'ianov, N.N. 153
Kassirskii, Isaac 178, 180–3
Kaufman, K.P. fon 149
Kavelin, K.D. 2
Kazakhs 13, 112–13, 246, 252, 256–7
Kazakhstan 9, 11, 86, 191. *See also* Virgin
    Lands movement
Kazan Khanate 61, 63
KazTsIK 245
Ketlinskaia, Vera 218, 223
Khakimbatov, Isabek 157
Khar'kov province 83, 89–90
Khatukhina (Khetagurovite) 223
Khetagurova, Valentina 213, 215, 217–20,
    234n29
Khetagurovite movement 9–14, 213–32, 274;
    gender boundaries in 220, 230–1; memoirs
    of 222, 227–32; men in 11,
    214–15, 217–18, 222, 225–6; patriotism
    and 214, 224, 229, 231; propaganda in
    214, 215–21; publicity for participants in
    227–8; reverse migrations and 215;
    skepticism over motivations and 230–1;
    volunteers for 215, 222–7; women in
    11–12, 214–15, 217–32, 274
Khetagurovki (film) 227
Khlopov, Aleksei Stepanovich 71
Khmelnyts'ky uprising 49
Khoja, Arif 157, 161
Khoziashev family 64–5, 70
Khrushchev, Nikita 9, 13, 196, 238–9, 241,
    248, 253, 255–6
Khvostov, N.A. 97

KIPS (Conference for the Study of
    Productive Forces) 174
Kirilov, Ivan 10
Kiselev, A.S. 195
Kivelson, Valerie 9, 11, 13–14, 265, 267
Kliuchevskii, Vasilii 1, 3, 7, 266, 271, 275
Koliasnikova, M. 223, 228, 236n75
Kolotskoi Monastery 24
Kol'tsov, Nikolai Konstantinovich 171–2,
    175, 180
Kolyvan-Voskresensk plants 111
Komarova, Mariia 232
Komissarzhevskaia, V.F. 159
Komsomol'sk (film) 218, 236n77
Komsomol'sk-na-Amure 218, 233n21
korenizatsiia. See indigenization
Koriaks 34
Korsakov, V.S. 117
Kostina, Kapitalina 228, 236n78
Kostychev, P.A. 97
Kotkin, Stephen 189
Kozlov family 70
Krasnov (Captain) 90
Krestovnikov, G.A. 155
Kristof, Ladis 52
Krivoshein, Aleksandr 9, 128–9, 131,
    134–2, 153–4, 271–2, 274
Kryzhanovskii, Nikolai 130, 132–3, 138,
    144n28
kulaks 189, 193–94. *See also* special villages
Kulomzin, Anatolii 130, 271
Kuropatkin, A.N. 150
Kuznetsov, Nikoali 179–80, 182–83

labor strikes 150–1, 160
Land and Agriculture, Main Administration
    of 154
land ownership: dekulakization and 189, 193;
    empty lands and 2, 8, 14, 26, 216;
    European concept of 21–2, 25, 34–6;
    lawsuits over 23, 24; Muscovite concept of
    23–5, 35–6, 47, 116; by nobility 131–2,
    138, 140; *pomest'e* grants and 8, 12, 44,
    47, 62–74, 266; population's value for 25;
    in Siberia 26–33, 35–6, 107, 116, 122, 132,
    135–8
landlords 23–5
Larin, Iuri 193
Las Casas, Bartolomé de 21
Lasaev syn Shukinchev, Shmamet 70
Lattimore, Owen 48
Latvians 133, 139
Law Code of 1649 *(Ulozhenie)* 25, 30, 45,
    47, 65–8
lawsuits 23, 32–3
Ledebour, Karl 117, 119–20
Levashev family 71
Lewin, Moshe 207–8
Lieven, Dominic 49

Limerick, Patricia Nelson 108
Liubavskii, Matvei 3, 266, 275
local autonomy 173; for Altai communities 115, 118; for Don Cossack Host 43, 48; for German exiles 254; for military servitors 62, 67–72; special villages' lack of 201, 203–5; in Tashkent 151–2, 161; for Ukrainians 48
London, Jack 217
Lotikova (Khetagurovite) 227
Luk'ianov syn Chufarov, Leontii 75n12
Lukin, Savva Fedorovich 76n33
Lutherans 249
Lyell, Charles 86

McCauley, Martin 256
Maev, N.A. 149
Mafeia, Metropolitan of Kazan 69
Makmametev family 70
Mallitskii, N.G. 152, 161
Manson, Patrick 176
maps and mapping 13–14, 29–30, 33–5, 95, 174
Marsh, George Perkins 86, 98
Martynov, Pavel 226
Matiunin, Iakov 66
Matveev, Boris 68
Mekishin family 70
men: acclimatization theory and 171, 177; in Khetagurovite movement 12, 214–15, 217–18, 222, 225–6
Mennonites 139, 249, 270
meteorology, agricultural 94
Mexico 21
Meyer, Gerhard 119
Middle Volga 9, 266; security for central state and 9, 61–7, 72–4; servitor negotiations in 67–72; settler characteristics in 61–2, 65, 73
Mikhail Fedorovich, tsar 44
Mikhailov syn Oshcherin, Mikhail 72
military reforms 62, 65, 73
military servitors: lawsuits by 23; mining in Siberia and 111; mobility of 45, 65–6; negotiations by 62, 67–72, 266; *pomest'e* land grants to 8, 12, 44, 47, 62–7, 72–4, 266; religious tolerance and 63–5; security in Middle Volga and 9, 61–7, 72–4
Miliukov, Pavel 3
Miliutin, Dmitrii 86
Miliutin, Nikolai 86
Miliutin, V.P. 193
Mill, John Stuart 138
mining industry 109, 111–12, 133, 191
Mirochnik, M.F. 186n35
Mironov, Boris 266
Mishalova, Efrosina 224–5, 236n76
mobility: free migration policies and 140; of Khetagurovites 221; of military servitors

45, 65–6; of peasants/serfs 24, 44, 86, 129–30, 134; of traders 50–1
Mochul'skii (Captain) 89–90
modernity 10, 106, 108, 121–2; Jadids and 161–3, 272; Khetagurovite movement and 214; "rock people" and 109; special villages and 189, 191; utopian visions of 270; women's role in 234n30
Molchanova (Khetagurovite) 223–4
Molokans 8
Molotov, V.M. 193–94
Moon, David 14, 271
Morozov, Boris Ivanovich 71
Moscow Irrigation Company 155
Moscow Trading Industrial Association 158
Moscow Tropical Institute 174
Mozhaisk 24
Murav'ev, Nikolai 10
Muslims 64, 149, 151–2, 156–62, 249, 257
Muzhestvo (Ketlinskaia) 218, 223

nationalism 86
nationality 13, 37, 128, 132–4, 138–9
natural environment *4*, 10, 14; climate and 89–94, 97, 99; human impact on 86–87, 89–90, 96, 98–9; as identity determinant 88, 139; irrigation systems and 90, 93, 97, 155, 271; land ownership concepts and 25; "stepmother" nature and 87, 95–6; of the steppes 81, 83, 86, 89, 267
natural selection. *See* evolutionary theory
navy, development of 53–4
Nekliudov, Grigor 68
Nerchinsk 191
New World 6, 21–22, 25, 34–6. *See also* Americas
Nicholas I, tsar 270
Nicholas II, tsar 134, 139, 151
Nikitkina, Vera 223
NKVD (People's Commissariat of Internal Affairs for the Russian Republic) 192, 195, 201, 218, 274, 276
nobles 63–4, 129, 131–2, 138, 140
Nomikosov, S. 92
North Caucasus Cossacks. *See* Cossacks
Northern Territory 199–200
Novokshchenov, Lukian 24
Nurkeev, Nurmamet 75n9

oaths 35
October Manifesto (1905) 134, 151
Odoevskii, Iakov Nikitich 71
OGPU (internal security police) 192–7, 200–201, 203, 205–7
OGPU PPs (provincial plenipotentiary representatives) 194, 197, 203–4, 206
Old Believers 12–13, 106, 112–13, 114, 117, 268, 270–1
Omsk 30

On the Shores of the Amur (Blanter) 227
oprichnina 63–4
Opryshko (Khetagurovite) 231
Orenburg Cossacks. *See* Cossacks
Orenburg province 81, 83, 96, 132
Oshanin, Lev Vasilievich 175–6, 179–80
Ostiaks 26
Ottoman Empire 8, 43
outlaws. *See* criminals and outlaws

Palen, K.K. 155, 161
Palimpsestov, Ivan 91–2
paternalism 106–8, 121–2
patriotism 9, 12, 214, 224, 229, 231, 242
Pavlenko, P. 236n90
peasants: ascribed 111–12; economic
    development, value to, of 25; emancipation
    of 86, 129; enserfment of 22, 25, 44–5, 47;
    land ownership and 24–5, 35, 135–6;
    mobility of 129–30, 134; uprisings of 130,
    134. *See also* serfs
pederasty 159, 161
Pelym 27
penal colonies. *See* special villages
People's Commissariat of Agriculture for the
    Russian Republic 195, 207
People's Commissariat of Internal Affairs for
    the Russian Republic. *See* NKVD
Perm region 26
Peru 21
Peter I, the Great, tsar 2, 10, 53–5
Petrov, Fedor 71
Petrov, Mikhail 68
Petrov syn Andreianov, Smirnoi 71
Piatakov, G.L. 191
Pipes, Richard 49
Plaskina (Khetagurovite) 230
Platonov, Andrei 189, 191, 196, 205, 208
Platonov, S.F. 266
plausible deniability doctrine 57n17
Plehve, V.K. 130–1, 134
Plymouth Colony (North America) 8
Pohl, Michaela 9, 11, 13, 266, 274, 276
Pokrov Convent 24
Poles, resettled 245
Poligonova (Khetagurovite) 229
Politburo 192–5, 206, 213
political exiles 9–10, 63–4. *See also* special
    villages; Virgin Lands movement
pomest'e land grants 8, 12, 44, 47, 62–74,
    266
Portugal 21, 25
Potanin, G. 118, 120–1
Potemkin, Grigorii 10
private property. *See* land ownership
propaganda 12, 244, 276
property rights. *See* land ownership
prostitution 12, 158–9
Pruth, battle of 55

Public Health, People's Commissariat for 171
Puritans 8
Pushechnikov, Kozan 68

Qari, Munawwar 162
Qing empire 8

race and racism 88, 170–2, 175, 177, 179–81
railway development 130, 148, 150–1, 158,
    168
Razin, Stenka 50, 72–3
Registry Offices (ZAGS) 207
Reiser, G. 152
religion 6; as identity determinant 88, 129,
    132–3, 139; purging of dissenters and 8, 9;
    tolerance of 13, 63–5, 112; utopian visions
    and 268, 270–1; Virgin Lands movement
    and 249, 257. *See also* Old Believers
Remezov, Semen 25, *29*, 29–30, 33–5
Resettlement Administration 128, 130, 135,
    139, 152
reverse migrations 15, 215, 242, 244, 253,
    276–7
Revolution of 1905 134, 151
Riabushinskii, P.O. 155
right to refuge 43
Ritter, Karl 120
Robson, Roy 112
"rock people" 12–13, 106–22; making of
    109–13; romanticization of 109, 118–21,
    270; settled alien status and 106, 109,
    113–18
Romadinovskii, Ivan 69
Romaniello, Matthew 9, 12–13, 25, 266
Romanov syn Kolitsov, Stepan 69
runaways. *See* unauthorized migration
"Russianness" 132–3, 138–9
Russo-Japanese War (1904) 134
Ruzhevskii, Mikhail 71

Sahadeo, Jeff 10–12, 272
St Simonians 271
Sakhalin Islands 191
salt industry 26
Saltykov-Shchedrin, M.E. 152–3
Samara province 83, 90, 96–7
Samsonov, A.V. 155
Saratov province 81, 83, 96
Sasov, Ivan 52–53
sciences, developments in the 86–7, 93, 99
Scott, James 191
seasonal migrants 6, 84, 192
security 8–9, 13, 266; in Middle Volga 61–7,
    72–4; in southeastern steppes 41–56; in
    Soviet Far East 139–40, 213–14, 274
Seleznova (Khetagurovite) 223
Semenov, Industrian 242, 251
Semenov deti Beklemeshev, Ivan 68
Semenov syn Bolkovskii, Nikita 69

Sepúlveda, Juan Ginés de 21
serfs: land ownership and 24, 33, 36; unauthorized migration and 9, 12, 26, 44, 47–8, 62, 109, 266
"settled aliens" status 13, 106, 113–18, 270
settler characteristics 7, 13; in Altai 109; Khetagurovite movement and 215, 222–7; in Middle Volga 61–2, 65, 73; in Siberia 26–7; in southeastern steppes 45, 84; Virgin Lands movement 241–2, 253
Severo-Dvinsk (Northern Territory) 199–200
Sharaia, Tatiana 223
Shchapov, A.P. 2
Shcherbachev, M. 114
Shirvindt, E.G. 195
Shmidt, V.V. 194–5
Shreder, R.R. 155
Shulman, Elena 9, 12–13, 265–6, 274, 276
Siberia 21–37; agricultural production in 271; economic development of 9, 10, 25–32, 34–5, 86, 267; indigenous peoples in 11, 22–3, 27–37, 106, 113–16, 267; land ownership in 26–33, 35–6, 107, 116, 122, 132, 135–8; mapping of 13–14, *29,* 29–30, 33–5; as penal colony 10; popular beliefs about 214, 216, 218, 230; resettlement policy for 128–9, 134–42; reverse migrations and 276; settler characteristics in 26–7; special villages in 199; subjecthood in 28, 32–7, 108, 115–16; women, treatment of, in 11, 31, 33. *See also* Altai region
Skrynnikov, R.G. 64
slavery and slave trade 11, 31, 33, 42
Smolensk War (1632–4) 45, 65
social estate categorizations 108, 115–16, 128–9, 131–2, 138
social reforms 9–10; as "civilizing missions" 10, 86–7, 120, 156, 160, 162–3, 169, 172, 216, 269, 271–4; purging of unwanted elements and 9–10, 63–4, 134, 189; utopian visions and 10, 118–21, 189–1, *202,* 208, 267–1, 273–4; Virgin Lands movement and 239
socialist realist aesthetics 208–9, 273–4
soil depletion and erosion 68–9, 92–3, 96–7
soil science 94–5
Sokolov, N.P. 179–80, 182–3
soldiers. *See* military servitors
Solov'ev, S.M. 2, 87, 95, 266, 271, 275
Solov'ev, Vladimir 95–6, 99
Sovnarkom. *See* Council of People's Commissars (SNK)
Spain 21–2, 25, 35, 53, 108, 171
Spanish Requirement 35
Spaso-Preobrazhenskii Monastery 64
Spasskii, Grigorii 119
special villages 10, 12, 189–209, 239, 276;

controls and 190, 205–8; disease/disease control in 190, 206–7; location/building of 190, 195, 199–200, 207; plans for 190, 196–205; rules of internal order for 200–5; special settlement and 191–6; transport to 190, 197–9, 206; utopian visions for 189–91, *202,* 208, 271, 273–4
Speranskii, Mikhail 106, 115–16, 124n22
Stalin, Joseph 10, 192–4, 224
statistical science 86
Statutes on Alien Administration (1822, 1892) 106, 115–17, 124n22
Stavropol province 81, 83
Steinwedel, Charles 9, 13, 271
Stenka Razin rebellion (1670–1) 50, 72–3
Stephen, Aron 107
steppes: agricultural production in 14, 41, 55, 81–99; disease in 14, 42, 54; maps of *82;* natural environment of 81, 83, 86, 91, 267; security for central state and 9, 41–56, 266; settler characteristics in 45, 84
Stilenev, Fedor 68
Stolypin, Petr 9, 10, 128–9, 134–42, 152–3, 156, 271–2, 274
Stroganov, Grigorii Anikievich 26
subjecthood 28, 32–7, 108, 115–16, 134–5, 137
suffrage movement, women's 220
Sufism 249
Sunderland, Willard 98
Surgut 30
Sviiazhsk 65
Sychov, Fedor 68
Syr-Dar'ia district 153–5
Syr-Dar'ia Statistical Commission 155–6

Tambov 52
Tania (Abruzov) 236n77
Tarasiuk, Galina 251
Tashkent 10–11, 148–63, 272; disease in 178; indigenous populations in 151–2, 156–62; pederasty in 159, 161; Russian elites in 148–56, 162–3; women in 12, 148, 158–60
Tatars 27–8, 41–3, 45, 54, 63, 83
taxation 13; of ascribed peasants 111–12; central tax rolls, protection of 26; of *iasak* people 27–28, 106–7, 112–18, 267; as proof of land ownership 23
Teleuts 117
Temporary Rules on resettlement (1904) 131, 133–4
Terek territory 83
Tikhonov Monastery 23–4
timar grants 8
timber industry 192, 199
Timofeev syn Voronkov, Savva 70–71
Tobol'sk 10, 30
Tolmachev, V.N. 194–5

Tomsk 10, 117, 137, 207
Tonashev, Tolubaik 67
Torpey, John 51
town-building 10–11, 149, 272
Trans-Siberian Railway 130
TsAGU (Central Asian State University medical school) 174
Tselinograd 239, 242, 253–5. *See also* Akmola/Akmolinsk
Tsvetkov, M.A. 85
Tungus people 35
Turkestan 11, 132, 150, 154–6, 171–7. *See also* Tashkent
Turkestan Agricultural Society 153, 155–6
Turner, Frederick Jackson 108, 267
Tverskii manufacturing company 158

Ufa province 83, 96, 132–3, 145n39
Ukraine 270
Ukrainians 15, 48–9, 84, 133, 139, 178–9
Ulala (village) 115
Ulozhenie. See Law Code of 1649
unauthorized migration 9, 12, 266; central tax rolls, protection of, and 26; controlling of 44, 47–8, 50–3; destruction of settlements and 55; right to refuge and 43; "rock people" and 109, 112–13, 117; volume of (19th-century) 130
Urakov, Dmitrii Vasil'evich 71
Ursati, A.I. 150
utopian visions 10, 267–71; of Khetagurovite movement 274; of "rock people" 118–21; of special villages 189–91, *202*, 208, 271, 273
Uzbek Republican Bacteriological Institute 181
Uzbek SSR 179
UzIEM (Institute for Experimental Medicine, Uzbek SSR) 179, 181

Vagin, V.I. 126
Valianskaia (Khetagurovite) 230
Valuev, P.A. 132
Valuev commission 92
Vasil'chikov, Viktor 92
Vasil'ev syn Davydov, Andrei 64
Vasilev syn Elagin, Andrei 66, 71
Vel'iamov, Andrei 66
Veselovskii, Konstantin 88–9, 91, 96, 99, 271

VIEM (All-Union Institute of Experimental Medicine) 178
Viola, Lynne 10, 12, 273, 276
Virgin Lands movement 9, 11, 13, 238–57, 271, 274; cultural life and 250–54, 256–7; evaluations of 255–6; identity and 251–3, 256–7; inter-ethnic contact in 239–51; patriotism in 242; propaganda in 244; recruits for 241–2, 253; religious life and 249, 257; reverse migrations and 242, 244, 253, 276
Vis Hadj *tarikat* 249
Voeikov, Aleksandr 93–4, 96–9
Volguls 27
Volodimer syn Volyskov, Ivan 66
Vologda (Northern Territory) 199–200, 207
Voronezh province 83
Vrevskii, A.B. 150
VSNKh (Supreme Council of the National Economy) 195
VTsIK (All-Russian Central Executive Commission) 201

western adventure stories 217–18
Western Mongol federation 109
White, Richard 108
"White Hats" sect 249
Witte, Sergei 130–1, 134, 271
women: acclimatization theory and 171; Don Cossack communities and 50; dowries for 12, 70, 71–2; indigenous, treatment of 11; Japanese 221; in Khetagurovite movement 11–12, 214–15, 217–32, 274; prostitution and 12, 158–9; in Russian/Soviet Far East 11; in Siberia 11, 31, 33; suffrage movement and 220; in Tashkent 12, 148, 158–61

Yellow Peril. *See* Japan

Zablotskii-Desiatovskii, A.P. 91, 99
ZAGS (Registry Offices) 207
Zhuk, Sergei 270
Zhukov, Lov 68
Zhurikhina, T. 227
Zhurin, Nikolai 241
Znamenski, Andrei 9, 13, 270
Zunghar "empire" 109, 113
Zyrians 2

Printed in the United States
145216LV00001B/27/P